MW00325847

Invested

Invested

How Three Centuries of Stock Market Advice Reshaped Our Money, Markets, and Minds

PAUL CROSTHWAITE, PETER KNIGHT,
NICKY MARSH, HELEN PAUL,
AND JAMES TAYLOR

THE UNIVERSITY OF CHICAGO PRESS   CHICAGO AND LONDON

The University of Chicago Press, Chicago 60637
The University of Chicago Press, Ltd., London
© 2022 by The University of Chicago
All rights reserved. No part of this book may be used or reproduced in any manner whatsoever without written permission, except in the case of brief quotations in critical articles and reviews. For more information, contact the University of Chicago Press, 1427 E. 60th St., Chicago, IL 60637.
Published 2022
Printed in the United States of America

31 30 29 28 27 26 25 24 23 22   1 2 3 4 5

ISBN-13: 978-0-226-82098-9 (cloth)
ISBN-13: 978-0-226-82100-9 (paper)
ISBN-13: 978-0-226-82099-6 (e-book)
DOI: https://doi.org/10.7208/chicago/9780226820996.001.0001

Library of Congress Cataloging-in-Publication Data

Names: Crosthwaite, Paul, 1980– author. | Knight, Peter, 1968– author. |
    Marsh, Nicky, author. | Paul, Helen J., 1975– author. | Taylor, James, 1976–
    author.
Title: Invested : how three centuries of stock market advice reshaped our
    money, markets, and minds / Paul Crosthwaite, Peter Knight, Nicky Marsh,
    Helen Paul, and James Taylor.
Other titles: How three centuries of stock market advice reshaped our money,
    markets, and minds
Description: Chicago ; London : The University of Chicago Press, 2022. |
    Includes bibliographical references and index.
Identifiers: LCCN 2022012505 | ISBN 9780226820989 (cloth) |
    ISBN 9780226821009 (paperback) | ISBN 9780226820996 (ebook)
Subjects: LCSH: Investments—History. | Investment advisors—Great
    Britain—History. | Investment advisors—United States—History. | Finance
    literature—Great Britain—History. | Finance literature—United States—
    History. | Capitalism—History.
Classification: LCC HG4516 .C76 2022 | DDC 332/.0415—dc23/eng/20220502
LC record available at https://lccn.loc.gov/2022012505

♾ This paper meets the requirements of ANSI/NISO Z39.48-1992 (Permanence of Paper).

Contents

Three Centuries of Financial Advice

In January 2021 the apes arrived. Users of WallStreetBets, a community of millions of retail investors on the discussion website Reddit, began buying en masse into GameStop, a struggling video game retailer whose stock had been the subject of aggressive short selling. The concerted buying spree, using online commission-free trading platforms such as Robinhood, saw GameStop shares leap sensationally by more than 2,000 percent over the course of a fortnight, from just over $20 to $483.[1] The "short squeeze" caught the hedge funds off guard, with some reportedly closing their positions at the loss of billions of dollars.[2] The episode turned a spotlight on the growing influence of social media on the stock market. Indeed, the watchword of the Reddit users—"Apes Together Strong"—both mocks Wall Street's dismissive attitude to supposedly ignorant outsiders and celebrates the (supposed) power of the internet to redress historic power imbalances in the market.[3] Other "meme stocks" quickly followed GameStop, including AMC Entertainment, to the mystification of market professionals, who bemoaned the "flight to crap" and anxiously asked, "Are the Apes Now Running Wall Street?"[4]

Though the apes were a new—and for many, unwelcome—player in the stock market menagerie of bulls, bears, stags, and lame ducks, there were historical parallels.[5] The most obvious one was hammered home incessantly by media commentators who insisted that meme mania was simply the latest in a long history of speculative bubbles, with the Dutch tulip mania of the 1630s and the South Sea Bubble of 1720 serving as favorite reference points.[6] Less commented on, however, was the way in which, though seemingly very modern, the GameStop saga provides an excellent vantage point from which to examine the long and poorly understood history of investment advice. The proliferation of tips and information in cyberspace is just the latest stage in a process going back three centuries, for the much earlier technology of print acted in a very similar way, explaining and popularizing investment for large constituencies of readers in the eighteenth and nineteenth centuries. The appeal of printed investment advice was always explicitly democratic, holding out the promise of access to privileged knowledge that would level the playing field and shrink the gap between outsiders and insiders. When hip-hop star Megan Thee Stallion announces in her 2021 YouTube tutorial "Investing for Hotties" that "Buying stocks isn't only for the big players. Anyone can start with as little as one dollar," she is repeating almost verbatim the assurances made by generations of market democratizers.[7]

Niall Ferguson sees in the anti–Wall Street rhetoric of the apes, typified by the rallying cry of "fuck the hedgies," the financial analogue of Donald Trump's insurgent populism.[8] Yet this aggressive celebration of the "little man" battling powerful vested interests is nothing new, finding precursors in the populist advertising of disruptive nineteenth-century brokerages which exhorted their clients to follow their stock tips and "SQUEEZE THE BEARS."[9] More generally, angry skepticism about the morality of "City" insiders and their "shills" in the media is prefigured in much eighteenth- and nineteenth-century writing about the stock market, laden as it is with lurid warnings about the tricks and dodges of the financial elites. Likewise, the machismo of many of the "Generation Z" traders ("Let's get fucking nuts . . . let's strangle these people out") reflects centuries-long habits of coding speculation as a masculine activity and the role of speculators as mastering a feminized market.[10] Though the history of printed advice has made genuinely useful information about the market more widely available, much of it has offered unrealistic visions of vast wealth easily won, and such visions are certainly widespread on social media today. Sports blogger turned day trader Dave Portnoy helpfully condensed his wisdom down to just two easy-to-follow rules: "1. Stocks only go up. 2. When in doubt whether to buy or sell see Rule #1."[11]

Portnoy's rise to celebrity status, with 2.6 million Twitter followers by July 2021 and regular appearances on CNBC, is nothing unusual in the history of investment advice, where telling people how to make money by investing in the stock market has usually proven a surer route to wealth than actually investing in the stock market. Once established, the reputations of individual financial gurus can survive adverse outcomes: indeed, anyone stung by following Portnoy's gung-ho approach and buying at the peak could not claim they were not warned, his Twitter bio pointing out,

"I'm not a financial advisor. Don't trust anything I say about stocks."[12] No matter how badly meme mania ends, it is unlikely to discredit the genre of investment advice, which over the centuries has shown a remarkable ability to survive crashes. The solution to bad advice has tended to be more advice, with countless competing providers promising to help retrieve investors' fortunes. In the wake of GameStop, the website of British bank Halifax warned its customers to "Stop Taking Investment Advice from Social Media," presenting instead a checklist "to help you avoid getting burnt."[13] Around the same time, research from F&C Investment Trust showed that recent events had encouraged 33 percent of Generation Z investors to start seeking out more information about investing.[14]

Explaining how investment advice has come to occupy such a central role in today's society is the central aim of this book. As such, it responds to a long-identified need. A decade ago, the historian of credit Lendol Calder observed that "the print culture that helped people make sense of money—through financial advice offered in books, newspapers, magazines, and advertisements—awaits its historian." The need for a study of this print culture is all the more imperative since, as he claims, "concerns about money—how to get it, how to save it, how to invest, multiply, and spend it—have likely sold more books in the last two hundred years than any other subject after religion."[15] Likewise, James Vernon has identified investment manuals as a historical "treasure trove" which remains "untouched by historians."[16] By paying far more attention to the canonical texts of political economy by authors like Adam Smith, John Stuart Mill, and John Maynard Keynes, historians have given us a partial and exclusive understanding of the development of economic knowledge. Certainly, the role of popularizers like Harriet Martineau, Jane Marcet, and Millicent Fawcett, influential "knowledge brokers" whose primers on political economy brought the ideas of these canonical writers to much larger readerships, is better appreciated than it used to be.[17] But a parallel literature, representing a grassroots economic wisdom written for those who were less interested in theories of how the economy worked than the practical issue of what to do with their money, has been largely neglected. This is particularly the case with investment guides to the stock market itself. By placing such advice literature center stage, this book offers an alternative economic history of the modern world.

Rather than beginning with Smith's *Wealth of Nations* (1776), our unconventional history commences with the texts that influenced Thomas Mortimer's pioneering guide to the stock market, *Every Man His Own*

Broker (1761). Instead of progressing through Mill's *Principles of Political Economy* (1848) to Keynes's *General Theory of Employment, Interest, and Money* (1936), it plots a very different course, taking in texts like Thomas Fortune's *Epitome of the Stocks and Public Funds* (1796), T. S. Harvey's *What Shall I Do with My Money?* (1849), Emma Galton's *A Guide to the Unprotected in Every-day Matters Relating to Property and Income* (1863), Moses Smith's *Plain Truths about Stock Speculation* (1887), Richard D. Wyckoff's *Studies in Tape Reading* (1910), Benjamin Graham and David Dodd's *Security Analysis: Principles and Technique* (1934), Ralph Nelson Elliott's *Wave Principle* (1938), Sylvia Porter and J. K. Lasser's *Managing Your Money* (1953), Louis Rukeyser's *How to Make Money in Wall Street* (1974), and Suze Orman's *9 Steps to Financial Freedom* (1997). Our study encompasses both well-known works and ones that have been long forgotten—around three hundred in total—to present the most comprehensive study of the development of financial advice writing to date.[18]

Though many of our authors, beginning with Mortimer himself, also gave financial advice in personal or professional capacities, our main interest is in print advice and its online equivalents today. Of course, print features prominently in many historical accounts of the development of the market and its extension beyond face-to-face relations. Printed "price courants" were a key constituent of early financial markets, facilitating the transmission of market data across space and time, while newspapers were crucial in communicating a wider range of financial information to market participants.[19] The nineteenth-century proliferation of forms of writing on finance has attracted much attention, as has the relationship between styles and genres.[20] Historians have shown how print could sustain financial fraud, cheaper printing and postal technologies permitting deception by mail order on a grand scale.[21] Likewise, the earliest economic forecasters used print and post to reach large followings.[22] Yet none of these works explore the origins, development, and implications of stock market investment advice in print over three centuries.

Print allowed the mass production of advice, and it is this phenomenon of advice transcending face-to-face relations and reaching first hundreds, then thousands—and eventually millions—of investors that we examine. Relatively cheap print democratized access to advice—investors did not need the cultural capital required to speak to a solicitor, banker, or stockbroker, simply the few shillings or cents to buy a pamphlet. Moreover, investment circulars were increasingly offered for free as the market expanded in the later nineteenth century. This had obvious implications for class but also for gender: print offered women opportunities for financial engagement even when social stigmas militated against this, and even when, as we shall see, such texts did not address them directly. Thus, the history of printed investment advice makes it possible to trace how authors and their publishers encouraged wider constituencies of investors to identify with the stock market, rather than restricting our focus to the activities of social and financial elites. Indeed, although we are interested in the forms of knowledge, institutions, and practices that constitute stock market investment advice in the broadest sense, the book focuses on advice written for ordinary citizens, rather than experts and professionals. Moreover, it is chiefly interested in the specific genre of the stock market investment advice manual and related varieties of investment advice in the financial press.

The term "investment manual" suggests a uniformity that would be misleading. This advice took many forms: from hefty and expensive catalogs of stocks and shares to single-page tip sheets, from treatises puffing a new technology to glossaries of stock market terminology, from hagiographies of successful market operators to descriptions of systems and methods for investment, and from airport best sellers to online blogs. Often a single text will contain several such elements. Indeed, the generic diversification of financial advice, which has become particularly apparent since the advent of the internet, is actually a feature of our story throughout its three-hundred-odd years. Mortimer's pioneering text did not emerge in a vacuum; rather, it drew on wider traditions of writing about money, and we therefore show how stock market advice texts at various points borrow from and relate to wider bodies of knowledge, whether broader currents of self-improvement writing, advice on other financial topics, fictional representations of the market, or academic economic writing.

Though some market manuals sought to provide basic instruction on how to invest rather than guaranteeing success ("how-to" guides rather than "how-to-win" guides), the appeal of the genre increasingly came to rest on the fantasy of easy profits and the certainty of success it promised, either explicitly or implicitly.[23] Our earlier chapters document the growing confidence and inflation of claims made by the genre while our later chapters explore how the genre survived—and thrived—despite the mounting body of evidence in the twentieth century that consistently "beating the market" was an impossibility. If it was true, as Burton Malkiel claimed, that "a blindfolded monkey throwing darts at a newspaper's financial pages" could select as good a portfolio as a professional financial analyst,

then why bother purchasing a guide to the stock market?[24] The resilience
of the stock market advice genre in spite of its very obvious limitations is
a puzzle that this book hopes to explain.

Ours is an Anglo-American rather than a global history. This is not to
deny the existence and importance of financial advice literature in other
parts of the world.[25] But there is a logic to confining ourselves to Britain and the United States. Our story begins in London with the set of
innovations commonly known as the Financial Revolution, which drew
on Dutch, French, and Scottish practices, in the late seventeenth century.[26]
The power of empire helped London to become the world's preeminent
financial center by the early nineteenth century, a century which saw the
London Stock Exchange flourish as the largest and most sophisticated
in the world. By the late nineteenth century, US markets had grown significantly in influence and, after World War I, London was clearly in the
shadow of New York. Our coverage consequently shifts to focus increasingly on the US market in the later chapters of the book, which is designed
to incorporate the two largest financial markets of the modern age in the
period when each was in the ascendant. Throughout, we place investment
advice in the context of the actual development of the stock market, and
we explore the changing relationship between the stock market, the wider
economy, and related forms of wealth creation and management.

The book makes five key arguments about stock market investment
advice. First, this advice literature is not a natural and inevitable result of
the growth of the stock market. Rather, it is the creation of opportunistic and entrepreneurial writers and publishers who see an opportunity to
make money not through the stock market itself but by creating a market for information and advice on it. Second, this investment advice does
not simply reflect the market unproblematically: it actively constructs
this market by embedding assumptions about it, thus creating a way
of seeing the market that begins to seem simple common sense. Third,
financial advice is not simply financial. It increasingly represents a form of
self-fashioning, borrowing from self-help literature to reach far beyond
the pecuniary and into the personal. More than just wealth, it offers its
readers the promise of self-mastery and self-fulfillment. Fourth, by the
twentieth century, advice literature begins to reshape the wider landscape
of personal financial advice more generally, reframing investment not as a
possibility but as a responsibility. Financial strategies, metaphorically and
literally, come to revolve around the stock market. Fifth, as we approach
the present, investment advice comes to reshape the whole self-help para-

digm itself, in its thoroughgoing financialization of the self. Investment advice's journey from subgenre to master category is the story that this book maps.

An interdisciplinary approach, bringing together financial history and literary studies, is critical to unlocking the significance of this large corpus of investment texts. This book is therefore both a substantial work of historical excavation, rediscovering a neglected but substantial body of writing, and also offers a methodologically innovative reading of these texts that models a new approach to studying writing about the financial market.[27] Stock market advice is not solely concerned with the technicalities of stock picking: it also does important cultural work. This book uncovers the desires that this advice taps into, the narratives and metaphors it mobilizes, and the assumptions it makes. Once invested in the stock market, readers became invested in a much bigger ideological project. Stock market advice came to shape a new kind of ideal citizen, for whom risk was individualized, the future turned into a revenue stream, and the self into an entrepreneurial project. Exposing this demonstrates how supposedly immutable economic laws are not timeless and natural but are constructed through social practices and cultural discourses. In short, the book explains how and why the genre of financial advice helped persuade Britons and Americans to think of their homes, their futures, and themselves as speculative investments.

CHAPTER ONE

Making the Market (1720–1800)

On April 22, 1720, as the South Sea Bubble began to inflate, an Irish-woman named Jane Ashe, recently widowed, wrote to a friend of the family, the Reverend Richard Hill. Hill was a prosperous diplomat and statesman who managed Ashe's investments. She was becoming concerned that she was missing out on a good opportunity, writing that she was "very sorry to find" from Hill's last letter

> that my little money was not in the South Sea, which might have amounted to something considerable, but at the same time must return my humble acknowledgements to you for your concern for me & I must still depend upon it. I am an intire stranger to any thing of that kind, & therefore cannot tell what to advice, but beg you will think of some secure way to advance my little stock.[1]

The letter reveals much about the early stock and share market. Sent from Dublin to Hill in London, it shows that investment even at this point was not confined to those living in the metropolis, thanks to regular packet boat services facilitating relatively swift communications across the Irish Sea. Nor did this market exclude women like Ashe who, at a time when they faced numerous legal and economic constraints, were in many respects able to participate on equal terms with men when buying and selling shares. Above all, the letter, and others that have survived, gives an insight into the personal connections that structured and sustained participation in the early stock market. Jane's late husband, St. George Ashe, bishop of Derry, had been friends with Hill, and Jane—together with her son-in-law Sir Ralph Gore—could tap into the wisdom of the well-connected Hill. These familial connections allowed those who knew little about the stock market to place their money in it with confidence. Gore, who conducted most of the family's correspondence with Hill, was thankful for the advice Hill gave Ashe and himself, "both she and I being intire strangers to ye funds and ye management of them."[2] With access to Hill, they did not need to trouble themselves with learning about how to invest themselves or coming to their own judgments: instead, Gore's repeated request in his letters is that Hill "dispose of her little stock as you do of your own."[3]

Ashe and Gore were lucky to know Hill. Enjoying the patronage of the earls of Rochester and Ranelagh, he had amassed a fortune by middle age, perturbing his father who reportedly observed, "My son Dick makes money very fast: God send that he gets it honestly."[4] He was well placed to benefit from the changes happening at the heart of the English state at the end of the seventeenth century. The government's need to leverage its tax revenues to fund foreign wars led to a series of innovations at the heart of which was the creation of a national (as opposed to royal) debt. A new financial infrastructure was constructed, with the Bank of England, chartered in 1694, the New East India Company (1698), and the South Sea Company (1711) all playing a part in servicing the state's enormous borrowing needs. Once described as the Financial Revolution, these reforms did not conjure the modern impersonal financial world into being.[5] Human intermediaries remained critical at every level of the eighteenth-century market, such as private loan-brokers who parceled government loans into smaller lots to sell to their private lists of investors, and men like Hill, who could find themselves handling the financial affairs of multiple family members and friends.[6]

In this environment, advice was something that circulated through personal circuits more than print. If they had wanted to teach themselves about London's market for stocks and shares, Ashe and Gore would have struggled to find a book explaining such things. The first manual to do so, Thomas Mortimer's *Every Man His Own Broker*, would not appear for another forty years. Yet the pair were not entirely innocent of financial matters, and their correspondence with Hill betrays an awareness of the choice of investments and their relative merits, some of which may have been gleaned from conversation with friends, but which also likely derived from newspapers. In the earliest letter that survives from Gore to Hill, dated late 1718, Gore explains that his mother-in-law "seems a little afraid of ye Silesia Loane tho it bears a great interest," and "would rather incline to have it in ye Banque annuities as more safe tho less profitable." But her attitude changed when reports of the South Sea boom reached them in early 1720. Dublin newspapers reported extensively on the rival schemes proposed by the South Sea Company and the Bank of England to convert national debt into company shares, and these reports did much to pique the interest of Dublin's wealthy, even if they did not entirely understand what they were reading.[7] Gore wrote to Hill in February suggesting that he convert Ashe's money from Bank of England and lottery annuities into South Sea stock, which "may make them of greater value than they are at present." The letter is filled with Gore's somewhat garbled account of what he has learned about the South Sea proposal, professions of his ignorance of "computations of this kind," and deference to Hill's superior judgment.[8] Hill seems to have advised against, but continued reports of the rising share price—leading to Jane's disappointed letter of April—made them insist on converting their annuities.[9] In July, Gore seems to acknowledge the risks involved, but these were not enough to dissuade them:

> neither she nor I are any way surprised at your not being concerned in ye South Sea, there being no shadow of reason (by ye best judgement we can make of it) for its growing into such a monster, however as ye world continues to run mad its possible there may still be something got by it.[10]

Accordingly, that month Hill switched their £2,000 of Bank of England and lottery annuities into South Sea stock.[11] But the market was close to its peak, and by early September, the price had begun to slide. Gore remained fatalistic about the future, writing that since "the prodidious [*sic*] rise of South Sea Stock proceeded more from humour than reason, no man living can know certainly whether it will rise or fall."[12] Yet fall it continued to do, and Ashe and Gore were among many who were to rue their decision.[13]

This correspondence shows that access to trusted family experts emboldened those unschooled in finance to place their money in the nascent stock market, yet it also hints that access to print could lead them to ignore the advice of these experts and behave independently. Print was thus becoming an important intermediary in the early market, and this chapter traces the diverse ways in which it disseminated information, news, opinion—and to some extent advice—about the market for stocks and shares. Though Thomas Mortimer's classic text is widely recognized as inaugurating a new genre, like the stock market itself, it too emerged out of earlier forms. This chapter shows how Mortimer borrowed elements from a technical literature, which dealt in "facts" or calculations, as well as literary responses to the increasing powerful financial class and the complexities of a developing stock market. It discusses how his book became the most important source of printed stock market advice for a generation of readers and, in doing so, seeks to identify the DNA of stock market advice literature.

A Projecting Age

An investing public existed long before the Financial Revolution, trading in the shares of early joint-stock ventures such as the Muscovy Company (established 1555), the Spanish Company (1570), and the East India Company (1600). But at this point there was no public secondary market for shares, which instead changed hands through tight-knit social networks.[14] This market began to develop in the seventeenth century, with shares being traded in public venues such as auction rooms and—increasingly—the Royal Exchange, London's major commodity exchange constructed in the late sixteenth century. But growing conflict with the other traders led the dealers in shares in 1698 to relocate a few yards away to Exchange Alley and the coffeehouses such as Jonathan's and Garraway's which lined it.[15] The coffeehouses were freely open to the public or charged a nominal fee for entry and were not designed to exclude people from the lower classes as the later formalized Stock Exchange would do. Nor were women barred from the coffee shops, despite an enduring myth among some historians that they were.[16] Brokers also congregated in the transfer offices of the Bank of England, South Sea Company, and East India Company, all located nearby.[17] Consequently, those who wanted to deal in stocks or shares could venture into this district themselves and attempt to find buyers or sellers directly. More common, however, was to find an intermediary who would transact business for the investor, in return for a commission.[18] Richard Hill, for example, despite living in London, employed the prominent broker Moses Hart to conduct his share transactions.[19] Specialization among such brokers was rare, and until at least the second half of the eighteenth century, they tended to ply their financial trade as an addition to their regular occupation. Among the brokers employed by the composer George Frideric Handel, for example, were men whose original or principal occupation included a draper, a tailor, and a blacksmith.[20]

One reason the share dealers left the Royal Exchange was the growing size of the stock and share market. The frequency of trading increased tremendously. Shares in the East India Company, for example, had changed hands on average only 44 times a year in the early 1660s: this rose to over 650 trades a year by the late 1680s.[21] And the number of companies to invest in was also growing. Besides the large chartered corporations, there was a wider set of joint-stock companies, a form of business that combined three attractive features: transferability of shares, separate legal personality of the company, and the limited liability of shareholders.[22] Although the financial historian W. R. Scott estimated that no less than one hundred new joint-stock companies appeared between 1688 and 1695, more recent research argues that the share market may have been more limited than this suggests, with trading concentrated in the shares of a much smaller set of companies.[23] Certainly, the chartered corporations brought together what were, by the standards of the time, large constituencies of shareholders: in 1688 the East India Company already had over 500 shareholders, while the ledger books of the Bank of England between 1720 and 1725 list the names of nearly 8,000 different investors.[24] Though the bank's shares had a face value of £100, they could be subdivided into smaller portions, and this meant that among the bank's shareholders were coachmen and servants alongside those of higher rank.[25] Other companies, including the South Sea Company, allowed investors to pay for shares in installments, which also diversified the occupational pool.[26] Impressive as the numbers of shareholders were, they were dwarfed by the holders of national debt. There were already an estimated 40,000 of these at the time of the South Sea Bubble in 1720, rising to 60,000 by the 1750s.[27] The state could tap into an even broader social base with lottery tickets. An important element in the state's fundraising efforts beginning in 1694, generating £144 million in their first ninety years, lottery schemes were an accessible method of state-sponsored speculation.[28] Tickets were split into smaller portions and sold again, becoming a form of currency in their own right and allowing widespread participation.[29] Advertisements for brokers often focused on the fact that they sold lottery tickets rather than other types of security, suggesting their widespread popularity.[30]

As Jane Ashe's example suggests, women played an active role in the early investment market. Under English common law, married women were subject to the rule of coverture. Women could protect their assets from coverture in a variety of ways, notably using contracts; otherwise, they were handing over most of their assets to their husbands' control and a portion would become his property outright. However, husbands did not

always insist on their coverture rights. As Amy Froide notes, Sarah Churchill, the Duchess of Marlborough, "was undeniably one of the most
influential public investors, male or female, in the first twenty-five years of
the Financial Revolution." Churchill handled all the financial matters for
her husband and "despite her coverture Sarah Churchill acted as a feme
sole."[31] There were also specialist publications available to them. Convey-
ancing manuals provided sample forms of a range of legal documents, including those relating to marriage. One, published in 1732, was entitled *A
Treatise of Feme Coverts or, The Lady's Law* and was aimed at "the fair
sex."[32] As the legal historian Christopher Brooks argues, "the doctrine of
coverture and its complications may have made women more, rather than
less, aware of their legal circumstances." The same could be said for their
financial circumstances. Early modern women were expected to keep accounts and to be involved in economic realities. Furthermore, married
women—like Ashe—were likely to be left widowed and were then charged
with looking after their families' economic affairs.[33]

The diverse range of paper securities available competed with more
traditional forms of investment; above all, land. Until this point, land was
the dominant mode of securing and increasing wealth, and, for men, the
only way to gain status and political power. It conferred voting rights
and the right to run for political office. It was also the key resource in
an economy which centered on the agricultural sector. There were numerous speculative schemes aimed at land improvements, such as enclosure or drainage of fens. The stock market needed to draw funds away
from this important competitor, and landowners had to be persuaded to
look further than their own districts. Investing had a number of practical
advantages. A share portfolio need not require the same kind of active
management as land. This was particularly appealing to female investors.
Although some women found it difficult to collect rents or payments on
personal loans from male debtors or tenants, they could claim dividends
or sell shares with relative ease. Moreover, unlike land, capital gains and
income were not taxed, and the returns could be huge. In the 1680s, the
Royal African Company was paying dividends of over 10 percent, while
some years shareholders in the Hudson's Bay Company and the East India Company received up to 50 percent.[34] And stocks and shares were
more liquid assets, with the developing London market making transferability relatively straightforward.[35]

But turning the stock market into an attractive proposition required
not only a financial revolution but also a conceptual one. Investors had to

believe that financial instruments, recorded on paper, could compete with the ownership of the ultimate symbol of tangible wealth: land. As Mary Poovey has argued, the fluid terrain of economic and imaginative writing from the late seventeenth to the late eighteenth century "helped Britons understand and learn how to negotiate the market model of value," based on the credibility of fictive forms of wealth in an economy increasingly centered on credit.[36] Alongside—and deeply connected with—the flurry of new trading ventures and corporate organizations in the period from roughly 1680 to 1720, there emerged new forms of economic writing, from literal forms of paper money such as credit notes to the development of the novel itself. Daniel Defoe, whose own writings encompassed both financial pamphlets such as *The Anatomy of Exchange-Alley* and *Robinson Crusoe* (both 1719), the first recognizably modern novel which told a tale of economic individualism, called it a "projecting age."[37] As Valerie Hamilton and Martin Parker put it in their study of the literal and conceptual connections between William Paterson's creation of the Bank of England in 1694 and his friend Defoe's writing, "corporations are fictions, and novels create worlds."[38]

In this period both the novel and new forms of financial transactions were shaped by and helped establish the idea that "property . . . has ceased to be real and has become not merely mobile but imaginary."[39] Like the broader credit economy, literature worked by creating trust in forms of value that were products of collective imagination: paper money, share certificates, bills of exchange, and even the national debt itself. As literary scholars have shown, credit was central to both the new financial world and the genre of the novel, relying on a belief in intangible and fluid projections of future value rather than the tangible property of the landowning class.[40] The emerging genre of the novel did not merely represent everyday life being transformed by market interactions, but instead made the mysteries of capitalist exchange intelligible for its readers who, like investors, came from an increasingly wide social background. The novel instructed readers—"emergent 'financial subjects'"—how to make sense of the strangers encountered in the rapidly expanding market: reading them as instances of conventional literary "characters" made the dissolving social hierarchies of class more manageable.[41] It therefore seems appropriate that Jonathan Swift was among the authors hired by the South Sea Company to write propaganda on its behalf, and that Swift, along with his contemporaries Alexander Pope and John Gay, sought to make money themselves from stock market investments.[42]

The Villainy of Stockjobbers

Though the emerging genre of the novel constituted a type of financial writing that helped smooth the way conceptually for an economy based on intangible forms of value, its progenitors were ambivalent about the implications of this change. Defoe railed against "the villainy of stock-jobbers" in a fiery 1701 polemic. The trade in new paper instruments, Defoe argued, had conjured up a formidable new enemy within the state that threatened national prosperity. Rather than wielding swords, muskets, or bombs, it posed a far more insidious danger:

> these People can ruin Men silently, undermine and impoverish by a sort of impenetrable Artifice, like Poison that works at a distance, can wheedle Men to ruin themselves, and *Fiddle them out of their Money*, by the strange and unheard of Engines of *Interests, Discounts, Transfers, Tallies, Debentures, Shares, Projects*, and the *Devil and all* of Figures and hard Names.[43]

By this point, jibes at stockjobbing were already common. Thomas Shadwell's 1692 play *The Volunteers; or, The Stock-Jobbers* satirized the projectors of wild and unlikely schemes whose sole concern was to profit from the sale of shares.[44] The term entered popular parlance, though its exact meaning remained indeterminate. Sometimes simply referring in general terms to the buying and selling of stocks and shares, it was more often used pejoratively as a shorthand for unscrupulousness and deviousness.[45] "Time contracts"—commitments to buy or sell stock after an agreed length of time—came in for particular censure. These were rarely settled by the actual transfer of stock but by payment of the difference between the price of the security when the bargain was struck and when delivery day arrived. This meant that the transaction was simply a bet on the future price of the stock—those "selling" did not even need to possess the stock—and was easily dismissed as a "fictitious" rather than a legitimate commercial transaction, one which contravened the laws against usury.[46] Such gambles created winners and losers, and the winners, critics argued, were always the insiders. Rhetoric against stockjobbing was fixated on the idea that the market was manipulated by "secret Cabals" of insiders who used "guileful Arts"—often spreading false reports—to manipulate the price of stocks for personal gain, ruining innocent outsiders in the process.[47] The quick profits they made threatened to undermine the social order. Defoe claimed that he could "reckon up a black List of 57 Persons" who had "rais'd themselves to vast Estates" from humble origins through their sharp practices. "Now they ride in their Coaches, keep splendid Equipages, and thrust themselves into business, set up for Deputies, Aldermen, Sheriffs, or Mayors; but above all, for Parliament-men."[48] As one satirical poem had it, "Stock-jobbing is the most bewitching Thing / 'Twill from a Beggar raise you to a King."[49]

The author of this poem described himself as a "Gideonite," a reminder that diatribes were often inflected by anti-Semitism. Indeed, "the Alley" offered opportunities not afforded elsewhere for outsider groups. Jews, Catholics, and Quakers faced restrictions on their legal freedoms, and those who could not, or would not, take Christian (that is, Anglican) oaths were blocked from various economic activities such as membership in livery guilds, holding public office, or opening retail businesses within the City's limits.[50] They benefited from the relative freedoms of the financial sector. In addition, religious minorities often had links to major trading centers through their coreligionists or family networks. The Sephardim in London, for example, had strong links to the Sephardi community in Amsterdam, which helped them to facilitate an international financial system. Sephardim made up a ninth of the original Bank of England proprietors with large shareholdings.[51] Samson Gideon (1699–1762), a Sephardic banker, was "the most noteworthy financier, Jew or Christian, of mid-eighteenth century England."[52] Gideon gave financial advice to the government but also involved fellow Jews in the government loan business.[53] In reality, only a minority of Jewish people were regularly trading in shares, which is not surprising given that "the great bulk of Anglo-Jewry in the Georgian period were desperately poor."[54] But high-profile exceptions like Gideon encouraged anti-Semitic conspiracy theorists to argue that this cosmopolitanism threatened the national interest. Jewish people were particularly associated with finance by their Gentile counterparts, and most of the depictions of Jewish financiers and shareholders came from their anti-Semitic opponents.[55]

Critics also thought the trade in stocks objectionable because it lured people away from honest enterprise. It was "a Nuisance worse than Pestilence / The bane of *Business, Trade* and *Diligence*," claimed one poet.[56] It unleashed dangerous passions, particularly avarice, thus corrupting the morals of the nation, and upsetting the "body-politic."[57] When the South Sea Bubble took off in 1720, such criticisms were endlessly repeated, one critic claiming that "the numerous Inhabitants of this great Metropolis, had for the most part deserted their Stations, Businesses, and Occupations; and given up all Pretensions to Industry, in pursuit of an imaginary Profit."[58] Indeed, the boom and bust provoked a multimedia explosion in commentaries and allegories on the bubble. That year, at least half a dozen plays about the stock market were published, including *South-Sea; or, The Biters Bit* and *The Broken Stock-Jobbers*, though not all of them were performed.[59] Spotting an easy opportunity to cash in, publishers offered the public pamphlets, broadsides, poems, satirical prints, and even playing cards moralizing on the episode.

Though some post-crash commentaries merely poked fun at recent events, others called for state intervention to punish the South Sea Company directors and reimburse investors. Such regulatory demands were not new: indeed, the authors of anti-jobber literature usually also offered policy proposals designed to drive out objectionable actors and to limit speculative activity.[60] Attempts by the City of London authorities in 1673 to regulate the market by means of a licensing system, which restricted the number of brokers (not just stockbrokers, but brokers in all commodities) to a hundred Englishmen plus twelve from the French and Dutch churches plus six "aliens," did not succeed in curbing unlicensed brokers, and pressure for parliamentary intervention grew through the 1690s.[61] The result was a 1697 act "To Restrain the Number and ill Practice of Brokers and Stock Jobbers," which confirmed the 1673 rules and built on them. To operate legitimately, brokers had to pay an annual fee of forty shillings and swear an oath before the Lord Mayor, and their number was limited to one hundred.[62] More ambitiously, the act sought to stamp out time bargains by restricting the period between contracts and transfers to three days. It also attempted to prevent conflicts of interest by forbidding brokers from dealing in stock on their own account: in other words, imposing a clear distinction between brokers as agents and jobbers as principals. However, despite the penalties imposed on anyone acting as a broker without a license as well as those caught dealing with such a broker, the legislation did not curb the activities of unlicensed brokers.[63] Neither did it succeed in its other objectives of thwarting time-bargaining or preventing brokers from dealing.[64]

Sporadic calls for regulation continued to flare up through the century. The Bubble Act of 1720,[65] sometimes erroneously believed to have been a post-crash attempt to regulate the market, was in fact passed at the height of the boom at the behest of the South Sea Company. Concerned that the number of joint-stock schemes being promoted was drawing capital away

from their company, the directors sought to outlaw companies not incorporated by act of Parliament or royal charter, in an attempt to monopo-
lize the market. Its impact on the stock market in the longer term was
limited.[66] A more serious attempt at regulation was spearheaded by
Sir John Barnard, a London wine merchant and Whig MP who entered
Parliament shortly after the bursting of the bubble. For him, the stock
market was nothing more than "a Lottery, or rather a Gaming-House";
worse, it was a rigged lottery, in which it was "always in the Power of the
principal Managers to bestow the Benefit-Tickets as they have a mind."[67]
Seeking to purge the market of speculative practices, he successfully secured the passage of an act in 1734 which outlawed the settlement of contracts by paying differences, voided contracts for the sale of stock which
the seller did not possess, and forbade options contracts, which gave the
option, but not the obligation, for the holder to either buy or sell shares at
a certain point in the future.[68] Though remaining on the statute book for
over a century, Barnard's act had only a limited effect, as suggested by a
succession of later bills over the next few decades, all unsuccessful, attack-
ing the same practices.[69]

While "tirades against jobbing" remained staple fare in the pamphlet
and newspaper press of the eighteenth century, it is important not to over-
simplify the attitudes of critics.[70] Even the strongest-worded invectives
betrayed a certain curiosity about the world they condemned. Though
mainly concerned with explaining the tricks and devices used by stockjobbers to fleece the public, Defoe's *Anatomy of Exchange-Alley* also seeks
to satisfy his readers' inquisitiveness as to what Exchange Alley and its
occupants were actually like. To this end, he provides a brief description of
the location of the coffeehouses and other landmarks along with sketches
of several of the leading "Alley-Men."[71] Defoe thus turns tour guide, albeit
a guide to enemy territory. Even critiques of the market could act as forms
of education, introducing to audiences unversed in finance the jargon of
the Alley. As early as 1718, Susanna Centlivre's play *A Bold Stroke for a
Wife* includes a scene set in Jonathan's, the dialogue incorporating the language of brokers and jobbers, including references to "bull" (a speculator
for a rise in prices) and "bear" (a speculator for a fall), which Centlivre
seems to assume her audience will be familiar with.[72]

Moreover, it was not the stock market itself but its manipulation that,
in many cases, was the target. When pamphlets condemned devices designed "to raise Stock to an excessive Price above its due and intrinsick
Value," they were not rejecting the stock market outright.[73] They believed

that paper securities *did* possess value but wanted market prices to reflect this core, intrinsic value rather than the machinations of the unscrupulous. The market could be stabilized and purified if it could be stripped down to these intrinsic values. As Prime Minister Robert Walpole put it when supporting Barnard's bill in Parliament in 1733, he hoped that as a result of the measure, "the Price of all Publick Stocks will become more certain and fixed, which will make them more valuable to all honest Purchasers."[74] The distinction that was beginning to form was between legitimate investment and illegitimate speculation—a distinction which was to become increasingly important in the coming years.[75]

Market Information

If anti-jobbing tracts only indirectly helped to normalize the stock market, then other forms of print did more to embed the market in popular culture. The wide circulation of price data is a key example. In early markets, information about the prices of commodities were jealously guarded, secrets to be shared or traded among private business networks rather than broadcast freely. In the sixteenth century, as John McCusker documents, the attitude of merchants changed, and they began to see the benefits of publishing prices using the new technology of print as a means of extending markets both spatially and temporally.[76] "Prices current" were first seen in European trading centers like Antwerp and Amsterdam in the sixteenth century and had reached London by the start of the seventeenth century. From the early 1680s, however, the compilers of a couple of these price lists, *Whiston's Merchants Weekly Remembrancer* and Robert Woolley's *Prices of Merchandise in London*, had begun to add the stock prices for the leading chartered corporations.[77] The inclusion of the stock prices of the East India Company, the Royal African Company, and the Hudson's Bay Company alongside more tangible commodities like wheat, hops, and coal clearly intimated that investors had nothing to fear from the immateriality of these kinds of intangible assets.

John Houghton's weekly periodical, *A Collection for Improvement of Husbandry and Trade* (1692), went further, covering a wider selection of companies than his predecessors did, eventually listing fifty-five companies by May 1694.[78] His stated objective in doing so was to extend the share market beyond the confines of the coffeehouses of Exchange Alley, which he believed would benefit the country as a whole:

Altho' they that live at *London*, may every *noon and night* on working-days, go to GARRAWAY'S COFFEE-HOUSE, and see what *prices* the *actions* bear of most *companies* trading in *joynt-stocks*, yet for those whose occasions permit not there to see, they may be satisfied *once a week* how it is, and thereby the whole kingdom may reap advantage by those *trades*.[79]

This was not merely a spatial extension: Houghton was writing chiefly for market outsiders, those who did not need to keep abreast of prices on a daily basis but who were being told that they could—and should— subscribe to such a publication that would give them weekly updates. This information, Houghton told his readers, would be of direct financial benefit to them. As he put it in his prospectus, his publication was intended "for Incouragement of those at distance to turn *Merchants*, and to inform them how their *Stock* goes, that they may thereby see when best to buy or sell."[80] Houghton was therefore a very early advocate of watching the market.

At a time when, as we have seen, concerns over the manipulation of stock prices were escalating, Houghton had to convince readers of the reliability of his data. As a fellow of the Royal Society, Houghton was able both to mobilize testimonials in his support and to present his publishing venture as part of a wider knowledge-making project.[81] As well as communicating information on prices, his periodical carried short essays on a wide variety of commercial topics. He encouraged subscribers to contribute their own pieces, creating the sense of his periodical as "a collective project" mobilizing the wisdom of the age.[82] Though the stock market occupied only a small fraction of the *Collection*'s overall coverage, which took in everything from the tending of cypress trees to the price of beans in Melton Mowbray, it was occasionally featured. Asserting his objectivity in relation to the market, telling readers that he himself was "not much concern'd in stocks," he presented himself as an expert who promised "to impart to others some mysteries in trade," rectifying common "errors and mistakes" made on the subject.[83] And though admitting that there were "many *cunning artists*" operating in the stock market, Houghton's broader aim was to persuade readers of the market's essentially benign nature and of the public benefits of joint-stock projects.[84] In a series of articles on the subject in the summer of 1694, Houghton explained how a "monied man" might deal with brokers in the coffeehouses. Rather than restricting himself to basic investment business, he explained many of the more exotic speculative transactions, providing a detailed example of an option contract and both "put" and "call" option types.[85]

Houghton's *Collection* was a landmark, made possible by what Miles Ogborn calls the developing "material geographies of information in late seventeenth-century England" — an impressive network of "printers, stationers, and booksellers."[86] At the low price of just a penny, his publication was very affordable, and, by the middle of 1693, he was boasting that his *Collection* was being sold by "most of the Booksellers in *England.*"[87] A commercial venture, financial imperatives fundamentally shaped the *Collection*'s content. When Houghton extended his coverage of stocks, he did not list prices for all of them, coyly informing his readers that "those that desire the Values of them to be Published may have them on very reasonable Terms."[88] Indeed, he did not try to conceal his own brokerage activities, which covered investments as well as jobs, property, goods, and even marriages.[89] He also included "thinly disguised advertisements for the prospects of certain companies" for which he was no doubt paid.[90]

In Houghton's wake, the circulation of stock prices continued apace. *Proctor's Price Current* first appeared in October 1694 and included commodity prices as well as prices for stocks.[91] But 1697 saw the arrival of a specialist financial price list with John Castaing's *Course of the Exchange.* Castaing's list, published twice a week but tracking daily price movements, was quickly recognized as the most reliable market source, with Houghton eventually copying his prices from Castaing.[92] Castaing's hegemony was challenged by John Freke's *Prices of the Several Stocks*, which began publication in 1714.[93] These price lists were compiled by brokers and were intended in part as advertisements for their brokerage services. Indeed, Freke's list informs readers that he "buys and sells Stocks, and all securities, and lends Money on the same." The frontispiece for one of the 1715 editions (see fig. 1.1) states that the work was "Sold by the Author, at his Office over against Jonathan's Coffee-house in Exchange-Alley." Inside, there is a manicule pointing to the following statement which appears at the bottom of every page: "Any Gentleman, on Notice, may have this Paper left at his House every Tuesday and Friday, for three Shillings a Quarter."[94]

Circulating chiefly in the coffee shops and their environs, these lists were mainly intended for small numbers of merchants and very wealthy metropolitan investors. But by the early eighteenth century, stock prices were beginning to appear in a wider range of publications, including the *British Mercury* (1710–15). Published by the Sun Fire Office and delivered free to shops, taverns, and coffeehouses as well as to the Sun's own policyholders, the *British Mercury* was reaching over 3,000 subscribers, including

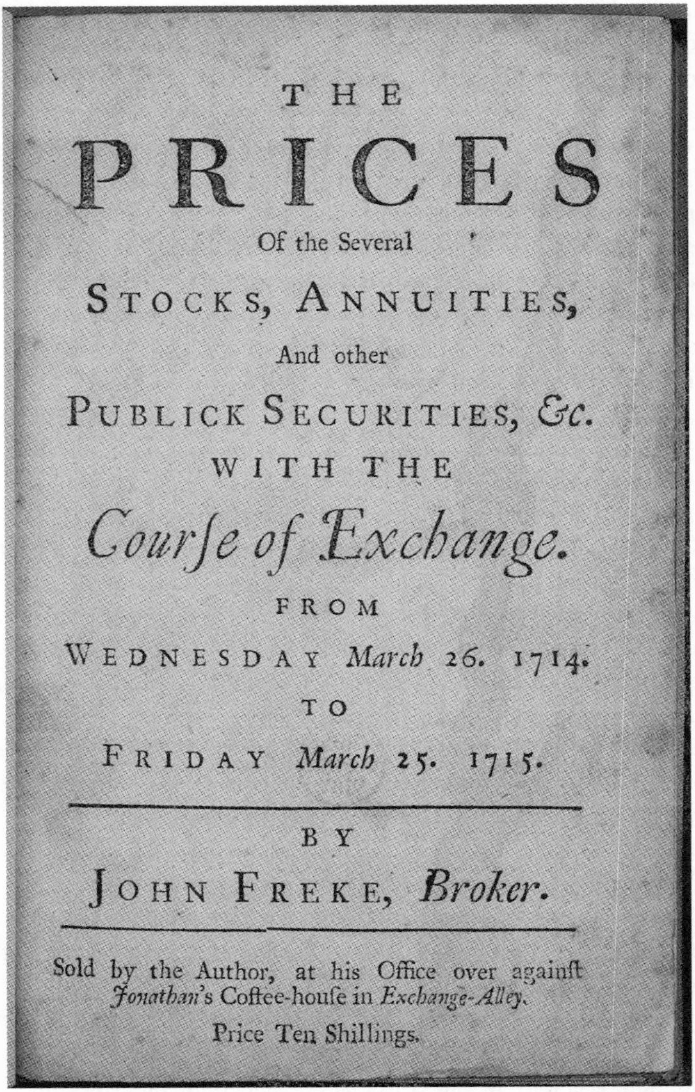

THE

PRICES

Of the Several

STOCKS, ANNUITIES,

And other

PUBLICK SECURITIES, &c.

WITH THE

Courſe of Exchange.

FROM

WEDNESDAY *March* 26. 1714.

TO

FRIDAY *March* 25. 1715.

BY

JOHN FREKE, *Broker.*

Sold by the Author, at his Office over againſt
Jonathan's Coffee-houſe in *Exchange-Alley.*

Price Ten Shillings.

FIGURE 1.1. Frontispiece of John Freke's published list of stock prices (1715). Reproduced
with the permission of the Senate House Library, University of London.

over 200 women.[95] By the time of the South Sea Bubble, stock prices were a familiar presence in general publications, including the *London Journal*, the *Daily Courant*, and the *Post Boy*.[96] Such papers also published company announcements and editorial opinion on the stock market. Printed news readily entered networks of private correspondence, with information read in newspapers shared in letters to friends and contacts functioning as "a social commodity," an element in "a larger system of gift exchange."[97] As the case of Jane Ashe showed, newspaper publicity could influence the decisions of early investors, particularly during the South Sea Bubble.[98] The press, with its commodification of financial information, certainly helped to develop a national stock and share market. But other forms of print were also integral in this endeavor.

The Calculating Investor

The publishing industry churned out manuals on topics that were closely related to the stock market without dealing with it specifically. There was a readership for technical and instructional texts on accounting and calculation which could be of use in investment activities. John Vernon's *Compleat Countinghouse* (1678) and John Ward's *Compendium of Algebra* (1724) explained how to calculate interest payments, despite displaying a certain caginess due to the traditional opposition to usury.[99] Between the two, and a year after the foundation of the Bank of England, Edward Hatton published the *Merchant's Magazine: or, Trades-man's Treasury* (1695), which also dealt with arithmetic, bookkeeping, and interest calculations. Hatton wrote that his book was useful for those "concerned with the Bank of England."[100] The content is similar to older works, but its marketing claims relate to the new financial world. And though chiefly aimed at actual or would-be businessmen, producers of such literature were keen to extend the market for it, and the title page of Hatton's manual suggests that though it was "Accommodated chiefly to the Practice of *Merchants* and *Trades-men*" it would also be "usefull for Schools, Bankers, Diversion of Gentlemen, Business of Mechanicks, and Officers of the King's Custom and Excise."[101] Some later guides were pitched more squarely at wider audiences. Roger North's *Gentleman Accomptant; or, An Essay to Unfold the Mystery of Accompts* (1714) tried to persuade genteel readers of the advantages of keeping their own accounts. Alexander Brodie's *A New and Easy Method of Book-keeping, or Instructions for a Methodical Keeping of*

Merchants Accompts (1722) was aimed at "Beginners" of both genders.[102] North included a section entitled "Of Stocks, and Stock-Jobbing; the Frauds therein detected" but, despite this bold claim, it merely amounts to a short entry in a glossary of terms. For North, corporations are "a Politick Essence, distinct from Human Nature, and contrived after a Popish model, for no purpose but Cheating" and brokers are "to Knaves, as Pimps to Whores."[103] Nevertheless, one of his examples has him purchasing East India Company stock, while Brodie's manual used many examples drawn from the world of stocks and shares.[104] The message was that sensible investment was linked to accuracy in calculation.

Dedicated calculating guides for the stock market also appeared. In 1700, the broker John Castaing published a small *Interest-book*, "not Five Inches long," consisting of tables to calculate interest between 4 and 8 percent. His book "gave no instructions on how to use the tables—the capabilities of the audience were assumed," and the tables were not explicitly presented as for investment calculations.[105] But later books of tables took a different approach. A few years after the South Sea Bubble had burst, George Clerke published *The Dealers in Stock's Assistant* (1725), while the following year saw the publication of Richard Hayes's *Money'd Man's Guide: or, The Purchaser's Pocket-Companion* (1726). Both authors were able to parade their credentials, Clerke pointing out that he was "of the South Sea House" and dedicating his volume to the governors and court of directors of the South Sea Company.[106] Hayes, meanwhile, was a London accountant and "writing-master" who had already published several volumes designed "to make People fit for Business."[107] Both Clerke and Hayes provided worked examples along with their tables to show how the face value of an investment might be translated into market value, with the further complication of pounds, shillings, and pence. These pocket guides were intended to be taken into the coffeehouses by investors as they traded because, as Hayes explained, it was difficult to do calculations "in a Coffee-Room among Company . . . where the Prices of things are continually varying."[108] They were therefore presented as essential information technologies for sensible investors. Despite this reference to the growing velocity of the market, Hayes claimed not to be writing for speculators, stating that despite the great interest in stocks "a few Years since," he chose instead to publish it "in these more composed Times" when people wanted to "lay out their Money to the best advantage, and not precipitately or inadvertently hazard the Loss of it, by a chimerical Notion of an exorbitant Gain."[109] Neither Clerke nor Hayes appear to have brought out further editions of their works, but Hayes also published *The Broker's Breviat* in 1734.[110] It included a range of examples to work out financial calculations relating to the stock market.

If books of tables gave people the means of calculating potential profits, then pocket books and memorandum books encouraged them to keep track of their investments. Easily affordable and aimed at a wide audience, much like pocket calendars today, they combined some printed information with blank pages so that the owners could record personal notes, including financial transactions. They constituted a kind of "ego document," similar to a diary, which encourages the owner to interact with it, while also allowing "their owners to participate in a growing trend for anticipating and recording their own movements within time," significant because the recording of transactions and the ability to envisage a future state are essential parts of successful investment strategies.[111] Some pocket books related to a particular city or trade. The *Liverpool Memorandum-Book* (1753) was clearly for the local market but also stated that it was intended for "ALL Sorts of People," presumably including women and lower-class men. It included space to enter details of "Bargains, Contracts, etc. of Business" as well as items peculiar to Liverpool, such as a list of the mayors.[112] The fourth section was given over to a list of slavers who were not part of the Royal African Company, as well as vessels employed in the "Guinea Trade," with details of how many enslaved people the ships could carry. The fifth section listed the ships involved in the West Indian, American, and foreign trades (involving slave-produced goods). The tenth section gave details about days for transacting business at South Sea House and other company offices. This pocket book gives no direct advice about investing in slaving companies, despite showing how much Liverpool was dependent on them and the plantation economy.

There was also a subgenre of pocket books aimed at women, in which ideals of femininity were linked to practical skills such as "prudent economy."[113] As women were often the bookkeepers of the household and "women of all social types were expert at haggling over exchanges at shops and market stalls," this linkage is perhaps unsurprising.[114] More strikingly, some publishers were selling pocket books which explicitly acknowledged the female investor in the stock market even when other authors generally ignored them. The *Ladies Complete Pocket-Book* (1760) states that it is a "methodical memorandum book," allowing women to keep a proper daily account of their money, including personal loans they made, and note down their appointments. It also includes instructions about

etiquette, including "precedency due to women; of doing the honours of
a table," and recipes including "particularly, one for love." Then come details of the new songs from Vauxhall Pleasure Gardens and twenty-four
country dances, not to mention a description of the sun and the moon, and
a chronological account of great events. The final item listed is an "explanation of the stocks." This gave worked examples to explain what printed
share prices in newspapers actually meant. For instance, "Bank Stock 117 *l.*"
meant "Every 100 *l.* of Bank Stock is sold for 117 *l.*" The heading given
to the explanation was "the same explained so as to be intelligible to the
meanest capacity." The author warns readers to take interest payments
(and their different timings) into account.[115] Though brief, this could be
taken as a form of rudimentary stock market advice. The 1762 edition
likewise includes an assortment of topics for a would-be genteel lady, including a list of transfer days, but again only a very brief mention of the
stock market itself.[116] It is sandwiched between instructions for the dance
"Party of Pleasure" and a table showing the prices of beef, mutton, veal,
lamb, and pork.

Later pocket books for women also indicate an embedding of the stock
market into wider popular culture. *Lane's Ladies Museum* (1792), for example, gives "an exact Account of the Times of buying and selling Stocks"
a prominent position in the second section, after a list of holidays.[117] The
list states when the bank and other important places such as East India
House will be closed. This information, along with the times and days of
transfers and dividends, appears before anything else. *The Ladies Most
Elegant and Convenient Pocket Book* (1790) likewise promised to record
the "Days and Hours for buying, accepting, or transferring Stock, and receiving Dividends" on its frontispiece.[118] These appeared immediately after the contents page and clearly before the table of precedency for ladies
and tables for sunrise and sunset. *The Court and Royal Lady's Pocket-
Book* (1797) has a similar arrangement.[119] Even the oddly named *Crosby's
Royal Fortune-Telling Almanack; or, Ladies Universal Pocket-Book* (see
fig. 1.2), published in 1796, lists days for transferring stock, along with sections on palmistry, dreams, and the inevitable list of new songs sung at
Vauxhall Gardens.[120]

Though interest tables and pocket books encouraged practices of calculation and recording investments, owners did not always use them in the
way they were intended. The copy of one such pocket book in the British
Library shows that its owner used it as a daily diary but did not list her
financial transactions, suggesting that "far from allowing the pocket book

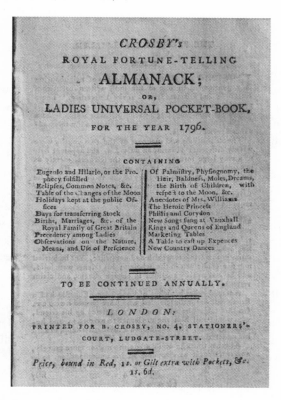

CROSBY's

ROYAL FORTUNE-TELLING

. ALMANACK;

OR,

LADIES UNIVERSAL POCKET-BOOK,

FOR THE YEAR 1796.

CONTAINING

Eugenio and Illario, or the Pro-
phecy fulfilled
Eclipses, Common Notes, &c.
Table of the Changes of the Moon
Holidays kept at the public Of-
fices
Days for transferring Stock
Births, Marriages, &c. of the
Royal Family of Great Britain
Precedency among Ladies
Observations on the Nature,
Means, and Use of Prescience

Of Palmistry, Physiognomy, the
Hair, Baldness, Moles, Dreams,
the Birth of Children, with
respect to the Moon, &c.
Anecdotes of Mrs. Williams
The Heroic Princess
Phillis and Corydon
New Songs sung at Vauxhall
Kings and Queens of England
Marketing Tables
A Table to cast up Expences
New Country Dances

TO BE CONTINUED ANNUALLY.

LONDON:

PRINTED FOR B. CROSBY, NO. 4, STATIONERS'-
COURT, LUDGATE-STREET.

Price, bound in Red, 1s. or Gilt extra with Pockets, &c.
1s. 6d.

FIGURE 1.2. Frontispiece of *Crosby's Royal Fortune-Telling Almanack* (1796). Courtesy of the British Library Board, RB.8.a.134, digitized by Google.

to fashion her character, its reader could fashion the pocket book to tailor it to her own concerns."[121] Moreover, there were clear limits to the help such publications offered new investors. The novice who ventured into a coffeehouse armed with a book of interest tables might still feel vulnerable. Indeed, Richard Hayes warned his readers that he could only help them with their sums: when it came to "the hazard and risque in Securities; that must be left entirely to a Man's own Judgment."[122] As for pocket books, the stock market ranks low on the list of items which their compilers thought readers would need. There is not much advice per se, as it is assumed that women already know what they must do. They know how to dance, how to transfer shares, and how to buy mutton; they simply need to refresh their memories as to dance steps, transfer days, and meat prices.

Advice Literature

This was not a culture short of printed advice. "Courtesy" or "conduct" books explaining matters of etiquette and giving moral instruction dated back to the Middle Ages, and the market for instructional texts of this kind grew in the early modern period, providing "a guide for literate readers to negotiate new sets of social possibilities."[123] Though originally promoting the courtier as the gentlemanly ideal, this literature became more and more part of the new urban, middle-class consumer culture that was increasingly setting the tone of polite behavior.[124] Female readers began to be targeted as well as male, particularly beginning in the late seventeenth century, a time when homegrown conduct books for women also started appearing in the American colonies.[125] And as literacy spread in the eighteenth century, so advice literature began to reach the servant and apprentice class.[126]

The purpose of much conduct literature was explicitly didactic, often inculcating an explicitly Christian morality, drawing on devotional texts which detailed how to live a life based on religious principles. Yet some authors catered to more material concerns, in particular addressing how to achieve wealth and success. The publication of guides such as *The Art of Thriving, or, The Plaine Path-way to Preferment* (1635), *The Ready Way to Get Riches: or, The Poor Man's Counsellor* (1673), *The Art of Thriving, or, The Way to Get and Keep Money* (1674), *Humane Prudence: or, The Art by which a Man May Raise Himself and Fortune to Grandeur* (1680), and *The Pleasant Art of Money-Catching, Newly and Fully Discovered* (1684) suggested a financially motivated and upwardly mobile audience.[127] Sometimes the lessons inculcated were traditional and pious—live within your means, avoid drink, womanizing, and gaming—but others purported to offer something different.[128] *The Pleasant Art of Money-Catching*, a volume which continued to be published into the middle of the nineteenth century, demonstrated many of the rhetorical traits that were to characterize modern "self-help" literature: the promise of magical secrets shared ("How to pay debts without Money"), shortcuts to success for the impatient ("How to get a great Estate in a little time"), and the hope of personal transformation ("Choice Rules, whosoever speedily follows, will certainly thrive, though they went down the Wind before").[129]

Besides these generalist texts, specialist manuals instructed ambitious young men on how to enter particular trades. Authors were keen to align mercantile pursuits with Christian faith in order to defend the pursuit of profit. Honor and virtue, readers were told, were the keys to attaining credit, and many early guides, such as William Scott's *An Essay of Drapery* (1635), were more philosophic essays than practical manuals. As urban and commercial society developed in the eighteenth century such guides became more focused on the particular skills that would-be businessmen needed to learn, particularly accounting, bookkeeping, arithmetic, and correspondence.[130] Simply the title of Thomas Watts's *An Essay on the Proper Method for Forming the Man of Business* (1716) spoke to the claims of this kind of literature to help readers fashion new business selves. The market for such texts was large and growing. After 1750, on average ten new trade manuals were published annually.[131] But neither these trade manuals nor the guides to "money-catching" tended to deal with the stock market. When they did mention it, it was generally to cast it as a dangerous distraction to aspiring businessmen, little different from gaming. In a chapter on "over-trading" in his *Complete English Tradesman* (1726), Defoe warned his readers against excessive boldness and greed, giving "the late South-sea calamity for an example, in which the longest heads were most over-reach'd, not so much by the wit or cunning of those they had to deal with, as by the secret promptings of their own avarice ... the cunningest, wisest, sharpest men lost the most money."[132]

Explicit stock market advice was therefore conspicuous by its absence for much of the eighteenth century, existing more in the imagination than in print. In an ironic essay in *The Spectator* in 1711, editor Richard Steele proposed a bold new plan. Rather than simply catering to "Men of Literature and superior Education," Steele said that he wanted his magazine to appeal to a wider audience, and therefore invited his readers who had prospered in different "Arts, Professions, and Trades" to send him articles explaining the path to "Greatness and Success" in their field. One of the subjects to be covered was the stock market. Steele asked:

> Is it possible that a young Man at present could pass his Time better, than in reading the History of the Stocks, and knowing by what secret Springs they have such sudden Ascents and Falls in the same Day? Could he be better conducted in his Way to Wealth, which is the great Article of Life, than in a Treatise dated from *Change-Alley* by an able Proficient there? Nothing certainly could be more useful, than to be well instructed in his Hopes and Fears; to be diffident when others exult, and with a secret Joy buy when others think it their Interest to sell.[133]

Though intended as a sarcastic gibe at more business-oriented periodicals and their perceived lack of moral integrity, particularly Houghton's *Collection*, Steele was in fact describing—with remarkable prescience—a type of literature that did not yet exist.[134] He captures the pleasures to be had from speculating in the stock market, but these were nothing to do with the transitory thrill of spinning the wheel of fortune, deriving instead from mastering the market through learning, by instruction from insiders, the hidden secrets of the seemingly random fluctuations of stocks. This command of the market extended to the command of the self—being "well instructed" in his own "Hopes and Fears"—setting the reader apart from the crowd and enabling him to get rich from it. As Steele put it at the end of his essay, if his plan worked, it would "produce a new Field of Diversion, an Instruction more agreeable than has yet appeared."[135] Later chapters will show it took a long time for reality fully to catch up with Steele's imaginings, but a significant step was taken in 1761 with the publication of Thomas Mortimer's *Every Man His Own Broker*.

Walking the Alley

In May 1761, advertisements started appearing for a new two-shilling volume, *Every Man His Own Broker: or, A Guide to Exchange-Alley*.[136] The book promised to explain "the Nature of the several Funds" as well as the "Mystery and Iniquity of Stock-Jobbing," and it quickly became a popular hit, racing through five editions in little more than twelve months. Initially appearing under the pen name "Philanthropos," the third edition was published under the author's name, Thomas Mortimer. Mortimer synthesized elements from many different strands of writing about the stock market to create something new.

First and most strikingly, he borrowed the lurid language used by authors of anti-stockjobbing literature to present the coffeehouses of Exchange Alley as sinful, devilish places. His aim, he explained in his preface, was "to teach astonished Britons the amazing art of thrusting their hands into the fire without burning their fingers," by which he meant instructing "people to walk thro' the fiery furnace of J——'s coffee-house unhurt." His portrayal of the market reflects the ad hominem diatribes common at the time. His animus against market professionals was partly anti-Semitic in nature: Mortimer claimed that it was "rare to see a Jew so much as singe his beard in this mansion of Belzebub." But he was also motivated by class prejudice—early on, he condemns the "medley of Barbers, Bakers,

Shoe-makers, Plaisterers, and Taylors, whom the mammon of unrighteous-
ness has transformed into Stock-Brokers." Ever since 1720, these men had
been "piddling with the public property, and enriching themselves at the
expence of the innocent and unwary."[137]

As Defoe had much earlier, but in a much more sustained way, Mortimer encourages a voyeuristic fascination for the seedy environment he
describes. He tells his readers he will instruct them in the art of "walking
the Alley," for which they needed to discard their companions' "Honor,
honesty, and ... good conscience."[138] The description that follows of a journey through the Alley with allegorical companions bears comparison with
Bunyan's *Pilgrim's Progress* (1678).[139] Bunyan sent his hero Christian on a
long journey with companions such as Hopeful and Faithful, meeting opponents such as Obstinate, Mr. Legality, and Mr. Worldly-Wiseman. Mortimer appropriates both Bunyan's naming conventions and his device of
a journey taken through an immoral landscape. While Bunyan describes
Vanity Fair and the Slough of Despond, Mortimer depicts the Alley as
an arena where personal morality is tested. More specifically, Mortimer
drew on a tradition of allegorical representations of finance that includes
Defoe's portrait of "Lady Credit" as well as satirical plays. Mortimer's fictional dialogues include figures such as Mr. Backward, Mr. Sharpset, and
Vanderdoubleface, who is clearly meant to be a Dutch jobber.[140] Similar
naming schemes were used in allegorical plays about the stock market in
the wake of the South Sea Bubble by authors such as Pieter Langendijk
and Colley Cibber. Langendijk's play *Quincampoix* (1720) has characters
called Bonavontuur (good adventure) and Windbuil (windbag); Cibber's
The Refusal: or, The Ladies Philosophy (1721) has Sir Gilbert Wrangle,
the unscrupulous South Sea director, dealing with Dr. Bullanbear. Mortimer's readers would have been familiar with the idea of the risky financial world being mocked and cut down to size.[141]

Mortimer reflects openly on how he, as "a prose writer, and only a bare
narrator of facts," can best convey the confused hubbub of the coffeehouses.
He claims that as "no borrowed style will suit it," he will simply allow the
characters to speak "in their own language."[142] The resulting depiction is not
done merely for comic effect but to show a world which is antithetical to the
Shaftesburian ideal of a society led by gentlemen who valued refinement,
gentility, and the right sort of company.[143]

Tickets—Tickets—South-Sea Stock for the opening—Navy-Bills—Bank Stock
for the rescounters—Long Annuities—(*here the waiter calls*) Chance—Chance—
Chance—*Mr. Chance is not here, Sir, he is over at his Office*—Here Tickets for

August—Omnium gatherum for September—Scrip for the third payment—3 per
Cent. consolidated, gentlemen.[144]

Afterward, he apologizes "for letting any thing so very low appear in
print" and claims that he only does so in order to act as a warning.[145] And
yet with the mixing of genres, *Every Man* evidently shares with the novels of this period the cultural function of helping to imagine into being
not only the new financial subjects created by a credit economy but also
the very idea of public credit (i.e., the national debt, underpinned by private banking and corporations) as legitimate, if corrupted by the brokers
and jobbers of the Alley. His description allows his readers to grasp an
abstract-yet-coordinated entity—"the market"—still coming into being,
rather than one already formed and fully functioning.

Indeed, though appropriating methods from polemical pamphlets, allegories, and satires, Mortimer did not write about the stock market simply
to condemn it. He wrote that he found it "amazing that this important
subject has never been touched, except in a few satirical pieces on the
fatal year 1720." Though these "lash the diabolical iniquity of that period,"
they "left no solid instructions." Mortimer saw that there was a gap in the
market: not simply to satirize the market but also to promote it. Mortimer
thus begins a long-standing tradition in popular investment advice manuals of taking contradictory stances about the market. The book, Mortimer
explained, "aims at instructing individuals, for their profit . . . by initiating
them into the secrets of 'Change Alley."[146] In doing so, Mortimer drew
on devices and conventions in advice literature, addressing his readers
directly and adopting a confiding persona, the man of experience who will
share his secrets for a couple of shillings.

Early editions were vague about the author's credentials, though they
claimed that readers could learn from the mistakes he had made on the
market—a footnote stating that he had "lost a genteel fortune, by being
the innocent dupe of the gentlemen of 'Change-Alley."[147] In the third
edition, however, Mortimer dropped his veil of anonymity and provided
a detailed account of his experiences to gain readers' trust. He had arrived in the Alley in 1756, in his mid-twenties, and quickly "swallowed the
baits" dangled by the Alley men, such as "how easy a thing it was to grow
suddenly rich." Youthful "vanity and self-conceit" led him to try "every
method that the Alley afforded" to make his fortune, but he only made
losses. These spurred him "to make a secret, but exact enquiry into the
causes of the continual fluctuations in the prices of the funds." He soon

found that the market was rigged: the fluctuations "did not arise from any critical situation of public affairs, but from the artful combinations of a set of men" who profited from them. Even worse, such men had given Mortimer advice only to trick him. "I have been frequently frightened out of my property in the Alley, and at the Coffee-houses near the Exchange, by men who seemed to me at that time, to be giving me the most candid advice," but "all this pretended friendship centered in self-interest," urging him to sell only to contribute to a fall in prices from which the "friend" would benefit.[148] His misfortunes, Mortimer concluded, were "all the consequences of having ventured into the Alley alone." But his readers would not face the same risks, because they had Mortimer's book to protect them. Indeed, it was printed in pocket form so that would-be traders could take it into the coffee shops with them. Mortimer hoped "it will become as necessary in the pocket of every merchant or gentleman, who has concerns in the funds, as the Tables of Interest."[149]

Unlike the tables of interest, Mortimer's book gave explicit advice. His central message was that readers should avoid the services of market professionals and conduct their own business in Exchange Alley. They did not need the services of a broker, because they had his book instead. Mortimer advanced several reasons for this advice. First, it was "almost impossible for a broker, to give any gentleman candid and disinterested advice, when to buy into, or sell out of, the funds."[150] The second reason was the enormous saving of unnecessary commission payments. Circumventing brokers, he claimed, would "save the public half a million *per annum*."[151] Third, it would diminish their baleful influence on public credit, rescuing "the best of governments from a slavish dependence on these sons of rapine."[152]

Erecting brokers as the villains in the market helped to legitimize Mortimer's own advice, which he presented as entirely disinterested, motivated solely by serving the public interest. Brokers could and should be replaced by the gentleman amateur. Mortimer argues that many men will have been executors of a will and should be able to move a legacy from one name to another without the assistance of a lawyer. They could therefore be their own brokers as well and act on behalf of their female acquaintances.[153] Like many later writers, Mortimer claims that women were particularly vulnerable in the stock market as they combined "ignorance, joined to a propensity for gaming."[154] He goes as far as to speculate that the practice of employing brokers originated for the convenience of women, who could not be expected to conduct their own business, thus indirectly blaming them for the corruption of the market. So, his advice is targeted only at male readers, whom he urges to "boldly and manfully" venture into the market to transact their own business.[155]

Mortimer was no stock picker. He was not trying to find undervalued shares or to identify future hot prospects. Instead, he advised patriotic investment in government securities ("absolutely preferable to all others whatever") and the major chartered corporations: investing in other companies was not recommended. Once invested, the reader should only sell shares to meet some cash flow requirement and not for the purposes of speculation. They should not be among "the vast crowd of people, who almost every transfer-day are to be found, one day selling, another day buying, and continually changing the situation of their money." He advised readers to ignore "idle rumors of bad news" in the press, as these were planted by stockjobbers to scare people into selling. In other words, Mortimer's is a conservative buy-and-hold strategy, which he believed was the only way to stay safe from the snares of the brokers and jobbers. His plan was "not founded on speculation, but on a twelve-months practice."[156]

Making the Expert

Early reviews of Mortimer's book were mixed. Some reviewers found his animus against brokers overdone—he "frequently expresses himself with a ludicrous acrimony" noted the *Monthly Review*—but conceded that one of the privileges of gamers who lost was "*the comfort of complaining.*"[157] More serious were concerns over Mortimer's real motives. In the second edition, Mortimer, seeing an opportunity to capitalize on his book's rapid sales, offered extra tutorials for the public, promising "to read a course of lectures early in the ensuing winter, in which the several branches of business in the funds" would be explained. He would then accompany his pupils to "the Bank, South-Sea, and India House," armed with the relevant acts of Parliament, to make sure the clerks conducted his pupils' transactions correctly.[158] The whole scheme, for which Mortimer's publishers would collect subscriptions, came perilously close to casting Mortimer as a financial intermediary himself, and indeed the *Critical Review* cited this section to challenge Mortimer's patriotic and disinterested motives. His maxims, it argued, "would carry more weight, and strike the mind with double the force, were it known that they had no tendency to private interest."[159]

Of course, Mortimer's self-interest was also served simply by selling copies of his book, and he was alert to ways of maximizing its commercial appeal. From the third edition on, he included a copperplate table displaying "the intrinsic value of the several Funds, and the Proportion they bear to each other, by which any Person may immediately know which is the cheapest to purchase."[160] The accompanying instructions to the table, called a "table of equation" beginning in the tenth edition, explained how investors could use stock quotations from newspapers to locate value investments. The aim was clearly to turn *Every Man* into the only book the calculating investor needed to purchase. Mortimer soon realized that, rather than having to give lectures and guided tours in person, his work could bring in a steady stream of income from sales alone. After the initial flurry, new editions of the book subsequently appeared every three to seven years—surely enabling him to pay off the substantial debts he claimed to have accrued from his unsuccessful speculations in the 1750s.[161] The tenth edition, published in 1785, was now priced three shillings and sixpence bound (fig. 1.3).

Though Mortimer had not coined the "Every Man" term—*Every Man His Own Doctor* had appeared in 1671, *Every Man His Own Gauger* (related to the drinks trade) in 1695, and *Every Man His Own Lawyer* in 1736—the success of his volume left a mark on the publishing industry. A spoof volume appeared in 1763 called *Every Woman Her Own Broker: or, A New Guide to the Alley*. Rather than redressing Mortimer's marginalization of female investors, this refers to a woman selling her body as opposed to trading in shares, as signaled by the subtitle: "*Containing Proper and Necessary Instructions for Every Woman, and Plainly Pointing out the Method of Making the Most of her Own Charms, Without the Assistance of Female Brokers, Tally-Women, etc.*"[162] It thus follows a familiar line of male commentators conflating female sexual license (and prostitution) with women's involvement in the stock market.[163] More substantially, over the following decades various publishers capitalized on Mortimer's success by releasing "Every Man His Own . . ." volumes on a tremendous assortment of (nonfinancial) topics. In 1785, a contributor to the *Westminster Magazine* complained that "For a few shillings, *every man may be his own physician, his own lawyer, his own horse doctor, his own broker, his own vermin-killer*, nay if he can weild [*sic*] a musket, he may be his own *standing army*."[164]

Already by the mid-1770s, *Every Man His Own Broker* had attained the status of commercial "scripture" which was "consulted oftner than the

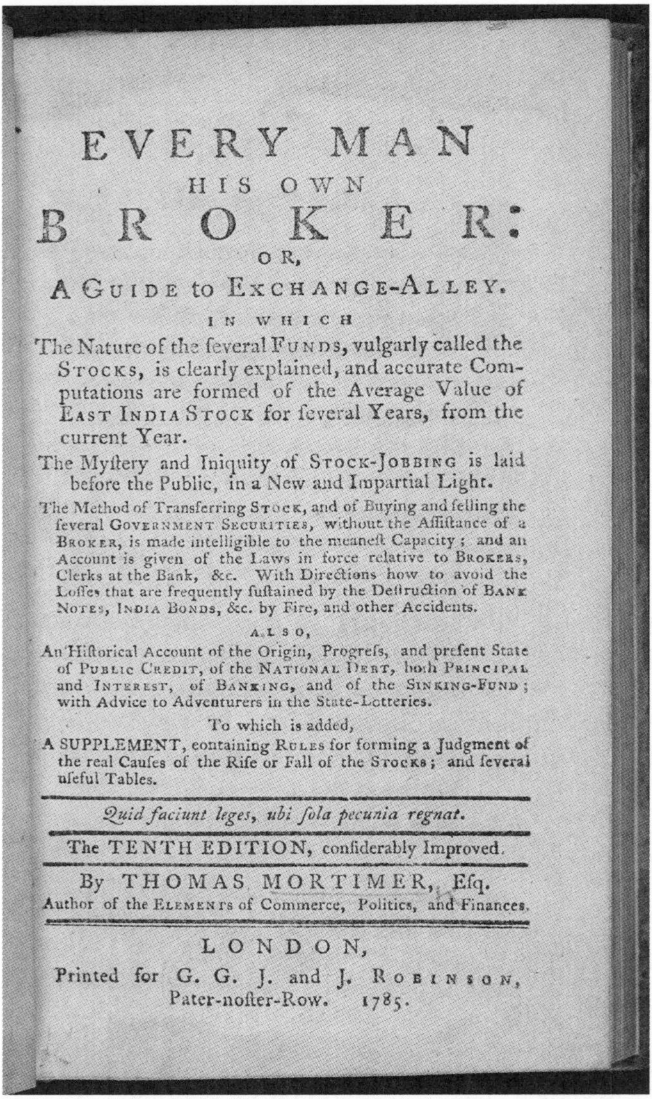

EVERY MAN
HIS OWN
BROKER:
OR,
A GUIDE to EXCHANGE-ALLEY.

IN WHICH

The Nature of the several FUNDS, vulgarly called the STOCKS, is clearly explained, and accurate Computations are formed of the Average Value of EAST INDIA STOCK for several Years, from the current Year.

The Mystery and Iniquity of STOCK-JOBBING is laid before the Public, in a New and Impartial Light.

The Method of Transferring STOCK, and of Buying and selling the several GOVERNMENT SECURITIES, without the Assistance of a BROKER, is made intelligible to the meanest Capacity; and an Account is given of the Laws in force relative to BROKERS, Clerks at the Bank, &c. With Directions how to avoid the Losses that are frequently sustained by the Destruction of BANK NOTES, INDIA BONDS, &c. by Fire, and other Accidents.

ALSO,

An Historical Account of the Origin, Progress, and present State of PUBLIC CREDIT, of the NATIONAL DEBT, both PRINCIPAL and INTEREST, of BANKING, and of the SINKING-FUND; with Advice to Adventurers in the State-Lotteries.

To which is added,

A SUPPLEMENT, containing RULES for forming a Judgment of the real Causes of the Rise or Fall of the STOCKS; and several useful Tables.

Quid faciunt leges, ubi sola pecunia regnat.

The TENTH EDITION, considerably Improved.

By THOMAS MORTIMER, Esq.
Author of the ELEMENTS of Commerce, Politics, and Finances.

LONDON,
Printed for G. G. J. and J. ROBINSON,
Pater-noster-Row. 1785.

FIGURE 1.3. Frontispiece of the tenth edition of Thomas Mortimer's *Every Man His Own Broker* (1785). Courtesy of the Copyright of the University of Manchester.

BIBLE," according to one disapproving critic.[165] In the prefaces to later editions, Mortimer noted with pride that his work had been cited in court by Lord Mansfield and had been translated into German, Dutch, French, and Spanish.[166] Not content with one mega-seller, Mortimer turned his hand to other genres, including pamphleteering (*The National Debt No National Grievance*), commercial dictionaries (*A New and Complete Dictionary of Trade and Commerce*), and even political economy (*The Elements of Commerce, Politics, and Finance*). Certainly, later generations did not rate his talents as an economist — J. R. McCulloch curtly dismissed his *Elements* as being "[o]f little or no value."[167] Yet Mortimer's network of self-referential publications helped him to become a trusted brand for late eighteenth-century investors and beyond.[168] In the 1807 edition, he was again offering his services as an investment adviser, advertising that "Advice respecting the most eligible time for buying into, or selling out of the Funds, and on the probable rise or fall of their prices, founded on long experience," could be obtained from the author by applying to the publishers by post.[169]

Despite the immediate success of *Every Man*, no directly competing titles emerged. This was partly because Mortimer took the opportunity of updating his volume, adding new material, and purporting to keep track of market developments. This may have helped to stave off competition. In the later eighteenth century, some other titles were beginning to provide alternative guides to the market but could hardly be described as rivals since they did not offer the breadth of Mortimer's manual. The second section of *The Lottery Pamphlet* (1776) provided a history of the public funds and a brief survey of the different securities available, the author's rationale being that "there are few Subjects of Conversation more general than the Value of Stocks, and hardly any Thing so little understood."[170] Toward the end of the pamphlet, the author explained how the prices of stocks were listed in the newspapers, which was for the benefit of "young Gentlemen and Ladies."[171] In 1782, *The Bank of England's Vade Mecum* gave a detailed tutorial, complete with maps, on how to transact business at the Bank of England, "without being obliged to ask any Questions of any Persons whatever."[172] This included an addendum explaining how to do business with stockbrokers in the rotunda. A different kind of volume, the nearly 600-page *General History of Inland Navigation, Foreign and Domestic* (1792), was compiled to capitalize on the boom in canal construction in the 1790s. Though covering the history of the sector, its focus was on current and projected schemes, so was of interest to investors in canals.[173]

The canal boom was a sign that the investment climate was changing. Aside from the growing number of different projects issuing shares to the public, in 1773 a group of brokers had removed from the coffeehouses to establish a "Stock Exchange" on Sweetings Alley. This was not yet an exclusive club—as with the coffeehouses, anyone could enter on payment of a daily fee of 6d.—but it was a sign of the growing ambitions of the brokers.[174] Mortimer belatedly caught up with the development—in 1791, the new subtitle to his book became *A Guide to the Stock-Exchange*. But he saw little need to scrap his description of what went on inside the coffee shops since he claimed that "the scene at the Stock-Exchange is just the same."[175] There were some signs of a softening of his blanket condemnation of brokers: by 1782, he was able to accept a limited role for the "reputable broker, who pursues only the legal duties of his vocation," claiming that "sensible, candid STOCK BROKERS, men of unblemished reputation" also approved of his work as it allowed readers to avoid dishonest brokers.[176] But his core message remained unchanged, and his insistence on a very narrow range of suitable investments began to make his work dated. Likewise, he failed to engage with the new thinking about the economy that contemporary political economists such as Adam Smith pioneered.[177] For Mortimer, the stock market functioned as a patriotic mechanism to help the state with its debts rather than as an aid to private enterprise. Where Smith argued that the self-interest of the butcher and baker allow society to be fed, Mortimer preferred the Shaftesburian view that a society should be run by gentlemen, and he railed against self-interest as a motive for brokering and engaging in the market. Like many later works in the genre of popular financial advice, *Every Man His Own Broker* therefore runs on different tracks from the developing body of writings on political economy. For Mortimer, there is no "Invisible Hand" guiding the market to a socially beneficial outcome: the would-be investor always needs to be on the lookout for the deceitful practices of the stockjobbers. Mortimer's approach to the market created opportunities for rivals, and, as the next chapter documents, in the last decade of the century a series of rival publications appeared, which were to represent investment in very different terms.

* * *

In the years before popular stock market advice literature, readers nevertheless had access to a host of different types of print which all played a part in making the market. At a fundamental level, investment was facilitated "by the same willingness to believe a fiction about the future" as inspired the growing novel-reading public of the eighteenth century.[178] More prosaically, but no less importantly, printed price lists imparted a sense of solidity, objectivity, and regularity to finance, allowing investors to gauge the state of the market and to calculate deals. As soon as these began to be published on a regular basis—in lay as well as specialist publications—market watching became possible, even at some physical remove from Exchange Alley itself. Printed tables of interest encouraged investors to make calculations, while pocket books and memorandum books taught them to record their transactions and track their financial health. At the same time, a voluminous body of poems, plays, pamphlets, and polemics familiarized readers with the stock market, even if usually taking a dim view of the brokers and jobbers who operated there.

Nevertheless, many Georgians clearly felt mystified by the powerful yet abstract forces conjured up by the Financial Revolution. As ever, Defoe put it best in his awe-tinged description of public credit:

> I am to speak of what all People are busie about, but not one in Forty understands: Every Man has a Concern in it, few know what it is, nor is it easy to define or describe it. . . . *Like the Soul* in the Body, it acts all Substance, yet is it self Immaterial; it gives Motion, yet it self cannot be said to Exist. . . . If I should say it is the essential Shadow of something that is Not; should I not Puzzle the thing rather than Explain it, and leave you and my self more in the Dark than we were before?[179]

The sense that this was a system which resisted all attempts to define it persisted, creating opportunities for those who claimed to be able to penetrate its secrets. Mortimer was the first to recognize this, applying the extravagant guarantees of advice literature to the mysteries of the market. As one critic argued, the key to such how-to guides was that they promised to boil complex subjects down to a few "easy and methodical rules" requiring neither genius nor hard work.[180] Above all, Mortimer promised *simplicity*: the title page of the very first edition promised to make the subject of stocks "intelligible to the meanest Capacity"—an "Investing for Dummies" for Georgian gentlemen.[181]

Mortimer's professed aim was that every man should be his own broker; his real aim was that every fundholder should buy his book. Indeed, advertisements for the tenth edition proclaimed that this was "A Pocket

Companion for every Person in the Kingdom who has Property in the Funds."[182] Though not quite achieving that objective, if we believe Mortimer's own figures, then combined sales of 50,000 for the various editions of *Every Man* suggest that a significant proportion of investors were coming to rely to some degree on his advice, likely smaller investors who were isolated from the social networks of personalized advice.[183] And it is possible that some of his readers were not investors at all. Given that the central tenet of Mortimer's approach to the market is that gentlemen should conduct their own share trading in London's financial district, only readers living within reach of the capital would be able to follow this advice. This did not limit the book's popularity, however, and it is likely that many of his readers were armchair investors, only visiting Exchange Alley in their mind's eye and experiencing it vicariously through his descriptions. Revealingly, at one point he admits that many of his readers were "not likely ever to see J——'s in reality."[184] His book was a shrewd combination of a technical survey of the investment market, which he admitted was a "dry" subject, leavened with more titillating fare on the evils of stockjobbing, which was explicitly included to amuse his readers.[185] The text thus needs to be understood both as an economic primer and a work of entertainment. The tacit message of *Every Man* was that the returns generated by the market were not simply financial in nature. This was an idea that later writers were to exploit to the full.

CHAPTER TWO

Navigating the Market (1800–1870)

I have, which will surprise you not a little, been speculating—partly in American FUNDS, but *more especially* in English stocks, which are springing up like mushrooms this year (in further-ance of every imaginable and unimaginable joint stock enterprise), are forced up to a quite unreasonable level and then, for the most part, collapse. In this way, I have made over £400 and, now that the complexity of the political situation affords greater scope, I shall begin all over again. It's a type of operation that makes small demands on one's time, and it's worth while running some risk in order to relieve the enemy of his money.—Karl Marx to Lion Philips, June 25, 1864[1]

W e do not know what financial advice Karl Marx sought, if any, when he ventured into the stock market in 1864, but his letter highlights many of the important developments which were transforming the mar-ket for stocks and shares in the nineteenth century. Though his depiction of prices as subject to the cynical manipulations of market insiders could have been taken straight from Thomas Mortimer's *Every Man His Own Broker*, his letter also alludes to the wider choice of investments, both domestic and international, and the rapid development of the joint-stock sector that made the 1860s market very different from that of the 1760s. Above all, Marx's letter vividly illustrates how outsiders had come to believe that, with the right strategy, there was easy money to be made by speculat-ing on the stock market. It seems that Marx's confidence was misplaced— there are no subsequent references to day-trading in his letters—and before long he was again milking Friedrich Engels for rent money.[2]

If we want to understand why people believed that it was possible to make money in this way, then the print culture developing around the stock market provides useful clues. Though eighteenth-century treatments of the market were notable for their variety, their formal diversity contin-ued and even intensified from the 1790s on, so that tracing the history of financial advice in the nineteenth century means reading across a wide assortment of genres. Despite their heterogeneity, one characteristic these writings shared is that they helped to construct the market they purported simply to reflect. Similarly, their authors were not merely responding unproblematically to demand when crafting their texts: their methods of writing about finance helped to cultivate curiosity about and fascination with the stock market, and encouraged their readers to see this market and their relationship to it in particular—and sometimes peculiar—ways. In other words, exploring the development of the financial system through this literature means recognizing the agency the authors and publishers of such texts had in shaping this system.

Though they often pulled in different, sometimes contradictory, directions, these texts did a number of things. At the same time as the London Stock Exchange was being formalized and enclosed, they consolidated the idea of the market for stocks and shares as a coherent and navigable domain made up not just of local or national but global securities, all of which were comparable, equivalent, even interchangeable. In doing so, they recast the market not as corrupt and chaotic but as rational and responsive to scientific modes of analysis. Data would render the market not only intelligible but predictable. As well as constructing the market, these texts also began to construct the investor. Readers were encouraged to imagine themselves as independent, calculating, and—almost always—male, and to base their investing decisions on hard data. Though rarely encouraging outright speculation, guides left it to readers to decide how much risk they wished to take on. "Running some risk," as Marx put it, was subject to less censure, and ostensible warnings about the dangers of the stock market, by underscoring the rapid profits that could be won (and lost), doubled as temptations to speculate. At the same time, these texts began to hint that the opportunities for self-determination—and stimulation— afforded by the stock market represented their own reward, aside from any actual profits made, a notion that was useful given the market's susceptibility to crisis. Indeed, that these guides helped to legitimize popular involvement in the stock market in the face of periodic panics in 1825, 1837, 1845, 1857, and 1866 is testimony to their considerable rhetorical power. This chapter explores the development of stock market advice over this period, focusing on Britain but also tracing parallel trends in the newly independent United States, where New York, though not yet rivaling London, was beginning to emerge as an important financial center in its own right.

Sanitizing the City

The British state's urgent and unrelenting demand for capital had transformed the stock market by the early nineteenth century. The requirements of financing the American Revolutionary and Napoleonic Wars meant that by the time peace came in 1815, the national debt had ballooned to £745 million, creating an abundance of new investment opportunities for the middle and upper classes. The state had little problem finding lenders, attracted by the safety, reliability, and liquidity of the funds, compared to mortgages or other private securities. Whereas there had been around 60,000 holders of national debt in 1760, by 1815 there were as many as 250,000, representing approximately one in forty-five citizens.[3] Obviously, the wealthy were most able to participate in this market, but there were further signs of social and geographical diversification: whereas fundholders had previously been heavily concentrated in London and the home counties, investment was becoming more dispersed across the country.[4]

High sales of Thomas Mortimer's *Every Man His Own Broker* eventually encouraged a growing number of enterprising authors to produce rival volumes. At the turn of the century, would-be investors could choose from a sudden profusion of market guides. Aside from Mortimer's *Every Man*, which reached its twelfth and thirteenth editions in 1798 and 1801 respectively, readers could also try three new manuals, all published for the first time in the mid-1790s: William Fairman's *Stocks Examined and Compared: or, A Guide to Purchasers in the Public Funds* (1795), Thomas Fortune's *Epitome of the Stocks and Public Funds* (1796), and Charles Hales's *Bank Mirror; or, A Guide to the Funds* (1796). This was to prove a turning point: although a fourteenth edition of Mortimer's manual was released in 1807, it proved to be the last, whereas Fairman and Fortune went on to dominate the early nineteenth-century market for this kind of book. Fairman went through seven editions to 1824, while Fortune lasted longer still, reaching a seventeenth edition in 1856. In turn, they spawned their own imitators. Despite its title, George Carey's 1820 handbook, *Every Man His Own Stock-Broker*, owed more to Fairman and Fortune than to Mortimer. While this guide did not progress beyond a second edition, another copycat, Charles Fenn's *Compendium of the English and Foreign Funds and the Principal Joint Stock Companies*, established itself as the most successful of its type. First published in 1837, it proved nearly as long-lived as the young Queen Victoria who ascended to the throne that year, its seventeenth and final edition being published in 1898.

The many editions of Mortimer's *Every Man* had been laced with observations on sharp practices in the City and tinged with anti-Semitism, and these outlooks continued to play well in the early nineteenth century. The migration of the trade in stocks and shares from the coffeehouses of Exchange Alley to a purpose-built exchange in 1773, and then to a new exchange in Capel Court in 1802 from which nonmembers were barred, was intended to exclude unreliable or fraudulent market participants. But this enclosure and privatization of the market also rendered the activities of brokers and jobbers more mysterious and less transparent.[5] The notorious Cochrane hoax of 1814, when a group of conspirators spread false rumors of Napoleon's defeat—allowing them to profit from the temporary rise in government funds—was a high-profile example demonstrating how easy it was for prices to be manipulated by secret cabals.[6] Fears about stockjobbing were expressed in a range of pamphlets around this time. Indeed, Mortimer's final work, published by his widow in 1810, was *The Nefarious Practice of Stock-Jobbing Unveiled*. Other titles, such as *Tricks of the Stock-Exchange Exposed* and *The Art of Stock-Jobbing Explained*, called for the abolition of the Stock Exchange and the reestablishment of an open market.[7]

Of the new investment guides, Hales's *Bank Mirror* carried something of this animus against City insiders, warning his readers to be on their guard against the machinations of dishonest brokers, whose "brotherly love" meant they looked after each other's interests rather than those of their clients.[8] Yet Fairman and Fortune, and later Carey and Fenn, developed a very different method of representing the market: the City as den of thieves was out, replaced by a safer, sanitized market. There were no warnings about the dishonesty of stockbrokers in Fairman and Carey: both assumed their readers would deal with them, as they included brokerage charges in their calculations.[9] Fortune went further, explicitly contradicting Mortimer's claims about brokers and urging his readers to use them since they would save them time and money: the commission they charged would be more than made up for by the better price a professional would be able to secure.[10] This new attitude was due in no small part to the relationship of the authors to the market: whereas Mortimer was a disgruntled outsider, Fairman was an accountant for the Royal Exchange Assurance Company, and Fenn was a stockbroker.[11] In early editions, Fortune claimed that his advice to deal with brokers was not self-interested, but the 1798 edition of Mortimer's *Every Man* asserted that Fortune was in fact a broker. Fortune denied this in his 1800 edition, yet subsequent versions of his manual silently dropped his denial of self-interest, and he was described as a stockbroker on the title page of a later book on life annuities.[12] These authors therefore had a vested interest in disinfecting the City.

In constructing their rational, benign market, they dispensed with Mortimer's literary and imaginative flourishes. In a subtle dig at Mortimer's discursiveness, Fortune noted in his preface that he intended his guide to be "Concise, Exact, and Clear ... with as little Deviation as possible," while Fairman stated that he had "altogether avoided political observations and conjectures, sincerely hoping that virtue and knowledge may ever triumph over vice and ignorance."[13] Though Mortimer's readers would have learned about the various securities on offer, they would have done so in a somewhat unsystematic way, and with their understanding influenced by the author's constant interjections. Purged of opinion, of advice, these guides seemed instead to offer objective knowledge. A sizable proportion of each was dedicated to providing detailed and unvarnished surveys of the array of securities available to investors, cataloging the market, and therefore making it legible. Just as the stock exchange was being spatially enclosed and defined, so these books aspired to encompass the entire market within their covers. Contents and index pages listed the securities available, while headed sections gave a potted history, key characteristics, and statistical information for each. By browsing the guide, readers were thus navigating the market, able to identify and distinguish between the various stocks and annuities issued by government and the chartered companies.

As part of their legitimizing mission, these authors targeted their manuals at calculating investors rather than reckless speculators. The proliferation of stocks, and their constantly fluctuating prices, encouraged the "time bargains"—contracting to buy or sell stock on a future date hoping to capitalize on rising or falling prices—that continued to give the stock exchange its bad name, particularly when the parties had no intention of delivery.[14] But the new wave of authors urged readers to benefit from these fluctuations in a different way. Fairman, for example, explained that by making "real purchases" when a stock's price had fallen comparative to the others, readers were far more likely to profit than by engaging in "speculations for time."[15] To this end, the guides provided tables of prices and interest and instructions on how readers could use these to calculate value. Fortune included his own version of Mortimer's "table of equation," a large foldout grid, which enabled readers to compare stocks yielding different interest rates in order to calculate which were underpriced. Fairman went further, providing a long series of tables showing the interest payable on the different funds and annuities according to date of purchase. The unruly mass of investments was by these means standardized and made comparable for the calculating investor.[16] The market they cataloged was made to appear rational, knowable, and safe.

Beneath their ostensibly bland surfaces, these manuals made big promises. Whereas Mortimer's ambitions had primarily been defensive, helping his readers to protect themselves against the jobbers and brokers who wanted to fleece them, the new books offered more. Fairman claimed that anyone "acquainted with the first principles of arithmetic" could "make accurate observations" in the funds, deciding when was the right moment to buy in order to secure "certain profits."[17] Carey purported to give his readers "rules for taking advantage of" price fluctuations: determining their impact on the value of stocks could "be done with mathematical certainty."[18] The promise of certainty out of confusion was appealing, helping to establish Fairman, Fortune, and Fenn as reliable and trusted brands, their books all outliving the original authors. Despite editorial control passing in time to other hands, the name of the original author was retained and prominently displayed, a talismanic guarantee of supposed security.

Longevity depended upon remaining up-to-date, and both Fortune and Fairman proved responsive to the growing importance of American loans on the British market after independence.[19] Fortune boasted that his manual contained a detailed appendix on US public funds and bank stock, "no other Book upon this Subject having ever yet mentioned them," and the 1808 edition of Fairman's guide followed suit.[20] Changes after 1815 posed a greater challenge to the ambition of these manuals to map the entire market. In peacetime, the British state's borrowing requirements fell, which enabled the government to reduce the interest on "consols" (consolidated annuities, the main type of government security) in 1822 and 1824.[21] From their high point of 5.7 percent in 1797, yields were closer to 3 percent by the mid-1820s.[22] Once closely linked with speculation, government securities began to be viewed very differently, as safe investments for the conservatively minded.[23] Indeed, many were dissatisfied with the reduction in interest, holders of £2.8 million in consols cashing in their investments in 1822 rather than accepting the lower rate.[24] They had a growing number of alternatives. European nations were hungry for capital to feed postwar reconstruction and saw London—now the financial center of Europe—as the best place to get it, while newly independent states in Latin America also began borrowing. Between 1822 and 1825, loans with a nominal value of £40 million were floated for twenty foreign states.[25] By 1824, the boom spread to joint-stock companies, both domestic and foreign.[26] The lingering presence of the Bubble Act of 1720 on the statute books gave companies unincorporated by act of Parliament or royal charter a dubious legal standing which may have acted as a slight brake on investment, but this obstacle was removed in 1825 when Parliament repealed the act.[27] Though investors in such companies still risked unlimited liability, joint-stock companies became a significant element in the mid-1820s boom. British investors had never before been faced with such a wide array of choice.

Though 1824 saw new editions of both Fairman's and Fortune's guides, neither did much to encourage speculation in the new securities underpinning the boom. Fortune's *Epitome* did provide a survey of foreign loans, but the editor's tone was faintly disapproving ("We trust . . . that the reader will find sufficient information in the following pages to guide him in the dealings he may wish to have in those Funds"), and his comments on particular loans stressed that political instability rendered them dubious investments.[28] Fairman's *Stocks Examined* ignored the new loan issues altogether, containing just a brief and dated coda on American stocks.[29] Moreover, both manuals ignored the joint-stock companies. But other authors stepped into this vacuum to help create markets for more speculative securities.

Imagining Wealth

The British had previously been advised, by Mortimer and by prevailing mercantilist thought, that international trade was a zero-sum game and that they should only invest at home. These mercantilist ideas were coming under attack in the early nineteenth century by political economists like David Ricardo, whose advocacy of "free trade" had implications for investment.[30] Though some conservative authors continued to oppose sending capital abroad, others argued that investing overseas was far preferable to overinvestment at home, which would only create an "unnatural and improvident demand for labour."[31] If such arguments were gaining traction, then other potential obstacles remained, notably the huge information asymmetries involved when investing at a distance. Yet this does not seem to have inhibited capitalists in the 1820s. In part, they relied upon the reputation of intermediaries in choosing their investments, trusting market leaders like Rothschilds and Barings to promote only reliable borrowers.[32] But rather than simply representing an obstacle to be overcome, lack of information may itself have been a lure to investors, particularly when it came to the Latin American states. The fact that so little was known about these territories in the years of Spanish and Portuguese rule created a space in which fantasy and imagination could thrive.[33] The region had been associated with incredible wealth at least as far back as Raleigh and Drake, and more recent accounts of explorers did nothing to alter this.[34] The most influential was German naturalist Alexander von Humboldt's *Political Essay on the Kingdom of New Spain*. Published in English in three editions between 1811 and 1822, and widely reviewed in the periodical press, Humboldt's detailed account of underexploited mineral wealth, together with the commercial potential of the region, gave a tantalizing glimpse of the fortunes that might be made in the region.[35]

Literature proliferated in the 1820s which recycled and embellished the writings of Humboldt and other explorers, and was designed to stimulate investment in the region, either in the form of loans or mining schemes. Thomas Strangeways's *Sketch of the Mosquito Shore* (1822), John Taylor's *Selections from the Works of the Baron De Humboldt* (1824), Benjamin Disraeli's *Inquiry into the Plans, Progress, and Policy of the American Mining Companies* (1825), and Henry English's *General Guide to the Companies Formed for Working Foreign Mines* (1825) presented more lucrative alternatives to investing in the funds. All were personally vested in the projects they described. Strangeways's text was commissioned by the soldier and adventurer Gregor MacGregor, who sought to attract settlers to Poyais, a territory on the coast of modern-day Honduras to which he had received title in 1820.[36] Taylor was a mining engineer and entrepreneur involved in Mexican mining ventures.[37] Disraeli was commissioned by financier John Diston Powles to promote the Latin American mines in which both men were invested in partnership with the publisher John Murray.[38] English was a stockbroker interested in talking up the market in general, who later went on to found the *Mining Journal*.[39]

The challenge they faced, therefore, was both to cloak their interestedness and to build public confidence in what were highly risky ventures. Their solution was to mobilize a welter of seemingly objective information in a performance of facticity. Strangeways announced that he would avoid making "any statement which might appear doubtful or exaggerated," confining himself "to such plain and positive facts, as are established beyond the shadow of doubt," quoting freely from existing authorities and drawing on his own knowledge of the region.[40] Likewise Taylor argued that he based his case on "facts as I found them, standing on authority which has not been questioned," and from which readers were free to form their own conclusions.[41] Disraeli and English quoted heavily from company prospectuses—hardly a dispassionate form of writing—while supplementing them with the latest information from letters, dispatches, and other sources. English insisted that he had drawn only on "the most authentic sources and original information," promising to give his readers the inside track on the progress of the companies, rather than merely trading in idle gossip.[42] But nearly all of his supplementary information talked up the prospects for profits, so did little more than amplify the hype contained in the companies' prospectuses.[43]

This cut-and-paste method, mixing fact and fiction, imbued optimistic fantasies with a compelling sense of textual solidity.[44] Facts are used as the launchpad for the reader's imagination. In Sketch of the Mosquito Shore, detailed but idealized descriptions of the territory provide the means for the "intelligent and industrious" readers addressed to imagine themselves as the adventurer-settlers—or rentier investors—ready to seize the wealth promised to them.[45] Taylor cited Humboldt's statistics demonstrating how productive Mexican mines had been under Spanish rule to invite readers to imagine how much more profitable they would be when modern steam technology—and British know-how—were introduced. The application of British "industry and intelligence," as Taylor put it, was sure to yield "extraordinary profit."[46] The certainty they offered was soon punctured. Strangeways proved an unreliable guide to Poyais's climate and resources: its settlers, facing disease and shortages of supplies, needed to be evacuated, and the value of its bonds plummeted.[47] The buried wealth lying in Mexico eluded the British companies established to mine it. The London directors underestimated the many challenges they faced and failed to delegate powers to the local management, while Taylor himself never even visited the mines. Investors in his main foreign venture, the Real del Monte, eventually faced losses of over $5 million.[48] Disraeli lost heavily in his own mining speculations, incurring debts that were to stay with him for decades.[49]

With their appeal based on the promise of privileged information that would give investors an edge, these texts were clearly hostages to changing circumstances. By the time that English produced a companion volume on domestic mining companies in early 1826, a crisis had struck.[50] Banks across the country faced runs from anxious depositors, leading to dozens of failures, and enthusiasm for company shares—as well as foreign loans—had cooled.[51] But by this point, more up-to-date forms of information had become available to investors. Enterprising newspaper proprietors exploited the demand for financial news after 1815 to a far greater extent than hitherto. Newspapers had long been vehicles for such news, from details of the arrival and departure of ships to tables of imports and exports and lists of stock prices. However, as we saw in the previous chapter, coverage was unsystematic, and papers did not give a running commentary on financial events. Recognizing financial news as a potentially lucrative commodity, in 1817 *The Times* hired Thomas Massa Alsager, a leading figure in London's cloth trade, to provide news from the City, which appeared irregularly in the editorial columns.[52] Ambitious newspaper proprietor William Innell Clement went further in packaging and marketing financial news, giving it a more prominent position first in his Sunday paper, *The Observer*, and then in the *Morning Chronicle*, a daily.[53] Early in 1822, under the heading "City," the *Chronicle* began collecting news to do with the financial markets together into one column. Initially quite brief, the column extended to occupy half a column or more and was prepared by a specialist member of staff, as frequent references in other parts of the paper to "our City Correspondent" attest.[54] When enthusiasm for company shares intensified in 1824, the *Chronicle* responded by reporting prices of Latin American mining companies, and coverage soon extended to domestic companies, enabling readers to track price movements of a host of corporate securities on a daily basis.[55]

Other papers followed this example, either by systematizing coverage in the form of a regular money article or simply by including greater coverage of financial news.[56] London papers devoted significant column inches to Latin American stories—over 20 percent of total news coverage in some cases, while the provincial press also began to include details of new issues.[57] The introduction of transatlantic mail packets in 1823 significantly increased the flow of information to investors. Hitherto culturally marginal, City affairs were now reaching investors across the country in unprecedented ways. Readers "from the tiniest of hamlets in rural Somerset to the fashionable spas of Bath and Cheltenham were tempted into the bond market" by this mainstreaming of financial news.[58] More than this, they were taught that the goings-on of London were by definition newsworthy, the daily rhythm of price movements reported faithfully in the press. The stock market now had a pulse, beating in homes across the country.[59]

But newspaper coverage displayed some of the same weaknesses as the puffing pamphlets discussed above. Deriving their authority as Strangeways and others did by mobilizing masses of seemingly objective information, City correspondents were not above using this data to hype the new investment opportunities, helping readers to dream of spectacular profits. "With respect to the States of South America, in particular, it is difficult to see, how Englishmen can better dispose of their surplus money, than in aiding them in the development of their resources," the *Morning Chronicle*'s correspondent opined in 1822.[60] When a Brazilian loan was introduced in 1824, the same correspondent reminded readers of "the immense resources of the Brazilian Empire" and commented that the loan was issued "under the powerful protection of" a respected London firm, which meant that "justice will be done to the subscribers in its management."[61] Comment was not always positive, and warnings could be found: when the first Mexican loan was floated, the *Bristol Mirror* struck a cautious note, urging its readers to learn "from the fate of the Spanish and Poyais bondholders."[62] But optimistic coverage outweighed the negative, and the distinction between editorial and paid-for content was not always transparent.[63]

However, though the collapse of 1825 and the growing number of foreign states which were defaulting on their loans dampened ardor for the stock market, the forms of writing that had sustained the boom were not discredited.[64] The daily City article did not vanish from the pages of the London press, and by the 1830s it was recognized as essential reading for "merchants, stockbrokers, and speculators of every shade."[65] Though foreign investment was slow to regain popularity, pamphlets designed to tempt investors into the more speculative sectors of the domestic economy were a feature of later booms in the 1830s and 1840s, as we shall see. And all the while, prospectuses continued to disseminate their optimistic predictions and promises to large audiences.[66] Yet the unreliability of much of the information in circulation in the mid-1820s encouraged some to turn to statistics in a search for certainty about the market, an approach that came to be increasingly associated with the London Stock Exchange and the financial press alike.

Statistical Thinking

Though briefly falling out of favor in the immediate aftermath of the 1825 crash, joint-stock companies were established as popular vehicles for both investment and speculation by booms in the mid-1830s and again in the

mid-1840s. Mainly centering on banks and railways, enthusiasm for companies nevertheless encompassed a wide variety of sectors, including mining, insurance, steam navigation, gas, water, and telegraphy.[67] From being
a relatively minor part of the London Stock Exchange's business in the
1820s, by 1838 over 40 percent of the Stock Exchange's 675 members were
involved in trading company shares.[68] And by mid-1845, most members
were active in the railway market.[69] Even before the so-called railway
mania of 1845, no less than 755 joint-stock companies were quoted on
the Stock Exchange, with a paid-up capital of over £150 million.[70] Further stimulus was given by the 1844 Joint-Stock Companies Act which
granted these companies a more secure legal footing than they had previously enjoyed, though unlimited liability was still the norm for companies
not incorporated by act of Parliament or royal charter.[71] The spread of
the joint-stock company was a nationwide rather than just a metropolitan phenomenon, and provincial stock exchanges began appearing from
the mid-1830s. The railway boom of the 1840s intensified this trend, and
though some exchanges were short-lived, others became major institutions, particularly in Liverpool, Manchester, and Glasgow.[72] Parliament
authorized 805 miles of new railway track in 1844, rising to 2,700 miles in
1845 and to 4,538 in 1846.[73] New lines were heavily oversubscribed.[74]

Across the Atlantic it was a similar story. Though many businesses remained small partnerships with unlimited liability, capitalized primarily
through kinship and local community networks rather than through the
stock market, Americans quickly saw the potential of the corporate form.
In the early years of the republic, a belief in the public benefits of corporate enterprise encouraged "rivalistic state mercantilism," whereby states
sought to attract businesses by liberal incorporation policies and other
benefits.[75] The result was that even before the Civil War (1861–65) the
United States had become "the consummate corporation nation."[76] The
nineteenth century also saw the formation of around 250 stock exchanges
across the country, concentrated in major population centers. Though most
were ephemeral and short-lived, others proved longer lasting, with New
York swiftly overtaking Philadelphia as the new nation's most dynamic
financial center. But like its rival markets, New York dealt primarily in
local stocks, and this only gradually changed. By the mid-1830s, local securities represented nearly three-quarters of the 124 stocks quoted.[77] As
in Britain, however, railroads had a transformative effect. The huge capitalization required for these ventures, along with their complexity as
large-scale bureaucratic organizations, meant that management became

separated from ownership and created a thriving trade in railroad stocks and bonds. Investment in railroads reached $400 million in the late 1840s and continued to rise thereafter.[78] Further boosting the range of investment opportunities was the passage of general incorporation statutes by individual states, making company formation easier and gradually turning incorporation from a privilege into a right.[79]

The rapid spread of joint-stock enterprise encouraged the development of a specialist business press. In Britain, the 1830s boom inspired several important titles, such as the *Mining Journal and Commercial Gazette* and the *Railway Magazine* (both established 1835), while the railway mania of the mid-1840s saw a glut of new railway periodicals. Most of the latter disappeared when the bubble burst, but this period also saw the establishment of one weekly paper which became an institution, the *Economist* (1843). The United States followed a similar path, with the formation of titles including the *American Railroad Journal* (1832), *Hunt's Merchants' Magazine* (1839), the *Bankers' Magazine* (1845), and William Buck Dana's *Commercial and Financial Chronicle* (1865), self-consciously modeled on the *Economist*.[80]

At a time when standards of financial disclosure in corporate accounts were patchy at best, these magazines were responsible for a significant improvement in the availability of statistics about the market. They were a product of a culture fascinated by the power of numbers, evidenced in the establishment of a host of statistical societies in London and the larger towns and cities as well as a statistical department at the Board of Trade in 1832.[81] This vogue for what Theodore Porter calls "statistical thinking" was driven by the belief that what seemed chaotic and disordered at the individual level "melted into unfailing regularity" when studied in the aggregate.[82] It was a credo that the *Economist*'s first editor, James Wilson, fully shared. Introducing his periodical's first statistical supplement in November 1843, Wilson denied that statistics were "dull and uninteresting," arguing instead that they could unlock surprising and profound truths to those able to "*read*" them properly.[83] Thus it was no surprise that when the railway boom developed, the Victorians were keen to make sense of the new technology through statistics. In January 1845, Wilson's *Economist* introduced a new section, the *Railway Monitor*, which promised to keep investors fully abreast of the latest data, while later that year, the London Stock Exchange established "a department for the registration of intelligence affecting English and Foreign Railway Shares and Stock," headed by Mihill Slaughter, a former coal merchant.[84] The ambitious plan was to establish the London Stock Exchange as the central information hub for railways, with companies invited to submit regular returns for the use of members.[85] Starting in July 1847, Slaughter was tasked with publishing a revamped *London Weekly Railway Share List*, which carried not only the market prices of railway shares but much of the information collected by Slaughter's department, such as traffic tables and mileage data. It also published innovative analyses of these data, penned by a young Bristol-born stockbroker, Robert Lucas Nash.[86]

There was a similar demand for data in the United States. *Hunt's Merchants' Magazine*, for example, carried a section entitled "Railroad, Canal, and Steamboat Statistics," which summarized—albeit not in a systematic fashion—the financial reports of listed firms, including earnings, dividends, fares, and operating expenses. At times it published more expansive pieces, such as an article in 1848 on Massachusetts railroads that included a table providing analytical details such as the net income per mile as well as more regular information on mileage and capitalization.[87] In such publications there was a frequent search for novelty in what was reported (especially if it could be advertised as providing something that competitors lacked), but this also meant that there was a lack of consistency in the information presented, making longer-term comparisons difficult. More systematic coverage was a feature of the *American Railroad Journal*, begun under Henry Varnum Poor in 1849. Poor, who later went on to found the financial research and credit ratings agency that became Standard & Poor, aimed to provide a more comprehensive presentation of commercial data in a form more readable and accessible than from piecemeal corporate accounts. By the later 1850s, readers of the *American Railroad Journal* could expect tabulated data on railroad earnings, bond interest, dividends, national and state securities, preferred and guaranteed stock prices, and daily prices on all the stock exchanges.[88]

This profusion of railway statistics could easily become overwhelming, which encouraged attempts at synthesis. In Britain, Henry Tuck's *Railway Shareholder's Manual* first appeared in March 1845 and quickly raced through six editions. Initially promising comprehensive coverage of British railways, by the fourth edition Tuck's guide was claiming to include every railway in the world. Reviews praised Tuck's manual for its sense-making power: "Every body is, or tries, or fears to be involved in the railway schemes with which the country, the legislature, and the newspapers, are now deluged," but in this volume, "everybody will find all the practical information necessary [for] being perfectly 'up' on the subject."[89] The

success of Tuck's manual encouraged imitators. William Frederick Spackman, who had already gained notice as a budding statistician, published
an *Analysis of the Railway Interest of the United Kingdom* toward the end
of 1845.[90] A little later, the London Stock Exchange began publishing a
detailed survey of the railway system, *Railway Intelligence*, offering a pan-
oramic view of the railway market, containing key information on every
company arranged alphabetically. Its scope swiftly grew to encompass details respecting authorized capital, debt, revenue, and management structure.[91] By the mid-1850s, it was well over 200 pages and had settled into
a pattern of publication every other year. Reviewers recognized Slaughter's innovations, noting that his volume's "utility increases with every
number."[92] The popularity of the statistical approach also influenced the
catalog guides which were still in print. Both Fortune's *Epitome*, edited
in the 1850s by the financial journalist David Morier Evans, and Fenn's
Compendium, now edited by another journalist, Henry Ayres, who also
edited the *Circular to Bankers*, began to include a much greater level of
statistical detail.

It was not long before similar statistical tomes began appearing in the
United States. The railroad boom here increased the nation's mileage of
track from 5,598 miles in 1847 to 30,626 miles in 1860.[93] The need to chart
this bewildering growth prompted the publication of *The United States
Railroad Directory* in 1856.[94] Though containing lots of information, the
volume lacked key data, including capitalization, debt, and earnings. It also
fell some way short of comprehensiveness, its compiler Benjamin Homans
noting that several leading lines had to be excluded, "every effort short
of downright importunity" having failed to secure returns from them.[95]
Though intended as an annual publication, this proved the only edition,
but the idea took root, and other volumes soon appeared. *The Capitalist's
Guide and Railway Annual for 1859* was a significant milestone, piecing
together from various sources an increased amount of information for
each railroad and including categories such as profit margins, return on
investment, and creditworthiness. In a significant development, its compiler F. H. Stow also began to offer an analysis of the information for
what it revealed about the suitability of each corporation for investment.
Like Homans's volume, though, Stow's experiment was not repeated.[96]
But Poor's entry into this market proved significant. His *History of the
Railroads and Canals of the United States of America*, published in 1860,
included digests of financial information on both railroads and canals, and
introduced novel categories such as comparative earnings data designed

to inform investment decisions. Though his plan to issue annual supple-
ments to the volume was thwarted by the Civil War, Poor returned to the
field in 1868 with the publication of his *Manual of the Railroads of the
United States*. It went on to become the longest running serial of its kind,
still published into the 1920s.

These increasingly ambitious exercises in quantification had important
ramifications. Providing better information was supposed to place readers' financial decisions on a more rational footing, which in turn would
elevate wild speculation into sensible investment. They thus were part of
a new information age facilitated by the rapid spread of the telegraphic
network, which consisted of over 10,000 miles of wire in the United States
alone by 1850.[97] Speedy news, claimed the *Economist*, left "no opportunity for promoting mischief by sinister reports," squeezing rumor and
falsehood out of the market, while the accumulation and dissemination
of data would make the market transparent.[98] The implied message—for
both readers and regulators—was that the changing fortunes of business
in general and the stock market in particular were the result of neither the
inscrutable unfolding of providence nor the whims of a cabal of powerful
insiders. Instead, with its faith in the power of numbers, the financial press
helped coalesce the belief that the market was governed by impersonal
laws that could be determined by scientific inquiry. This notion appeared
to tame the volatile financial system, disturbingly prone to panics and
crises, recasting it as stable, benign, and—perhaps—even predictable.[99]
Indeed, it was a short step from unveiling the "hidden laws" governing
the market to being able to predict the market's future direction. Thus, it
was significant that market statisticians proved particularly interested in
collecting historical price data. From this point the market, as Alex Preda
notes, "developed a history, from which its future could be inferred."[100]

Yet the much-vaunted objectivity of statistics was an illusion.[101] The
idea that they would insulate the market from manipulation soon proved
idealistic. For a start, the railway statisticians were far from disinterested
collectors of data. Tuck was publisher of one of the leading railway periodicals, the *Railway Times*; his manuals aimed to hype the railway share
market, and—as the mania developed—to defend it from its many critics, arguing "that nothing but the most absurd prejudice, the most stupid
obstinacy, or the most corrupt venality, can be opposed to the Railway
system."[102] Spackman also had a financial interest in railways but seems to
have been a "bear," advertising in the press to buy up the shares and scrip
of struggling and defunct companies on the cheap.[103] Statistics became a

battleground between the two. Tuck accused Spackman of plagiarizing statistics from his *Railway Shareholder's Manual* but skewing them to exaggerate the amount of capital required to construct all the proposed railways, thus helping to trigger the panic of autumn 1845.[104] Numbers did not speak for themselves, and what they were made to say could be controversial. The London Stock Exchange came under fire for Nash's dissections of railway accounts that it printed in its *Weekly Railway Share List*. Criticized by railway boards and the railway press alike for establishing a publication "to run down shares," the Stock Exchange succumbed to the pressure and axed Nash's editorials in October 1849.[105] But without accompanying interpretation, the numbers left many investors baffled. Slaughter's successor at the statistics department of the London Stock Exchange, Henry Burdett, recounted a story told him by a stockbroker friend. The broker's client wanted to invest in tramways, so the broker advised him to read the tramways section in the *Official Intelligence*. A week later the client returned and told the broker he did not think much of the book. "Asked why, the client explained that after careful comparison and study he found that, except for the names of the different tramways, the particulars given were practically the same, the only difference being the figures in each case." When the broker tried to explain that this was the point, the client replied that "as he had no head for figures, a book of this kind was of no value to him."[106] Assuming a financially literate, calculating investor, these statistical manuals, together with much of the business press, appealed most obviously to market professionals and experienced investors rather than wider constituencies. Numbers alone were not enough to help such readers: what they needed was interpretation and advice. As we shall see, there were many willing to provide it.

Fashioning the Self

If the nineteenth-century passion for statistics generated a literature that, though significant, was only ever read by small numbers, then the concurrent zeal for self-improvement generated a far more widely read print culture. The attention devoted by historians to Samuel Smiles's canonical *Self-Help* (1859) overstates its uniqueness: Smiles was merely restating, albeit very profitably, ideas long in circulation.[107] Print culture had long sustained what Stephen Greenblatt terms "self-fashioning"—"an increased self-consciousness about the fashioning of human identity as a manipulable, artful process."[108] For some time, conduct manuals had fueled "fantasies of mobility through self-fashioning—the idea that each (white and male) individual has a 'self' that could be 'fashioned' independently of social and economic realities."[109] Such literature boomed in the nineteenth century, a response to the insecurities generated by rapid industrialization and urbanization. This emerging "society of strangers" was mobile, and young. By 1851, over 60 percent of the population was under twenty-four.[110] With so many moving to urban areas in search of work, family and regional ties weakened. Inexperienced, and less able to access the counsel of older family members, these young migrants eagerly consumed printed advice to help them navigate modern life.[111]

A pronounced strand in this literature was economic self-improvement. Guides such as Leman Thomas Rede's *Art of Money Getting; Showing the Means by Which an Individual May Obtain and Retain Health, Wealth, and Happiness* (1828), *The Book of Economy; or, How to Live Well in London on £100 Per Annum* (1832), and *Open Sesame! or, The Way to Get Money, By a Rich Man Who Was Once Poor* (1832) taught strategies for money acquisition and money management. Business success was the goal for growing armies of upwardly mobile mechanics and aspiring clerks, and texts catering to this ambition flourished particularly strongly in the United States.[112] Edwin Freedley's *Practical Treatise on Business; or, How to Get, Save, Spend, Give, Lend, and Bequeath Money*, first published in Philadelphia in 1848, had a wide circulation on both sides of the Atlantic. It included sections entitled "Habits of Business," "Getting Money," "How to Get Customers," and "How to Become Millionaires." Freeman Hunt, the founder of *Hunt's Merchants' Magazine*, followed in 1856 with *Worth and Wealth: A Collection of Maxims, Morals, and Miscellanies for Merchants and Men of Business*. This covered a similar range of topics, including "How to Prosper in Business," "Effects of Ostentation upon Credit," and "Self-Reliance, the Main Spring of Success."

Such texts addressed the reader directly, providing explicit instruction and advice, often in strongly didactic fashion. Narrators of self-help literature often "assumed a guise of avuncular omniscience," elevating the wisdom they contained as unchallengeable.[113] They used aphorisms and maxims as repeated textual devices not only to make their points easily intelligible but to "put the weight of tradition and common sense behind social values and interpretations which were in reality peculiar to Victorianism."[114] Optimistic texts in the sense that they told readers that they had the power to mold their own destinies, the process of "self-making" they offered represented, Michael Zakim argues, "another of the great production projects of the age of capital . . . resting on an infrastructure of self-study, self-satisfaction, self-observation, self-esteem, self-respect, self-confidence, and self-acquaintance."[115] These manuals thus enshrined a manly self-reliance as the cornerstone of their strategies of the self. For these authors, as for their eighteenth-century predecessors, the stock market was a dangerous distraction from the goal of self-improvement. Freedley's compendium of business advice did include the chapter "How to Get Rich by Speculation," cut-and-pasted from the *Boston Courier*, though this concerned speculation in commodities and was hedged with cautions.[116] Other guides conveyed traditional warnings against the stock market. "Do not leave a legitimate business for financiering," Hunt urged his readers: "Be content with such things as ye have."[117] And though the author of *Open Sesame!* presented Francis Baring, founder of Barings Bank, as an example of what could be achieved by "sober energetic habits," he did not intend to encourage speculation, which could prove "a dangerous and fatal field of action," even to the most wary.[118]

Yet other authors borrowed the methods of this genre of writing but subverted its message, representing the stock market as a golden path to self-improvement, for those bold enough to follow it. Railways were the initial subject of this literature, which hyped the new technology and enticed investors with visions of the spectacular profits that could be made. The mania for railway shares that developed in 1845 was thought to be attracting a range of new participants into the market—"Needy clerks, poor tradesmen's apprentices, discarded serving-men, and bankrupts"— and while such claims were no doubt exaggerated, lower share denominations and partly paid-up shares played a major part in democratizing speculation.[119] These pamphlets were accessible, written explicitly for novices joining the market for the first time, and easily read in a single sitting—a far more realistic point of entry than intimidating compilations of railway statistics. The two most prominent, *A Short and Sure Guide to Railway Speculation* (1845) and *The Railway Investment Guide* (1845), priced at just a shilling each, went through multiple editions.[120] Pocket books were also published designed to help people keep track of their trading activity, including *The Railway Speculator's Memorandum Book, Ledger, and General Guide to Secure Share Dealing* (1845) and *The Railway Shareholder's Pocket Book and Almanack* (1845), and these also carried snippets of advice. With newspapers publishing extensive extracts, their reach was considerable.[121]

Whereas previous manuals had rarely addressed the reader directly, these railway guides very consciously spoke to new investors. Adopting the personal tone characteristic of self-help literature, they addressed themselves to the concerns of the neophyte operator. Critics of railway speculation—of which there were many—painted it as a dangerous and delusive pursuit.[122] Far from representing a problem to the authors of these works, it offered an opportunity. The anonymous author of the *Railway Investment Guide* framed new investors as acutely vulnerable due to the lack of advice available to them: "there is no hand-book, no guide, no *vade mecum*, for them . . . a want which may be the disappointment, ruin, and beggary of entire families."[123] Reveling in hyperbole, in an echo of Thomas Mortimer's lurid prose, he portrayed the railway market as a perilous place, where there were "thousands of bubbles," all of which had the appearance of solidity. The path to wealth was hazardous because it had "an imperceptibly-diverging branch that winds away also to RUIN!" But this guide would "rescue the public from this chaos of bewilderment, confusion, and uncertainty."[124]

Indeed, all these texts coached readers more explicitly than previous literature. Rather than providing data, they talked readers through the practicalities of investment, such as applying for letters of allotment, how to understand share quotations, and tips on dealing with stockbrokers. They offered advice on picking stocks. Company directorates, they argued, were a shortcut to distinguishing between solid and ephemeral schemes, illustrating the continuing importance of social status in the investment market. The reputation of the directors was key for two reasons: respectable men would never lend their names to undertakings unlikely to succeed, plus there would always be a ready market for the shares in schemes with good directorates.[125] But these guides also embraced speculation, albeit advising differing levels of caution. The author of the *Railway Investment Guide* was the most bullish: while acknowledging that some predicted a panic on the scale of 1825, the fact that it was impossible for one in ten of the schemes promoted to be carried out successfully mattered little to the canny operator, for serious money could be made even from bubble companies by dealing in letters of allotment and scrip. There was little risk involved, as constantly rising prices meant that the winners greatly outnumbered the losers.[126] Others recommended a slightly more conservative approach. "A Successful Operator" told readers to steer clear of shares in newly projected lines, speculation in which was likely to leave them "shipwrecked."[127] Instead, they should stick to shares in authorized lines, making sure that they could afford future calls (part-payments) on their shares, otherwise they risked having to sell out at a loss when such a request for payment was made. Those who could pay the calls, however, had "only to hold on steadily, and sooner or later (unless the line was a mere *bubble*), he will have an opportunity of selling at a profit." Resourceful speculators could buy up shares at bargain prices when calls forced overcommitted holders to sell.[128]

The guides promoted the idea that amateur operators could employ simple strategies and basic rules of thumb to ensure profit, just as many self-help books promised simple routes to success. Though the author of *The Railway Shareholder's Pocket Book* conceded that it was "difficult to lay down any system to secure profits," in the very next breath he recommended "a very reasonable plan" pursued by many: "hold until the price begins to fall, and then sell directly."[129] Slightly more cautiously, *The Railway Speculator's Memorandum Book* urged "Never be too eager of gain. Thousands of pounds have been lost by greediness. Sell stock when it is rising, having attained a moderate height." The book also briefly addressed the "characteristics necessary for a successful speculator," which were "Patience, Caution, and Promptitude." Self-reliance was a better strategy than listening to market gossip: "If you pay too much attention to rumours . . . you will often find yourself deceived! Rely upon your own judgment, founded upon all the facts that you can collect."[130] By following these simple rules of thumb you would be transformed into "A Successful Operator" and "One of the Initiated."

But events soon overtook them. The sharp fall in the price of shares which occurred in late 1845 made association with speculation toxic.[131] Though *A Short and Sure Guide to Railway Speculation* survived the crash, it was rebranded to harmonize with the more sober public mood, the eighth edition appearing under the new title of *A Short and Sure Guide to Permanent Investments in Railways*. The author tried to persuade readers that despite the crash, they should not lose confidence in the long-term prospects of the sector: many bargains were there for "the experienced capitalist" to seize.[132] But this was optimistic: hundreds of projected schemes were abandoned, prices continued to slide, and it slowly became clear that the railways would never be as profitable as the hype had claimed. The exposure of dubious accounting practices at the lines of George Hudson, the "railway king" who had been the public face of the boom—and to whom *A Short and Sure Guide* had been dedicated—further depressed confidence.[133] New books on the sector explicitly condemned speculation.

One such, posing the question "Are Railways a Good Investment?," did so "not for the satisfaction of the *speculative* portion of the public, but for that numerous class, who have been induced to *invest* monies in these undertakings, with a view to *permanent* dividend."[134] Another stated that "We do not encourage, on the contrary we greatly deprecate, that vicious spirit of gambling, which is far too prevalent."[135] They believed that the future of the sector lay in recasting railway shares as safe, dependable investments appealing to long-term investors.[136]

These railway guides were ultimately ephemeral, compromised by the crash, and were limited to one sector, enthusiasm for which chilled with the steady and prolonged decline in prices after 1845.[137] But if railway shares fell out of favor, then this new approach to writing about investment did not; with some modifications, it was applied to the stock market as a whole in a new wave of investment manuals which emerged just as the railway mania faded.

Mass-Producing Advice

The aftermath of the railway mania had created a climate of uncertainty about investment, with large numbers of shareholders enmeshed in costly and long-running lawsuits to settle liabilities.[138] Those who had not lost heavily in the falling railway share market faced an extensive range of alternative investments. The national debt represented an ever-shrinking proportion of the total securities traded on the London Stock Exchange as more and more domestic and foreign securities obtained official listings.[139] The number of potential investors was also growing. More middle-class investors had the resources to invest, but they were less likely to have the requisite "knowledge, connections or expertise," and the ability of face-to-face advice to cater to them all was doubtful.[140] Investors in smaller towns and rural areas were at a particular disadvantage: one rural resident argued that though local farmers and traders were no longer content to deposit their savings under a brick or "in the recesses of some ancient and curiously contrived bureau," the absence of local stockbrokers meant that they were effectively frozen out of the stock and share market.[141] Even when advisers were available, not everyone had the confidence to approach them: stockbrokers were often assumed to be uninterested in smaller clients and impatient with female investors whom they regarded as needy and time consuming.[142]

Enterprising authors and publishers believed there was a demand for investment advice that was not being satisfied by personal advisers, and they maneuvered to fill this gap. In 1846, the publisher and advertising agent Charles Mitchell commissioned banker Gavin Mason Bell to write *A Guide to the Investment of Capital.* Three years later, London stockbroker T. S. Harvey published *What Shall I Do with My Money?* with the small London firm D. Steel. And in 1852, the much larger house, Effingham Wilson, based at the Royal Exchange, published solicitor Robert Ward's *A Treatise on Investments.* All three were written and packaged to appeal to novice rather than experienced investors. Bell's *Guide to the Investment of Capital* was a relatively substantial clothbound volume with gilt lettering and was rare among early investment guides in having a pictorial cover (see fig. 2.1). The imposing gold sovereigns lent a reassuring solidity to the intangible practice of investment, while depicting coins from the reigns of the three most recent monarchs, George IV, William IV, and Victoria, imparted a sense of prestige and longevity to a stock market still belabored by charges of disreputability and ephemeralness.[143] The book was positioned as a work of self-improvement, taking its place alongside Mitchell's other guides helping readers navigate aspects of modern life, covering everything from oratory and authorship to etiquette and dancing the polka.[144] Effingham Wilson too had a track record dating back to the 1820s of publishing self-help works (with topics including punctuation and vegetarian cookery) and had already shown interest in building a market for investment advice by publishing both Charles Fenn's *Compendium* and the *Short and Sure Guide to Railway Speculation.*[145]

The authors of these guides presented the rapidly expanding market for securities, and the ignorance of many who bought these securities, as necessitating a new kind of advice literature. Bell noted that there were

> thousands upon thousands of persons in Great Britain depending entirely upon the interest realised from the investment of their capital in lands, houses, and the various stocks and public undertakings now so numerous, there are thousands upon thousands wholly ignorant of the nature of the securities they possess, and of the various sources and modes of investment within their reach.[146]

Similarly, Harvey observed that the wide variety of shares available by midcentury "appear to a stranger under such varied and difficult aspects, that the task of selection requires more than ordinary discernment and calls for help."[147] The profusion of investment opportunities was such a

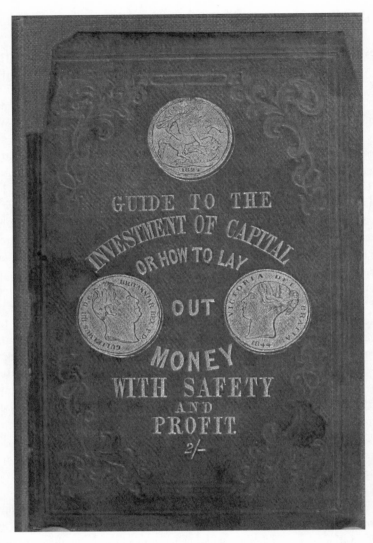

FIGURE 2.1. Front cover of G. M. Bell, *A Guide to the Investment of Capital* (1846). Courtesy of the British Library Board, Digital Store 1390.a.12, digitized by Google.

problem because of the dangers inherent in the market. Yet, rather than an embarrassing problem for these guides to overcome, the recent railway mania, together with other contemporaneous examples of fraud and instability in the corporate economy, were presented—implicitly or explicitly—as justifying their existence.[148] Far from seeking to downplay risk, they drew attention to it, reminding readers of the speed with which fortunes could be lost as well as won.[149] "Hundreds have been suddenly enriched, and others have as suddenly sunk into poverty," wrote Bell of the railway mania.[150] Harvey resorted to a variety of metaphors to underline the presence of risk, writing both of "the quicksands that occasionally engulph a fortune," and the "the rocks ahead, sunken or visible" that investors faced as they navigated the market.[151] Ward provided the most extended warnings on the subject, in doing so unconsciously echoing fiction of the time that highlighted the unreliability of signifiers like luxurious offices, teams of well-dressed clerks, and fancy circulars when it came to the corporate market.[152] Just as Charles Dickens's *Martin Chuzzlewit* (1844) documents the sham solidity of the Anglo-Bengalee Disinterested Loan and Life Insurance Company, which "started into existence one morning, not an Infant Institution, but a Grown-up Company," complete with dazzlingly luxurious offices and bombastic circulars, so Ward, albeit more prosaically, described fraudulent companies that were concocted by plausible schemers. They seemingly flourished "until some unfortunate shareholder in the concern gets too impatient, and begins to suspect all is not right: then suddenly the clerks are dismissed, the offices abandoned, the trustees and directors are no where to be found: the shareholders find they are swindled."[153]

Emphasizing the bewildering array of investments—and the unreliable signifiers which made choosing the right one so difficult—served to underline the indispensability of these guides. Whereas earlier texts were chiefly concerned with cataloging the market, these new manuals were not content with simply gathering and presenting data. Although they borrowed to some extent the now-traditional catalog structure, with chapters or sections on different categories of investment and sectors of the economy, these texts very much saw their role as furnishing advice, advice that would keep the novice investor safe.[154] Perhaps unsurprisingly, given the long shadow cast by the railway mania, this advice was relatively conservative. Ward, for example, was far from enthusiastic about the prospects of the new companies being established for working mines in California and Australia.[155] And at a time when the laws against usury were still nominally (though not practically) in force, capping the legitimate rate of return at 5 percent, he advised that investments offering more than this were "to be looked upon with great suspicion ... such an investment cannot be a first-rate security; if a person choose to seek after such, he must, in a greater or less degree, jeopardize his capital."[156] Though slightly more tolerant of securities yielding over 5 percent, Harvey still suggested that they "should cause a misgiving so far as to stimulate searching enquiry into their safety."[157]

Yet rather than simply shepherding readers toward the lowest-yielding investments, the authors of these guides invited them to reflect upon their circumstances, needs, and attitude to risk, and to select their own investments accordingly. Bell presented a typology of five different types of investor, each with their own set of recommended investments, asking readers to identify themselves in the schema:

1. Those who desire to obtain the highest rate of interest without much risk ...
2. Those who would prefer a high rate of interest, and are willing to run the risk that securities yielding high rates generally involve ...
3. Those who are not in a position to invest their money for any lengthened period, but may require to call it up suddenly ...
4. Those who desire to obtain a steady and uniform rate of interest, and to be secure of their capital in a few years ...
5. Those who are willing to be content with a low rate of interest, and to be entirely secure from risk ...[158]

Similarly, Ward's book envisaged multiple types of investor, including those who "prefer security of capital to a large annual return" and those who wanted "a greater annual rate of interest than that usually paid on first-rate securities, without wishing to enter into wild speculations."[159] The idea was that individual attitudes and circumstances would shape the behavior of each investor, rather than the preferences of the author.

It followed that these guides did not tell readers exactly what they should do—as Ward put it, he was not setting himself up as a prophet who could predict "the probable increase in value of this or that species of property"—but rather purported to train them to become self-reliant investors.[160] This meant not simply trusting to published statements, since these were not always reliable, but going beyond them to assess the character of the directors and investigating how the company was regarded in its own locality.[161] Similarly, Harvey's readers were furnished with a "List of Inquiries" to make of any joint-stock company investment, ranging from the character of the directors and managers to the size of the reserve fund.[162] The texts thus framed successful investment as a skill which could be learned, distancing it from wild speculation and embedding it in a tradition of the private partnership, in which shareholders were responsible for ensuring that their companies were managed responsibly. Investors were thus imagined as active partners in their companies rather than simply passive dividend-receivers.[163]

Harvey went furthest in presenting investment as a repertoire of skills to be learned, sometimes underlining his point with a proverb to ground it in common sense. Thus, he urged the importance of spreading risk across several securities: "let not any rest content with merely *one* safe investment — experience daily proves that to have 'two strings to the bow' is only common prudence in ordinary affairs."[164] When counseling those who wished to speculate, he stressed the need to be content with small profits rather than grasping for big wins, "on the principle, that 'a nimble sixpence is better than a lazy shilling.'"[165] Anticipating later trends, he even offered some contrarian advice on reading the market. Although it was impossible to predict when the market would rise or fall, generally speaking it was "*the safer course to invest during times of despondency, and to abstain during times of excitement*," because "those who start before the multitude, by getting a little in advance," were the most likely to succeed.[166] He encouraged his readers to adopt a "scientific" approach: investment, "if sifted and studied properly as a science," would allow the reader to avoid "much of the loss that frequently is found to fall upon families from untimely and ill-considered" choices.[167]

Penned by a banker, a stockbroker, and a solicitor — the three main professions responsible for giving investment advice to their clients — these handbooks were imagined as something more than just poor substitutes for face-to-face advice.[168] The *Stamford Mercury* went so far as to claim that the comprehensiveness of Ward's book might deprive his fellow solicitors of clients.[169] Indeed, Ward played up the idea that his book offered something that face-to-face advice could not. Though solicitors were well able to advise clients on their investments, "what may be a very advantageous investment for one person may not be so for another; and a solicitor cannot advise his client to seek a particular kind of investment in preference to another, without inquiring too minutely into all his circumstances." By contrast, reading his book not only allowed investors to decide for themselves what kind of investment suited them best, but also equipped them to evaluate the reliability of advice given them by others.[170] Reviews praised the educational functions of Ward's book, the *Newcastle Guardian* noting that where he "stops to offer counsel he does it in few words; furnishing the reader with the means for arriving at conclusions rather than the conclusions themselves."[171] In a remarkable sign of finance's growing cultural cachet, the education these texts offered was thought to be relevant not only to investors but to everyone. "Even the general reader, who has no money to invest, and is not likely ever to have a personal interest in the subjects treated of, will derive from its perusal a store of information capable of being turned to good account," wrote the *Sunday Times* of Ward's manual.[172]

In the mid-nineteenth century, readerships for this kind of writing were relatively modest but growing. Such was the demand for Ward's guide that it was reprinted in enlarged form just months after the first edition.[173] Bell's tome was less successful, not reaching a second edition despite a positive review in *The Times*'s City column.[174] Harvey's *What Shall I Do with My Money?*, by contrast, was a popular hit, its title, echoing words which must have been uttered many times by confused capitalists, helping it to garner lots of press attention.[175] It ran through seven editions between 1849 and 1858, growing from a sixpenny pamphlet to a two-shilling manual, its success confirming the growing commercial viability of mass-produced stock market advice.

Sensation and the Stock Exchange

This new popular advice literature developed in tandem with fictional works satirizing and condemning the financial market, whose ambiguous morality became a topic of fascination for novelists.[176] They were responding to the growing importance of finance in the Anglo-American world. In the United States, a total of over 22,000 corporate bodies had been specially chartered by 1860, while in the United Kingdom, legislation between 1855 and 1862 made it a far simpler process to form companies with limited liability.[177] Over 5,000 limited companies were registered under the new laws in the first ten years of their operation.[178] The railway boom and bust inspired novelists in the 1850s to weave morality tales around the dangerous passions unleashed by the mania.[179] Later in the decade, novels like Charles Dickens's *Little Dorrit* (1857) and Charles Lever's *Davenport Dunn: A Man of Our Day* (1859) exposed the hollow "Mammon worship" that underpinned the fleeting material success of speculators and financiers, who are exposed as mendacious swindlers.[180] It was a similar picture in the United States, where fictive forms were quickly adopted to explore—and satirize—the emerging financial sector. Two early plays, *Wall-Street, or, Ten Minutes before Three* (1819) and *Wall-Street as It Now Is* (1826), the latter involving a corporate plot to take over the nation's treasury, helped establish Wall Street as a shorthand for immoral money-making.[181] A little later, Frederick Jackson's *A Week in Wall Street* (1841) used colorful novelistic devices to engage readers in its depiction of the dangers of "stock gambling," which is described as a "whirlwind" destroying the savings of ignorant outsiders.[182] Around midcentury the sensationalist genre of city mysteries—such as George Foster's *New York by Gaslight* (1850) and Thomas De Walden's play *The Upper Ten and the Lower Twenty* (1854)—claimed to lift the veil on urban sin and corruption, including the dark arts of financiering. They combined the appeal of a guide to unchartered territory with a gothic account of shady business practices. George Francis Train's *Young America in Wall Street* (1857) condemned the city's elite whose wealth was founded on financial speculation. In a similar vein, melodramatic novels presented the stock market as a place of dangerous temptations and immoral acts, for both men and women. Plots often turned on reversals of fortune in the market, with women frequently the victims of seduction at hands of evil financiers. While most novels cast women as innocent victims of masculine financial chicanery, others blamed female speculators as dangerously addicted to gambling fueled by greed, thus perpetuating the long-standing problematization of women's involvement in the markets. The implied financial advice in these works was seemingly clear: participating in the stock market was not only economically risky but also led to depravity.[183]

Despite their overt moral condemnation, however, fictional denunciations of the market operated ambiguously. Their sensationalism made the stock market seem dangerously enticing. Even if morally dubious, the happenings on Wall Street made for a compelling story; even if most speculation seemed to lead to ruin, and the market was manipulated by powerful insiders, there was nevertheless the possibility that a fortune could be made in a heartbeat. Some stock market advice deployed this double play of condemnation and titillation. This can be seen in the first US investment advice manual, William Armstrong's forty-page pamphlet *Stocks and Stock-Jobbing in Wall-Street, with Sketches of the Brokers, and Fancy Stocks* (1848). Like his British contemporaries, Armstrong explained that his aim was "to present in a clear and simple manner, the nature of stocks and stock transactions, so that they may readily be understood by every one." He claimed that "hitherto there have been no means for an uninitiated person to acquire such knowledge" except through experience, "which is generally a dear schoolmaster." In addition to lists of information on specific securities and brief profiles of leading brokers, it includes descriptions of how the stock market works, with accounts of bulls and bears, corners, and other forms of market manipulation. Like the compilers of railroad manuals, Armstrong advised focusing on both company fundamentals (their "intrinsic value") and wider economic conditions.[184] He distinguished between natural and unnatural price fluctuations in the stock market, with the latter a result of insiders gambling in so-called "fancy stocks" whose true value was either obscure or unknowable (for example, failed railroad lines no longer paying dividends or issuing statements). Although keen to portray investment on the stock markets as a rational activity, Armstrong also admits that it is not a fair game, because of the potential for swindling. In places he characterizes the stock market as involving an ongoing contest between the bulls and bears, each side recklessly puffing the market or foretelling its doom. In that situation, Armstrong concedes that outsiders may as well just toss a coin.[185] Nevertheless he does give some advice, a mixture of general business maxims and practical rules of thumb: do not put all your eggs in one basket; always get stock market contracts in writing and secured with a deposit; use trustworthy brokers; and only invest in stocks of known value.

The author, designated on the title page anonymously as a "reformed stock gambler," offers pious pronouncements on the dangers of speculation, acknowledging that "the excitement and infatuation which it induces is not surpassed by any description of gambling."[186] He also makes a point of eschewing lurid tales of the unsavory practices of the big Wall Street operators that were becoming the staple fare of popular journalism—the "spicy materials which are furnished in such abundance by Wall-street speculators."[187] Nevertheless, he provides an insight for the curious into how "fancy stocks" are traded and even includes in an appendix detailed information on ten such stocks, presumably to allow the outside investor to make a rational choice on what has been framed as irrational speculation. Moreover, his text affords readers titillating glimpses of forbidden activity: the warnings can be read as an enticement, sowing the seed of easy fortunes in the mind of the reader.

Midcentury Britain saw the growing diversification of print advice. Fortune's *Epitome of the Stocks*, now edited by financial journalist David Morier Evans, went through three more editions in the 1850s. Evans updated it to reflect the changing securities market, with brief sections on railways and joint-stock banks widening its scope beyond domestic and foreign funds for the first time—even if most of the data on railways were culled from Slaughter's *Railway Intelligence*.[188] Though the 1856 edition proved to be the final one, the baton for this type of guide passed to Fenn's *Compendium of the English and Foreign Funds and the Principal Joint Stock Companies*, which raced through four new editions between 1854 and 1860. Though the market for such reference works—with their increasingly statistical focus—clearly persisted, it had definite bounds, the genre alluded to disparagingly by the author of an 1861 article in the *National Magazine* on the Stock Exchange:

> Perhaps, dear reader, you have been expecting or dreading a description of all sorts of "Foreign Stocks," "Railway Stocks," and all other Stocks that are bought or sold here; but we do not intend it. There are very dry books that profess to do this, and which very few people read.[189]

More accessible "how-to" guides aimed at novices, following the model established by Bell, Harvey, and Ward, had a much greater commercial potential. Mainstream publishers moved into the market, publishing *Practical Hints for Investing Money* (1855) by Francis Playford and *A Handy Guide to Safe Investments* (1858) by the pseudonymous "Gresham Omnium."[190] The former was published by Smith, Elder & Co., a big-spending house which outbid rivals to secure some of the nation's best-loved authors, including Anthony Trollope and George Eliot; the latter was published by Groombridge and Sons, a newer house which already had a hand in the self-improvement market with the popular magazine *Family Economist*.[191] Aided by extensive advertising, both manuals found a readership: Omnium's went to a second edition in 1860, while Playford's became a standard text, reaching its sixth edition in 1869. This may be partly because it broke with the monotonous catalog-like structure of rival handbooks which was followed by Omnium, opting instead for short, themed chapters on practical matters, from the remuneration of brokers to the causes of fluctuations in the price of stocks. This may have rendered it more convenient to use, and reviews praised Playford's ability to unravel "in language which is intelligible to the most 'unbusinesslike' mind, all the mysteries of Capel Court."[192]

Both books adopted a conservative stance on the new limited companies. Omnium barely acknowledged the new laws, while Playford was

actively hostile to limited liability, arguing that it contravened the law
that those who risked for gain should also be responsible for losses if a
venture failed. Rather than steering investors toward the new companies, Playford preferred "to recommend investment in the Public Funds
as the safer means of employing spare money, particularly in small sums
and for uncertain periods." And while he was keen to defend the more
speculative transactions on the stock market, such as time bargains, on
the grounds that these provided the public with a fair and liquid market,
these were not suitable for his book's readers. Small investors should "buy
and sell within their means of paying for, or delivering whatever they deal
in." If they dabbled in time bargains, they would only experience "loss, of
time, money, and character."[193] These authors also sought to protect their
readers from other dangers, particularly unsuitable agents. Both Playford and Omnium, members of the London Stock Exchange, stressed the
need to deal with well-established stockbrokers—men like themselves.[194]
This would protect readers from fraud, since members were bound "by
the laws and customs of the Stock Exchange." Those who were not members could ignore these rules and were free to combine the functions of
brokers, jobbers, and speculators, which meant that their interests would
rarely coincide with those of their clients.[195] Such outsiders were "not to
be trusted under any circumstances."[196] Drawing a distinction between
lawless outsiders and honorable insiders was both a way to establish credibility and to try to protect member brokers from the competition the
outsiders threatened.[197]

The advice of authors like Playford and Omnium was conservative and
paternalistic, urging small investors to stick with the safest securities and
to deal only with the most reputable intermediaries. (Rare texts in this
period advising on working-class investments were more cautious still,
recommending that readers place their savings in the Post Office Savings
Bank, benefit societies, or building societies.)[198] But this was not true of all
print advice. If the boosterish railway guides of the 1840s had only briefly
flourished, then the literature on domestic mining proved hardier. Usually
written by the kind of outside dealers Playford and Omnium had warned
against, and often privately printed, they deployed a host of strategies to
make mining seem a safe investment as well as well as staggeringly profitable.[199] Capitalizing on a number of bank failures in the mid-1850s, they
argued that the risk of loss was in fact far less in the mining sector than
in banking.[200] They held up domestic mining as more patriotic than putting money in foreign mines, since only the former would develop the

nation's resources and augment national wealth. While they admitted that money had in the past been lost in Cornish mines, scientific innovation and investigation had rendered modern mining far less risky.[201] These authors also sought to blur the boundaries between investment and speculation. "Everything," one author helpfully remarked, "is . . . more or less a speculation," and prudent investors would manage the inevitable risk by spreading their money across several undertakings.[202] Alongside detailed treatises were pamphlets amounting to little more than tip sheets recommending particular mining stocks to "small and large capitalists" alike.[203]

Other guides also encouraged readers to take a more speculative approach to the stock market. Purporting to come from the pen of "A Late MP," *How to Make Money, and Plenty of It; or, Hints on Speculation* (1857) positioned itself as a self-improvement text.[204] Its front cover (see fig. 2.2) promises "success in life!" but with little of the moral earnestness that characterized the Smilesian branch of success literature. Though overlaid with a thin veneer of traditional sermonizing ("when we envy the happiness of rich and great men, we know not the inward canker that oftentimes eats out their inward joy and delight"), the pitch here was not moral uplift but material enrichment, explaining to readers how to make money—"and plenty of it," as the title unapologetically boasted. The pamphlet's democratic mission was overt, aimed at "needy persons and their families" who wanted to emulate those "thousands of lucky individuals" who had become millionaires in "the present age of speculation." It therefore casts the stock market as an instrument of social mobility. Though the pamphlet's structure was conventional, consisting of a run through various types of asset including land, the content was anything but, with assessments of the possibilities each security presented for speculation on short-term fluctuations in prices. For example, the funds were recommended not on the grounds of security but because "there is perhaps no description of property liable to greater vicissitudes of fluctuation as stock, it is constantly on the move, and therefore ever feeding the thousands who play upon its surface."[205]

Rather than framing speculation as little better than spinning the wheel of fortune, the pamphlet presented it as a skill which had to be diligently learned. Would-be speculators needed to acquire the habits of constant vigilance and be prepared to "unceasingly watch the market," which meant a close study of prices. They were advised to observe "the daily fluctuations of the share list" and to be on the hunt for further sources of information: railway speculators were thus recommended Slaughter's *Railway*

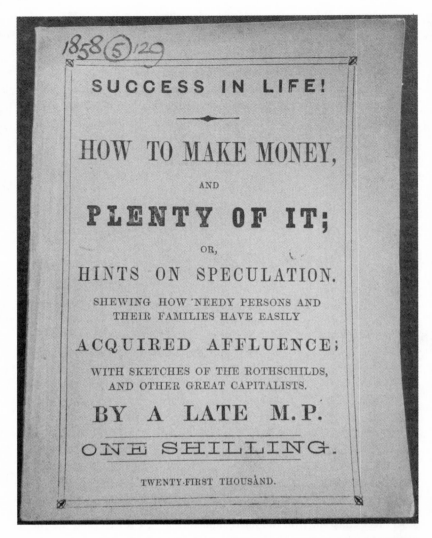

FIGURE 2.2. Front cover of A Late M.P., *How to Make Money, and Plenty of It* (1857). Bodleian Library. Image provided by James Taylor.

Shareholders' Manual, while those who preferred mining companies were told to take the *Mining Journal*. Success in speculation was thus like success in any other field of business endeavor—the result of study, work, and self-tutoring—and just as morally justifiable. There were further borrowings from the genre of self-improvement. The manual concluded by sketching three brief biographies of the Rothschilds, John Law, and George Hudson, the "railway king." Far from cautionary tales, these were celebrations of upward mobility, intended to demonstrate to the reader "that wealth is within the reach of every shrewd speculator who takes proper advantage of the events and changes always occurring in every man's life."[206] More fundamentally, by incorporating figures from the world of finance into one of the key devices of self-help literature — the inspiring biography of the self-made man — the author was attempting to moralize speculation, suggesting that such men were admirable role-models (even though Law had fled France in disgrace and Hudson was locked in a legal battle with one of his former companies).

Published not in London but by the Birmingham bookseller William Cornish, its unabashed advocacy of speculation made *How to Make Money, and Plenty of It* something of an outlier in the 1850s, and it is difficult to know how popular the pamphlet was.[207] Cornish's claim that the pamphlet had gone through twenty-one editions are belied by the absence of references to the pamphlet in the press. But the more relaxed attitude to speculation it embodied was to become more mainstream in the middlebrow press of the 1860s. Typical of the traditional critical stance were Malcolm Laing Meason's fictionalized tales of City speculation, such as *The Bubbles of Finance* (1865), first serialized in Dickens's *All The Year Round*, and his *The Profits of Panics* (1866).[208] These charted the rise and fall of the kinds of companies being promoted in the craze for limited liability companies that had tempted Marx to try day-trading; indeed, the second volume was rushed out to capitalize on the panic which engulfed the leading financial house Overend, Gurney & Co. in May 1866, which had been floated as a limited company just months previously.[209] Meason's tales sought to save the public from "share dealing dishonesty," but at the precise moment that *All The Year Round* was publishing his dire warnings, its rival *Chambers's Journal* was presenting speculation not so much as a dangerous vice as an absorbing hobby.[210] The author of an article on the Stock Exchange did not seek to deny its association with frauds and market rigs, but these were apparently no impediment to participation: "if you want a little reasonable and interesting excitement, there is nothing like dealing with the Stock Exchange." Those who speculated with money they could not afford to lose were fools, because the emotional strain they would endure would not compensate for any amount of gain they might make. But for those who understood and could bear the risks, "there is excitement about speculation which may be reckoned as a kind of profit."[211] In other words, readers were being offered an emotional, rather than a strictly financial, payoff for dabbling in the market—a kind of return which was to become increasingly central to the genre of advice literature, as later chapters will show.

Protecting the Unprotected

Whether advocating safe investment or riskier speculation, or seeking to blur the boundaries between the two, midcentury guides to investment had much in common. They told readers that their responsibility was to educate themselves to become more proficient economic agents. At the same time, they tended to encourage readers to depend on the guidance and advice of professionals. They presented the Stock Exchange— rather than alternatives such as banks or land—as the best destination for the spare cash of small investors. And they also invariably gendered their readers as male. As such, they were consistent with traditions of encoding the market as feminine, dating back at least as far as eighteenth-century ideas of "Lady Credit," and speculators as masculine, whose job was to master the market. As Urs Stäheli notes, casting the market as a scene of heterosexual seduction "necessarily turned the speculator into a man . . . female speculators occupied an impossible place in the discourse of speculation."[212] Though women frequently featured in the Victorian imagination as the victims of financial fraud—the oft-invoked "widows and spinsters"—it seemed harder to imagine them as active and independent agents, on the point of investment, judging by their absence from the financial advice genre.

We might take this gendering as evidence of the growing influence of ideas about "separate spheres" in the Victorian era. "Bourgeois notions of gentility required that women remain ignorant of money matters," notes George Robb, and the legal system continued to divest wives of control of their property (unless secured by a separate estate or other legal maneuver) until 1870.[213] Middle-class women were bombarded with a growing avalanche of advice literature in the nineteenth century that set out to explain to them "their proper duties as daughters, wives and mothers."[214] Household books could take a multitude of forms, including "compendiums, miscellanies, dictionaries, encyclopaedias, school textbooks, narratives, collections of receipts, anecdotes or letters," and instructed women on a range of topics, including etiquette, medicine, childcare, and managing servants.[215] These texts did envisage an important economic role for their readers. Domestic economy was a prominent topic, with women instructed how to keep proper household accounts as a means of curbing extravagant expenditure, avoiding debt, and ensuring domestic serenity.[216] Sound money management and skill with figures were presented as core feminine responsibilities in the century's two best-selling domestic manuals: Maria Rundell's *New System of Domestic Cookery* (1806) and Isabella Beeton's *Book of Household Management* (1861).[217] Though such manuals had an empowering rhetoric—Beeton likened the mistress of a house to the commander of an army or the leader of a business enterprise—women's responsibility for money management actually represented an obstacle rather than a bridge to greater autonomy, "one of several feminine tasks which comprised a time consuming diversion from a woman's aspirations to engage in the public domain."[218] In these years, the issue of investment of capital was conspicuous by its absence in this kind of literature. Yet this did not reflect the reality of large and growing numbers of women investors, principally single women, who had a greater degree of agency over their finances. They made up 34.7 percent of fundholders in 1810, increasing to 47.2 percent by 1840.[219]

Where did these women learn about investment? Clearly, they faced disadvantages in not being able to tap into male business and social networks in which information about investment circulated.[220] Yet personal networks of family and friends did represent significant sources of information and advice for women.[221] Women could also access the services of professionals, such as solicitors, bankers, and increasingly, stockbrokers. However, commentators at the time doubted women's ability to negotiate on equal terms with male advisers and stressed their consequent vulnerability both to fraud and to bad advice.[222] Nevertheless, women faced few formal bars on investing their money, certainly compared to other fields of activity, and in most cases they could attend general meetings of shareholders and vote along with their male counterparts.[223] Rather than deferring to men, many women actively managed their own financial interests. Women's correspondence with brokers in both Britain and the United States reveals examples of well-informed and assertive investors who were well able to form their own opinions and act independently.[224]

References to the press in such correspondence suggest that print culture was an important source of information for female investors. Yet women's magazines played only a marginal role here, rarely acknowledging that their readers might be interested in finance and offering only occasional snippets on the subject. *La Belle Assemblée* carried one such morsel when it reported in 1822 that Lord Mansfield, when asked by a lady how to place her cash to the best advantage, replied: "If you want principal without interest, buy land; if interest without principal, lend your money on mortgage; but if principal *and* interest, purchase in the stocks."[225] A little later, the *Lady's Newspaper*, established in 1847 and noted for covering political and imperial news as well as more traditionally "feminine" fare, carried a weekly "Money-Market" report, but this was a terse affair of just a few lines, and finance did not feature prominently elsewhere in the paper.[226] But even if women's periodicals rarely discussed investment directly, the language of finance could influence how they talked about other subjects, in ways that foreshadowed the more overt financialization of the self that we discuss at more length in later chapters. Thus, one article recommending that ladies take up charitable giving argued: "here is an investment of money which, in the long run, will yield the investor cent. per cent. A gift to the poor is a loan to One who never forgets to repay the lender."[227] The most frequent metaphor, however, involved women's investments—or speculations—on the "marriage market," echoing masculine discourse which insisted that the best investment any woman could make was to marry a wealthy man.[228]

Such metaphors were double-edged, at once rhetorically excluding women from the financial markets but also assuming a familiarity with the language of investment, and it is likely that women were learning about the subject from the same daily and weekly newspapers that their male relatives were reading. These papers carried a growing amount of financial reportage, thus bringing the stock market into the domestic sphere. Men rarely considered such reading appropriate for the fairer sex. In one 1840s short story about the railway mania, for example, the male narrator calls on a lady in St. John's Wood and finds her reading a morning newspaper.

> "Nothing in that, certainly," you'll say; but wait till you hear what part of it she was reading. Not the deaths, births, and marriages; not the court-circular; not the fashions of the month; not the column of advertisements . . . no, not on any of these features of the daily romance of the world was my lady's attention fixed; but on the city article and the railway share list!!![229]

Described mockingly as "The Railway Queen" in the story's title, her obsessive tracking of share prices and aggressive pursuit of profit render her unladylike in the narrator's eyes—indeed she tells him she wishes she were a man so that she could become secretary to a railroad. The ridicule of women who took an interest in the financial columns was part and parcel of a culture that sought to regulate and control women's choice of reading matter.[230] But male censure was no obstacle for women who wanted to read about investment in their newspapers. In 1842, the Brontë sisters were left railway shares in their aunt's will, and Charlotte recorded that her sister Emily took control of their investments, mastering the subject "by dint of carefully reading every paragraph & every advertisement in the news-papers that related to rail-roads."[231] The easy availability of such material meant that newspapers and periodicals were likely to have been a significant gateway into the market for novice investors of both genders.

Though press coverage might spark an interest in the stock market, there were limits to its educational role. Financial journalists saw exposing fraud as an important public duty, but they tended to assume a knowledge of market basics and often wrote in a jargon that some found impenetrable.[232] And while newspapers had long dispensed advice to their readers on a remarkable variety of topics in the form of "Answers to Correspondents" columns, they generally refused to take on the role of financial adviser in this period.[233] *Lloyd's Weekly Newspaper*'s curt response to one inquirer in 1861 that "we decline to advise as to the investment of money" was not unusual.[234] This diffidence fed the popularity of advice manuals, and in 1863 a significant milestone was reached with the publication of *A Guide to the Unprotected in Every-day Matters Relating to Property and Income*, the first investment manual explicitly for women. Written anonymously by "A Banker's Daughter," it was the work of Emma Sophia Galton, daughter of a Birmingham banker and elder sister of the eugenicist and statistician Francis Galton.[235] Galton explained that "many young people, especially widows and single ladies" were frequently calling on her for help with financial matters, and their ignorance highlighted the paucity of advice aimed at them. As a result of this want, she decided to go into print with her own manual. "Numerous excellent works are published," she admitted, "but the mistake their Authors generally make is in supposing the Reader to know something of business. I write for those who know *nothing*."[236]

A Guide to the Unprotected covered the basics of keeping accounts, writing checks, making calculations, composing letters to bankers, and selecting investments. The overarching lesson was the necessity for caution.

Inexperienced investors, Galton said, typically wanted to secure the highest rate of interest, but they should instead seek safety. Yet, in a sign of the times, this did not simply mean sticking with consols. Galton recommended railway bonds and debentures as good investments, and shares in joint-stock companies could also be contemplated, provided they were established with limited liability, and only once "very careful inquiries have been satisfactorily answered."[237] These would secure returns of up to 4 percent, the most that could be safely received. Speculation was not countenanced, and she urged a buy-and-hold strategy.[238]

Galton's book was an immediate success and remained in print for the rest of the century, reaching its seventh edition in 1900.[239] It thus established a new market of financial advice for women, yet by defining its audience of "those who know *nothing*" as female, it served to entrench stereotypes about feminine financial incompetence. Galton imagined her book as complementing rather than replacing face-to-face advice, which the reader should seek from "a sensible and upright Friend." But she was scornful of the idea that her readers should ask a woman for advice, since "they usually know little or nothing of business. It is much like the blind leading the blind."[240] In reality, many men were financially uninformed too, a point acknowledged in some reviews of the book which suggested that "a great many of the more business-like sex . . . will gain something from it"—though they might not care to admit it.[241] Indeed, certain types of men—clergymen, half-pay officers, small tradesmen—were habitually imagined as being as vulnerable as the archetypical widows and spinsters when it came to the financial markets.[242] Galton herself seems to have recognized this when she produced a spin-off volume, *First Lessons in Business Matters* (1875). This recycled much of the contents of *A Guide to the Unprotected*, but repurposed it as advice for both women and men, presenting "Maria Jones" and "Edward Jones" as its typical investors.[243]

Nevertheless, dedicated financial advice for women in this period continued to insist upon feminine financial frailty. The *Englishwoman's Domestic Magazine*, published by Isabella Beeton's husband Samuel, carried a long article on "Ladies and their Money" in 1864, which took an even more conservative stance than that of Galton. The anonymous male author dismissed joint-stock companies, whether new or established, with limited or unlimited liability, as requiring "too much discrimination for ladies to venture on a safe selection." It also warned that "a lady's *money is never quite safe while being handled*," and therefore counseled against any investment which required too much "handling" by others, which

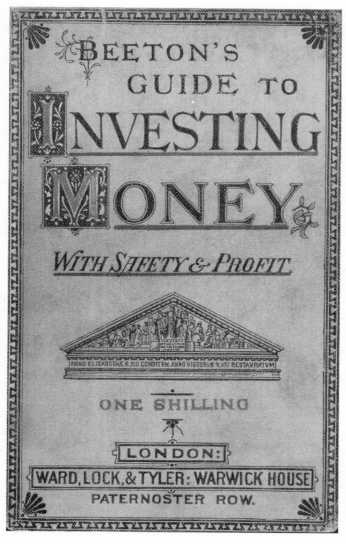

FIGURE 2.3. Front cover of *Beeton's Guide to Investing Money with Safety & Profit* (1870). Courtesy of the British Library.

also ruled out debentures and preference shares. This left the funds as the most appropriate investment for ladies.[244] By directly addressing a female reader—unlike the vast majority of financial advice on the market—such literature helped women to imagine themselves as financial actors. But by insisting upon women's vulnerability, it also served to foster uncertainties and anxieties in the minds of readers, which both created a dependence on the advice and severely limited women's investment options. Critically, advice in this period did not draw links between women's responsibilities for managing household budgets and their role as investors. Arguing that the former equipped them for the latter might have been a strategy for making women feel more confident in the financial markets. Instead, though ostensibly empowering their readers, these texts were more interested in confirming masculine market sovereignty.

The denial of female agency was at its most overt in another Beeton production, *Beeton's Guide to Investing Money with Safety and Profit* (1870). Part of a series of popular shilling reference books issued under the Beeton brand, its decorative cover (see fig. 2.3) sought to imbue investment with dignity and, featuring an illustration of the pediment of the Royal Exchange, promised to place readers in the heart of the City. That the book contained a short section on investments for women seems at first glance an explicit acknowledgment, rare for the time, that women had a legitimate place in the financial world. However, it framed investing as something done *for*, not *by*, women: "Such investments should be chosen for women as are most simple—that is, such on which the interest is easily received, also that do not fluctuate in price, and that do not require to be watched."[245] That the manual's probable author, Samuel Beeton, had been obliged to sell both his business and his name to a rival publisher, Ward, Lock, and Tyler, in 1866 following his disastrous investments in Overend & Gurney, was an irony upon which he understandably chose not to dwell.[246]

Virgin Fields

Emma Galton's insistence that 4 percent was the highest rate of return that could be safely achieved was becoming a tough sell by the early 1860s, given the growing difficulty of maintaining middle-class lifestyles on the limited incomes generated by such investments.[247] This tempted investors to look for opportunities abroad, and defaults by Latin American states in the 1820s and by US states following the panic of 1837 did not knock confidence for long.[248] Indeed, sending capital abroad was becoming more popular after midcentury, a trend which commentators noted.[249] "Not only enterprising men but *un*enterprising men and women invest in Indian securities, in the securities of Colonial Governments and foreign industrial undertakings," observed one provincial paper in 1864.[250] The same year, the *Economist* detected a new confidence among the wealthy to send their capital overseas that coincided with a weakening of the automatic distrust of foreign securities that had previously kept so much capital in the funds.[251]

Nineteenth-century print culture made it much easier for British investors to imagine taking their money out of local and national securities and placing it abroad. Catalog guides were relatively quick to incorporate foreign investments into their coverage of the market. Their inclusion in such manuals, and the amount of space dedicated to them, encouraged readers to treat them as part of the legitimate market. Thus, in the first edition of Fenn's *Compendium* in 1837, the section on foreign funds was longer than that on domestic, and while coverage of joint-stock companies was chiefly focused on the United Kingdom, significant coverage was also given to US joint-stocks, and British companies for overseas development were also included. This idea of equality between domestic and overseas investments was reinforced by the way daily stock and share lists were presented in the press. As we have seen, newspapers were quick to carry the prices of foreign stocks and displayed them prominently. Though domestic and overseas investments were typically listed in separate categories, this was not always the case. By the 1860s, for example, *The Standard*'s daily list of prices included a large "Miscellaneous" category in which the Eastern Assam Tea Company lined up alongside the Ebbw Vale Company and the Rhymney Iron Company sat beside the Rio De Janeiro City Improvements.[252] Such blending made it easier for investors to imagine very different types of investments as, in some ways, equivalents, even interchangeable.

But investors needed means of discriminating between the many foreign investments open to them, and authors of advice literature were happy to supply them. Empire, of course, played an important role, and investment guides usually presented colonial securities as safer than foreign ones.[253] This was partly because of greater trust in and familiarity with the legal systems in these territories, and partly because of the belief that, if it came to it, the British government would bail out investors in the case of a crisis.[254] Colonial loans were also regarded as a better proposition because they were used to support infrastructural development and were therefore "reproductive," whereas foreign states too often borrowed to fund military campaigns or to service debts.[255] But rather than schooling readers automatically to favor imperial investments, advice literature encouraged readers to judge loans to foreign states as they would loans to individuals, where assessments of "character" were paramount.[256] Thus, *The Investors' Guardian Almanack* (1869) distinguished between reliable and unreliable borrowers within the empire. It gently chided Australia for its level of debt, but observed that the funds borrowed had not been wasted since "they have been fairly expended in reproductive works . . . and her resources . . . exceed her expenditure." British Columbia, by contrast, was to be avoided at all costs: there was "little trade to support the pretensions of the place, which affects to be a leading port and emporium on the Pacific Coast, which it is not." Moving on to foreign states, Belgium was praised for her "good character and credit," and Russia for her "admirable" financial policy which meant that "her credit is unimpeachable." On the other hand, Turkey was "known to be honest, but is not to be quite depended upon," and as for Spain, "the less said the better. There is not a good point about her."[257] The engaging anthropomorphism framed lending to a foreign state as little different from assessing the creditworthiness of a local business, and therefore much easier to contemplate.

More important still were traditions of writing about overseas territories as places of fantastical untapped resources simply waiting for the application of modern scientific expertise. Just as Humboldt's writings had influenced investment in Latin America in the 1820s, so E. George Squier's writings stimulated later financing in the region. A US archaeologist, diplomat, and prolific author, Squier's surveys of Honduras in the 1850s painted an idealized picture of its potential and prospects. It had gold and silver mines aplenty, which had been "but little worked, for want of scientific knowledge, intelligence, machinery, and capital." The abundance of the country's natural resources was "favorable to nurturing and sustaining a large population, and point unerringly to the ultimate, if not the speedy development here of a rich and powerful state."[258] Not coincidentally, Squier played a leading role in attempts to promote a Honduras Interoceanic Railroad in the 1850s, which failed despite obtaining support from influential figures in London.[259] Though he moved on to other pursuits, his writings continued to influence investors. So, when in the late 1860s the Honduran government contracted a series of large loans on the London market to finance the railway, Carlos Gutierrez, the Honduran minister in London, was eager to secure the republication of Squier's writings on Honduras, telling his backers that this would be "of more use to us than all the weekly articles published in the London newspapers."[260] Such was the power exerted by this kind of writing on the imagination of investors.

Proponents of investment in other parts of the world tantalized readers with visions of easy wealth. "A Manchester Man," author of 1861's *A Guide to Indian Investments*, used sexualized imagery to depict an India ripe for economic exploitation. This was "a virgin field" for English capital, a "vast and fertile country" whose development would allow it to "contribute enormously towards feeding and clothing the European communities."[261] Around the same time, "An Anglo-American" portrayed the United States using similar language, bewitching readers, again cast as male, with visions of abundance. Here, "the riches of Nature, unbounded and inexhaustible, offer themselves spontaneously to all who will be at the trouble involved in gathering them." This was "a country of vast magnitude and of undeveloped resources so immense and various, that to describe the facts relating to them would appear more like romance than reality."[262] Indeed, the "romance" of such texts was just as important as the data they marshaled, for their function was to seduce as much as persuade.[263]

Though the American Civil War disrupted the westward flow of capital, this proved only a temporary setback.[264] After the war, North American mining promoters established outlets in London, such as the British and Colorado Mining Bureau, occupying an office just behind the Bank of England and displaying "more than 560 ore specimens, numerous Rocky Mountain newspapers, books, maps, annual reports, and prospectuses."[265] Such materials purported to lessen the information asymmetries involved in investing at a distance, but in reality maximized them, since they were assembled by those with a stake in tempting the public to invest. Those who turned to the press for more objective perspectives were just as vulnerable because it was easy for promoters to plant favorable stories to sway investor sentiment. *The Times* facilitated efforts to promote the ultimately unsuccessful Glasgow and Cape Breton Coal and Railway Company, publishing letters making the company's coalfields appear, as Donald Nerbas puts it, "an emerging mecca of successful imperial investment." A rival engineer noted privately how the company had been "puffed up in the London papers," and marveled at "how easy it is to gull the English capitalists!"[266]

Eschewing opinion altogether in favor of data was no safeguard. Promoters hired "armies" of London brokers and jobbers to buy and sell
securities on the London Stock Exchange to create the appearance of
an active market and to keep prices rising.[267] These fictitious quotations
were reported in the daily papers, and investors who relied on them were
fooled. As one MP explained before a select committee to investigate
loans floated in the late 1860s and early 1870s, if you invested in a loan to
a South American republic,

> you are wholly unacquainted with any of the arrangements which are made,
> which would enable you to judge whether it was a fraudulent, or reckless, or a
> prudent transaction; and accordingly persons fly to the only source they have,
> namely, the newspaper, to see what premium it bears upon the Stock Exchange;
> they go to that, and that alone.[268]

The fact that quotations could not be trusted worried even market insiders. The extent to which the market for Honduran bonds was rigged would
surprise even experienced businessmen, believed the *Economist*, "and it
will amaze theoretical economists to find how much 'market price,' with
which they have dealt as something regular and controllable, can, even for
a considerable time, be arranged by speculators, and guided by them to
suit the very worst of purposes."[269] Such an admission, by one of the century's key devotees of the science of statistics, is revealing. It seemed that
any "scientific" approach to the market—indeed, any attempt to draw
hard-and-fast distinctions between fact and fiction—was doomed to be
thwarted by the fundamental unreliability of the market's textual signifiers. Yet rather than stemming the production of investment advice, such
anxieties provided the ideal environment for it to flourish, as the next
chapter will explore.

*   *   *

The print culture explored in this chapter undoubtedly helped to normalize investment in the stock market, persuading readers of the benefits
it possessed over more traditional outlets such as land. As the century
progressed, print facilitated the diversification of investment beyond the
funds, with pamphlets and manuals helping to draw the capital of those
who wanted higher returns than consols could provide into both foreign
loans and joint-stock companies. In doing so, they obscured the harsh re-

alities of expropriation and exploitation, including slavery, and reaffirmed racial hierarchies. Though there are clear limits to the "democratization" of investment in this period, these guides sought to reach wider constituencies of uninformed investors, tutoring them in the absolute basics of how to invest, even as they continued to gender them as male. To reach such readers, these texts did what Mortimer had done in the previous century and borrowed from other genres. In particular, they emulated the large and growing literature of self-improvement by addressing investors and their concerns directly and by actually advising rather than merely informing. Major publishing houses began to print popular stock market advice, and these titles took their place in the multitude of self-help writings targeted at mass readerships.

The implications for people's understanding of investment were profound. With the argument that hard work, self-control, manly self-reliance, and, increasingly, scientific study—all typically prescribed for success in other domains—were just as applicable to the stock market, would-be investors were led to understand that their success (or failure) was very much their own responsibility.[270] An increasing tendency to wrap the advice up in homely proverbs and recognizable maxims helped to make the impenetrable financial world deceptively familiar and encouraged investors to assess it by the same standards they applied to other aspects of their lives. Alternative forms of writing, whether pamphlets exposing stock exchange iniquities or novels dissecting City corruption, may not have acted as the brake on investment one might assume. Advice literature neutralized these threats by incorporating a sense of danger. Acknowledging the hazards attendant on investment helped to establish the indispensability of the writers' advice, while also admitting that the shady reputation of the Stock Exchange could give speculation a thrilling charge.

Though the genre had not yet become generic—investment guides took too many forms and were not produced in sufficient numbers in this period for this to happen—it was certainly becoming very recognizable. We can perhaps detect just a hint of weariness in *The Times*'s review of Playford's *Practical Hints*, which remarked that the book consisted of "a familiar exposition of the modes of transacting business at the Bank and Stock-Exchange."[271] Yet the growing sense of familiarity and the repetitious nature of these manuals were no obstacle to success. While some investors may have satisfied themselves with just one guide, the logic of self-help pulled in another direction. Ostensibly empowering readers, advice literature is more interested in creating dependency, projecting a reader who is "anxious, perpetually in need of reassurance and information," thereby "encod[ing] the necessity of return and continued reliance."[272] That readers were encouraged to fill their shelves with financial advice is underlined by the suggestions for further reading which authors sometimes helpfully provided: Galton, for example, directed her readers to, among others, Omnium, Ward, and Playford.[273] These texts were increasingly weaving a mutually reinforcing and self-referential web in which readers could become entangled. The more tomes you possessed, the more inoculated you could imagine yourself to be against the ever-present perils of fraud and crisis.

These trends, embryonic in this period, were to intensify in the later nineteenth century as the stock market continued to expand and standards of living continued to improve. The desire to make the stock market come alive for outsiders, with a shift in focus from numbers to narrative and from impersonal economic laws to personality and drama, was more in evidence. Emerging simultaneously was a more theoretical approach which did not see stock market movements as representing underlying economic conditions but rather viewed the fluctuation of prices as a world unto itself. These developments were particularly visible in the postbellum United States, where our focus now begins to turn.

CHAPTER THREE

Playing the Market (1870–1910)

"You are a wealthy woman, and I intend to make you far wealthier." Thus wrote renowned American financier John Pierpont Morgan to close family friend Marie Josephine Leslie in 1906. Morgan, who had taken care of Leslie's finances since she was a girl, had invited her to join a confidential syndicate he was forming "with some of the richest men in America." For every £1,000 invested there would be a £25,000 return, as well as 12 percent interest. Though Morgan had sworn her to secrecy, Leslie, who was now based in the south of England, was generous enough to share the opportunity with a couple of her friends, Annie Blount and Maria Stokes. The women, who could not believe their luck, paid in a total of £13,000 between them. But they were destined to be disappointed. Their money did not make it into Morgan's syndicate, instead finding its way into the pockets of bookmakers, outside stockbrokers, dressmakers, and a private detective Leslie was employing to follow her estranged husband. Morgan, it transpired, had never met Leslie—as the financier was obliged to testify in court—and Morgan's letters, which Leslie had read out to the two women to persuade them to invest, were fake.[1]

Yet such was the magic of Morgan's name that the fantastic returns Leslie promised were entirely believable to the pair—even though Leslie was working as a humble kennel maid in a guest house outside Maidenhead when she met them. As Stokes later admitted in court, "I had, of course, heard of Mr. Pierpont Morgan for many years, which, I think, influenced me because he is such a very successful financier."[2] The case shows how, by the early twentieth century, the fame of the "financial kings" of Wall Street had reached as far as the home counties of England and was able to unlock the purses of otherwise cautious investors.[3] Though Wall Street was not yet the financial capital of the world, the dynamism of the US market was widely acknowledged, with Morgan recognized as "one of the mightiest private individuals on earth."[4] At once vilified and celebrated, what men like Morgan actually did remained distinctly hazy in most people's minds, but what no one doubted was their ability to make money. It was this association of the stock market with colossal wealth, obtained ethically or otherwise, that helped fuel growing popular fascination with the financial world and was cultivated by a booming print culture. An outpouring of stockbroker memoirs, financial journalism, City fiction, and investment advice manuals promoted a culture of market watching in Britain and—even more strongly—in the United States. Whereas earlier in the nineteenth century reports on the stock market had enjoyed a relatively small readership, now a popular culture of finance came to matter to an increasingly large mass audience.

These varied publications about making money in the market were themselves primarily concerned with making money, by making their readers feel that this advice was necessary. Though in these years only around I percent of British and American households actually held stocks and shares, these varied genres of popular financial writing encouraged a much broader emotional investment in the stock market.[5] Once presented as an ephemeral, even fraudulent, adjunct to the "real" economy of agriculture and industry, the fortunes of the stock market were now understood to affect the fates of millions. Financial advice literature worked to persuade readers (and, further, potential buyers) that learning how to invest was almost a duty of the modern informed citizen, making the market matter even for the vast majority of people who were not formally involved. The British stockbroker George Gregory's *Hints to Speculators and Investors in Stocks and Shares* (1889), for example, noted that the vast scale of stock exchange business meant that "every human being is, more or less, directly or indirectly interested in these transactions; yet, of the countless millions of people throughout the world, those who understand them, even imperfectly, may be reckoned as only a few thousands."[6]

Gregory's text is emblematic of other key trends in these years. The easy conflation of investment and speculation in the title nods to the legitimization of the latter that was one of the main projects of financial advice in this period. Indeed, the guide was one of literally hundreds published in both Britain and the United States by firms like Gregory's that sought to make speculation intelligible and accessible to larger numbers—not only to encourage them to buy into the stock market but also to sell more advice books. Capitalizing on the new technology of the ticker tape, which used the telegraph to broadcast price information at unprecedented speeds, these brokers' guides told a mass readership that speculation was, for the first time, within their reach. Deploying a populist rhetoric, they encouraged readers to think of themselves as savvy, risk-taking individuals who deserved a share of the riches—and the excitement—previously reserved for the elite. Though this writing nearly always coded speculation as a male activity, women were undoubtedly participating in growing numbers too. Indeed, it was in one such brokerage, the London and Paris Exchange, that Leslie spent a slice of the money she obtained from her unfortunate friends. In important ways, then, the print culture of this period laid the groundwork for the larger-scale popularization of the stock market that was to follow the Great War. What it purveyed was largely a fantasy, but it was no more fantastical than other writings about economics and finance.

For the Benefit of THE MILLION

As with the growth of joint-stock companies in Britain, large-scale corporate organization became an increasingly important and normal part of economic activity in the United States in the second half of the nineteenth century. This chapter considers the development of financial advice in both Britain and the United States in the period from roughly the Civil War to the First World War, and it marks the moment of transition as New York begins to eclipse London as the financial capital of the world. (As chapters 4 and 5 explain, the economic, social, and cultural significance of stock market investing played out very differently in the two countries during the twentieth century, and the most significant trends—in both publishing contexts and the content of the books—are to be found in the United States.) During the Civil War, private bankers such as Jay Cooke persuaded many citizens to purchase government bonds to help fund the war, helping to give investment a patriotic gloss. But Cooke's firm itself went bust in 1873, triggering a national panic whose ripples were felt around the world, temporarily curbing enthusiasm in Britain, Germany, and elsewhere for American investments.[7] From the late 1870s, however, investment in government and municipal bonds by the wealthy and the middle class was increasingly supplemented by involvement in corporate securities. In the United States this was enabled by changes in the regulatory regime, which saw a rush to the bottom as states such as Delaware and New Jersey competed to make the rules of incorporation ever more favorable.[8]

As in Britain, the rapid expansion of the railroads was the driving force. The huge capitalization required for these ventures created a thriving trade in railroad stocks and bonds. By the late 1860s in the United States there were 360 railroad stocks and 700 bonds being traded, commanding the lion's share of stock market activity; in 1870, for example, 87 percent of shares traded were railroad ones.[9] On each side of the Atlantic, both the volume and the variety of shares traded mushroomed. The average annual volume of shares traded on the New York Stock Exchange (NYSE), for example, more than doubled between 1875 and 1882; the daily volume skyrocketed from 1,500 in 1861 to 500,000 in 1900.[10] Likewise, on the London Stock Exchange the number of securities quoted rose more than tenfold between 1853 to 1913, from under 500 to over 5,000.[11] Even if the popular investment manuals sold a fantasy of stock trading to ordinary citizens, nonetheless the size and importance of the financial sector in the American and British economies were growing considerably. In the late 1890s and early 1900s corporate lawyers in the United States used the *Santa Clara County v. Southern Pacific Railroad Co.* Supreme Court decision of 1886 (which affirmed the notion that corporations enjoyed some of the same legal rights and protections as individuals) to argue that corporations could own shares in other companies. This decision paved the way for the creation of massive trusts and holding companies in the Great Merger Movement from roughly 1895 to 1905, with a shift from railroads to industrial stocks. In 1885, 81 percent of trading on the NYSE was in railroad shares and bonds, but by 1905 it was only 49 percent. In their place, industrial and utilities stocks expanded from 16 to 41 percent, while the total volume of trading doubled in the 1890s.[12]

The securities market was thus both broadening and deepening in terms of the variety of shares offered, the volume of shares traded, and the liquidity of the market. Though this looked like the "democratization" of share ownership, to a large extent growth was supported by the wealthy— including a growing number of wealthy women—moving more of their money out of land and property and into the stock market.[13] Indeed, the stock exchanges were cautious about the prospect of a genuinely "democratized" investment. Though share denominations were gradually falling in Britain, the standard level in the United States remained at $100, and they were typically traded in lots of 100 (i.e., a minimum trade of $10,000), hardly conducive to a culture of mass investment. Moreover, neither the

London nor New York Stock Exchanges made an effort to publicize or promote investment to a wider public. With brokers keen to obtain professional standing, self-promotion was frowned upon as ungentlemanly. Exchanges gradually limited members' ability to advertise, with the NYSE restricting most forms of advertising by member firms in 1898.[14] One American society magazine made it clear why advertising by brokers was regarded as so inappropriate:

> So long as the candle burns within the legitimate precincts of Wall Street and the vicinity of the Stock Exchange, and the moths, well knowing the inflammable nature of their plumage, will insist upon singeing it, I have no fault to find with those who furnish the flame. But when a broker and a banker . . . deliberately goes about lighting his speculative tapers all over the city and employing agents to shoo unknowing and unsuspecting moths into their blaze, I moved, out of sheer pity, to raise a voice of warning.[15]

The subject of this warning, Henry Clews, enjoyed cultivating a prominent public persona, even though he was a member of the New York Stock Exchange. But his approach was unusual, and though members were permitted to publish on matters related to the markets, anything which smacked too much of touting for business was frowned upon by their respective supervisory committees.[16] So while inside brokers did compile investment manuals, these tended to be of the "catalog" type—in the tradition of making information on particular types of security more available, rather than interpreting it, let alone explaining and encouraging investment for novices.

Though stock exchanges discreetly refrained from publicizing investment, others proved more comfortable assuming the role of interpreters and popularizers of the stock market. Investment advice continued to take many forms and could be found in newspapers and periodicals, polemical pamphlets, novels and short stories as well as general guides to business affairs. Though various reference works and sector-specific handbooks carried on being published in large numbers, more accessible and well-rounded guides to stock market investment, especially for novice investors, became much more common. These guides addressed investors of more modest means for the first time. Those who had their money lodged in a savings bank or building society were told that they were wrong to think that stock exchange securities were out of their reach. The guidebooks tried to persuade them that they could get much higher rates of interest by investing their money in the stock market.[17] The trickle of accessible general-purpose stock market advice therefore became something approaching a flood in the later nineteenth century. Indeed, already in 1877 authors of new guides were feeling the need to apologize "for adding to the very numerous works on financial operations."[18]

Authorship of such guides remained diverse. Some of the more sensational were penned by former speculators (following in the tradition of "reformed gambler" narratives), while professions responsible for giving financial advice, such as accountancy and law, contributed more sober guides, including William Relton's *Saving and Growing Money*, R. Denny Urlin's *Hints on Business, Financial and Legal*, and William Harman Black's *Real Wall Street*.[19] Financial journalists, who had not hitherto taken a leading role in authoring investment manuals, ventured more confidently into this market in the 1870s, with Robert Giffen, Walter Bagehot's assistant editor at the *Economist*, Robert Lucas Nash, also at the *Economist*, and Arthur Crump of the *Pall Mall Gazette* all appearing in print.[20] By the turn of the century, financial journalists were turning increasingly frequently to this form, with Charles Duguid, Francis Hirst, Hartley Withers, and Henry Lowenfeld in Britain all penning major texts in the years before the Great War. In the United States, a number of guides published by John Moody popularized the investment theories of Charles Dow, the founding editor of the *Wall Street Journal*.[21] But such contributions were dwarfed by a group who became in this period the market leaders in the financial advice genre: stockbrokers operating outside the official stock exchanges. Untrammeled by any rules against advertising, they became assiduous disseminators of printed advice and tips in the form of weekly and monthly circulars as well as the "how-to" guide.

Despite the formalization and enclosure of markets in the nineteenth century, a thriving trade in stocks and shares continued in "curb" markets in the United States and the United Kingdom. These were the kinds of dealers that conservative guides inevitably warned their readers against, but despite being regarded as disreputable and untrustworthy, they became an increasingly visible and influential part of the market in this period. Their role in providing facilities for "the common people" to speculate on stocks and shares in the "bucket shops" that caused such a moral panic in the closing decades of the century has been documented.[22] Less appreciated, however, is their role in transforming the information and advice landscape. They made it more accessible, more plentiful, and cheaper—in many cases, free. Just as importantly, they gave it a stridently populist tone. Whereas the "size, intricacy, and technicalities" of the weightier catalog-style manuals repelled "ordinary readers," the more accessible guides of the outside brokers explained investment in clearer language.[23] Though they had published guidance before the 1870s, they now became more ambitious, writing guides which gave an overview of the entire investment market, claiming to provide the uninformed and undecided everything they needed to begin dabbling in stocks and shares. These guidebooks were not issued out of altruism, of course: at heart, they were extended advertisements, enticements to speculate, often with the writer's firm. Offering a cheap or free guide to the ways of Wall Street or the London Stock Exchange as a promotion for an outside brokerage business was a standard strategy. US firm Tumbridge & Co.'s *Secrets of Success in Wall Street* (1875) is an early example. Its overall aim is to make the alien world of speculation appear normal and businesslike and, in effect, to make the market legible: "Persons unacquainted with Stock Speculation may become perfectly familiar with the intricate machinery necessary for its operation by a careful study of these pages," the guide explains. "They will also attain a knowledge of financial matters useful in any pursuit, and may be the means of their making many safe and profitable investments; even those who have had an interest in stocks will find information and hints unknown to them before, which will greatly aid and increase their gains in future operations." In addition to a brief summary of stock market devices such as puts, calls, spreads, and straddles, the guide—in the hope of making the stock market seem less forbidding— includes satirical newspaper cartoons, along with photos of the brokerage premises showing not only the solidity of its furnishings but the clubability of its customers' trading room.[24]

That such guides proved successful in drumming up business is suggested by their rapid profusion. On a typical Sunday in 1903 the *New York Times* included multiple such advertisements: J. L. McLean & Co. offered "our new Eighty Page Illustrated Wall Street Guide"; W. E. Woodend & Co. urged readers to "send for our weekly Market Review"; Joseph Cowan & Co. recommended to prospective customers its new book, *"Reveries of a Trader," with Side Notes on Successful Speculation*; and Henry B. Clifford, a banker and broker, offered his booklet "Fortunes That Grow in a Night." The most prominent advertisement, however, was from Haight & Freese, which by this point was the largest operator of bucket shops in the United States, with branches throughout the nation.[25] In the preface to a revised and expanded edition in 1898 of its *Guide to Investors* (see fig. 3.1), the company claimed that the previous edition of 100,000 had

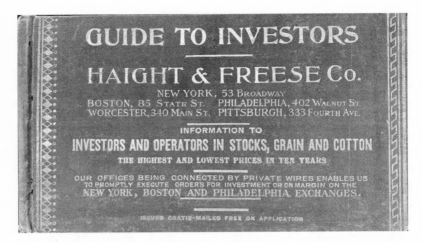

FIGURE 3.1. Cover of Haight & Freese, *Guide to Investors* (New York: printed by the author, 1898). Image provided by Peter Knight.

sold out. Even if that figure is exaggerated, it is clear that free booklets such as Haight & Freese's reached a far larger and more diverse audience than the traditional counterparts issued by recognized publishing houses.

The manner of address of Haight & Freese's guide was explicitly populist, not because it presented a muckraking condemnation of the corruption of Wall Street but because it made appeal to ordinary Americans: they too could have a slice of the profits that had up to now been confined to the financial elites. The booklet is expensive-looking, in a sumptuous red cloth binding with silver text and decorations, proudly listing the company's five premises and the fact that they are connected by "private wire" to the various exchanges. At the same time, the cover includes the prominent announcement that the guide is "Issued gratis—mailed free on application." As their advertisement stated: "Our manual is designed for the benefit of THE MILLION of busy people to whom the subject is of interest, but who require to have lengthy, tough details correctly explained and 'boiled down' for immediate and easy consumption." Being familiar with the ins and outs of the stock market was thus, according to Haight & Freese, not a danger but a duty for all citizens: "It has become a necessity for all classes to be so informed if they are to have a fair chance of securing a portion of the immense profits which, year by year, are distributed by means of the rapidly accumulating number and value of Exchange securities."[26]

Chains like Haight & Freese were able to spread so rapidly because of the opportunities presented by mass advertising. The *New York Times* was not at all unusual in carrying ads for outside brokers who wished to reach wide audiences. Full-column, half-page, and eventually full-page advertisements for brokerages were becoming common in general-interest titles. The advertising matter was just one element in the mix of market materials presented to readers of the newspaper press. From midcentury, financial journalists on both sides of the Atlantic began to move away from factual, objective description and occasional exposures of fraud to a more subjective, interpretive, and advice-giving mode.[27] They endeavored to provide an explanatory framework for the lists of printed stock prices that were, for many readers, inscrutable. They strove to make the mysteries of the market engrossing and intelligible to their readers, especially for those who were not City or Wall Street regulars, by focusing on personalities and melodrama. They also increasingly responded to public demand for market tips. While claiming to demystify the market, these new forms of financial advice writing in fact created new myths about it, as they cultivated a risk-taking, investment-positive sensibility in their readers.

The popular financial press found a ready market in the last quarter of the nineteenth century, expanding from nineteen titles in 1874 to ninety-two by 1904 in the United Kingdom, for example. These years saw the establishment of several popular financial dailies, including the *Financial News* (1884) and the *Financial Times* (1888) in the United Kingdom and the *Wall Street Journal* (1889) in the United States.[28] Toward the end of the century, American middle-class magazines such as *Harper's Weekly* and the *Saturday Evening Post* began to include financial columns along with illustrated, melodramatic short stories and serialized novels about business and finance by writers such as Edwin Lefèvre, Frank Norris, and Harold Frederic. After the turn of the twentieth century, more specialized popular magazines emerged that were aimed at investors of modest means and bucket shop speculators, such as *Pit and Post* (established in 1902), *Financial World* (1902), *Moody's Magazine* (1905), *Ticker* (1907; later renamed the *Magazine of Wall Street*), and *Commerce and Finance* (1912).

As Mary Poovey has argued, popular financial journalism in the earlier nineteenth century served to naturalize the workings of the market, even when it adopted a critical stance. "The new City columns treated the financial world as a distinct culture," Poovey notes, "which writers strove to make interesting even to readers who did not need to know about international exchange rates or economic theory."[29] In explaining the market's perplexing ways to lay readers, Poovey argues, popular financial journalism served to make the chaotic fluctuations of the markets seem normal. Yet, as this genre of writing evolved later in the century, it did not simply serve to build trust among lay investors in the stock market by explaining its seemingly arcane ways. It also tapped into the emotional wellsprings of fear and excitement that attracted growing numbers of would-be speculators to the stock market. One ideological function of the new financial journalism, then, was to make the market seem of vital, daily importance to casual readers, even in those times when panics, corners, and booms were not making the headlines. It helped create an imagined community of market watchers, persuading them that it was their duty to check the money page obsessively and to identify emotionally with the rise and fall of prices. It made increasing numbers of people emotionally invested in the stock market, even if they were not financially invested themselves.

Though the press constantly published warnings to readers about the dangers of speculating in bucket shops, the relationship between brokers and newspapers was far from straightforwardly antagonistic. Newspapers published bucket shop advertisements on a gigantic scale as well as paid-for "puffs"—promotional matter masquerading as editorial content. Moreover, there was a growing porousness between financial journalism and outside brokerages. One manifestation of this is what Dilwyn Porter calls "bucket shop journalism." To take an example, in its combination of seemingly objective market commentary, instruction, and advice, *Pit and Post* echoed the style and format of other monthly magazines for speculators from the period. However, it was written not by a financial journalist but by a brokerage firm (Knight, Donnelley & Co. of Chicago) and acted as a promotional vehicle for that business. Indeed, each issue included a full-page advertisement for the firm on the back cover.

But if brokerages were shifting into journalism, then there was also movement in the other direction. Newspapers gradually lost their earlier reticence about giving investment advice, partly in response to the incessant demand from readers for tips. Published advice was increasingly expected, but some periodicals went further, setting up bespoke advisory services for their readers and so encroaching on the roles normally performed by brokers. One British weekly, *Financial Truth*, offered its subscribers an Inquiry Bureau, designed for "investors who have no available means of acquainting themselves with the under-current of the financial world."[30] Going further still, the *Financial Answers* Bureau undertook not only to advise on investments but to buy and sell shares on behalf of readers, to monitor the progress of their investments, and to collect their dividends.[31] In this market, then, brokers were journalists, journalists were brokers, and readers were clients. The fluidity created a more dynamic—but less transparent—ecosystem of financial advice that was instrumental in paving the way toward a wider social base of investment. Indeed, the "democratization" of the stock market depended upon the democratization of access to financial advice. The nature of this advice helped to re-shape popular understanding of investment, speculation, and gambling, with profound consequences.

Speculative Investments

One of the key aims of the developing genre of popular investment advice was to redraw the boundaries between investment, speculation, and gambling—and, in the process of legitimizing the stock market, sell more advice books. As various historians have noted, these categories were becoming increasingly unstable in the later nineteenth century.[32] Historically, most forms of stock market activity had been condemned as not much better than gambling. To the respectable classes in the United Kingdom and the United States, gambling was seen as antithetical to the cherished values of thrift and hard work, even if the prospect of getting "something for nothing" continued to appeal to many at the fringes of society.[33] As we have seen, supporters of the stock market had for a long time tried to legitimize investment by disassociating it from anything that smacked of gambling, speculation included.

Some guides in the later nineteenth century continued to pursue this line, urging readers to prefer good security to high interest, to hold stocks for the long term, and to steer clear of speculation. Despite the sensationalist title, Thomas A. Davies's *How to Make Money, and How to Keep It* (first published in 1867 and reprinted in 1884) contains cautious advice restating the boundaries between investment and speculation. A self-help manual which tackled the subject of investment over two chapters, Davies's book cautions his American readers that investment is not a route to riches but rather presents opportunities to secure and increase the money that they have already made. Up to this point his book has showed how various forms of labor can produce a living, but he notes that "purely making money, with money, is a distinct trade."[34] Recognizing that his audience might be vulnerable to unwise investment decisions, he suggests that if readers have made money, they need to know how to make it work, or it will soon disappear and go to someone else who knows that "trade" better: "There is no trade so intricate as the investing of money safely; but, like the mechanic art, when once learned, how easy, and how simple!" He errs on the side of caution, recommending a savings account and ten-year endowment policies (including life insurance) that give a yield of 6 percent. For those with larger sums to invest but no experience in "financiering," the recommendation is for bonds and mortgages on real estate, at 7 percent per year return, albeit with the proviso of using a lawyer to check that the security is worth it. For Davies, the next safest investment is dividend-paying bank stocks, but he advises that readers (or their proxies) will need to examine closely the books of the firm and, more importantly, the character of the bank officers, rather than being taken in by their fancy premises alone. In his pecking order of safety, next come government bonds, then dividend-paying railroad bonds and stocks, because "such stock and bonds, judiciously purchased, cannot fail to be productive of income." In general, his stock market advice is "*Never invest in any stock until it has paid a dividend.*" He therefore warns readers to avoid most mining stocks, because "it is doubtful as a class whether they have ever paid a profit," and also life insurance stock because it has likewise "proved speculative." Davies's following chapter, "How Money Is Lost," covers unwise practices such as placing money into "new and untried enterprises" with no track record of dividend payment, no matter how convincingly they are promoted. In nearly all cases these are deemed to be "as likely to be profitable as a railway to the moon." For Davies, "speculation in stocks" was "the quickest and surest means of getting rid of money that is known." Yet he nevertheless recognizes that there is "a fascination about making a sudden fortune that will continue to find devotees in such hazards"—and the inclusion of these two chapters on financial matters in a self-improvement manual is testament to that fascination.[35]

Other guides, even those that framed themselves as warnings against stock market speculation, indulged this fascination more overtly, hedging their bets by providing practical information for novice outsiders who might want to try their luck. The entirety of financial journalist Arthur Crump's guide, *The Theory of Stock Exchange Speculation* (1874), for example, was an attempt "to show to persons who may contemplate trying their hand at Stock Exchange Speculation, the improbability of their hopes being realized."[36] Nevertheless, his guide was a sign of changing times. Despite arguing that amateur speculators were almost certain to fail, by dissecting the various methods of operating, by pointing out the many pitfalls that existed—and by sharing the secrets of rich financiers—it could also paradoxically be read as a guide on how to succeed at speculation. Indeed, outside brokers subsequently used quotes from the book in order to vindicate their approach to the market.[37] Moses Smith's diatribe, *Plain Truths about Stock Speculation: How to Avoid Losses in Wall Street* (1887), could also be read in more than one way. Styling itself as "a revelation and exposure of the trickery and sharp practices which prevail in the marts of speculation," it brims with familiar Biblical imagery of temptation and idolatry. "The god of Wall Street is Mammon; money is its idol," Smith announces. "Men bow down in homage to the 'Golden Calf.' In no other place in no other business is the world so cold, cynical and heartless in the presence of misfortune." Like many writers from earlier in the century, Smith compares the stock market to gambling: "morally there is no difference whether one makes his commissions on a stock gamble, or on pool selling at a horse-race." In short, *Plain Truths* is "a warning to keep out of Wall Street." At the same time, however, it purports to reveal to readers "the only true and generally safe way to deal in stocks and make money." Smith's lengthy and detailed book thus combines a potted history of some of the more notorious episodes of panics and swindles as a warning to the unwary with practical information on how to buy and sell stocks. He includes an introduction for the uninitiated to the terminology, forms of dealing, and varieties of exchanges, and he discusses, for example, which stocks are well capitalized and paying regular dividends and therefore unwise to short. Likewise, he advises that those seeking investment rather than speculation should look to "certain classes of stocks which are almost as safe as a mortgage," such as the Rensselaer and Saratoga Railroad.[38] The book also includes a "Directory" for those seeking to visit New York—as if the author was aware that the previous 300 pages of dire warnings would not deter the endless waves of curious outsiders.

In contrast to earlier in the nineteenth century, the most common strategy in stock market advice of this period was to deny any distinction between investment and speculation. The aim was to make speculation legitimate by distancing it from gambling and assimilating it with investment. The insistent message of these texts was that to invest was to speculate and to speculate was to invest. Unlike the earlier genre of "city mysteries," H. M. Williams's *Key to Wall Street Mysteries and Methods* (1904), for instance, is not a melodramatic exposé of vice in lower Manhattan but is instead a user-friendly guide for the public on investment and speculation, with no obvious moral distinction between the two. Williams adopts an informal tone, addressing his readers in the second person and using confessions of his own costly experiences on Wall Street to illustrate his points.[39] Harking back to the autobiographical stance in Mortimer's pioneering guide in the eighteenth century and drawing on the ambivalent genre of "reformed gambler" memoirs earlier in the nineteenth, works of financial advice like Williams's appealed to the authority of personal experience rather than abstract or credentialed knowledge to make them appear trustworthy.[40] Guides written for a variety of audiences argued that "all business is speculation" and that risk was an inevitable part of life—and of investing.[41] Pursuing robust returns on capital was not necessarily incompatible with safety, reasoned these guides.[42] Investment and speculation, according to London outside dealers W. W. Duncan & Co., for example, were "twin sisters, and so nearly alike that it is almost impossible to discriminate between them," since both activities aimed to maximize returns and minimize risks. The rational response was a policy of "speculative investment."[43] The question remained of whether only professionals should engage in speculation, with the fear that the involvement of outsiders in stock markets was no better than gambling. However, popular financial writing slowly—albeit not without contest—began to make speculation seem normal and legitimate for all.

A growing number of writers of financial advice, especially in the United States, endorsed the idea that speculation was a completely necessary and legitimate part of the nation's economic machinery. Lewis C. Van Riper's *Ins and Outs of Wall Street* (1898), for example, was a promotional booklet liberally advertised in the Sunday newspapers. Van Riper insisted that "speculation is a profession" and that the brokers of Wall Street are marked out by their "strict integrity and honest dealing."[44] Appealing to the patriotic bull sentiment of most amateur investors, he maintained that speculation was not mere gambling because the real value of American industry was indeed increasing. For Van Riper, the problem was not with speculation as such but with the lack of authoritative guidance—and he tried to persuade readers that his was the only guide they needed. "There are no standard works on speculation written by experienced, successful speculators," he insisted, thereby insinuating that other guides were based merely on theory or a moralizing stance by those without direct involvement. In a similar vein, J. Overton Paine's pamphlet *Speculating in Wall Street on Margins* (1900) offered instruction via chatty anecdotes taken from the author's own experience. It argued that speculation would allow the humble provincial to feel connected to the pulse of global commerce:

Just pause and reflect up on this for a moment! Do you not feel interested in the possibilities of speculation? Judiciously conducted operations in Bonds, Stocks, Cotton and Grain upon moderate margins enable one to invest a small sum so that it will yield very large profits; it also puts you in touch with the financial and commercial interests of the world.[45]

Neither Van Riper nor Paine was a stranger to criminal action, but that does not mean that such arguments remained confined to the seedy margins of finance.[46] Rather, through endless repetition and amplification in the press, the rehabilitation of speculation began to achieve widespread circulation and growing credibility.

Readers were receptive to this rebranding exercise for a number of reasons. First, it coincided with a sustained period of declining returns on government debt. In the United Kingdom, the yield on consols entered a sustained decline from the 1880s until 1910, prompting investors to reconsider their approach to the market.[47] Likewise in the United States, ten-year Treasury notes, which had provided a yield of 5.3 percent in 1864, declined after the panic of 1873, reaching a low point of 2.9 percent in 1900.[48] "Safe" investment, it was clear, came with its own risks, namely sacrificing income that could be obtained elsewhere. A second factor was the rise of consumer society, creating emulative pressures that could only be fed by conspicuous consumption.[49] Lower returns on investments squeezed incomes and made it harder to "keep up with the Joneses."[50] Moreover, dreams of upward mobility, particularly among rising armies of ambitious clerks and other go-ahead young men, made the quest for higher returns a pressing priority.[51] Playing the stock market could become contagious at a local level, as captured by one financial journal: "Every hamlet in the country presents examples of independent fortunes amassed through fortunate investments, and the instinct of emulation impels thrifty men to buy stocks as the most available way to augment their savings and to lay the foundations of future wealth."[52]

On the supply side, a key factor helping to normalize speculation was the new technology of the ticker-tape machine, which began entering brokers' offices and gentlemen's clubs from the early 1870s. Speculation on price movements, previously only feasible for the wealthy, now moved within reach of the far greater numbers who could watch the stock market action unfolding on the clacking machines even as the prices were chalked up on the quotation boards. Anyone could walk into a bucket shop and monitor price information minute by minute.[53] Stock tickers proliferated most rapidly in the United States—one estimate suggested that there were 23,000 subscribers in 1905—but they were also a feature of the London financial landscape once a skeptical London Stock Exchange was persuaded to grant the Exchange Telegraph Company access to the floor in 1872.[54] The drama of tape watching thus became a common feature of both fictional tales and nonfictional profiles of stock market operators; though some writers depicted reading the ticker tape as addictive and thus akin to gambling, others presented it more positively as a form of leisure, framing speculation as an exciting pastime.[55]

Critically, rather than characterizing tape speculation simply as a species of gambling, outside brokers couched its appeal in terms of "prudent speculation"—something that would previously have been dismissed as oxymoronic.[56] Time bargains and futures contracts had long been associated with the worst excesses of gambling on the stock exchange on both sides of the Atlantic.[57] Yet some manuals began to present options trading not as the road to ruin but as a sensible and cautious strategy. A British pamphlet from 1877, for example, explained that options "gave the fullest scope . . . for benefitting by favorable fluctuations in the market, whilst at the same time the *possible* loss is a small fixed sum," preventing "the disasters which unprotected risks must occasionally lead to."[58] Likewise many outside dealers highlighted the benefits of the "cover" or "margin" system (as it was called in British and American parlance respectively): a way of speculating on the rise or fall of stock prices by only depositing a fraction of the price, often just 1 percent. Condemned as reckless by critics, who pointed out that such a small margin easily "ran off," its proponents denied that it was a form of gambling. Instead, they argued that it was a sensible method of limiting liability, for if the speculator's predictions were incorrect and the price moved the wrong way, he or she would be subjected to no further risk once the cover was exhausted.[59] The further benefit was that, by knowing that liability was limited, the investor "avoided the worry and anxiety which would otherwise have tended to warp his judgement, and prove detrimental to his success."[60]

Though not showing up in share registers, bucket shop patrons were invested both financially and emotionally in the stock market. With their low margin requirements and availability of small quantities of shares ("odd lots," not available on the official exchanges in the United States), bucket shops afforded their patrons a sense of the excitement of stock market speculation, even if they were in reality only betting against the house on the rise or fall of prices.[61] Nevertheless, the volume of business conducted by bucket shops far exceeded that transacted by the legitimate exchanges in the United States. By 1889, for example, bucket shop clients were estimated to be betting on the equivalent of one million shares per day, seven times the volume traded on the New York Stock Exchange.[62] Further boosting this kind of speculation for capital gains in the United States was the fact that, unlike in the United Kingdom, the retained profits of corporations were not taxed, and therefore there was less incentive to provide generous dividends.[63]

Importantly, the rhetorical reconfiguration of risk was not witnessed solely in bucket shop literature. Even guides that condemned practices such as speculating on low margins affirmed that there were forms of risk-taking that were perfectly sensible. A growing number of writers recommended readers steer a middle course between the poles of excessive caution and excessive risk-taking. In an exhaustive analysis of returns on hundreds of securities through the 1870s, the *Economist*'s Robert Lucas Nash, for example, concluded:

> It is not either the slight risks (that is, the safe investments) nor the extreme risks which have been the most profitable to our investors. The *moderate risks have certainly paid the best during the past ten years*; and doubtless they will do the same in the decade to come.[64]

Later, William Barker outlined the predicament faced by many. Chasing the "fabulous dividends" promised by advertising brokers was too dangerous, but by going to "an honest, old-fashioned stockbroker," the erstwhile investor would probably be told to put everything in safe but low-yield government bonds. Yet, he argued, there was "a happy *via media* between these two courses," which offered decent returns for minimal risk.[65] Likewise, financial journalist Henry Hess represented the task of investors as "pilot[ing] their finances safely between the Scylla of low yield and the Charybdis of great risk."[66] Thus, ideas that were present in their most extreme form in bucket shop literature were amplified in a far wider range of writing, thereby helping them to achieve greater currency.

By the turn of the twentieth century, then, the boundaries between investment, speculation, and gambling had been redrawn in a profound way in popular financial advice writing, in which ordinary investors were rhetorically persuaded that "speculative investments" were not only morally legitimate and economically rational but within their grasp. But readers of this literature were faced with a major problem. Once untethered from the security and predictability of government stock, how far into

the realms of risk dare they venture? How did they square the circle of
safety and profit in practice? Various, and often contradictory, approaches
to these problems were suggested by different strands of financial advice
writing.

The Celebrities of Wall Street

If one important function of writing about the stock market in the second half of the nineteenth century was to lessen the traditional moral op-
probrium attached to speculation, then another was to make the stock
market come alive for outsiders. The period saw a shift in focus from
numbers to narrative and from impersonal economic laws to personality
and drama. Popular guides promised to introduce readers to the mysterious world of the stock market, humanizing its abstractions. John Francis's
Chronicles and Characters of the Stock Exchange (1849) set the tone for
subsequent works, with its chatty and anecdotal approach making the history and functions of the London Stock Exchange comprehensible to the
layperson. In the United States, a number of memoirs and guidebooks
followed this model, promising to expose the mysterious world of Wall
Street. Popular volumes included James K. Medbery's *Men and Mysteries of Wall Street* (1870), William Worthington Fowler's *Ten Years on Wall
Street* (1870), Matthew Hale Smith's *Twenty Years among the Bulls and
Bears of Wall Street* (1871), and Henry Clews's *Twenty-Eight Years on Wall
Street* (1887), many of which went through numerous editions.[67]

Although not designed as practical guides to investment, these books
nonetheless served to instruct readers by making the jargon, mechanics, and personalities of Wall Street familiar, and by reassuring them that
speculation—at least in the hands of professionals—was not inherently
wicked. These memoirs provided a far less judgmental portrait of Wall
Street than earlier accounts. Although they condemned some sharp practices of the "king operators," their dramatic tales of the legendary corners and pools organized by the "celebrities of Wall Street" conveyed an
impression of awe. "All along the pathway of the street," Smith wrote,
"are noble characters who stand like light-houses on the tall, rocky cliffs,
unchanged and unmoved by the agitation, turmoil, and ruin, that play
around their feet."[68] Despite seeming to provide ammunition for reformers who felt that the protection of vulnerable investors was best achieved
by educating the public in the specifics of stock market activity, these

compendiums of Wall Street lore nonetheless tended—in part by sheer repetition—to legitimize the stock market by lionizing its larger-than-life "characters." These books were, however, still some way from the tomes produced in the twentieth century by celebrity financial advice writers with their proprietary "systems." Although their combination of historical summary, technical explanations, lively anecdotes, philosophical musings, and investment wisdom can seem jarring at times, the formula of these biography-cum-guides proved enduringly popular with readers. Clews's memoir, for example, went through multiple editions and was later expanded to become *Fifty Years on Wall Street*.[69]

This popularity derived at least in part from these texts' promise of demystifying an otherwise opaque financial world. Medbery, for instance, presented the enigmas of the financial district as something that could be explained and made less mysterious by a knowledgeable guide. Although including a reasonably detailed description of the mechanics of investment in its various forms, *Men and Mysteries of Wall Street* functioned chiefly as a Baedeker to Wall Street for curious outsiders. This quasi-anthropological primer provided an insider's account of the quirks, customs, and japes of brokers, together with dramatic descriptions of activity on the floor of the New York Stock Exchange, comparable to visiting Niagara Falls:

> The first impression on entering the Stock Exchange is upon the tympanum. A genuine tourist almost inevitably has a dreamy reminiscence of Niagara. . . . Peering down through the high-vaulted, dim-lighted space, the eye sees nothing but excited faces, arms flung wildly in air, heads appearing and disappearing—a billowy mob, from which surges up an incessant and confused clamor.[70]

Like other writers of guidebooks to Wall Street in this period, Medbery adopted an ethnographic stance toward the seemingly barbaric battles and exotic rituals enacted on the exchange floor. As well as exoticizing the alien world of Wall Street, he also domesticated it, characterizing the stock market as both a sporting contest and a theatrical spectacle, with the plush, red velvet chairs in the visitors' gallery completing the effect. Often the memoirs and guidebooks focused on the view from the visitors' gallery and the chaotic scenes of trading that would otherwise seem incomprehensible to outsiders.[71] Medbery provided an early example of practical advice on how to visit the New York Stock Exchange: "You can reach the Long Room from the antechamber on Broad Street," while the

New Street entrance presents "a better opportunity to the spectator."[72] An actual Baedeker travel guide to the United States for 1893 likewise recommended that "strangers, who are admitted to a gallery overlooking the hall (entr., 13 Wall St.), should not omit a visit to this strange scene of business, tumult, and excitement, a wilder scene probably than that presented in any European exchange."[73] The firsthand guides from this period thus helped the armchair traveler navigate the strange lore of this unfamiliar land, dramatizing and humanizing the abstractions of the market.

The financial world seemed mysterious to those on the outside because there was an inherent informational asymmetry between amateur investors and corporate insiders, especially in the United States.[74] It would not be until the New Deal financial reforms of 1933–34—in the wake of the crash of 1929—that corporations were required to provide systematic accounts to their shareholders. Before then, the amount of financial information provided by corporations was scant, especially for manufacturing firms. *Pit and Post* lamented this situation, noting in 1903 that "unfortunately there is no law at present which compels industrial corporations to make affidavit-certified reports in classified detail; hence the kind of reports issued and the range of facts covered by them depend entirely on the sweet will of the managers."[75] As late as the 1880s, the New York Central and Hudson River Railroad, for example, refused to issue a single report to its shareholders.[76] Even something as straightforward as clear statements of sales or profit-and-loss figures were not consistently included until at least the 1890s. The NYSE, for example, did not require listed companies to file annual reports until 1895 (and earnings-and-balance sheets beginning in 1900), but it was still possible for newly established corporations to avoid this by applying instead to the unlisted department of the exchange, or to bypass the requirements altogether by trading on alternative markets such as the curb market or the Consolidated Stock Exchange.[77]

This lack of transparency meant that, in the decades either side of the turn of the twentieth century, the mythical figure of the vulnerable investor of modest means became central to debates about the legitimacy of the stock market, especially in the United States. Reformers insisted that small investors should be protected from the manipulation of insiders and from the dangers of fraudulent overcapitalization of corporations through the active intervention of the government in regulating new stock offerings and requiring the public incorporation of the stock exchanges themselves. The Senate's Industrial Commission (1900–1902), investigating what was termed the "Trust Question" (about the corporate abuse of monopoly power), identified the outside investor of modest means as central to the emerging notion of an American industrial democracy. The hope was that ordinary citizens would be able to own a modest stake in the newly formed industrial trusts, reinventing the dream of proprietorial democracy for the age of corporate capitalism. The commission argued that, without full transparency of financial information, outside investors were investing merely on blind faith, with the implication that financial advice guides were no better than prayer books.[78] After the Wall Street panic in 1907, the Hughes Commission went further, recommending a number of measures designed not merely to enforce corporate financial transparency but to actively protect vulnerable outsiders, such as tightening control over quotations and forbidding trade in potentially risky, unlisted securities that made no financial disclosures at all. Likewise the Pujo Committee (the congressional inquiry into the so-called Money Trust in 1913) recommended "complete publicity as to all the affairs" of listed corporations on the stock market.[79]

These concerns translated into reforms. Common standards for corporate accounting were introduced with the Hepburn Act of 1906.[80] Following the Hughes Commission, some western states—for example, Kansas in 1911—introduced blue sky laws (as these state regulatory interventions were called), requiring specific forms of corporate financial transparency. But many of the recommendations for national securities reform failed to gain purchase. This was partly because defenders of the market successfully insisted that the best way to promote American values of democracy and independence was for the market to be left free and unfettered, with "caveat emptor" as its guiding principle: it should not be up to the government to save the "lambs" from their own folly. In his landmark 1905 ruling on bucket shops, Justice Oliver Holmes famously made the distinction between "speculation which is carried on by persons of means and experience, and based on an intelligent forecast, and that which is carried on by persons without these regular qualifications."[81] Stock market apologists thus argued that instead of protecting *inexperienced* speculators, any reforms should be aimed at discouraging *unqualified* investors from participating in the market. Holmes thus sets up amateur outsiders as a "negative analogue" to professional insiders and their "intelligent forecasts," part of a long-running rhetorical maneuver that tried to claim that some forms of stock market investment were rational and scientific, more than mere guessing about unknowable futures. The governors of the New York Stock Exchange and their defenders insisted that the market should indeed be left to professionals, as the only ones who had the financial means and the knowledge to carry the financial risks. By contrast, reformers complained that the market was being manipulated by professionals, putting the wider public off investing.

Though sometimes providing muckraking exposés that ostensibly buttressed the case for reform, much popular writing on Wall Street actually had a different emphasis. By documenting the influence that powerful individuals and secret cliques could exert on the stock market, authors like Medbery, Fowler, and Clews certainly stressed the importance of hard information to the investor. But whereas earlier manuals had argued that knowledge was to be derived by studying market statistics, these new guides emphasized instead a different kind of knowledge, acquired through experience and connections—and for those who had neither, the books promised to provide an affordable proxy. As with Mortimer's groundbreaking guide to stockjobbing in London, these memoirs increasingly portrayed Wall Street as a game whose rules and quirks needed to be mastered by the novitiate, with the implication that learning from experienced guides was the best way of avoiding being fleeced. This was an idea which animated the emerging genre of City and Wall Street fiction, and which was also integral to the new financial journalism.[82] The popular press now presented the stock exchange in terms of human melodrama rather than the impersonal abstractions of economics. What distinguished successful financial reporters, according to Wall Street writer and broker Edwin Lefèvre, was that they were "able to deduce from dry statistics facts of interest to human beings." Key to their pose of credibility, therefore, was "knowledge obtained at first hand, of the men whose personality so dominates the financial markets that it is very hard to disassociate the men from the events."[83]

So, though sometimes urging regulatory protection of the "lambs," or condemning speculation as gambling, the main message of popular guides to the stock market in this period was that the savvy outsider could—if armed with the right information—get even with powerful insiders. Their promise was to equip the inexperienced speculator with the necessary knowledge to compete with the market manipulators. This style of reporting was particularly apparent in the society magazines that began to be published in the 1870s and 1880s in both Britain and the United States. Coupling drawing room scandal with stock market gossip, two of the most successful examples were *Truth* (established by Henry Du Pré Labouchere in Britain in 1877) and *Town Topics* (established by Colonel William

D'Alton Mann in the United States in 1885; see fig. 3.2).[84] Labouchere and Mann were flamboyant figures who often blurred the boundary between respectability and disreputability, and the story of their journals is remarkably similar. Elegant, authoritative, jaunty, and urbane, the magazines' accounts of the stock market are very much in tune with the brisk reports of the society column, with both sections issuing stern reprimands for behavior deemed to be beyond the pale of accepted norms. Both the society and financial columns promised intimate knowledge of these exclusive realms. The exposure of scandal was integral to their appeal, with an avowed faith in the power of publicity to fight corruption. While both Labouchere and Mann styled themselves as reformist outsiders, their publications also repeatedly emphasized their insider status, with their easy familiarity with the inner workings of high society and *haute finance*. The magazines provided their readers with the vicarious pleasure of feeling that they were "in the know," along with a sense of moral superiority from learning about the fall from grace of social leaders. In the same way that the gossip pages both helped constitute the spectacle of high society while also condemning it, so too did the muckraking financial columns help sustain the very markets they appeared at times to criticize.

On the one hand, they insisted that investment decisions could be made rationally by developing an understanding of fundamental economic indicators and principles. Labouchere, for example, insisted that the market was "no recondite mystery" and that readers could learn to calculate the "intrinsic value" of financial instruments.[85] On the other hand, society magazines repeatedly presented the stock and commodity markets as a clubbish world of cliques and cabals, with market movements usually the result of insider manipulation. The fluctuations in prices of stocks are frequently described in *Town Topics* in mock-heroic terms, a perpetual and personal struggle between the bull and the bear factions, with the focus on the dominant personalities of the exchanges, emphasizing the writer's personal knowledge and privileged connections. The market is often presented as under the personal influence of a masterful player, a bold and energetic character: "You have doubtless concluded that Mr. Gould is at the back of this market, and I think that such a conclusion, if arrived at, will be proven a fact ere many days have passed. . . . I know for a fact that both Cornelius and William K. [Vanderbilt] are opposed to the payments of any such large amounts to stockholders."[86] *Truth* and *Town Topics* thus presented high society and the stock exchange to their curious readers as both extremely exclusive institutions, yet made those readers feel as if they

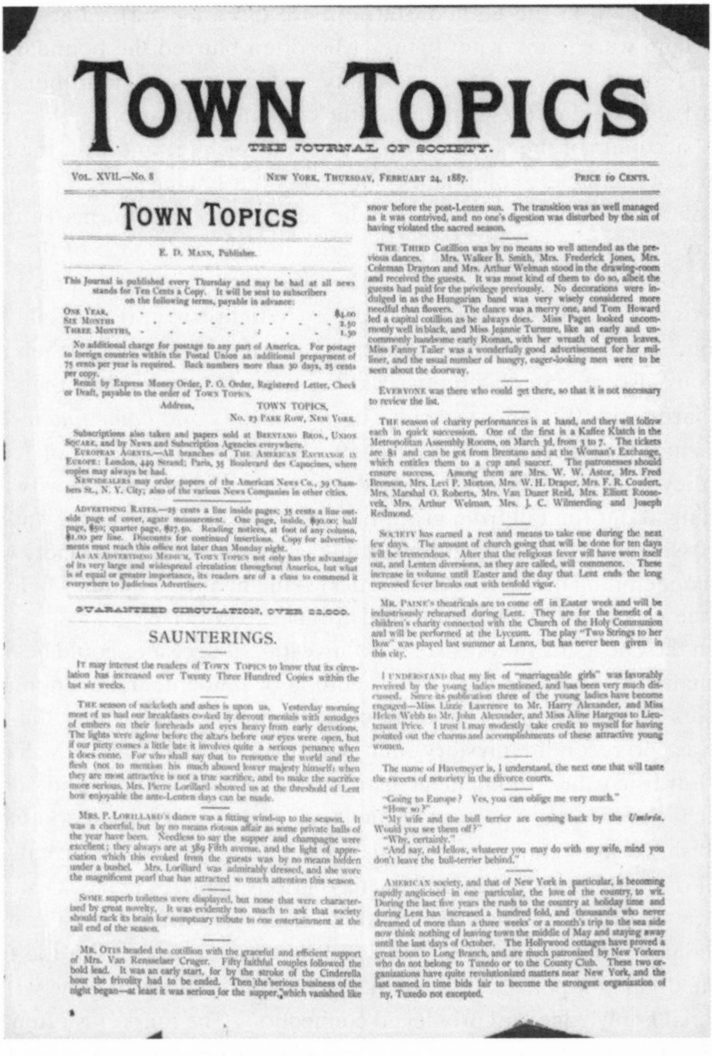

TOWN TOPICS

THE JOURNAL OF SOCIETY.

VOL. XVII.—No. 8 | NEW YORK, THURSDAY, FEBRUARY 24, 1887. | PRICE 10 CENTS.

TOWN TOPICS

E. D. MANN, Publisher.

This Journal is published every Thursday and may be had at all news stands for Ten Cents a Copy. It will be sent to subscribers on the following terms, payable in advance:

ONE YEAR,	$4.00
SIX MONTHS	2.50
THREE MONTHS,	1.50

No additional charge for postage to any part of America. For postage to foreign countries within the Postal Union an additional prepayment of 75 cents per year is required. Back numbers more than 30 days, 25 cents per copy.

Remit by Express Money Order, P. O. Order, Registered Letter, Check or Draft, payable to the order of TOWN TOPICS.

Address, TOWN TOPICS,
No. 23 PARK ROW, NEW YORK.

Subscriptions also taken and papers sold at BRENTANO BROS., UNION SQUARE, and by News and Subscription Agencies everywhere.

EUROPEAN AGENTS.—All branches of THE AMERICAN EXCHANGE IN EUROPE: London, 449 Strand; Paris, 35 Boulevard des Capucines, where copies may always be had.

NEWSDEALERS may order papers of the American News Co., 39 Chambers St., N. Y. City; also of the various News Companies in other cities.

ADVERTISING RATES.—25 cents a line inside pages; 35 cents a line outside page of cover, agate measurement. One page, inside, $90.00; half page, $50; quarter page, $27.50. Reading notices, at foot of any column, $1.00 per line. Discounts for continued insertions. Copy for advertisements must reach this office not later than Monday night.

AS AN ADVERTISING MEDIUM, TOWN TOPICS not only has the advantage of its very large and widespread circulation throughout America, but what is of equal or greater importance, its readers are of a class to commend it everywhere to Judicious Advertisers.

GUARANTEED CIRCULATION, OVER 22,000.

SAUNTERINGS.

IT may interest the readers of TOWN TOPICS to know that its circulation has increased over Twenty Three Hundred Copies within the last six weeks.

THE season of sackcloth and ashes is upon us. Yesterday morning most of us had our breakfasts cooked by devout menials with smudges of embers on their foreheads and eyes heavy from early devotions. The lights were aglow before the altars before our eyes were open, but if our piety comes a little late it involves quite a serious penance when it does come. For who shall say that to renounce the world and the flesh (not to mention his much abused lower majesty himself) when they are most attractive is not a true sacrifice, and to make the sacrifice more serious, Mrs. Pierre Lorillard showed us at the threshold of Lent how enjoyable the ante-Lenten days can be made.

MRS. P. LORILLARD'S dance was a fitting wind-up to the season. It was a cheerful, but by no means riotous affair as some private balls of the year have been. Needless to say the supper and champagne were excellent; they always are at 389 Fifth avenue, and the light of appreciation which this evoked from the guests was by no means hidden under a bushel. Mrs. Lorillard was admirably dressed, and she wore the magnificent pearl that has attracted so much attention this season.

SOME superb toilettes were displayed, but none that were characterised by great novelty. It was evidently too much to ask that society should rack its brain for sumptuary tribute to one entertainment at the tail end of the season.

MR. OTIS headed the cotillion with the graceful and efficient support of Mrs. Van Rensselaer Cruger. Fifty faithful couples followed the bold lead. It was an early start, for by the stroke of the Cinderella hour the frivolity had to be ended. Then the serious business of the night began—at least it was serious for the supper, which vanished like snow before the post-Lenten sun. The transition was as well managed as it was contrived, and no one's digestion was disturbed by the sin of having violated the sacred season.

THE THIRD Cotillion was by no means so well attended as the previous dances. Mrs. Walker B. Smith, Mrs. Frederick Jones, Mrs. Coleman Drayton and Mrs. Arthur Welman stood in the drawing-room and received the guests. It was most kind of them to do so, albeit the guests had paid for the privilege previously. No decorations were indulged in as the Hungarian band was very wisely considered more needful than flowers. The dance was a merry one, and Tom Howard led a capital cotillion as he always does. Miss Paget looked uncommonly well in black, and Miss Jeannie Turnure, like an early and uncommonly handsome early Roman, with her wreath of green leaves. Miss Fanny Tailer was a wonderfully good advertisement for her milliner, and the usual number of hungry, eager-looking men were to be seen about the doorway.

EVERYONE was there who could get there, so that it is not necessary to review the list.

THE season of charity performances is at hand, and they will follow each in quick succession. One of the first is a Kaffee Klatch in the Metropolitan Assembly Rooms, on March 3d, from 3 to 7. The tickets are $1 and can be got from Brentano and at the Woman's Exchange, which entitles them to a cup and saucer. The patronesses should ensure success. Among them are Mrs. W. W. Astor, Mrs. Fred Bronson, Mrs. Levi P. Morton, Mrs. W. H. Draper, Mrs. F. R. Coudert, Mrs. Marshal O. Roberts, Mrs. Van Duzer Reid, Mrs. Elliott Roosevelt, Mrs. Arthur Welman, Mrs. J. C. Wilmerding and Joseph Redmond.

SOCIETY has earned a rest and means to take one during the next few days. The amount of church going that will be done for ten days will be tremendous. After that the religious fever will have worn itself out, and Lenten diversions, as they are called, will commence. These increase in volume until Easter and the day that Lent ends the long repressed fever breaks out with tenfold vigor.

MR. PAINE'S theatricals are to come off in Easter week and will be industriously rehearsed during Lent. They are for the benefit of a children's charity connected with the Church of the Holy Communion and will be performed at the Lyceum. The play "Two Strings to her Bow" was played last summer at Lenox, but has never been given in this city.

I UNDERSTAND that my list of "marriageable girls" was favorably received by the young ladies mentioned, and has been very much discussed. Since its publication three of the young ladies have become engaged—Miss Lizzie Lawrence to Mr. Harry Alexander, and Miss Helen Webb to Mr. John Alexander, and Miss Aline Hargous to Lieutenant Price. I trust I may modestly take credit to myself for having pointed out the charms and accomplishments of these attractive young women.

The name of Havemeyer is, I understand, the next one that will taste the sweets of notoriety in the divorce courts.

"Going to Europe? Yes, you can oblige me very much."

"How so?"

"My wife and the bull terrier are coming back by the *Umbria*. Would you see them off?"

"Why, certainly."

"And say, old fellow, whatever you may do with my wife, mind you don't leave the bull-terrier behind."

AMERICAN society, and that of New York in particular, is becoming rapidly anglicised in one particular, the love of the country, to wit. During the last five years the rush to the country at holiday time and during Lent has increased a hundred fold, and thousands who never dreamed of more than a three weeks' or a month's trip to the sea side now think nothing of leaving town the middle of May and staying away until the last days of October. The Hollywood cottages have proved a great boon to Long Branch, and are much patronized by New Yorkers who do not belong to Tuxedo or to the County Club. These two organizations have quite revolutionized matters near New York, and the last named in time bids fair to become the strongest organization of ny, Tuxedo not excepted.

FIGURE 3.2. Cover of *Town Topics* (February 24, 1887), 2. Document provided by the New York Public Library and made available through *Everyday Life & Women in America*, ca. 1800–1920.

were included, part of a select band who know what the gossip is about. Although society figures were supposedly the subject of Mann's attack, they almost certainly read the magazine (even if they would not admit to doing so), with the magazine finding its way "into almost every cottage in the Park [Tuxedo Park, an elite, Gilded Age resort in New York], as it did into the cottages, villas, and mansions at Newport." At the same time, however, it was read, according to the son of the etiquette-guide writer Emily Post (herself a victim of Mann's scandal mongering), by everyone in the household, masters and servants alike: "upstairs, downstairs, and backstairs."[87] Although reliable evidence of the actual readership of the magazine is scant, it is likely that the rapidly growing readership consisted not only of high society but those who delighted in mocking the scandalous behavior of their supposed betters, and who wanted the illusion that they too were part of the inner sanctum of society. *Truth* and *Town Topics* thus played on the contradictory desires for privacy and publicity, secrecy and transparency, which made the realms of both high society and finance tick. In short, they provided an imaginary resolution to the long-standing and persistent problem of asymmetrical information in the stock market, by rhetorically making outsiders feel like they were insiders.

Labouchere and Mann promised readers valuable stock tips, usually framed as studiedly insouciant accounts of their own dabbling: "Having a trifle to invest, I have bought myself a few more Egyptian Preference Bonds," a column in *Truth* noted in 1878.[88] Likewise in *Town Topics*, the "Room-Trader" gave personal investment advice whose selling point was its supposed accuracy: "Since I last wrote, I have sold a few of my Richmond and West Point Terminals at a profit of four points, and now intend holding the balance. . . . Without any prospect of a settlement of the Transcontinental difficulty, with the absolute certainty that the company is in urgent need of new steamers, and with the undeniable fact that there will be no dividend on the stock for many weary months, perhaps for years, to come, I cannot consistently ask you to buy it around its present price."[89] *Town Topics* soon went further, establishing a Financial Bureau, offering investment advice by letter and telegraph to subscribers, which was advertised as an exclusive, personal service. In effect, the bureau promised to deliver what the rest of the paper could only gesture toward, namely, inside information and trading advice based on well-placed intelligence. Its regular advertisement assured readers that its "sources of information are more complete, more from the 'inside,' and hence more accurate than those of any other paper or institution in the country."[90]

Labouchere and Mann alike denied that there was a conflict of interest in their own stock market activity. Labouchere insisted that it was precisely the transparency of his financial conduct that distinguished it from the corrupt practices of other money-page writers who, he claimed, kept their trading secret. The irony, however, is that both Labouchere and Mann were indeed up to their necks in shady dealings. Despite having made public remonstrances against financial journalists using their columns to secretly feather their nests, Labouchere was himself the subject of an exposé in the 1890s that made public some of his private letters (from twenty years prior) that seemed to reveal his cynical disregard for the public. It also made clear that Labouchere, like other unscrupulous financial writers, used his column to manipulate the market, relying on the fact that readers eagerly followed his tips.[91] In a discussion of Anglo-American Telegraph stock, for example, he confessed to his correspondent that:

> It seems to me that the money on the up & down scale is to be made between 58 and 68. Our object now ought to be to send them down, then let a lot of people sell at 56, 57 or lower if possible, and at once start negotiations & send them up again. It seems to me that this can be renewed several times.[92]

Labouchere's critics accused him of being a "heartless share-rigger, a man who prostituted his position as the trusted writer on financial subjects in the *World* in order to swell his own pockets at the expense of the public."[93] More egregiously, a court case in 1905–6 brought out the revelation that Mann had in effect been running *Town Topics* as an extortion racket.[94] He would blackmail the great and good in exchange for suppressing salacious stories about them, and he recorded the bribes from his wealthy victims as "loans" which he most likely never intended to repay. In return for burying a story, he would even sell shares in the magazine at vastly increased rates, although it was not always clear whether any actual shares changed hands. In neither case did the revelations seem to affect circulation, with *Truth* enjoying sales of 30,000 in the 1890s and *Town Topics* reaching 140,000, so Mann claimed, in the 1900s.[95] Their mode of representing finance encouraged a cynical knowingness in their readers which assumed that they would be less likely to be shocked when the financial and sexual peccadilloes of their guides were exposed. After all, the thinking went, such behavior was only to be expected from market manipulators, and if the game was rigged, then to level the playing field ordinary readers needed the inside knowledge these gossip magazines provided all the more.

In this way, the popular press in the late nineteenth century helped to normalize and dramatize stock market investment for ordinary citizens. The new style of journalism emerged out of, and spoke to, the fundamental ambiguity at the heart of financial knowledge in this era. On the one hand, readers were made to feel that they needed an expert guide to the unfamiliar laws of the market, whose impersonal rhythms and patterns were not immediately obvious to the casual observer. On the other hand, the market was presented as a place of scandal and intrigue, requiring trustworthy insider knowledge. Financial writers thus figured the market as a place of both safety and danger, both rationality and emotion, and both abstract process and human spectacle.

The principles that animated the society press's financial coverage were also becoming much more prominent in national dailies and weeklies. The chattiness and wit of the *New York Herald*'s money column, the direct financial guidance offered by *Harper's Weekly*, and the brightness and crispness of the *Daily Mail* all testified to the mainstreaming of this new presentation of the market. On the one hand, the stock market is a remote realm in which financial titans do battle on a scale that dwarfs humble individual investors. On the other, it is a familiar place that ordinary people can understand through homely metaphors. The financial press combined a quasi-anthropological distance from the exotic customs of the City and Wall Street with a gossipy appeal to readers, as if they were insiders in this tribe. By making outsiders feel like they were insiders, popular financial journalists could both condemn the depravity of stock speculation and offer their readers a supposed shortcut to riches. The goal of this coverage was to teach lay readers how the stock market works, not so much in the name of objective reporting, but in order to persuade them to participate — and, of course, keep buying the advice. Thus, *Harper's* told its readers in 1899 that "with due care in the selection there are many opportunities presented in times like these on the Stock Exchange, and the man with funds to invest will not be slow to see them."[96] Making concrete the structural abstractions of political economy was part of the rhetorical trick that persuaded ordinary readers to enter the market. Indeed, commentators at the time credited the press with effecting a wholesale transformation of middle-class attitudes to the market, one writer noting that the "country squire" and the "impecunious widow . . . who not long ago would have been horrified at anything but a three per cent. investment have now become so hardened as to try their luck at 'bulling' and 'bearing.'"[97]

The Simulation of Personal Advice

Popular financial journalism thus provided a simulation of personal advice for a mass audience. It aimed to make readers feel that they were "in the know," privileged recipients of insider information that would enable them to beat the market. The paradox of such advice was that the more people who bought it, the less plausible it was that it could provide a competitive advantage. However, the huge popularity of some financial writers meant that their prognostications had the power to move the market in a self-fulfilling prophecy, in turn persuading more readers of its power. The most dramatic example is the stock promoter turned muckraking journalist and novelist, Thomas Lawson, whose apocalyptic fantasy scenarios ended up producing just the market collapse in real life that his fiction had projected. Lawson was at one point the sixth richest man in America. He made his fortune as a stock promoter, organizing large corporate mergers. However, he was soon sick of what he saw as the corrupt stranglehold that a clique of big businessmen had on the American economy. Instead he turned to muckraking journalism, and in 1906 he published *Frenzied Finance*, a searing exposé of the scandal surrounding the Amalgamated Copper deal. But Lawson soon realized that journalism does not pay as well as finance, so he returned to stock promotion. This time he tried to move the market not by insider dealing or an advice manual but by writing a sensationalist novel, *Friday the Thirteenth* (1907). It predicted an apocalyptic crash of the stock market. His avid readers took his warnings at face value and ended up creating in the real world the panic that the fiction had imagined—and Lawson pocketed the profit.[98]

At the same time that the burgeoning newspaper press was insinuating this seemingly personal market advice into hundreds of thousands of homes, the free pamphlets and guides of the outside brokers were engaged in a similar mission. Such guides claimed that they would allow outsiders to avoid becoming "lambs" at the mercy of insiders and manipulators. For example, William E. Forrest (who distributed "Hoyle's Market Letter") emphasized the language of republican simplicity and plain speaking in *The Game in Wall Street, and How to Play It Successfully* (1898). Yet the guide hypocritically promised to protect the "lambs" at the very moment that it was trying to fleece them:

In putting forth this pamphlet the Author has no scheme to work. He has tried to give, in plain language, the facts, or some of them at least, about the game in Wall Street. He has made no effort at style in writing. Simple English and the "calling a spade a spade" is what he has striven for. He does not set up to be a reformer. He accepts human nature as he finds it. He hopes that this little work may save a "lamb" or two from the sacrifice. . . . Possibly, if the public learn something about the game, they may avoid making fatal mistakes. If the public should learn to play the game so as to win, that in itself would do more to break it up than anything else could.[99]

The guides encouraged investors of modest means to think of themselves as heroically seeing through the smokescreens put up by stock market professionals by cultivating a stance of ruggedly independent thought and feeling. The irony, however, was that these freebie publications were in fact designed to entice readers to hand over discretionary control of their investments to the broker. Though claiming to equip novices with the information they needed to operate independently, they explicitly acknowledged that some readers might welcome "help" in figuring out which securities to buy—even to the extent of leaving that decision entirely at the discretion of the broker to whom they had entrusted their money, with little chance of challenging their decisions when the market turned against them.

It was therefore critical for brokers to persuade the public to trust them. As we have seen, investment advice for the elite had traditionally taken an intimate form, whether in person or in writing, from a relative, family friend, solicitor, banker, or broker. Archives contain letters from clients and replies from their brokers that range from the short-and-informative to the highly individualized, often intermingling personal and financial news. For example, a letter of September 18, 1877, from George Bliss of Morton, Bliss & Co. to a Mr. Grenfell, a client in London, begins:

My dear Mr. Grenfell:

I received your letter of the 4th yesterday, and am glad to learn that you are refreshed & better for your little trip and holiday. I find myself pretty well again, and hope, as the cool weather comes on, that I shall recover my usual vigor.

Prices of securities have advanced very rapidly with us, and, at first thought, one would conclude that a reaction would soon take place. Such economies in the management of corporate interests have been introduced since 1873, on account of the depressed condition of business, that an improving business tells in the net result rapidly. This is especially the case with railways. . . . It is proper to consider cotton at the current rates as better security than when higher prices ruled.[100]

Even though Bliss's letters often got straight down to brass tacks, they nevertheless helped sustain a relationship with the client. In his letter of January 13, 1882, for example, Bliss gently admonished the lack of financial knowledge of his correspondent—a family member:

> Dear Theodore [Bliss],
>
> I have yours of yesterday's date.
>
> I have not seen any quoted sale of Milwaukee St. Paul Southern Minnesota in 6's at less than 103 since you were here. I think if you saw a quotation at 103 it was a <u>bid</u>.[101]

It is significant, then, that investment advice guides written for a mass audience often attempted to provide the kind of personal touch found in Morton, Bliss & Co.'s letters. Advertisements for outside brokers often addressed the reader directly and emphasized the human face behind the corporate facade.[102] For example, in April 1906 *Red Book* magazine featured a full-page advertisement for W. M. Ostrander Inc., with the entreaty to "Send for MY BOOK FREE." A photograph of Ostrander's earnest-looking face takes up half the advertisement, inviting a sense of personal connection to this Philadelphia broker and real estate agent who advertised liberally in the press. He addresses the reader directly: "I want to send *you* my magazine six months free" (emphasis added; fig. 3.3).[103]

Infrastructural and technological developments offered brokers new methods for simulating a personal bond with investors.[104] Attractively produced mass-mailed circulars enticed aspirational respondents to take part in schemes that would supposedly guarantee spectacular profits. Like earlier confidence tricks (the very term "confidence man" first emerged in 1849), these misrepresentations-by-mail often made appeal to a traditional idiom of personal connection, even though they were conducted in the anonymous mode of mass consumerism.[105] For example, in his exposé of mail frauds published in 1880, the New York postal inspector and prominent anti-vice campaigner Anthony Comstock told the story of Lawrence & Co., a fake brokerage office set up by Benjamin Buckwalter, a former snake-oil salesman. Buckwalter's newspaper advertisements

Copyright © 2015 ProQuest LLC. All rights reserved.

FIGURE 3.3. Full-page advertisement for W. M. Ostrander, Inc., *Red Book* 6, no. 6 (April 1906): 164. Image published with permission of ProQuest LLC. Further reproduction is prohibited without permission.

would declare that it was "just your time" to "make money safely, easily, and rapidly" in the stock market through the "combination method" of speculation.[106] Those who replied to the advertisements would be sent a lengthy circular that included both a confusing explanation of the combination system and a direct, friendly approach to the reader. The scheme supposedly allowed small investors to pool their capital, so they could collectively engage in a large-scale speculation that would put them on an equal footing with Wall Street titans. Suckers who accepted the bait would send in their money to Lawrence & Co., along with a signed form that gave the broker complete legal freedom to make investment decisions on the client's behalf. Discretionary brokerages were open to abuse, and, indeed, Lawrence & Co. did not actually invest the pooled money in the stock market on behalf of its trusting clients. Buckwalter would instead merely pocket the money sent in by the public. Investors were then strung along with a series of seemingly personal form letters, asking them to send further money to keep the winning streak going. Once a sucker had been bled for as much as Buckwalter thought he could stand, the "Royal Bounce" letter was sent, explaining that, sadly, the latest combination had failed and the victim's account was therefore wiped out.

When Comstock raided the firm's office, he discovered a "sucker list" of more than half a million names and seized some 40,000 letters from victims, the most tear-jerking of which Comstock reprinted. In addition to the legion of bucket shops, other scams from this period included "1 percent margin syndicates" (in which participants would be asked to stake a risibly small margin that would inevitably get wiped out); "stock promoters" (who would mail out elaborate prospectuses for firms whose prospects were grossly exaggerated, or even for firms that did not exist); "guarantee brokers" (who would faithfully return all the money from failed investments, minus an eye-watering 12.5 percent "insurance charge" each month); "investment syndicates" (such as E. S. Dean & Co. and the Franklin Syndicate, which operated a Ponzi scheme long before Ponzi himself, paying out up to 10 percent in weekly returns to early investors, simply by handing over the money received from subsequent ones); and the "advance-information brokers" (who promised, for a fee, "inside and advance information" on the future course of grain and stock markets, but who would instead use the clients' money to bet on both sides of the market, take a cut from the winners, and offer commiseration to the losers, all the while happily pocketing the regular subscription fees from both). The scale of these late-century frauds operating through mass mailings and advertising was astounding. Writing in 1904, John Hill, a director of the Chicago Board of Trade tasked with combating bucket shops, estimated that $100 million was invested in fraudulent stock promotions in 1902, while another $100 million annually was lost by the public in other get-rich-quick schemes, not including the rapid proliferation of bucket shops themselves, whose organization was increasingly complex.[107]

These scams employed a pseudo-personal appeal to their victims as part of their operations carried out on an industrial scale. The letters sent out by firms such as Lawrence & Co. took advantage of modern litho-graphic printing techniques to make them look handwritten. In his exposé published in the Pinkerton Detective Series, George McWatters warned "youthful readers" that these mass-produced copies were designed to fool the recipients into believing that they were handwritten for their benefit: "Probably one-third of those who receive these letters do not know that they are in fact 'printed,' and each ignorant receiver feels flattered as he reads the letter that the 'speculator' has taken pains to write to him so extendedly."[108] The mimicry of intimacy was now doubly false: the fake appeal to a personal connection was itself cast deceitfully in pseudo-authentic lithographic "handwriting." Even large bucket shop chains, like Christie Stock & Grain, continued to rely on a chummy tone even as they gave their postal clients the brush-off. "Well, old friend," one missive be-gan, "we got in wrong this time, even though your corn was sold at what seemed to me an outrageous high price last evening."[109] The scams often combined what looked like impartial details of the success of the invest-ment scheme, as if the numbers spoke for themselves, with an appeal that rested on placing trust both in the people that ran it and those who sup-posedly had profited by it. One correspondent of Lawrence & Co., for example, confessed that "I have read your circular carefully; and though I do not fully understand some of the terms, and methods, yet *I* BELIEVE YOU; and this doubtless is better than if I believed myself and doubted you."[110] Most of these fraudulent schemes thus relied on a populist appeal, both by offering the semblance of participation in the stock market for would-be investors of very humble means, and also by evoking the democratic sentiment of average Americans being able to enjoy a share of the same successes as the elite. As an ad for an advance-information bureau put it, its aim was "to furnish a service that will put the small investor on an equal footing with the large trader, or, to use the parlance of the 'Street,' the 'in-sider.'"[111] In contrast to the political faith in transparency and regulation that was becoming more prominent in the early twentieth century, part of the appeal of this financial advice was that it would combat the inequalities produced by Wall Street by allowing outsiders to become insiders. It also used forms of mass communication to convince readers that they—somehow—were not one of the masses. It was an industrialized form of the con trick.

Financial Advice as Conspiracy Theory

In humanizing the stock market, these forms of popular financial writing drew upon—and also helped reinforce—the notion that the market was moved more by powerful individuals than impersonal economic processes. Often they did this by turning their account into a melodramatic conspiracy theory that claimed to find a hidden agency behind structural forces. In contrast, the money page in *Harper's Weekly* usually tried to show that financial fundamentals and economic laws, rather than investor psychology or insider manipulation, were the real operative forces behind stock market movements. A column summing up the year 1900, for example, concluded that "the end of the year finds us in a strong position industrially, commercially, and financially, with a much better prospect for continued prosperity than appeared at the beginning." Yet *Harper's* money page also at times acknowledged that market movements could not always be explained in terms of economic fundamentals alone. Instead, it admitted that manipulation by insiders was to blame, particularly when the general public were not active in the market. In December 1901, for example, it noted that:

> Irregularity was the principal characteristic of the trading in stocks last week. Outside interest in speculation continued at a low ebb. This left the market in the hands of the professionals, who are prone to govern their actions by technical conditions, and to respond readily to rumors of all sorts.[112]

The column also warns that the canny market reader must learn to recognize that the price signals have been deliberately manipulated through wash sales by a small group of professional traders in order to look like a genuine market movement. The trick, it suggests, is to discover malign intentionality beneath what has been made to look like impersonal economic forces. Readers are thus taught that rising share prices do not necessarily provide a realistic reflection of increased productivity or value, because the market might merely have been manipulated in order to make unsophisticated outsiders *think* so. Even though its focus on economic fundamentals made *Harper's* closer in tone and outlook to the financial press aimed at business professionals, it nevertheless instructed its lay readers in how to identify the hidden hand of market manipulation behind what at first sight seemed to be the Invisible Hand of supply and demand.

Highlighting the power of secret machinations should in theory have deterred lay investors from getting caught up in the stock market. Yet readers responded enthusiastically to the revelations of scandal, fraud, and manipulation in part because they believed that they were learning the unvarnished truth about the City and Wall Street from guides with firsthand knowledge, but also because they flattered themselves into thinking that they were too savvy to be fooled by such duplicitous practices. At first sight William Stafford Young's *Safe Methods in Stock Speculation* (1902), for instance, seemed to offer a muckraking exposé of the stock and commodity markets as a rigged game. Its title promised to square the circle of removing risk from speculation (safe methods!), but the lengthy subtitle suggested a more concerted attack on the stock market: "Practical information of the methods used by which the Wall Street millionaires have amassed vast fortunes, filched from the public, and explaining fully matters regarding manipulations that have heretofore remained a secret." However, Young's real purpose was to convince readers that, precisely because the market was manipulated by powerful insiders, amateur speculators could take advantage of this insight to chart a route to riches—a route that began, naturally, with buying his book. In a clear break from the religious and moralistic diatribes against unproductive labor that were popular in the nineteenth century, Young acknowledged the psychological attraction of speculation for those unwilling to abide by the usual endorsement of the slow and steady accumulation of wealth: "Stock speculation is a very seductive game, at once fascinating and offering more opportunities for quick returns than any other line of business. . . . It is of interest to business men in all walks of life, who are attracted by the 'get-rich-quick' possibilities, and who may have tired of the slow, plodding method of commercial business." Because powerful syndicates were seemingly able to manipulate the market at will, there was an information asymmetry between insiders and outsiders. "Information is unreliable," Young noted, "because the people who are doing the work never divulge their plans." The "only safe plan" was "to follow the manipulators." At the outset of the book, Young gestured toward the idea—widespread at the time—that unwitting outside speculators must be protected from unscrupulous insiders. This might suggest that his volume was written, as he asserted, "in the hope that some of the lambs may receive a little light on the subject." However, instead of recommending laws to protect the innocent investor, the real message of the book was to make sure that they were not naively taken in by the ruses of the manipulators: "The author assumes that the reader knows the stock market to be a game that is played in the same manner as a game of chess—the purpose being to always fool the other fellow."[113] Earlier in the century financial advice manuals worked hard to persuade readers—in contrast to the prevailing moral condemnation of speculation as gambling, and in the face of repeated panics and scandals— that the stock market was a rational and honest place. But Young takes a different line: precisely because the market was manipulated, amateur investors could use that insight to their advantage, outwitting the professional sharks.

Young seems at times to regard the market like the weather, obeying the laws of nature: "These sharp breaks are like a spring shower, when it rains hard but soon is over." At other times he suggests that the market follows its own regularities, like a dependable mechanism or creature, the telltale signs of which become familiar to the careful observer: "when these two stocks [St. Paul and Union Pacific] do not show the right springy movement, it is well not to be on the bull side." Ultimately, though, for Young the rhythms of the market are not a natural or mechanical phenomenon but the result of manipulations designed to *look* natural. "All of these movements," he warns, "are to mystify the outside and give the impression that something stupendous is going on." The insiders are thus not merely manipulating the general direction of the market: they are making the evidence tell a different story precisely in order to sucker in the unwary. The savvy amateur speculator must therefore learn to decode the clues that are hidden in plain sight. "By watching closely for the signs," Young counsels, "one may follow every movement of the manipulator and ascertain exactly what he is trying to accomplish, without the aid or advice of anyone."[114] Through independent analysis the outsider can thus come to understand what is happening on the inside.

Having successfully worked out what is really going on, the would-be speculator can then safely take action. Young insists that the patterns of manipulation are repeated and therefore reliably predictable, and he provides both instruction and evidence, including several charts of particular market events (e.g., a twenty-point movement in St. Paul stock, September 1901–January 1902). Despite a similar appeal to graphical presentations, this was a far cry from the more full-blown development of what would become known as "technical analysis" in the early twentieth century, which aimed to show the repeated patterns that were endogenous to the market. Instead, Young provides a retrospective narrative gloss, translating the seemingly random or self-activating fluctuation of prices into an account of malign manipulation by insiders. For Young, the behavior of the stock market is neither chaotic and unpredictable, nor even simply marching to its own tune, but is instead governed by the repeated campaigns of secret maneuvering that produce telltale signals. "After stocks have advanced three days and close at top and open high the next morning," Young asserts, "there is almost sure to be a reaction of a point or two." Ironically, in planning their campaigns to manipulate the market, the syndicates in Young's view are relying on the unreliability of human reason, allowing them to predict and profit from the foolishness of the masses: "Manipulators expect this behavior [the 'ignorant' 'mass of speculators' failing to recognize that an 'inactive' but slowly declining bear market is about to collapse], for they know human nature well enough to count upon it."[115]

In essence, then, Young develops a conspiracy theory of stock market movements: nothing happens by accident, nothing is as it seems, and everything is connected.[116] He insists:

> This panic may seem to the uninitiated to have been one of accidental nature. But this is indeed a delusion. Nothing that happens in Wall Street can be attributed to accident. These men lay their plans and look far into the future. They guard their secrets with great tenacity, confiding in none except those trusted few of the inner circle.[117]

Like many conspiracy theorists, Young wavers between pessimism and optimism. On the one hand, the system is rigged by conspirators too powerful to even be named. "The author will not venture to point out some of the means adopted to attain ends," Young warns cryptically, "as it might cast reflection upon people in high places." The market is not the self-sustaining and self-directed entity envisioned by technical analysis; instead it is like a beast or a slave, completely under the control of its master: "the manipulators, who make it a practice, for their own protection, to keep the market in check and not permit it to become over-taxed." According to Young, there were at the time he was writing very few small-scale

investors left, and instead a handful of millionaires owned a large part
of the stock in particular corporations. Indeed, Young's evidence that the
"Milking Process" had been going on for at least two decades is the visible
increase in millionaires, with all the small investors slowly swallowed up.[118]
Yet Young insists that lone, autodidact speculators can use their mental
prowess to make money and thus get even with the shadowy cabal pulling the strings of the market. Young's account of market manipulations
provided a compensatory fantasy of individual masculine agency, precisely at the historic moment when the corporate reconfiguration of the
American economy made the independent proprietor or producer far less
significant. This cynical take on how the market "really" worked was also
what Young hoped would make his guide stand out from an increasingly
crowded field.

The Art and Science of Investment

Chance played no part in the market as conceived by Young: every price
movement was preordained by the wire-pullers. Yet other writers who did
not share Young's conspiracy-tinged views also denied the role of chance
in the financial world, though for different reasons—not least because acknowledging that the stock market was a lottery undermined the very
premise of "expert" advice. "Luck," argued one guide, "has far less to do
with business in general, and with investing in particular, than is commonly supposed. What is often attributed to luck, or chance, or to fate, is
really the product of prompt judgment and common sense."[119] Downplaying luck helped to distinguish trading from gambling by reframing it as a
matter of skill, which could be acquired and perfected, with the right guide
and for the right price. Writers insisted that, although the ignorant and the
stupid acted blindly and would inevitably lose in the long run, risk could
be managed and tamed by those who knew how, a crucial weapon in the
armory of the successful speculator: "When danger is known it can be provided against."[120] Such beliefs were characteristic of a growing tendency in
the late nineteenth century to recast financial knowledge as a science. As
Alex Preda notes, stockbrokers and would-be financial professionals promoted a new, economic conception of the market as "governed by objective laws, similar to those governing natural phenomena" in order to challenge critiques of the stock market as (in the words of one guidebook) the
plaything of "powerful men who are behind the scenes, the directors, and

wire-pullers, and financial magnates, who, possessing through their wealth enormous leverage on the markets, exercise it remorselessly."[121] On this line of thinking, the market was not inscrutable but could be read, and its future could be calculated, by investors willing to observe, analyze, and act accordingly. This skill had to be carefully cultivated through "study and effort," which the advice manuals insisted they could teach.[122]

The development of self-vaunted scientific approaches was particularly in evidence in the growing interest shown in historic price data.[123] Though tables of historical highest and lowest prices had long been available in specialist publications, from the mid-1870s such tables gained greater currency (especially in the United Kingdom), being published both as stand-alone reference lists and also as elements in more general invest-ment guides.[124] Though authors admitted that such tables did not allow you to predict the future exactly, they did enable you to judge probabili-ties of particular securities moving upward or downward, for (the theory went) in most cases history provided a good guide to the future. As one guide put it, "prices are like billiard balls—they reach their limit and re-bound."[125] Resting decisions on historical price data legitimized specula-tion, differentiating it from buying the shares of new companies, which was closer to gambling, given the high mortality rates of new promotions.

From this it was a short step to contending that price movements fol-lowed regular, predictable patterns. This belief underpinned one of the most idiosyncratic but persistently popular works of financial advice in the late nineteenth-century United States, Samuel Benner's *Prophecies of the Future Ups and Downs in Prices*, which went through multiple editions after its first publication in 1879.

Benner was an Ohio farmer who developed a homespun, quasi-divinatory account of business cycles affecting the entire economy, based not on any theoretical economic understanding but the authority of ex-perience. Unlike later guides to market movements written by financial insiders who claimed to possess scientific expertise, Benner's system was rooted in a farmer's observation of the rhythms of nature.

With the aid of charts, Benner claimed that there were "cycles of 11 years in the prices of corn and hogs, 27 years in the price of pig-iron, and 54 years in general business."[126] With little evidence to back up his obser-vations, Benner trusted that science would eventually provide the causal explanation for what he tellingly styled a "prophecy." The cover of his book depicted Benner as the oracular prophet of profit, atop his pile logs, gazing down at hogs, corn, and copious coin. Despite Benner's claim to have identified statistical patterns that operated at a level far removed from individual human intention, he nevertheless insisted that the business cycles he discovered were ultimately governed not by economic law but providential destiny, and were a matter of faith rather than formula:

> The author firmly believes that God is in prices, and that the over and under production of every commodity is in accordance with His will, with strict reference to the wants of mankind, and governed by the laws of nature, which are God's laws; and that the production, advance, and decline of average prices should be systematic, and occur in an established providential succession, as certain and regular as the magnetic needle points unerringly to the pole.[127]

Benner's book aimed to provide a form of homegrown risk management for the farmer, but also for the "manufacturer, and legitimate trader, as well as the speculator."[128] Although his book was dubbed "Cammack's almanac" because it was allegedly consulted by Addison Cammack, the famous Wall Street trader, Benner's prophecies were based on long-term cycles rather than the immediate churn of prices coming over the stock ticker. The book was therefore less obviously of immediate use to those interested in short-term speculation. Yet it remained influential in part because of its deployment of charts as a way of uncovering patterns and regularities in market prices not otherwise visible to the human observer, which fed into the development of what became known as technical analysis. More broadly, Benner's book emerged out of, and contributed to, a shift in thinking about the nature of economic life. It helped convince people that the economy could in theory be predicted. Persuading the public that financial forecasting was a science required the development of technological, institutional, and intellectual structures of authority which all began to emerge at the tail end of the nineteenth century. A work of financial advice, however, merely had to convince its buyers that its system was scientifically sound.

For all its talk of a "science of *price cycles*," Benner's book had more in common with astrology and the tradition of farmers' almanacs for predicting the weather than with the development of actuarial science or the fledgling discipline of meteorology.[129] Benner's book demonstrates that modern methods of prediction did not so much replace traditional, superstitious ones as become fused with them, applying a veneer of scientific rigor to folk practices. Vernacular methods of financial prognostication thus took on the language of economic determinism and promised to make stock market investment seem rational rather than a matter of blind faith. They also suggested that everyone—even a humble Ohio farmer—could learn the secrets of the market, from the very book they had bought.

Quasi-scientific ideas about prices and how to read them made their way into other guides. In his 1898 pamphlet, Van Riper informed readers that a speculator must learn to read the signs and symptoms of market movements, conjoining (in a wayward clash of metaphors) the skills of the weather forecaster and the physician: "Wall Street may be said to be the financial pulse of America, and it is the first to scent a coming storm." Speculative values are presented as natural phenomena governed by the laws of nature, having "their ebb and flow just as surely as the tides of the ocean."[130] H. M. Williams's *Key to Wall Street Mysteries and Methods* (1904) presented readers with specific schemes for trading based on the seemingly scientific techniques of ticker-tape reading and chart analysis.[131] Williams compared speculation to astronomy and weather forecasting, noting that scientific principles in all three disciplines now permitted a transition from superstition to modern modes of rational and probabilistic prediction. Yet for writers such as Williams and Riper, successful speculation remained as much an art as a science, to be achieved, like other professions such as medicine, through both education and on-the-ground experience.

Rather than representing a movement away from conspiracy theories about the market toward more "scientific" understandings, this kind of proto-technical analysis could also sit quite comfortably alongside conspiracy tropes. Forrest's *The Game in Wall Street*, for example, avers that speculation is a science, and that "one ought not to play this game at haphazard." He recommends "keep[ing] an accurate record of the fluctuations in prices," but emphatically denies that the prices of stocks are governed by rigid laws of supply and demand. Instead he insists that "these fluctuations are not due to chance but are *the result of design*," and learning to interpret the charts of market fluctuations will enable "a fairly good idea of what the pools are doing."[132] If speculation is a science for Forrest, it is because price movements are governed by the reliably predictable human nature of the greedy pools of bulls and bears battling for control of the market. On the other hand, the knowledge to be cultivated by the amateur speculator is like the knowledge of an expert card player, who understands both the rules of the game and the psychological traits of the expert players:

> When once this point [that the accumulation and distribution of stocks is orchestrated by pools of powerful investors] is clear in your mind all the mysteries will become plain to you. The game in Wall Street is a GAME OF HUMAN

NATURE. The pool generals are men who study crops and politics, both domestic and foreign, and legislation and finance. They know when the time is ripe to start a bull or a bear campaign, and when they can afford to end it. . . . The cards they use are both "marked and stacked," and they take no chances.[133]

Although amateurs cannot hope to go head-to-head with the market makers, readers are led to believe they can nevertheless use their home-grown knowledge of human nature to turn speculation into a game of skill rather than chance. In a similar vein, though promising a scientific approach, A. N. Ridgely's *Study and Science of Stock Speculation* (1901) reinforces views of the market as rigged—which the genre of financial advice itself had helped cultivate—by giving an insider's account of "Wall Street's Big Game," and "how it is played." Asserting that 90 percent of fluctuations are manipulated, Ridgely promises to tutor purchasers of his ten-cent pamphlet in the methods of the market manipulators so that they could profit by them. Readers were instructed to "Keep accurate charts and records of the most active stocks," so that they could use them "to learn what the insiders are doing." Price movements gave clear pointers to action for the informed chart-keeper: for example, it was dangerous to buy a stock on the third day of a rise, for "the market generally moves two or three days in one direction and then either rests or reacts." The price-tracking reader was then in a position to follow two "systems, or rather methods," which Ridgely named "Catching the Fluctuations" and "Limited Pyramiding." Profits could be made, but only through hard work: the reader who kept charts needed to "keep them *properly*, and learn how to read them."[134]

The scientific mode could also inform quite different approaches to the stock market. Price information was, of course, just one type of data available, and methods of analysis were beginning to be built on other sources. As we saw in the last chapter, the financial press had long sought to make economic data available to its readers, and in this period was beginning to interpret it more rigorously. Investment was a rational operation, they argued, if research was carried out on the economic fundamentals. Lamenting in 1903 the lack of a binding requirement for industrial corporations to make detailed, legally certified reports, *Pit and Post* saw its mission as compiling the necessary information to guide readers in their investment choices:

In the hope of discovering some useful principles underlying industrial stock values we have subjected to rough analysis a group of thirty of the most conspicuous industrials, and have tabulated them: First, in the order of their apparent merit, based on the most complete reports available; and, Second, in the order of their apparent merit judged by their prices on the exchange.[135]

Though interested in patterns of stock price movements that seemed to move through a logic of their own, the magazine encouraged readers to look beyond the daily fluctuations to consider instead the intrinsic economic conditions: "It is the purpose of this magazine to induce investors and traders to look below the surface, away down into the realm of causes so that they may detect in advance the developments which in a few years will give great profits to the far-seeing man." Its catechism was that "the Science of Values is the fundamental fabric on which all successful buying and selling must rest."[136] Indeed, this kind of approach prefigured later forms of "fundamental" analysis, but it rested as much on a blind faith in an underlying financial order as technical analysis.[137]

Yet, just as proto-technical methods of analysis often drew on more traditional approaches to the market, *Pit and Post*'s approach was often more intuitive than methodical. It recommended, for example, purchasing Colorado Fuel and Iron because Rockefeller had bought the firm, and the financial titan would ensure that it succeeded in the long term. At times it makes confident recommendations: "whether dealt in speculatively or investment-wise, these stocks [Chicago bank shares sold on the curb market] have been found to yield handsome returns on the brain and cash outlay involved, and they are so secure that scarcely any hazard is involved in handling them." It also frequently refers readers back to previous issues to "confirm" the accuracy of its predictions and recommendations. Yet it often hedges its bets, revealing that financial advice is often more like the ambiguous pronouncements of horoscopes, which retrospectively can be taken as confirming any interpretation:

> This immense shrinkage on top of twelve months of lowering values seems to us to be, for the moment, sufficient, and there should logically be a handsome upturn from these quotations. It would not surprise us to see $10 per share added to the best things, but we are frank to say that we are more confident of ultimately lower values than we are of even temporary enhancement of magnitude.[138]

Like the cliff-hanger of a serialized novel, the market predictions in these monthly magazines created a sense of financial suspense—sometimes confirmed, at other times thwarted—which the next issue would then masterfully (albeit spuriously) incorporate into an unfolding narrative, whatever the outcome. Like millennial prophecy cults, financial advice is never wrong: it is always able to reinterpret any temporary misfortune or seemingly contradictory evidence through the lens of its existing explanatory framework.

A seemingly more scientific method also influenced other approaches to investment. Though primitive ideas about portfolio diversification had long been in circulation in the shape of general references to not putting too many eggs into one basket, more sophisticated ideas on diversification as a strategy for minimizing exposure to risk began to appear.[139] An early example was *Beeton's Guide to Investing Money* (1870), which advised readers wanting to secure a high yet safe rate of interest from foreign loans to divide their investment five ways in, say, Turkish, Italian, Spanish, Egyptian, Guatemalan, or Argentine loans. "By dividing his capital in this way the investor reduces his risk to a minimum, as it is unlikely all these countries should stop paying their interest, although it is not unlikely that any one might do so."[140] The proliferation of investment trusts in Britain after the establishment of the Foreign and Colonial Government Trust in 1868 also helped to disseminate the principle of spreading risk.[141] Some guides praised trusts as good investments particularly for small investors: they "do very completely what each individual investor tries to do imperfectly for himself," argued George Bartrick-Baker, for example.[142]

By the 1890s, diversification was taking more complex forms. Duncan's of London stressed the importance of "distributing capital in a scientific manner over various investments." Their recommended method of doing this was to divide the available capital in four quarters. The first could be locked up in "some absolutely safe and permanent security," to pay around 3 percent. The second quarter was the "Reserve or Contingent Liability Capital," for use in emergencies, to be placed in convertible 3 percent securities, such as consols or railway debentures. The other half could be used for speculative purposes: of this, the third quarter was for "permanent speculation," where the capital was not entirely secure but the interest was anticipated to be large. The final quarter was to be used for "temporary speculation"—finding opportunities to benefit from short-term fluctuations in prices. This method meant that you could never lose everything—one-half of your capital was entirely safe, while the other was "very nearly safe, because being used in so many different channels it is hardly likely that they will all fail." By acting in this way, individual investors could emulate banks and finance houses, thus creating a "true system of prudent investment."[143] Henry Lowenfeld, the main mover behind Duncan's, developed these ideas further at the Investment Registry, which advertised itself as "the largest combine of private investors in the world."[144] Writing during a prolonged lull in the market, Lowenfeld argued that dividing investments along geographical lines allowed investors both to conquer risk and maximize returns. "The recent years of depression have taught many important lessons . . . the application of which will protect the investor, who remodels his investment list in a scientific fashion, from the risk of future loss."[145] Learning the correct method was a serious undertaking, however, which involved buying the Investment Registry's numerous other publications and subscribing to its monthly journal, the *Financial Review of Reviews*. Together, these represented "A Complete Outfit for Investors."[146] Thus, proponents of scientific methods were at once genuinely interested in developing more sophisticated approaches to the stock market and also very much alive to the financial opportunities that marketing these approaches to wide audiences presented.[147]

Mastering the Market

If the "scientific turn" helped to legitimize speculation, it also helped to marginalize women, on the grounds that they were not sufficiently rational for the market. The financial advice of this phase remained as heavily gendered as it had been in earlier periods, with perhaps even more brash assertions of women's shortcomings as investors. The Wall Street memoirs of William Fowler and Henry Clews, for example, have much to say on the "dowagers and damsels" who "talk of little but the stock market," but who "do not seem to have the mental qualities required to take in the varied points of the situation upon which success in speculation depends." They are, "by nature, parasites as speculators," too "impulsive and impressionable," and, without a man to advise them, "they are like a ship at sea in a heavy gale without compass, anchor or rudder."[148] In a similar vein, the bucket shop promoter John B. McKenzie's *Bulls and Bears of Wall Street* declared that "women make poor speculators. Without the assistance of a man a woman in Wall Street is like a ship without a rudder. . . . With all due respect to the modern woman and her ability in the world of commerce, in addition to being too impulsive and impressionable, she does not possess the mental equipment of her brothers."[149] The implicit message of such works, however, was not that women must never engage in stock market investment but that, if they were to do so, they would need the "assistance of a man," which the advice manual offered to supply in proxy form.

In a variety of cultural forms—from financial journalism to investment advice books and from melodramatic fiction to stockbroker memoirs— women were portrayed as marginal figures in the market. They were deemed to be ignorant of how finance worked, lacking the requisite rationality, and were believed to be by nature alternately naive and vulnerable or impulsive and emotionally unstable. But at other times, women were eulogized as the bastions of domestic sanctity and moral purity, providing a domestic gravitational force that could counter the reckless speculative habits of their husbands.[150] According to the authors—both male and female—of this popular financial literature, these innate qualities made women especially vulnerable to fraud. The specter of female victimization was conjured up by conservatives and progressives alike. On the one hand, stock market apologists argued that the world of finance should be self-regulating, with investment left to professionals rather than the amateurs who were blamed for causing market instability. On the other, progressives, including (in the United States especially) those women who embraced the social gospel movement, favored government regulation of the stock market precisely to protect the weak and vulnerable, the widows and orphans of popular imagination. Even though by the end of the nineteenth century many writers had begun to view the City of London and Wall Street not as dens of thieves and gamblers but as necessary parts of the engine of national economic success, the advice for women in the prescriptive literature remained moralistic and patronizing: the price for succeeding in this man's world would involve becoming "unsexed."

It was thus a common trope in both the advice manuals and financial fiction of the period that women were not merely ill suited to speculation but cut a ridiculous figure if they tried to master the market. The humorous stories create an atmosphere of jocular, manly camaraderie, as the reader is invited to laugh with the (male) narrator at a woman's folly. Lefèvre's short story "A Woman and Her Bonds," for example, tells the tale of a widow who repeatedly visits her friend and broker every time she reads in the paper that the price of her modest investment has fluctuated.[151] Eventually, to assuage her anxiety, the broker sells her bonds, only to be confronted by the widow when their value has suddenly soared. She insists that he sell the bonds back to her at their original low price, and the reader is invited to sympathize with the resolutely reasonable broker's frustration at the irrationality of the widow, who is presented as simultaneously vulnerable, ignorant, and greedy. In a similar fashion, in *The Sayings of Rufus Hatch* (a miscellany of the wisdom of a supposed Wall Street operator, penned by the journalist Amos Cummings), the entry "Uncle Rufus's Virtuous Advice to a Lady Contemplating Speculation in Wall Street" tells the lengthy story of a well-to-do daughter of a farmer who writes to "Uncle Rufus" for advice on speculation:

> You see I favor buying and holding on some time in hopes of making a large sum, but if you think it better to buy and sell often, why, I rely on your good judgment and experience. If you think there is but little chance of my making and more chance of my losing, I trust you will candidly write me so. For this reason I have written you, thinking that knowing of me and how I am situated you would perhaps be so kind as to take an interest in investing for me carefully, different than the firm would on receiving a short business note. If you invest for me, would it not be best for you to sell any time, if necessary, without first advising me, and so losing precious time? Then, if that same stock seemed about to rise, you could immediately invest again.[152]

The moral of the anecdote is that, for women investors, a little knowledge is a dangerous thing: the farmer's daughter claims to be placing all her trust in the famous financial expert, but at the same time insists that he speculate for her. The advice from "Uncle Rufus" is to brush her off, claiming that she has mistaken him for a different broker, and that she should put her money safely into bonds.

Although popular financial writing from the period thus repeatedly tried to portray women as unsuited to finance, the reality was somewhat different. With the changing legal status of married women's property, increasing numbers of women did have capital to invest, and the stock market was a more likely venue than becoming a partner in a business venture.[153] However, the reality of women's lives as investors in this period remains underexplored. George Robb's *Ladies of the Ticker* manages to shed some light on "women's investment choices, their levels of expertise, their sources of information, and the nature of their interactions with financial agents."[154] Robb demonstrates that the well-to-do female clients of two stockbroking firms in the United States—Morton, Bliss & Co. (in the 1870s and 1880s) and George P. Butler & Brother (in the early 1900s)—were active as investors, making informed decisions about their portfolios. Women constituted approximately a quarter of each firm's clients. They tended to be more cautious than their male counterparts, following conventional wisdom that bonds with their reliable payment of interest were more appropriate for women than the supposedly more volatile world of shares. Women were also more likely to maintain diverse portfolios rather than engage in endless rapid speculations like their male counterparts. The correspondence with their brokers also shows that these women were reasonably well-informed and thoughtful investors, unlike the figures in the popular imagination. Furthermore, women (more so in the United Kingdom than the United States, in part explained by geography) were often active investors, attending and speaking at shareholder meetings.[155]

Despite the late nineteenth-century upsurge in popular financial advice writing, very little addressed women investors. This was even true of some of the content appearing in women's periodicals. For example, "Buying a House without Cash" in the *Ladies' Home Journal* advises that investing in the stock market is indeed a viable way to achieving the capital to buy a house, but the piece is addressed to men, and only mentions women in parentheses: "I will consider, by way of illustration, that a man (or woman) wants to buy or build a house."[156] At best, magazine articles tended to offer general advice on the ways that the "New Woman" from the 1890s onward might begin to make her own money (e.g., through employment in a shop or by giving language classes) or use judicious means to make the little money she had go further (e.g., by better management of the household budget).[157] When it addressed women and stock market investment, it did little to provide useful information and instead peddled clichés and ridicule.[158] Such articles tended to argue that because women could not become members of the exchanges, they were more likely to hold an exaggerated sense of the power of inside information. Women wanted sure returns, the advice writers insisted, because they had limited capacity to assume risk.

Nevertheless, some strands of financial advice writing did try to cultivate a distinctive "feminine" culture of financial investment, no doubt with an eye to developing a new market for their advice. We can detect, for example, the beginnings of an ethical investment literature in this period (especially in Britain), in which women were imagined to play an important role. In the pamphlet *Where Does Your Interest Come From? A Word to Lady Investors* (1886), the progressive writer Caroline Haddon condemned "the airy way in which women habitually ignore all the responsibility attached to the source from which they draw their wealth." Combining the traditional view of investment—that when you bought shares in a company, "you have become virtually a partner in that Company" — with a strong belief in the growing public role of women, she argued that female shareholders should use their influence within the company to ensure that it behaved responsibly, particularly to its workers: "its acts are your acts; its crimes, its cruelties are on your head." She told her female reader that, when trusting a man to advise her on investing her money, she should ask him not only "Is it *safe*?" but also "Is it *rightly* used?" — even if this meant accepting a lower rate of interest. Yet investors who wanted to invest responsibly had few guides. "Day after day our breakfast tables are strewn with prospectuses of new companies, and with periodicals that offer themselves as safe guides in the intricacies of the stock and share markets." None of these advised on ethical investments, Haddon complained. Yet responsible investors did have a growing number of options, particularly the cooperative ventures discussed in the *Co-operative News* and the philanthropic housing schemes developed by Octavia Hill.[159]

Indeed, women were heavily involved in profit-making housing programs on both sides of the Atlantic, not only as investors but also as rent-collectors who doubled as "friendly visitors" giving advice to tenants. Such schemes tried to harness the profit principle and the corporate form to charitable ends, offering investors dividends capped at 5 percent (in Britain) and 7 percent (in the United States).[160] Though driven by charitable impulses, such schemes were examples of what Maltby and Rutterford have termed "the financialization of philanthropy" in the later nineteenth century, where potential beneficiaries were assessed exactly like any other investment opportunity. "It was individual *return*, not individual *need*, that would decide the outcome when they appealed for help."[161] Hill's ruthless application of business principles enabled her to keep up the 5 percent dividends to her investors, unlike many earlier such schemes which had seen disappointing yields. But this came at the cost — so her critics claimed — of imposing an unreasonable degree of moral and financial discipline on her tenants.[162] Yet Hill's success was a high-profile example of how, despite the assumptions embodied in much popular financial advice, women were well able to comprehend and apply scientific principles to the management of money.

The focus on the sovereignty of the self also meant that these writings (especially in the United States) appealed implicitly to a fantasy of white manhood.[163] In this period, the genre of popular financial advice rarely, if ever, directly addressed the issue of race, even though the question of black citizenship through economic self-determination was crucial to the postbellum era. For example, white philanthropists and financiers founded the Freedman's Savings Bank in the aftermath of the Civil War in the hope that it would turn former slaves into (implicitly masculine) sovereign citizens through the discipline of saving and the assumption of risk for oneself. The initial charter for the Freedman's Bank in 1865 had mandated that the funds could only be invested in comparatively safe government securities, and that the bank's customers should be questioned about any withdrawals to ensure that they were to be used for worthy purposes. In 1870, however, Congress approved a change in the bank's charter to allow it to invest in railroad shares, real estate, and other speculative ventures. In a corrupt fashion, much of the bank's business was funneled through the Jay Cooke & Co. brokerage firm, and, with the spectacular crash of Cooke in 1873, the bank failed in 1874. As the historian Jonathan Levy has argued, the failure of the Freedman's Bank highlighted the way that the prospect of individual freedom and self-ownership for African Americans had become entangled with the systemic risk of the national financial system that was beyond the control of any individual. However, Shenette Garrett-Scott has shown that the bank's customers—including women—were not merely the passive victims of white paternalism and financial fraud but were using their savings to help take control of their lives (coupled with the fact that the white-controlled bank played a less significant role in black women's lives than collective savings vehicles through churches and other community-organized societies).[164] Despite the intrusive checks on withdrawals, there is also evidence that some customers were using their saved funds to invest in new businesses and engage in market speculation.[165]

In a similar vein, Ann Fabian, for example, has documented how African Americans used "dream books"—compendiums of dream interpretations that linked the visions to particular numbers—to guide their play in the policy numbers game, creating a form of vernacular financial knowledge of risk and gain. At the surface level these dream books are very different from the genre of investment advice, but they served a parallel function of providing a mechanism for laypeople to manage financial uncertainty. Indeed, they functioned as a "negative analogue" for supposedly more respectable financial advice which claimed that it was not mere gambling, but at the end of the day they were both divinatory systems for rationalizing the hazards of fortune. Fabian asks: "Why did people bet on numbers in spite of the enormous odds against them? Why, in effect, did they waste their money? Why did they defy tremendous cultural pressure to save and accumulate?" Her answer is that the numbers game provided a utopian, antirationalist revolt against the dominant ideology of economic discipline, patient accumulation, thrift, and self-help for people who were victims of a rigged system: "Those who ventured had chosen quick gain over delayed savings, waste over accumulation, idleness over work or leisure, and superstitious interpretation over calculation."[166] As we have seen, that was often the very same appeal made by investment advice manuals. In general, however, racial difference was conspicuously absent in much investment advice literature of the period, and the role of nonwhites remains under-researched in histories of stock market participation.

Against the Crowd

In most financial writing, women and nonwhites were rhetorically disbarred from the stock market by the focus on scientific investment; they were also excluded by the ubiquitous language of masculine, sovereign individualism deployed by the guides. The implied reader of these volumes is often the ambitious white male clerk for whom the promise of getting rich quick was particularly alluring, and for whom the fear of slavishly following others weighed heavily.[167] Manly self-reliance was the prescription: "It is well to learn to form one's own opinion, and to trust to one's own judgment. The man who shrinks from entering the water will never learn to swim," exhorted one manual.[168] The language of financial advice invoked independent, autonomous investors who, once they had committed their money, "ought to know why they have invested, accepting no man's verdict but their own"—excepting, of course, the verdict of the very work of financial advice they were reading.[169] It followed that the independent operator was best advised to tune out what others were doing and saying (with the usual irony that if everyone bought the advice writer's book, then they would all be following the same star). One financial journalist, for example, advised his readers to "avoid as much as possible following the fashion of the hour in the investment of money. . . . To buy what everybody is running after is always to buy dear." It was far better, he advised, to scour the lists of securities for "obscure or neglected stocks" which might be undervalued and represented far better value.[170] Even the few guides written for women could suggest developing a contrarian sensibility. The author of *Counsel to Ladies*, for instance, told readers: "Never follow the crowd in either buying or selling. When the public is sanguine and expecting still higher prices, it may be wise to sell."[171]

Nevertheless, the ability to resist the crowd was usually coded as a masculine trait, though not one that was possessed by all men. Arthur Crump, whose manual was published in both Britain and the United States, provided a thorough examination of the temperament and mentality supposedly required to be a successful operator. "It is necessary," he wrote,

> that a speculator should possess a coolness that is not affected by the excitement into which others are thrown by unexpected events; that he should cultivate the art of concealing the dissatisfaction felt on sustaining a loss, which is read at once in the face of a nervous or excitable man; and that he should have the power of calling forth emotions which are the opposite of those commonly manifested under given circumstances.[172]

According to Crump and other financial advice writers, most haphazard speculators were entirely unsystematic in their approach, overly excited by gains, shaken by losses, and too likely to be swayed by others. Successful speculators, by contrast, were able to "emancipate" themselves from the "frailty of human nature" by laying down fixed principles for behavior and sticking with them. Moreover, complete ruthlessness was a prerequisite quality for the effective speculator: such a person must have "a concrete hardness of indifference" which would allow him "to start a Juggernaut, and drive it over the crowd, if thereby he can do it profitably." These depictions of the speculator posited him as an individual standing against the crowd, a fantasy of uniqueness repeatedly sold in mass commercial form in the guides. "He must systematically not only disregard the interest of other people," Crump insisted, "but deliberately calculate upon the weaknesses of human nature which characterize the crowd, in order to work upon them for his own ends."[173] The successful speculator owed loyalty to no one but himself. In a passage titled "The Cold-Blooded Speculator," another market veteran confessed, "Yes, I have made money out of my country's blood. I beared Consols as would any alien amongst us."[174]

Crump was skeptical about the potential for many people to cultivate these qualities. But other manuals were more positive that amateurs could train themselves to speculate successfully. They thus embodied the central promise of the self-improvement literature that was flourishing at this time: that following the right prescription would transform the reader.[175] That vacillating and ignorant outsiders would be turned into confident and self-reliant operators was suggested by a passage that appeared almost verbatim in the booklets of both Gregory & Co. and Haight & Freese, the leading bucket shops in Britain and the United States respectively: "when so instructed upon every detail (which, before perusal of our work, will have appeared to him like mystery), the general reader will be in a position to operate with confidence upon his own judgment."[176] Yet this highlighted the contradiction that lay at the heart of such guides, which had them constantly walking a fine line between insisting that readers develop independent judgment and issuing endless series of prescriptions that had to be closely followed before the hapless lamb could metamorphose into a Wall Street wolf. Thus, although readers were taught to be skeptical about other sources of expertise, this did not extend to the guide itself, whose authority was repeatedly emphasized. Van Riper even went so far as to dub his rules to investors "The Ten Commandments."[177] Advice manuals had once been intended as complementary to professional advice; now they sought to usurp that role, positioning themselves as the only thing readers needed to fulfill their potential as successful speculators.

Rationality, reason, and decisiveness were the watchwords of this literature. One author warned against being overly hasty in making investments: "always have a good reason for buying or selling . . . a reason which will bear being written down on paper."[178] Once you had made up your mind, you should stick with the decision rather than wavering: "Do not act contrary to your judgment, after reasoning a matter out."[179] Applying such prescriptions, however, was not necessarily a simple matter: in what circumstances should you trust your instincts, and when was reason a better guide? How easy was it to avoid both hesitation and rashness? And at what point did decisiveness become stubbornness? But this was more a problem for the reader than the author, for failures could be blamed not on the advice in the book but on the reader for not internalizing it properly. Indeed, this literature was full of reminders about the hard work involved in self-mastery. "The way to success," advised Young, is "through the medium of concentration," and was only "for those who have sufficient will power to wait for opportunities and then take advantage of them."[180] A "Cosmopolitan Speculator" agreed: "intensity of concentration . . . alone can inspire the second-sight that you need for quick and right decision."[181] Here too, they had something in common with other genres of self-improvement. Samuel Smiles denied in later editions of *Self-Help* that his book was a guide to material success, arguing instead that the habits it sought to inculcate were the whole point. Results were less important than "the aim and the effort, the patience, the courage, and the endeavour" involved in pursuing them.[182] As one historian of Smiles puts it, *Self-Help* can therefore be seen as "a Romantic work, in that the activity and struggle of the individual was all."[183] Similarly, though many of them promised to help their readers get rich quick, what stock market guides actually offered was more complex, a fantasy of self-realization in which the (implicitly white male) individual became master of his own destiny. Such a message had particular resonance for many in *fin de siècle* Britain and America at a time when the rise of mass culture and collectivist politics threatened to submerge the individual.

The implied fear in these guides is not so much the failure of losing money as losing control of oneself. The mastery of money was synonymous with the mastery of self, which was only possible if emotions were kept firmly in check. Investment, Lowenfeld told his readers, was "a business, like any other, from which sentiment, obstinacy, and individual fancies should be excluded."[184] The financial journalist Richard Wyckoff emphasized in 1910 that, alongside "nerve to stand a series of losses" and "persistence to keep him at the work during adverse periods," the ideal trader requires "self-control to avoid overtrading and a phlegmatic disposition to ballast and balance him at all times."[185] In these texts—some of which drew on the new development of crowd theory—there are copious warnings about the unmanning, hystericizing influence of financial contagion during a panic.[186] However, both fictional and nonfictional accounts of strong-willed speculators often suggested that they become so attuned to the rhythms of the market that they begin to merge with it.[187] The tape reader, Wyckoff insisted, is so ruthlessly in control of his emotions that he "evolves himself into an automaton which takes note of a situation, weighs it, decides upon a course and gives an order." He elaborates further on the "proper mental equipment" required by this new breed of scientific speculator, above all "the power to drill himself into the right mental attitude; to stifle his emotion, fear, anxiety, elation, recklessness, to train his mind into obedience so that it recognizes but one master—the tape."[188] In this way the speculator's independence begins to erode as he becomes an "automaton," subservient to the spectral, quasi-divine power of the ticker tape.

In the self-consciously modern financial advice literature from the first decade of the twentieth century, the professed aim is not simply to gain inside information through personal connections with the powerful cliques supposedly pulling the strings of the market, nor to follow a sure-fire system, nor even to inculcate an attitude of steely self-reliance. Instead, these publications insist that you must also turn yourself into a recording machine, much like the ticker itself. The goal is to eliminate emotion and personality, and thus become totally in tune with the mechanical rhythm of the market. Advice manuals and Wall Street fiction alike turned repeatedly to a climactic scene in which the heroic speculator is intensely reading his own fate — and, by extension, the fate of the nation — on the symbols coming over the ticker tape. The trancelike reading of the ticker tape by these "Napoleons of finance" allows them to possess the secrets of the market, but they in turn are possessed by its seemingly unfathomable, inhuman — and also implicitly feminizing — forces. A magazine profile of the speculator James R. Keene, for example, characterizes him as the "high priest of the ticker," whose scrutiny of the tape is "so intense that he appeared to be in a trance while mental processes were being worked out."[189] If these guides present speculation as modern, technical, and objective, they also describe it in terms of intuition, supernatural possession, and something approaching mystical divination.

*   *   *

The history of stock market advice in this period is riven with tensions and contradictions. Those who took charge of educating the public in stock exchange matters were mostly not members of these exchanges but outsiders working in competition with them. Though the era was full of muckraking exposés of the stock market, these acted as much as enticements to speculation as deterrents. As the market became ever larger and more abstract, those offering financial services adopted an increasingly personal appeal to investors. Though a growing number of authors claimed to be documenting the "science" of investment, this was a science characterized by intuitive, superstitious, and even magical thinking. Despite an increasingly aggressive tendency in advice manuals to define the ideal investor as male, in reality women were becoming a more active, visible, and confident part of the market. Although explicit recognition of racial difference is almost entirely absent in these works, the assumptions they make about the financial subject are often racially coded. And though writers urged the necessity of ruthlessly driving emotion out of business, many were clearly drawn to the stock market precisely because of the emotional thrills offered by speculation.[190]

Despite these many dissonances, one thing that united the financial advice of this period was the conviction that the stock market was legible, that its movements were predictable, and that they would respond to the right kind of analysis. As such, despite their many differences, these works can all be seen as strategies for coping with the growing power and the seeming arbitrariness of the market. As Audrey Jaffe puts it, such writing "constitutes a collective denial of the possibility that the market may conform to no decipherable logic and be subject to no controlling authority: that there may be no narrative at all in the stock-market graph."[191] It became almost a matter of faith for some authors to imbue the stock market with a logic, a narrative, and, above all, a comforting sense of meaning: convincing readers of this was central to the project of getting them invested.

The search for meaning led writers to draw very different conclusions. Some insisted that the market was controlled by a few financial titans, but—with a good feel for human nature—knowledge of the telltale signs of market manipulation could be turned to the advantage of the canny amateur speculator. Others insisted that the impersonal numbers-driven logic of the stock market transcended the power of any individual to control it. One branch insisted that the market was best approached through analysis of the underlying economic fundamentals, while a newly professionalizing cadre of analysts began to argue that there was a hidden pattern to stock market movements that could be uncovered by the emerging discipline of technical analysis. In many cases, however, the writers hedged their bets by offering a pragmatic smattering of all kinds of advice. As the next chapter shows, in the first decades of the twentieth century financial writing adopted more doctrinaire positions. Yet the turn to more "scientific" forms of financial knowledge never fully escaped their association with folk and occult ways of knowing. Popular guides to Wall Street increasingly presented the stock market as a supernatural realm as much as one governed by the laws of nature.

Critically, much of the advice literature of these years was not simply encouraging new ways of seeing the stock market, it was also fostering fresh ways of understanding the self. This point is easy to miss, given that the outward appeal of the genre was squarely to the pocket. Yet stock market advice further converged with other forms of self-improvement writing to promise not just wealth but also personal transformation, offering its readers a fantasy of the speculator as self-reliant and ruthless risk-taker, a fantasy that made contentious assumptions about gender and race. The idealized portrait of the heroic market player was, for many, a comforting illusion. As the market for stocks and shares grew and became ever more complex, and as the world of work became increasingly anonymous and disempowering, financial advice held out the fantasy of empowering the individual investor or speculator, peddling a dream of individual, white, masculine agency. This view of the investor as master of his own fate had important implications. It implied that market regulation was unnecessary because the informed individual was well equipped to protect himself: indeed, a completely fair market might cease to provide profitable edges for the astute operator.[192] It also entailed a particular way of viewing other people—as members the herd-like "crowd" from whose bovine stupidity the savvy speculator would benefit—which may have influenced other social interactions but was central to the "value proposition" of an author trying to sell instructional manuals of financial advice.[193] And in it we also detect the seeds of the financial responsibilization of the individual, the logic of which was to be worked through after the Second World War.

CHAPTER FOUR

Chartists and Fundamentalists (1910–1950)

In the spring of 1922, a young man leaves his Midwest home for New York to learn the bond business, since everybody he knows is doing the same. He buys "a dozen volumes on banking and credit and investment securities," which stand on his shelf "in red and gold like new money from the mint, promising to unfold the shining secrets that only Midas and Morgan and Mæcenas knew"; each evening he devotes a "conscientious hour" to "stud[ying] investments and securities." These volumes convey a promise to the twenty-nine-year-old Nick Carraway that the investment genre as a whole sought to communicate to his generation, and to older Americans too: that between the covers of an investment handbook might be found privileged knowledge providing a route to riches, and that, in the 1920s, the moment had arrived to access such knowledge and put it into action. In committing himself to his reading regime, Nick visualizes and seeks to realize a better, more informed, and wealthier version of himself. The narrator of the defining novel of Jazz Age America intuits that to partake of the era's rewards he must seek out veiled information concerning the workings of the financial system: this was a message that investment advice writers were at pains to promulgate in the period. It is fitting that F. Scott Fitzgerald should depict his character working through a stack of investment guides in order to gain enhanced insight into the operation of the securities markets, since such books insistently promoted themselves as the indispensable primers for trying one's hand on Wall Street. In this, as in so many ways, *The Great Gatsby*, published in 1925, is a signal text of its era. It is telling, too, that the novel's protagonist, Jay Gatsby, fantasizes about reinventing himself from plain old James Gatz via a Benjamin

Franklin–style self-improvement regime.[1] As we'll see, the connections between investment advice writing and the culture of self-help and personal transformation became all the stronger in this period.

This chapter places investment advice texts of the "Gatsby decade" within the wider evolution of the genre, providing an account that extends from just prior to the First World War to the middle of the twentieth century. It focuses on the United States while also considering parallel developments in the United Kingdom. The outbreak of the Great War was a turning point for popular participation in financial markets, drawing unprecedented numbers first of Britons, and later of Americans, into securities investment via the issuing of government war loans. In the United States, in particular, the twenty-year era culminating in the Wall Street crash of 1929 saw ownership of common stocks increase sharply. The US government's successful promotion of Liberty Bonds during the war stimulated citizens' appetite for financial investment, but for the best part of a decade this enthusiasm only moderately spilled over into participation in the stock market: following the war, bonds (both government and corporate) remained the preferred vehicles for most amateur investors, being widely considered the conservative, reliable alternative to stocks, which were seen as inherently speculative and the preserve only of risk-taking "operators."[2] As we saw in the previous chapter, financial authors' writing for a mass market during the late nineteenth and early twentieth centuries placed Wall Street at the center of popular culture: no longer a remote and shadowy place, it was read about, discussed, and debated by Americans of varying social and geographical positions. It was only in the 1920s, however, that this cultural prominence translated into something approaching a "democratization" of actual share ownership. The (relative) prevalence of stock market investment evident by 1929 was to a very large extent a product of the Roaring Twenties themselves, and especially of the latter half of the decade, fueled (as we'll see) by a new consensus that common stocks were in fact superior instruments to bonds—even for the nonexpert investor.

Throughout the period, though, laypeople keen to try their luck at Wall Street speculation were amply catered to by an array of investment advice guides, which proliferated alongside the expansion of public involvement in the stock market during the 1920s—and helped to promote it. In the post–World War I era, the field of investment advice literature was defined by an increasingly entrenched standoff between the authors and publishers of technical analysis–based guides—which urged readers to attend to indicators in financial prices themselves—and those touting forms of "fundamental" analysis geared toward the underlying conditions of individual companies or the economy at large. The Great Crash of October 1929, however, dealt a devastating blow to the field of investment advice as a whole. The crash both undermined writers' claims to privileged professional insight into the future direction of the market and—at a stroke—shrank the potential readership for guidebooks advising on the buying and selling of stocks, since, in the Depression years, far fewer Americans had the means or inclination to invest, their worst fears about the risky nature of Wall Street having been realized. The trauma of the crash was registered especially acutely by investment advice writers, who had seen their professional reputations tarnished and their business models damaged, as well as—in many cases—their own stock holdings wiped out.

The challenge for investment advice writing in the 1930s and 1940s was to recover from the harrowing and ignominious experience of the crash. The events of October 1929 vastly magnified a perennial problem for investment advice writers: how to account for the fact that the market often exhibits behaviors—from minor spikes or dips to full-blown booms or panics—that writers' methods and predictions demonstrably fail to factor in. We thus approach the Great Crash as a case study via which to foreground how writers put their rhetorical resources to work to attempt to re-legitimize their field in the wake of market events that negatively impacted their credibility. Though the crash presented major challenges for both technical and fundamental analysts, the post-crash period was in fact the heyday for both forms, as authors in each tradition invoked the lessons of 1929 in order to render their fields increasingly sophisticated, systematic, and codified. By midcentury, both camps would have their own canonized textbooks and established (and sharply distinct) philosophical outlooks on the worlds of investment and speculation. By the end of the period, though, neither tradition had resolved certain basic conceptual and practical challenges to its validity. These challenges would leave the two established forms of investment advice vulnerable to the more theoretically refined approaches to finance emanating from academic economics and business departments from the 1950s onward.

Britain vs. the United States

The first half of the twentieth century saw the United States decisively outstrip the United Kingdom as the financial advice genre's hub, both in terms of the sheer abundance of titles produced and in terms of the innovativeness and distinctiveness of the guidance offered. As we've seen, there has always been an audience for investment advice writing, even among readers with little or no actual involvement in or connection to the stock market. But we also know that readers are more likely to consume such books if they are investors themselves, or if they are acquainted with people who are. The more rapid expansion of investment writing in the United States in this period can thus be attributed to a widening gap between shareholder numbers in the United States and the United Kingdom, which meant that the British market for advice writing became gradually smaller by comparison. Additionally, certain peculiarities of the British capital markets made them unconducive to the proliferation of new technical forecasting methods seen across the Atlantic. However, one particular preoccupation remained markedly pronounced in British investment guides: the importance of foreign investments and the status of Britain as an imperial power with both political and financial dominion over large parts of the world.

As Janette Rutterford and Dimitris Sotiropoulos have shown, prior to World War I stock market investment was markedly more "democratized" in the United Kingdom than in the United States. While the number of shareholders in each nation was roughly equal in absolute terms—at probably a little over 1 million—this figure constituted 2.4 percent of Britons as compared to a mere 1 percent of the US population.[3] British stockowners, moreover, tended more closely to resemble the archetypal investor of "small or moderate means"[4] in having, on average, smaller but more widely spread holdings than their American counterparts.[5] Both countries ran successful bond campaigns during the Great War, which significantly increased levels of ownership of financial securities. In Britain, the three major issues of war loans attracted over 13 million subscribers.[6] While there is some evidence that this novel experience stimulated British interest in securities investment more generally, it had nothing like the effect on wider financial activity of the US Liberty Loans.[7]

British markets saw sustained bursts of activity in new issues in the years immediately following the war and again in the mid to late 1920s. The latter phase mirrored (albeit on a more modest scale) the Roaring Twenties US bull market and culminated in the so-called Dirt Track Boom[8] of 1928–29, symbolized by the criminally overextended London stock promoter Clarence Hatry, whose downfall in September 1929 was a precipitating factor in the Great Crash that struck Wall Street a month later. The crash was less severe in the United Kingdom than in the United

States, however, with the London Stock Exchange experiencing a 16 percent fall in the months following the initial collapse, while the New York Stock Exchange saw prices tumble 40 percent.[9] The British market also recovered more quickly: the LSE returned to pre-1929 levels in 1934, whereas the NYSE would not do so until 1954, and the number and value of new public offerings in the United Kingdom in the mid-1930s were similar to those of the late 1920s.[10] Yet despite phases of intense stock market activity in the United Kingdom, and despite the British market enjoying a relatively soft landing after 1929, the pool of British investors never significantly expanded in the manner seen in the United States in this period. In 1926, when the second postwar new issue boom was well underway, UK shareholder numbers were estimated at 1.3 million[11]—only marginally higher than a best estimate of prewar levels—and when the first formal study of British popular investment was undertaken in 1949, using 1941 registers, it arrived at a figure of 1.25 million shareholders or 2.6 percent of the population, levels "surprisingly similar to more ad hoc estimates made much earlier in the century." Rutterford and Sotiropoulos attribute this plateauing of stock market participation to the particular political trajectories of the United Kingdom in the post–World War I period: "the relative stagnation of UK shareholder numbers after 1914 can be explained by financial repression of government in terms of high taxation on investment income, capital and dividend controls, expropriation, and nationalization."[12] The divergence between the United Kingdom and the United States over taxation was especially significant: the 1920 US Supreme Court declaration "that stock dividends did not qualify as income under the Sixteenth Amendment" made stocks markedly "more attractive," as Phillip G. Payne notes. Also significant was the decision of brokerages and the London Stock Exchange not to transfer the aggressive marketing tactics used to sell war loans to the postwar promotion of stock investment (as their counterparts in the United States did).[13]

The most obvious reason why the United Kingdom did not see writers armed with novel techniques pouring into the investment advice genre in the post–World War I decades, then, was that investor numbers simply did not grow sufficiently to attract the profusion of volumes that hit the market in the United States: in short, among Britons "share investment remained the domain of the privileged few."[14] There were also, though, aspects of how British stock trading was reported and administered that discouraged the development of innovative methods of investment analysis of the kind that swelled the field in the United States. As we saw in the last chapter, the advent of the stock ticker was key to the growth of popular interest in the stock market in the late nineteenth century. The ticker was introduced to the London Stock Exchange in 1872 (only five years after its appearance in New York).[15] But well into the twentieth century, British tickers carried considerably less information than was customary in the United States. As one leading American author of investment advice complained in a stock market guidebook published in 1917: "The London stock tickers do not attempt to print the price of each sale nor the quantity sold. They merely give at intervals the 'bid and asked' quotations on each stock. The American stock trader in London feels as though he had no information about the market worth mentioning with only these meager figures to go upon."[16] "The Stock Exchange ... hardly encouraged popular capitalism," David Kynaston observes in his history of the City of London, noting that when, in 1923, the BBC asked for permission to broadcast prices, the request was only finally granted three years later "with the utmost reluctance," and the "concession [was] rendered almost useless by the stipulation that no prices were to be broadcast prior to 7 pm, long after the end of trading."[17] This resistance to transparency on the part of the London Stock Exchange was symptomatic of a culture in which financial information was something to which only "insiders" were entitled to have access. Insiderdom in the City of London was of course closely correlated with upper- or upper-middle-class status in an age when what P. J. Cain and A. G. Hopkins call British "gentlemanly capitalism" still held sway.[18]

The fine-grained, real-time price and volume data widely disseminated in the United States, and on the basis of which American advice writers developed an array of distinctive techniques for detecting market patterns and indicators, were thus more difficult to access in the United Kingdom (for one American technical analyst or "chartist," it was a crucial fact that "price fluctuations compiled from newspaper openings, highs, lows, and closes, are not nearly as dependable as the information garnered directly from the tape," since "a great number of full point changes may be missed").[19] In part because only those actually on the floor of the exchange had access to the market's current technical conditions, few British stockbrokers, other City professionals, financial journalists, or academics—the typical authors of advice guides—were involved in investment analysis in the formal sense in which that field was being defined and codified by writers and practitioners in the United States. A minority of brokers did set up research departments in the interwar period, and the Exchange Telegraph Company, the firm which ran the ticker in the United Kingdom, produced cards from the early 1920s that carried basic data on individual firms; brokers who subscribed to this service could use these cards when advising on investments or send them on to clients. Most members of the Stock Exchange, however, simply relied on access to the circulation of tips, gossip, rumors, and what we would now call inside information, rather than building on the methods of either technical or fundamental analysis, as developed by writers across the Atlantic in this period. Insider dealing only assumed a clear social stigma, and began to carry legal penalties, in the United Kingdom in the 1960s (in the United States, by contrast, anti-insider dealing legislation was first introduced in the 1930s). In Britain in the early decades of the twentieth century, "the reputation of many brokers stood or fell by their ability, on the basis of inside information, to provide their chosen clients with profitable tips." Thus "from a broker's point of view . . . there seemed little point in spending money on analyz-ing the form—even if one had the ability or inclination to do so—when instead it was possible, for the most favored brokers anyway, to go straight to the horse's mouth."[20] Tight restrictions on the wider public's access to trading data went hand in hand, then, with what now looks like a remark-able tolerance for the free circulation of information within a select group of individuals. These individuals—though they may rarely if ever have set foot physically on the floor of the Exchange—were nonetheless construed as market insiders according to the prevailing conceptual boundaries of the day.[21]

While popular investment advice writing always implicitly carries the appeal of access to privileged knowledge, a central precept of the genre as it developed in the early twentieth century was that it was unnecessary— and indeed could be outright dangerous—to rely on access to insiders for success in the market: few nuggets of guidance are as frequently offered as "pay no attention to tips!" American writers, as we shall see, could plausibly suggest that readers look instead to the financial information stamped out in black and white on the ticker tape. The British market's comparative lack of transparency in the dissemination of trading volume and price information, and structural and temperamental resistance to new analytical methods, presented fewer such opportunities. As a conse-quence, the British guides that did appear in this period—volumes such as *The Book of the Stock Exchange* (Armstrong, 1934, 1939, 1949), *The Stock Exchange: A Short Study of Investment and Speculation* (Hirst, 1911, 1913, 1932, 1948), *Investment and Investors* (Hardinge, 1935), *Stocks and Shares* (Withers, 1917), *The Business of Finance* (Withers, 1918), and *The*

Shareholder's Manual: An Elementary and Non-Technical Treatise on the Investment of Capital in Stocks and Shares (Bassett, 1922)—tended to be broadly consistent with nineteenth-century templates in offering extensive information on the administrative arrangements of the London (and sometimes provincial) exchanges, and on the practicalities of transacting with a broker, claiming dividends, and so on. However, they gave only general, commonsense guidance to the actual methods by which one might select stocks—in contrast to the increasingly complex analytical techniques touted by American advice writers. The target audience was the—by US standards, relatively small—constituency of investors who wished to place their money in stocks or bonds but lacked access to the upper- and upper-middle-class networks that dominated the City's financial business. A rare example of an attempt to provide guidance on the use of new investment analysis methods—both "technical" and "fundamental"—in the British context is Hargreaves Parkinson's *Scientific Investment* (1933), to which we return shortly. The title of this book raises a further issue—the "scientific" (or otherwise) status of investment advice—which we will also take up in detail, since an invocation of "science" was one of the most common, and most vexed, rhetorical maneuvers among writers in this period.

Imperial Investments

One way in which British guides did clearly distinguish themselves in this period was in their continued preoccupation with imperial—and more broadly foreign—investment. Like the genre's treatment of gender, this is an example of a divergence between popular investment advice writing's ideological commitments and the empirical realities of the stock market, for this period in fact saw an uneven but marked trend away from overseas and toward domestic investment on the part of British shareholders. Prior to the First World War, British capital funneled abroad outweighed that invested at home around four to one. The inevitable wartime limitations on foreign investment were prolonged by strict capital controls in the war's immediate aftermath. During the 1920s, after the lifting of these controls, the London overseas market partially recovered, seeing trade in reconstruction loans for foreign states, new issues on behalf of governments and public bodies in the empire, and bursts of interest in commodities such as rubber and coffee. At the end of the decade, though, the value of home issues was greater than that of issues for foreign concerns.

Foreign lending declined further in the wake of the Depression: by the
mid-1930s, the four-to-one prewar ratio in favor of overseas issues had
almost exactly reversed.[22]

The key long-term cause of this decline in foreign lending was Britain's supersession by the United States as the world's creditor. Ironically,
though, while American investment guides rarely even mentioned the
possibility of buying foreign securities (an exceptional case does so only
to state that "foreign investments or American investments abroad are a
foolish venture for the ordinary investor"),[23] British texts persisted in giving them pride of place and expounding at length on the various classes of
overseas securities. Such writings continued, that is, to inhabit a turn-of-
the-century mindset in which the British investor naturally looked toward
the distant territories of the empire or the developing economies of the
New World before the more mundane commercial concerns that made up
the domestic market, even as actual investors' attentions were in fact becoming focused much closer to home. Again, then, we see the cultural and
ideological work that investment guides did, over and above—or even at
odds with—their ostensible practical applicability to participation in the
securities markets. In this case, they performed a crucial compensatory
function, cultivating a fantasy of continued British hegemony over the
globe in the face of the nation's diminishing world status and increasingly
fragile hold on its empire.

Consistent with this function, British guides echoed nineteenth-century
distinctions between "sound" and "unsound" foreign investments, the latter often characterized using the racially coded language of "delinquent"
southern states—places whose populations supposedly lacked the indus-
triousness, dynamism, and sense of honor to be reliable debtors.[24] The
prolific financial author and editor of the *Economist*, Hartley Withers, for
example, referred to the tendency of governments that had "outrun the
constable without any care for balancing [their] budget[s]" to bite back
churlishly at accusations of "levity and improvidence" with "plentiful
charges of exploitation and capitalist blood-sucking."[25] On the opening
page of his *Shareholder's Manual* (1922), Herbert H. Bassett introduces
the imaginary Republic of Lithalia—an "undeveloped country just growing in agriculture and industry"—before pointing to Honduras as a real-
world "example of a country with a dishonest record which is unable to
borrow under any conditions."[26]

Few publications display British financial writers' staunchly imperialist
mindset more clearly than *Investment and Investors* (1935), published by

the City of London–based issuing house Investment Registry. The book grandly flourishes the firm's imperial and establishment credentials, listing past and present chairmen and directors whose offices include Secretary of State for the Colonies, First lord of the Admiralty, Home Secretary, Minister of Information, Prime Minister of Newfoundland, and Viceroy of India (the latter the then-chairman and nominal author of the guide, Lord Hardinge of Penshurst). The list of the various "Types of Investment" that appears at the start of the book is unequivocal in identifying British government loans as "in point of security the best investments that can be obtained." "It may be argued," the book acknowledges, "that circumstances might conceivably arise owing to which there might be a default even in British Government loans, as has been the case in other countries." However, "we will not pursue this line of argument. If British Government loans were to prove unsafe we believe that all the theory advanced in this book would prove unsound, and that the term, 'security of capital,' applied to any investment, would cease to have any meaning." If loans issued by the British state constitute the absolute baseline of financial security—indeed, give that very notion its meaning—then other investments are graded in a descending order of political, institutional, and cultural affiliation to the mother country. Thus, close behind British government loans are those of the British dominion governments and the dominion municipal loans of the "big cities" of Britain's settler-colonies, "such as Quebec, Ottawa, Cape Town, Sidney [sic], [and] Wellington." In the "foreign investment field," however, "there are few countries, the political and economic conditions of which can be considered sufficiently stable to justify investment by those who wish to pursue a 'safety-first' policy." Those seeking "stability of capital value" are cautioned not to stray beyond "the British Dominions and a few of the very soundest foreign countries."[27]

One far more speculative category of investment to which British financial writers were habitually drawn is gold mining—that archetypal form of colonial resource extraction. These writers hark back to the 1895 boom in "Kaffirs" (as shares in South African mining companies were known), which accompanied discovery of the potential extent of the Witwatersrand goldfields.[28] In introducing this sector in his guide to the stock market, Herbert Bassett casually explains to readers how "the Kaffir market" is shaped not only by the output of the mines but also by the supply of the "boys" who work them.[29] Hartley Withers conjures up what readers might expect were they to step onto the floor of the London Stock Exchange through a vivid dramatization of the "boiling whirlpool of the Kaffir Circus."[30] Though overseas investment in general contracted sharply during the 1930s, gold mining shares saw something of a resurgence, as a rise in the price of gold following sterling's departure from the gold standard in 1931 stimulated a host of new ventures.

According to F. E. Armstrong, a partner in a stockbroking firm whose guide to the Stock Exchange went through four editions in the first half of the twentieth century (two in 1934 alone), nothing "holds a spell for speculators because of its rich prizes" like "a hole in the ground." "Many millions have been won from the bowels of the earth," he adds, noting that "men still talk with bated breath of the Kaffir boom of '95, the equal of which has probably not been seen in recent history." Gold mining—this crucial aspect of the economics of imperialism—is thus, for Armstrong, the quintessential object of financial speculation. And it follows that, on his account, imperial exploration, pacification, and conquest are themselves salutary expressions of the speculative impulse now most clearly seen at the Stock Exchange. Referring to "Columbus, Cook, [and] Livingstone," he observes that "all pioneer effort is by its very nature speculative, and efforts to deprecate this natural urge and impulse must, to be consistent, frown on the noblest achievements of man."[31] Another major, multi-edition investment guide of the period, by Francis W. Hirst (who preceded Withers as *Economist* editor), similarly points to the close interrelation of the British imperial project and the ambitious, far-sighted ethos of the Stock Exchange: no "territorial limit [can] be set to British investments. Our merchants and shippers seek profit in every corner of the globe; our investors large and small have interests in every continent, and the London Stock Exchange List is in itself a sort of key to the distribution of British trade and capital," he writes. "It will, therefore, be proper within a small compass to take a wide view; for, as Burke says, 'Great empire and little minds go ill together.'"[32] For Hirst, as Alexander Zevin comments, the City of London was "a bastion of free trade dynamism and British 'soft' power—uniting the Empire and the world through investment and trade."[33] Invoking the notion of an "Anglosphere" shaped by British settler-colonialism, Hirst suggests that "an English book on the stock markets appeals directly to our American kinsmen in the United States, to Canadians, Australians, and New Zealanders, as well as to the peoples now drawn together in a United South Africa."[34]

Hargreaves Parkinson concludes his book *Scientific Investment* (1933) with an extended metaphorical description of stock market activity as a colonial project in which participants explore, survey, map, exploit, and compete over territory. He distinguishes, however, between the speculator-prospector or pioneer and the investor-colonist:

> Investment is a territory which has been frequently explored but seldom surveyed. Discoverers . . . have been generally too anxious, as it were, to reach the North or South Pole of High Income or Capital Appreciation, to spend much time with theodolites in the *terrain* through which they have passed. . . .
>
> Investment is no El Dorado, where unlimited gold nuggets are available. . . . Investment is a territory for the colonist, not the prospector. . . . Parts of the territory may yield abnormally rich results to those who first enter them, but rewards above the average invariably bring in other settlers and cannot be maintained in the face of the world-wide levelling force of competition.[35]

While "the life of a pioneer is essentially speculative" and "large gains and heavy losses cancel each other," the investor (like the "colonist") seeks instead to "achieve an income, not a fortune."[36] It's hard to imagine that Parkinson would have so vividly cast speculation and investment in the guise of colonial reconnoitering if that very process had not played such a central and long-standing role in the promotion of overseas financial opportunities on the British stock market. As Marc Flandreau writes, in the latter half of the nineteenth century, "a patch of land, once its human and material surroundings had been sorted out, could be sold and bought, and as a result of the geographer's or anthropologist's structuring of the world, financial products could be devised."[37] By the time Parkinson was writing in the 1930s, trade in overseas securities made up a much smaller portion of business at the London Stock Exchange; but his account, like those of other investment writers of the period, suggests how crucial an imperialist worldview remained to the mythos of British finance. In this, investment writing partook of the wider popular culture of the period, which already—decades before Britain began to decolonize, but amid a mounting sense of the empire's precariousness—looked back nostalgically to a supposed prewar imperial heyday.[38]

The Expansion of the US Market

As we've seen, levels of British share ownership—whether in home or foreign markets—grew only modestly in the early decades of the twentieth century. In the United States, in contrast, the pool of stock market investors—and hence the pool of those likely to have an especially active interest in educating themselves about the workings of the market—expanded sharply in this period. The exact magnitude of that rise is difficult to determine with certainty, however.[39] Oft-cited contemporaneous figures suggest an increase in the number of American stock owners from 4.4 million in 1900 to 12 million in 1920 to 18 million in 1928:[40] the latter figure would represent around 14 percent of the population, though it is almost certainly an overestimate, given that these figures do not take account of individuals holding stock in multiple companies. A more conservative (though still striking) estimate suggests that by 1929 around one-quarter of American households held corporate stocks.[41]

The number of individuals actively trading stocks, even at the peak of the late 1920s boom, was perhaps no higher than 1.5 to 2 million,[42] but the millions more Americans who bought stocks as investments through employee or customer share ownership plans, investment trusts, or bank securities affiliates such as National City Company naturally had a keen interest in understanding the forces that caused their holdings to rise or fall in value. Moreover, in this period, given the wide diffusion of investment across social groups,[43] it was increasingly certain that even individuals who did not own stocks themselves would have friends or neighbors who did. Stock market investment, then, moved from being an activity that most Americans could imagine only in hypothetical or fantasy terms to one that individuals from many walks of life could quite realistically envisage participating in themselves, if they were not in fact already invested. The audience for investment advice literature was swelling due not only to the growing ranks of actual investors, that is, but also because of the increasing familiarity, accessibility, and cultural visibility of investment more generally.

The 1920s witnessed new levels of middle-class participation in the stock market, typically among those—such as car dealers, salespeople, lawyers, small business owners, engineers, and mid-ranking clerks—liable to have at least a passing professional concern with the nation's financial fortunes.[44] And the decade also saw significant involvement on the part of what Cedric Cowing identifies as a "special class" of working men and women, including barbers, chauffeurs, maids, typists, speakeasy waiters, elevator operators, valets, and indeed the famous bootblacks—the exemplary "little men" of the era.[45] Such jobs, at least in centers like New York, Chicago, Boston, San Francisco, and Cleveland, brought those who performed them into regular contact with financial professionals whose high living and knowledge of securities markets tended to "stimulate [the] speculative itch."[46] It was such middle- and working-class Americans — interested by, in certain key ways proximate to, but decidedly not insiders within the financial world—who made up the core market for investment advice literature. We can get a sense of the scale of that market from circulation data for the leading amateur investors' periodical, launched in 1907 as *The Ticker* and renamed the *Magazine of Wall Street* in 1912: by 1927, the magazine boasted regular sales of 75,000—a substantial figure for a nominally "niche" or special-interest publication in a period when only a select few of the top-ranking general-interest titles sold more than a million copies.[47]

A number of factors help to explain the growth of stock market participation during this period. Especially significant is the novel experience of securities ownership that huge numbers of Americans gained during World War I. The Treasury's favored method of financing the costs of conflict in Europe—the four Liberty Loan and one Victory Loan drives that it initiated between 1917 and 1919—attracted an estimated 20 million subscribers: around 82 percent of US households or 20 percent of the population.[48] As Lizabeth Cohen, Cedric Cowing, Steve Fraser, Julia Ott, and others have shown, the spectacular, celebrity-backed war bond campaigns gave many Americans a crucial first taste of financial investing and instilled a perception that securities ownership might be a legitimate, admirable, and indeed patriotic act.[49] These campaigns brought in $21.4 billion, while a further $1 billion dollars was raised from the estimated 34 million people (men, women, and children) who bought War Savings stamps and certificates. Together, these schemes covered around 60 percent of the cost of the United States' involvement in the war.[50] As Vincent Carosso puts it, Liberty Bonds "taught people to buy securities": millions of individuals "had discovered the magic of coupon-clipping and the desirability of bonds as a form of wealth."[51] The war bonds set the stage for later developments in other ways too. As James Grant describes, "to augment the stock of real capital, the government directed the banking system to loan would-be investors the price of their bonds. The Federal Reserve, in turn, would lend to the banks." In effect, then, "the worker-investors would buy on margin—an experience some of them would repeat in the stock-market boom of the 1920s."[52] After the war, brokerage firms, banks, investment houses, and the New York Stock Exchange used marketing and publicity techniques developed to promote Liberty Loans to stimulate public interest in stock market investment.[53] They promulgated an ideology of "shareholder democracy" or the "New Proprietorship," according to which it was both the right and the duty of every American to seek to benefit from and contribute to national prosperity through ownership of corporate stocks.[54]

Another key factor in encouraging new levels of securities ownership in the mid- to late 1910s was the decline of the bucket shops. In the last decade of the nineteenth century and the first decade of the twentieth, legitimate brokers and the major exchanges (especially the New York Stock Exchange and the Chicago Board of Trade) became increasingly exasperated by these rogue establishments, whose business was parasitic on their own but often dwarfed it in scale many times over, and besmirched their reputation with the taint of gambling, deception, and sharp practice. Several decades of campaigning by the exchanges eventually culminated, in 1909, with the passing of a federal law banning bucket shops in the District of Columbia. An ensuing federal investigation saw several of the major bucket shop chains with operations in Washington, DC, shut down, and by the end of 1915 the age of the bucket shop as a popular fixture of the American city was effectively over.[55]

One of the reasons why bucket shops had proven so attractive over the previous decades was the disdain with which many brokerages treated "odd lot traders"—those wishing to deal in bundles of shares smaller than the standard 100-share lot. As late as 1916, David Hochfelder notes, "only 80 of the New York Stock Exchange's 600 brokers accepted trades of less than 100 shares," but the impact of the closure of many bucket shops on demand for odd lot trading was almost immediate: in April 1916, the *New York Times* reported a "remarkable increase in the odd lot business" on the Stock Exchange, since "thousands" of those who had once frequented bucket shops, "practically all of whom were small speculators, have opened accounts with branches of Stock Exchange houses."[56] Recognizing that bucket shop customers shut out of their old haunts represented a significant pool of potential new clients, brokers quickly expanded services catering to the odd lot trade over the following years. This development was hailed by many investment advice writers as a sign of Wall Street's increasing openness to the common man. According to Harold J. Aldrich, writing in his 1923 book *The Stock Market Investor*, for example, "the odd-lot business of small brokerage houses has assumed a dignity and position of influence hitherto unknown." Where once "Wall Street had a welcome only for the man who was capable of buying in lots of 100 shares or more, it has now been made equally responsive to those who buy in lots of ten, twenty, and thirty shares."[57] In the unprecedented bull market that brought the decade to its close, a clear indicator of the high levels of public participation was the prevalence of odd lot trading: one odd lot house, for example, handled close to 1.2 million shares over two days during the late 1920s "Hoover Market."[58]

The extension of stock trading to a more socially and geographically diverse clientele also encouraged, and at the same time was encouraged by, the ever-wider distribution of means of monitoring the real-time performance of one's holdings. There were around 840 stock tickers in operation in 1900 and close to 1,300 in 1906;[59] numbers at the end of the 1920s have been put at 3,772 New York Stock Exchange tickers, 650 Trans-Lux Movie Tickers (devices that projected the ticker onto a big screen), and 5,650 other devices for communicating prices.[60] Tickers were no longer confined to brokerages, banks, or bucket shops but became increasingly familiar sights in spaces ranging from restaurants and beauty parlors to railroad depots and even ocean liners.[61] The increasing familiarity of the device in public spaces reinforced a sense that stock investment was a legitimate activity in which ordinary citizens might participate.

Of course, even as stock market investment assumed a new popularity, visibility, and cultural centrality, Americans continued to deploy their money for more prosaic purposes, from securing installment credit to paying into savings accounts or pension plans to taking out mortgages or annuity or life insurance policies. However, a striking feature of general works of personal financial advice in this period, which sets them apart from earlier books of their ilk, is the way in which the topic of securities investment is not simply confined to a designated chapter—as merely one of a number of more-or-less reliable ways of making use of one's money—but instead emerges as the paradigmatic model for financial management as such. This development reflects the dominance of the securities markets in the popular economic imagination and represents a crucial phase in the emergence of a stock market conception of subjectivity, which our study traces across the twentieth century and into the twenty-first. The standard personal finance guide for two generations of Americans was David F. Jordan's *Managing Personal Finances: How to Use Money Intelligently*, which went through three editions and multiple printings between 1936 and 1951 (with a second author, Edward F. Willett, making additions following Jordan's death in 1942) and spawned a slew of imitations. A New York University finance professor, Jordan already enjoyed a sufficiently

high public profile by 1920 for the stock market manual he published that
year to be titled simply *Jordan on Investments*. Though this book was primarily targeted at professional investors, by the mid-1930s Jordan could
boast of having sold 60,000 copies.[62] By casting its often somewhat worka-
day subject matter in terms of Wall Street investment, *Managing Personal
Finances* tapped into the glamour that the stock market still carried, even
post-crash, as a site of daring economic strategizing and risk-taking. At
the same time, Jordan acknowledged the reality of ordinary Americans'
diminished capacities to purchase stocks and bonds, cannily squaring this
circle by casting virtually any constructive financial outlay as effectively
equivalent to a judicious investment in the securities markets.

In his book's opening chapter, Jordan asserts that "any expenditure
that gives a satisfactory return is a good investment, regardless of whether
the money is spent for the purchase of a bond or an article for the home."
He continues:

> One hundred dollars paid for a good bond will provide an income of four dol-
> lars a year, but the same money invested in a good bed will provide a degree
> of comfort and satisfaction far beyond the value of four dollars a year.... A
> comfortable pair of shoes and an accurate watch are investments of the highest
> grade. An ample supply of self-confidence producing clothing is an investment
> in the "gilt-edge" category. In the rather prosaic field of home furnishings may
> be found dividend-payers that outrank Government bonds as investments.[63]

Jordan goes on to extol the virtues of books, education, and travel "as investments." Perhaps unsurprisingly, given his own professional identity as
the author of instructional volumes, Jordan argues that books offer especially stellar returns, since "a book costing three or four dollars can be sold
for as many thousands after the contents have been digested."[64] Jordan,
then, propounds nothing less than a stock or bond market model of the
self, in which every purchase is—or should be—an investment made with
the aim of enlarging what later economic theorists would refer to as an
individual's "human capital."

One of the major guidebooks that followed in Jordan's wake and
mimicked the format of his work—John A. Leavitt and Carl O. Hanson's
Personal Finance (1950)—similarly views domestic financial dealings in
general through the prism of securities investment. Having explained the
principle of stock diversification, for example, they urge readers to use this
approach as a template for their finances as a whole:

Diversification of investment is obtained in ways other than the purchase of the securities of several different corporations or government units. . . . The man who owns a house, gasoline station, insurance, and 10 shares of the preferred stock of the local gas and electric company has also diversified his investments. In contrast, the prosperous farmer who purchases more farms as his wealth grows is not observing the principle of diversification. If the income from one farm disappears, the income from the other farms will likely do the same. Similarly, the prosperous druggist might do well to invest his funds in an annuity, rather than another drugstore.[65]

In the first half of the twentieth century, then, we see glimmerings of an approach that will become hegemonic in personal financial advice writing over the following fifty years: the installation of principles drawn from stock market investment advice as the primary models for financial—but also personal and familial—well-being and security in general.

Financial Print Culture

Just as, in the early decades of the twentieth century, the stock ticker could be heard tapping out its first draft of financial history in smaller and more far-flung places, so the wider financial print culture also expanded in this period, disseminating information about the market to a broad and eager public readership. An awareness of growing popular interest in securities investment during the 1910s led the nation's leading mainstream newspapers—the likes of the *New York Times* and the *Chicago Tribune*—to boost their coverage of developments on Wall Street or LaSalle Street (Chicago's financial hub), while mass-market, general-interest magazines such as *Harper's*, *The Century*, *World's Work*, the *Saturday Evening Post*, and *The Outlook* added new financial content to their pages. As we saw earlier, a specialist business press had been operating in the United States since the mid-nineteenth century. Titles founded before 1900 saw their readerships expand substantially in the early decades of the new century: from a circulation of just a few thousand copies in its early days, the leading paper, the *Wall Street Journal* (established in 1889), boasted a circulation of over 50,000 by the end of the 1920s. New titles also quickly gained large readerships: *Barron's National Financial Weekly* (later *Barron's* magazine), launched in 1921 by Dow Jones & Co. owner Clarence W. Barron, was selling 30,000 copies by the latter part of the decade.[66]

Coverage of the stock market in these and similar publications was largely devoted to listing and reporting on the latest movements in particular stocks and sectors and the changing business and political conditions liable to impact the market over coming weeks and months. It was on the whole assumed that readers had a basic grasp of the core processes and functions of the market and the underlying mechanisms shaping its day-to-day dynamics. Consequently, columns presenting what was demonstrably investment *advice* usually circumvented elementary discussions of the workings of the market in favor of proceeding straight to recommendations of companies or industries that presented buying or selling opportunities. Though undoubtedly widely read and often influential, such content had long been dogged by rumors of corruption and conflicts of interest, and in the 1920s public trust in newspaper advice was severely damaged by a series of revelations about writers having been bribed to tout particular stocks, including two of the *Wall Street Journal*'s most widely read daily columnists, William Gomber (author of "Broad Street Gossip") and Richard E. Edmondson (who penned the "Abreast of the Market" feature).[67] Other publications were frauds through-and-through. Pools of stock operators—the so-called pirates of promotion—compiled what scammers and regulatory authorities alike referred to as "sucker lists," to which they mailed bogus newspapers extolling the virtues of the stock of dummy companies, which the promoters would quietly unload as prices rose.[68] Part of the appeal of investment advice manuals, then, was that— rather than offering potentially conflicted "tips"—they provided general techniques, strategies, and approaches for stock selection, and encouraged readers to put them to use themselves.

If the pirates' cheaply produced and freely distributed tip sheets formed one pole of the period's financial print culture, then at the other end of the scale stood the business reports, ratings, and statistics produced by companies including the Standard Statistics Bureau, Poor's Publishing Company, Moody's Investors Service, the Fitch Publishing Company, the Harvard Economic Service, and Babson's Statistical Organization. Subscribers to these services received regular updates in the form of hefty and highly detailed statistical analyses of the business situation at both sector-wide and corporation-specific levels, which sought to identify and forecast economic trends. As Walter A. Friedman describes in his recent history of this field, the subscription companies stressed "what today we would call the 'real economy'—upcoming changes to production, employment, trade, and services—rather than trends in the stock market,"[69] though statisticians did carefully track equities and bond prices, and much of their analysis was geared toward identifying moments in which "real" economic conditions made buying or selling in the securities markets propitious. However, these services' subscription lists were almost exclusively made up of industry professionals: the bankers, brokers, financiers, and executives who had the money to afford the high subscription fees (the Harvard Economic Service, for example, cost $100 a year when the average income was about $1,400) and the time and knowledge required to make sense of the bulletins' densely printed tables, graphs, and indexes.

Instead, the print culture targeted at ordinary citizens centered, more than ever, around inexpensive manuals that explained investment from first principles in commonsense terms and with a minimum of technical detail. Some of these books were published by well-known, mainstream presses, such as Doubleday, Henry Holt, Macmillan, and Houghton Mifflin, though they largely appeared with smaller, specialist publishers with finance- and business-oriented lists. The vast majority of these houses were located in New York (with premises clustered around lower Broadway and Wall Street), though some were based in other financial centers, including Boston and Chicago. Available by mail order from publishers as well as from bookstores and newsstands, books typically cost around $1 to $2, representing something more than a casual purchase but promising a relatively affordable means of accessing the insight into investment that was increasingly seen as a key form of cultural capital (and a viable route to capital proper). The investment advice guide or manual was often a stand-alone artifact, but it could also lend new longevity, stature, and visibility to otherwise ephemeral writings and at the same time provide platforms and markers of authority and expertise for writers as they pursued subsequent activities.

Many guides (including several of the best-selling and most influential) incorporated material initially published in the likes of the *Wall Street Journal*, the *Saturday Evening Post*, or *Barron's*, or one of the more niche periodicals such as the *Magazine of Wall Street*, *Financial World*, or the *Financial Review of Reviews*. Of course, republication of previously serialized material in book form is a perennial publishing practice; only a small fraction of the abundance of periodical writing devoted to the stock market received such treatment, however. When a series of articles was revised for book publication (usually by a press affiliated with the paper or magazine where it originally appeared), it was invariably because the series had elicited favorable correspondence and inquiries from readers:

such publication is therefore a clear signal of writing that struck a chord with the investing public. Amid the huge quantity of financial print material produced in the period, then, one of the best ways to trace the emergence, development, and dissemination of significant and influential ideas is by tracking those that made the transition from periodical into monograph form.

Manuals were also central to the popular investment culture of the period in the way they served to legitimate, underpin, and promote other services for investors. The most influential authors-cum-publishers developed investment advisory agencies that, in contrast to the likes of Moody's Investors Service or the Babson Statistical Organization, were targeted at the amateur as well as the professional investor. Companies such as the Richard D. Wyckoff Analytical Staff, the W. D. Gann Scientific Service, and the R. N. Elliott Educational Service sought to capitalize on the public circulation of the books produced by their founders. They offered services ranging from market letters and annual forecasts to correspondence courses, seminars, and in-depth appraisals of subscribers' stock holdings. A month's worth of weekly stock or commodity newsletters might cost just a few dollars, whereas subscription to a bespoke service including a full-scale portfolio consultancy could cost as much as $500 a year. Lists of these companies' provisions appeared at the backs of their books: their output was consistent in insisting that while subscription services might provide guidance on emerging opportunities for profit in the markets, these could only be successfully exploited once the theoretical lessons, principles, and methods outlined in the mass-market manuals had been fully internalized. The manual, that is, provided the key to unlocking the otherwise opaque figures, charts, tables, and technical commentary that appeared in the subscriber-only materials. As Enoch Burton Gowin puts it at the end of *Developing Financial Skill* (1922), the first in a series of investment guides,

> while the textbooks are being studied, and the client is thus broadening his financial vision, he is also able to apply the principles contained in the texts, through actual commitments in the market, based on recommendations given through the "WEEKLY INVESTMENT AND SPECULATIVE ADVISORY BULLETIN." When the course of study has been completed and the principles of scientific operation in the securities market clearly understood, the client is then prepared to make the most complete use of the current studies and forecasts of the Institute's staff.[70]

Similarly, one of the leading investment gurus of the 1930s and 1940s, Ralph Nelson Elliott, presented his major monograph, 1938's *The Wave Principle* (which retailed at the relatively expensive price of $15), as the "Treatise"—the essential theoretical text necessary for anyone hoping to make sense of his $60-a-year Interpretive Letters. By examining the changing concerns of the investment advice manual, then, we can track the evolving paradigms within which investors were being encouraged to perform their detailed, day-to-day analyses of market data.

Some light may be shed on the particular appeal of advice manuals— which provided *methods* for buying and selling in the market but left it to readers to determine *what* to buy and sell—by a study conducted at a typical brokerage house in the mid-1930s. Brokerages would regularly issue tips bulletins, and this research found that, had clients consistently followed the firm's recommendations, they would have accrued average returns of 142 percent on their capital per month; in fact, however, most recorded overall losses during the two-year period under examination.[71] As Cedric Cowing suggests, "the great discrepancy between advice and results indicates that the public preferred to make its own judgements even when expert advice was available."[72] The period's investment advice manuals were, ironically, perfectly keyed to this kind of advice-resistant mindset, since they provided readers with basic practical knowledge and analytical methods for trading in the stock market, while at the same time insisting that the most crucial piece of advice for all investors was that they must learn to make up their own minds. This strategy served at once to endow readers with a sense of capability and empowerment and to exculpate authors should an individual's own experiments in investment go awry.

Henry Howard Harper's *Psychology of Speculation* (1926) is typical of this double movement in elaborating an account of how "the human element in stock market transactions" may be factored into investment decisions, while "set[ting] down as an axiomatic truth that no one can learn the art of making money in the stock market by reading statistics, charts, precedents, theoretical disquisitions, and instructions." "Those who would make money speculating in the stock market," instead, must exhibit "the rare faculty of maintaining a complete mastery over one's impulses, emotions, and ambitions under the most heroic tests of human endurance."[73] In *The Business of Trading in Stocks* (1917), John T. Brand (writing under the pseudonym "B.") explains that "I take the position that all I can do is to suggest principles, to be worked out by each trader for himself, and do not suggest any hard-and-fast rules by which to trade."[74] Similarly, according to Thomas Temple Hoyne in *Speculation: Its Sound Principles and Rules for Its Practice* (1922), one of the "great rules for speculation" is that "every speculator must learn to think for himself" through "introspection and experience."[75] Investment advice writers of the early twentieth century sought to endow their readers with the ability to operate as self-governing subjects whose greatest failure was not losing money (since even the expert speculator inevitably did so on occasion) but rather slavishly following others' prescriptions.

Race, Gender, and the Market

This ethos of achieving mastery and sovereignty over self and others is of course heavily freighted with racialized and gendered implications. It is not simply significant that such texts were almost exclusively written by white men, but also that they consistently projected an implied reader who was likewise white and male. In refusing any recognition that the reader might be a person of color, and by approaching female investors as individuals to be discussed (if at all) over their heads—as objects of skeptical male appraisal—rather than addressed directly, these texts distort the realities of stock market participation in the period in ways that are revealing of prevalent assumptions about the "true," "authentic," or "essential" (as opposed to actually existing) nature of investment.

The Liberty Loan drives of the war years—which placed particular emphasis on the obligation of ethnic minority groups to demonstrate their loyalty to the nation by buying its securities[76]—might be thought to have gone some way toward eroding such assumptions, but the large numbers of minorities who answered their government's call made it no easier for financial writers to imagine the archetypal investor as anything other than white. These assumptions likewise withstood the emerging (if still marginalized) presence of nonwhite participation in the stock market (on the rare occasion that one does find a reference to racial difference in such writing, it is in the use of a racial epithet as a metaphor for "suspicious" trading activity).[77] There is evidence of African American equities ownership stretching back to the early nineteenth century, but it was only in the early twentieth century that black Americans began to establish any kind of professional footing on Wall Street. Initially, that presence was precarious indeed: just one African American broker, W. Fred Thompson, is recorded as having been active in the early years of the century.[78] During the 1920s and 1930s, several African American–owned securities firms (some run by and specifically catering to black women) opened in New York and elsewhere, and this period was also distinguished by a number of successful African American speculators, most notably the Harlem-based H. R. George (whose nickname, "the Black Wolf of Wall Street," reflected both racist animosity and a certain grudging respect for his tenacity as a trader) and Chicago's brothers Edward and George Jones.[79] The luxurious and flamboyant lifestyles of such figures attracted interest in the black press, but George, the Joneses, and the few other black speculators operating in the 1920s were wiped out by the crash of 1929. During the Great Depression, the particular economic hardships faced by African Americans meant that fewer than ever had money to spend on stocks, while the provision of financial services by black professionals would not revive until the late 1940s, when the first black registered stockbrokers began to work on Wall Street.[80]

The unspoken but pervasive assumption of the investor's whiteness in stock market writing of the period is perhaps to some extent unsurprising, given not only the acute racial prejudices of the era but also the infrequency with which the brokers, speculators, and financial journalists who were the authors of investment guides would have had professional dealings with African Americans, who gained only very limited access to the culture of Wall Street. More glaring is the fact that such authors aligned the stock market almost as closely with masculinity as with whiteness, since women investors were in fact a visible and growing constituency throughout the period. Again, definitive figures are hard to come by, but as early as 1910 women probably represented 20–25 percent of American shareholders.[81] At this time, the typical female investor was an upper-middle-class widow who would conventionally entrust the administration of her portfolio to a male banker, lawyer, or other agent.[82] (This paternalistic approach lived on in a work published in 1940, *Investing for a Widow*, which printed selected plans devised by readers of *Barron's* magazine for "the investment of $100,000 which is assumed to be the entire fortune of a young widow with two children.")[83]

At the beginning of the century, then, while women might be owners of shares, a "separate spheres" model continued to apply to the extent that they were subject to strong societal pressure to hand over active management of their holdings to trusted male professionals, who were assumed to be more capable in the cut-and-thrust dealings of the stock market.

However, the female professionals and middle-class housewives who began to enter the market in numbers after the First World War took a more hands-on approach to their holdings, and as the late 1920s bull market approached its peak they were joined by many young working-class women.[84] A 1927 survey of a hundred corporations showed that in many cases female shareholders were in the majority; according to a 1928 study, 20 percent of new securities issues went to women buyers; and by 1929 it was reported that women made up 35 percent of the nation's shareholders.[85] Some brokerages sought to cultivate a clientele that, earlier in the century, the industry had tended to spurn: they opened dedicated "women's departments," often located in smartly appointed rooms at fashionable hotels; ran advertising campaigns targeted at female investors; and hired growing numbers of women brokers.[86]

These developments attracted much—usually amused and condescending—commentary in mainstream newspapers and magazines. However, investment advice writing that recognized the existence of female investors and addressed their distinct needs and the particular obstacles they faced in participating in the market was almost entirely confined (besides the occasional short piece in the specialist financial press)[87] to women's periodicals, especially the *Ladies' Home Journal* and *Good Housekeeping*. This hiving off of advice writing responsive to the female investor from the genre's mainstream reflects the prevailing view among investment writers that women shareholders were, at best, a peripheral concern and, at worst, an outright affront to sound financial practice. The *Ladies' Home Journal* was a great advocate of women's investment in Liberty Bonds during the Great War,[88] and in the following decade it encouraged its readers to see responsible and prudent investment in stocks as an appropriate means by which wives might support their husbands in strengthening their families' domestic finances.

"The Management of Money" in the *Ladies' Home Journal*'s November 1928 issue suggests that while "no woman goes shopping without some notion of what it is she wants to buy," many women lack such clear objectives when it comes to the stock market: an accompanying illustration depicts a plaintive-looking young woman appealing "helplessly" to a male financial professional to invest her money (fig. 4.1). In this and other pieces published in the 1920s, the *Ladies' Home Journal* sought to alleviate such a plight by instilling basic principles of commonsense investment in its readers, whom it—unlike the vast majority of financial authors—recognized as likely to be involved in the stock market in considerable numbers.[89]

BUT SHE WILL TAKE AN AMOUNT OF MONEY
REPRESENTING MORE THAN SHE HAS EVER
SEEN IN HER LIFE TO A GOOD BANK OR BROKER
AND HELPLESSLY SAY SHE WANTS IT INVESTED

FIGURE 4.1. Illustration by E. McNerney Jr., *Ladies' Home Journal* (November 1928): 33. "The Management of Money" by Samuel Crowther provided courtesy of Meredith Corporation, Ladies' Home Journal®, © 1928. Image published with permission of ProQuest LLC. Further reproduction is prohibited without permission.

Good Housekeeping also published a flurry of articles on the stock market in the late 1920s and early 1930s, almost all written by the magazine's investment specialist, Ruth Boyle. In several of them, Boyle positions herself as a mediator between the resolutely male-oriented field of investment advice manuals and the magazine's female readers: her role, that is, is to "translate" the discourse of male-authored investment advice into terms assumed to be accessible and relatable for the magazine's female readers. For example, in a 1929 piece Boyle puts a query from a reader who wishes to "invest my money as a businessman does" to Edgar Lawrence Smith, the author of *Common Stocks as Long Term Investments* (1924), one of the most influential financial guidebooks of the period. Smith—"on his way to talk to an audience of college girls"—is described as "smilingly" replying that the inquirer should initially buy "just one share," thereby minimizing the damage "if she happens to choose the wrong one." Boyle concurs with this advice, observing that "a young college graduate would undoubtedly find both the financial page and the stockholders' report dull if she owned no stock, but the possession of just one share will sharpen her interest."[90] In a piece in the October 1929 issue, Boyle notes that "recently . . . women have begun to show a real desire to know at least as much about investments as the average man does": she encourages readers to seek out reliable guidebooks on the subject so as to avoid stumbling on "a book written by a crank, somebody exploiting a 'system' for coming out on the right side of the market, or some one carried away by a theory that looks all right on the surface but proves to be thin ice when the skeptic puts the weight of knowledge and experience on it."[91] In a piece published the following year, Boyle recommends "an interesting new book, written since the stock crash last fall," J. George Frederick's *Common Stocks and the Average Man* (1930).[92] Even while communicating the book's key ideas to her overwhelmingly female readership, Boyle reproduces the strongly gendered slant implied by Frederick's title, continually using masculine pronouns to refer to the hypothetical investor in common stocks.

The most famous finance-themed women's magazine article of the period appeared in the *Ladies' Home Journal* in August 1929 and suggests similarly gendered presuppositions. This piece was one of the signal artifacts of the "New Era" ideology of the late 1920s: an interview with the financier John J. Raskob entitled "Everybody Ought to Be Rich." The piece abounds in ironies, not only because of its timing (published just two months before the Great Crash, it finds its subject looking forward to ten years in which "the wealth of the country is bound to increase at a very rapid rate"),[93] or because Raskob had in fact liquidated most of his own holdings by the time the article was published,[94] but also because, in spite of the venue in which it appeared, the hypothetical amateur investor around whom Raskob frames his discussion is a man named Tom, while a female presence is registered only fleetingly in a disdainful reference to Tom's "wife's sister" who is bound to contrive some "emergency" with which to "draw . . . forth" the two hundred dollars in his savings account.[95]

The logic whereby, even in a piece recommending securities investment to the readers of a women's magazine, the governing perspective is naturally male is all the starker in the period's investment manuals, and nowhere more so than in virtually the only such guide written specifically for a female readership (a volume equally unusual in also being written by a woman): Elizabeth Frazer's *A Woman and Her Money* (1926).[96] Based on a popular series of articles published in the *Saturday Evening Post*, Frazer's book was well received, with the *New York Times*, for example, praising the author for having "used with skill and good effect a striking method for making her book readable and giving to her material fresh, dramatic, personal interest."[97] This method is, though, a remarkably self-effacing one: insisting on her own lack of specialist expertise in the field, Frazer emphasizes that her advice on navigating the world of stock investing is based on extensive conversations with (male) bankers, brokers, and other financial professionals; and she goes further in writing the book from the point of view of a male persona—an avuncular investment counselor who recalls his consultations with female clients, casting a wry but indulgent eye on their foibles and perplexities. Though written by a woman for women, Frazer's book is consistent with the general tendency in the period to defer to a masculine voice as the source of authority, expertise, and assurance in matters relating to the stock market.

This gendered hierarchy was certainly an unquestioned assumption for the great mass of investment guide writers, who were of course male. When, as these authors' texts consistently do, stock market investment is reduced to its bare essentials—the eternal elements that make the market what it is—for the instruction of the lay reader, the agent of investment is always implicitly, and sometimes explicitly, male. On the rare occasions when such writers considered the topic of female stockholders, they insisted on their fitness only for the least risky forms of investment[98] or disparaged women for being so "used to protection" that they took losses "in a manner so distressed and so distressing" that it exhausted the patience of their brokers.[99] In *Making Money in the Stock Market* (1930), Orline D. Foster insists that "there are certain people who should never enter into speculation," among them women, who "as a rule are not fitted for the nervous strain which necessarily accompanies all hazard." For Foster, "it is essential that women's money should be placed within the margin of safety" because "the average woman is not fitted by education to analyze and determine business value and risks." Foster concedes that a woman might conceivably "fit" and "accustom" herself "to business matters" so as to "educate herself to speculate as intelligently as a man," but the standard against which she would be measured is, again, presented as necessarily a masculine one.[100] In the period's investment advice guides, then, a separate spheres ideology remained firmly in place, even as the boundary between those spheres was in fact being rendered increasingly porous by the rise of a cohort of active female shareholders. That these writers were so determined to ignore or belittle women investors—even as this constituency represented a large and growing market for their works—speaks, again, to our key claim that such texts were animated more by ideological investments than by the empirical realities of stock market investment (or even, at times, authors' own financial self-interest). The female stock market participant, then, largely remained an absence in the investment advice literature of the period.

Technical or Fundamental?

Early twentieth-century investment advice writing in the United States thus systematically excluded substantive engagement with female investors or investors of color. The field was at the same time deeply riven by an internal schism between two competing paradigms of investment analysis. Every system, method, and technique of the period ultimately came down on one side or other of this divide. Writers either advocated a "technical" analysis approach—in which the goal was to identify cycles and patterns in market data in order to predict future price movements—or they were proponents of "fundamental" analysis: the attempt to determine whether companies were under- or overvalued on the stock market and trade accordingly. The terms "technical" and "fundamental" analysis began to be commonly used in the early decades of the twentieth century (the *Oxford English Dictionary* dates their first appearances in print to 1902 and 1917 respectively, with "fundamentalist" appearing—in the context of the stock market—a little earlier, in 1912): the period saw concerted efforts, by both camps, to define and systematize their approaches.

Though both technical and fundamental approaches to investment advice put great store on their hard-headedness and rigor, writings emphasizing attention to underlying, fundamental factors tended to place particular emphasis on their reliability, security, and conservative affiliation to sources of real, stable value—in contrast to a speculative ethos concerned only with the undulations of share prices themselves. Such moderate advice, with its appeal to commonsense understandings of what would make a particular stock valuable, spoke to what was, in the 1910s, a predominantly risk-averse investing public (as evident in the prevailing preference for the supposed reliability of bonds), and its loudest and most influential voice was that of John Moody. Moody had built his reputation by establishing Moody's Investor Service, a subscription service that was targeted at professional investors and others employed in the financial sector, and which offered detailed information on companies that issued bonds and stocks (insofar as such information could be obtained, given that mandated corporate disclosure was limited, and many companies issued only flimsy periodic reports on their performance, if they issued them at all).[101] Moody's avowed goal in developing the forerunner of what is now one of the world's leading ratings agencies was to bring greater transparency to the corporate and investment worlds and give investors more informed grounds for their decisions than the insider tips, access to pool manipulations, or intuitive hunches that had tended to shape much activity on Wall Street in earlier decades.

In a series of generically titled books published in the early decades of the century (*The Art of Wise Investing* [1904], *The Art of Wall Street Investing* [1906], *The Investor's Primer* [1907], *How to Invest Money Wisely* [1912], and *Profitable Investing: Fundamentals of the Science of Investing* [1925]), Moody expressed his desire to inculcate a similar focus on sound fundamentals in a wider, lay investing public. In *How to Invest Money Wisely*, Moody tellingly prioritizes bonds in outlining the various classes of investment, and in turning to stocks asserts that "in the long run" the investor "greatly adds to his principal by taking cognizance of these two great factors in selecting investments, viz., a study of the general trade and commercial cycles, and an intelligent analysis of intrinsic values. . . . If he pays a little too much for a stock of real intrinsic merit (but has bought it in the proper period) all that he has got to do is to hold it as an investment and receive his dividends; in time it will sell up to or above his cost price again."[102]

Another figure whose activities were largely dedicated to catering to professional investors and businesspeople, but who also sought to provide the benefits of his experience and market understanding to general readers via affordable, accessibly written handbooks, was Roger W. Babson. Catering more to investors hoping for "short-term" returns than those adopting a "buy and hold" strategy, Babson stressed, in the recurring preamble to his serially produced manual *Business Barometers*, the need for the investor to attend to "fundamental statistics relat[ing] to underlying conditions of the country": his guide aimed to "show the importance of considering underlying and fundamental conditions before buying or selling securities or merchandise."[103] As another fundamentals-focused investment expert, Thomas Gibson, candidly noted in *Simple Principles of Investment* (1919), however, the kind of "exhaustive inquiry" necessary to judge "the individual merits of various securities" is "a formidable task even for the experts. It would be a flat impossibility for the best posted layman. And an insufficient investigation would be worse than none at all, as error or miscalculation on one important point might prove fatal." Gibson promised to equip the would-be investor with "a few fundamental principles . . . a knowledge of which he may acquire at no great expense of time or effort" and acquaintance "with the influence of important basic conditions on values and prices of securities."[104] Yet the reader could be forgiven for wondering whether these lessons could really be sufficient for successful action in the market, or whether the fundamental analysis route might require a level of sustained research that would effectively turn the amateur investor into a professional as well as further outlay in obtaining the kinds of corporate ratings and reports that Moody, Babson, Gibson, and others sold (at considerable cost, as we've seen) to their professional and institutional subscribers. To a greater or lesser extent, then, such guidebooks were also advertisements: Moody's preface to *How to Invest Money Wisely* is explicit in directing readers to "the back pages of this book [where] will be found a detailed description of our Investment Service."[105] Hence the appeal of the other key investment paradigm of the period, technical analysis, which held out the promise that an investor might be able to make do simply with a guide to principles and tactics, a pencil and graph paper, and the latest market prices, rather than access to the mass of other business data that (presumably) lay behind those prices. In this way, technical analysis held a strongly populist, autodidactic, and democratizing appeal: it offered to level the playing field and allow anyone (or at least anyone who had purchased the correct instructional tome) to play the markets.

The foundational figure in the technical analysis tradition was Charles H. Dow, co-deviser of the Dow Jones Index of leading stocks and founding editor of *the Wall Street Journal*. In 1902, the financial journalist Samuel Alexander Nelson published *The ABC of Stock Speculation*, which reprinted fifteen of the more than two hundred "Review and Outlook" columns written by Dow for the *Wall Street Journal* between 1899 and 1902 (the year of his death). These selected pieces, Nelson proposed, collectively constituted a coherent body of ideas identifiable as "Dow's Theory."[106] George Charles Selden, a former Fellow of Political Economy and Finance at Columbia University, elaborated on Dow's ideas (though without directly acknowledging the connection) in articles for the *Maga-*

zine of Wall Street and a series of books derived from them (*Psychology of the Market* [1912], *Investing for Profit* [1913], *The Machinery of Wall Street* [1917], and *How to Select Investments* [1918]), before, in 1920, publishing an annotated edition of this same selection of Dow's editorials under the title *Scientific Stock Speculation*. Alex Preda has explored how the pioneers of technical analysis sought, in the early to mid-twentieth century, to carve out a scientifically legitimate space for their activities within the financial sector. Preda emphasizes technical analysts' desire to be recognized as professionals deserving of the respect of fellow professionals as well as their establishment of processes of credentialization and institutionalization designed to validate their field within both academic and industry environments.[107] The wide dissemination of Dow Theory in the 1910s and 1920s is indicative of the ways in which technical analysts also sought to present a scientifically grounded image of their work not only to the community of financial insiders Preda analyses but also to the lay investing public, whose confidence in the soundness of technical approaches was crucial to their willingness to consume and use them.

The title Selden chose for his 1920 edition of Dow's writings clearly signals this intent, though precisely how far financial speculation could be defined as a science was a question requiring some finesse on the part of the field's proponents. Dow himself had acknowledged the inherent incongruity between speculation—with its necessary epistemological limits and indeterminacies—and the appeals to objective truth associated with scientific method, while suggesting (in "Scientific Speculation," the lead piece in both Nelson's and Selden's collections) that "within limitations, the future can be foreseen," since "the present is always tending toward the future and there are always in existing conditions signals of danger or encouragement for those who read with care."[108] Similarly, in his introduction to *Scientific Stock Speculation* Selden averred that "science in speculation must deal with tendencies rather than with exact mathematical conclusions." While "the mathematician is always seeking some invariable rule or fundamental principle of fluctuations," "all speculative rules must be approximate." Nevertheless, Selden insisted, "it is quite possible to estimate the importance of the principal elements in the situation" and "to see in advance some of the changes which are impending" so that "results are obtained which may properly be called scientific in a correct sense of that word."[109]

The science of speculation—as defined by Dow Theory—sought to advance beyond the loose rhetorical appeals to "scientific" authority that had become common among American financial writers in the late nineteenth century by establishing the existence of a set of objective tendencies (if not invariant laws) in the stock market. Absolutely central for Dow himself was the claim that the market was subject to three trends: the main or primary movement, which could persist in a generally bullish or bearish direction for as long as several years; the countervailing "medium swing" or secondary reaction running from a couple of weeks to a month or more; and the "narrow movement" of prices' moment-to-moment or day-to-day fluctuations.[110] All the more crucial to Dow Theory as it was popularized in the 1920s was the idea that a scientific approach to the stock market entailed viewing it as a "barometer" of wider economic conditions. This idea was the key concern of William Peter Hamilton, a protégé of Dow's, who edited the *Wall Street Journal* from 1908 until his death in 1929. Hamilton's position at the *Wall Street Journal* (whose circulation would reach more than 50,000 copies under his editorship) gave him as prominent a platform as any financial writer of the period. While he largely confined his regular editorials to reflections on the present position of the stock market in its various phases, he took the opportunity of a series of articles in the *Wall Street Journal*'s sister publication *Barron's National Financial Weekly* in 1921 to lay out the underlying philosophy of the market that he had derived from his mentor.

Published in book form as *The Stock Market Barometer* in 1922, the series anticipated full-fledged academic theories of the "efficient market" by several decades in asserting that "the price movement represents the aggregate knowledge of Wall Street and, above all, its aggregate knowledge of coming events." While Hamilton acknowledged that "the adolescent science of reading [the stock market] is far from having attained perfection," he went further than Dow in insisting that "the laws we are studying are fundamental, axiomatic, self-evident." "In this higher truth," he continued, "surely there is something permanent that would remain if the letter of the Constitution of the United States had become an interesting study for the archaeologist. . . . Such a foundation is permanent because truth has in it an element of the divine." The metaphor of the stock market as a "barometer" registering shifts in economic confidence had been common in the late nineteenth century, but for Hamilton the term had a very precise significance: the market was a barometer—rather than a mere "recorder"—because, in discounting "everything everybody knows, hopes, believes, anticipates," it did not represent "what the condition of business is to-day" but "what that condition will be months ahead"—a "function of prediction" performed with "almost uncanny accuracy." Of course, as efficient market theory would later emphasize, the idea that the stock market is consistently "right" tends to exclude the possibility of any systematic method of outsmarting it, presenting something of a problem for a writer purporting, at least in part, to offer practical guidance to the would-be speculator (a circle Burton Malkiel would seek to square in *A Random Walk Down Wall Street* [1973], discussed in chap. 5). Thus, while Hamilton is evidently intellectually committed to the idea of the market's "omniscience," he conveniently admits that "major bull markets and bear markets alike tend to overrun themselves," thereby leaving open a window of opportunity in which shrewd operators might act contrary to the crowd and find themselves in profitable positions once the market snaps back into conformity with the objective "line of values."[111]

Hamilton thus identifies the holy grail of technical analysis as it developed in the 1920s: not so much to anticipate the momentary fluctuations of individual prices, as in the formative technical analysis practice of "tape reading" (such opportunistic "scalping" being seen as nigh-on impossible to perform reliably), but rather to identify the pivotal moment when the general trend of the market has begun to shift from a "line of accumulation" to one of "distribution" (or vice versa), with those still following the existing "line" consisting merely of the "uninformed public" trading "on prospects only."[112] The linchpin of the print culture of technical analysis–based investment advice in the period was Richard D. Wyckoff, editor of the *Magazine of Wall Street* (formerly *The Ticker*). A key shift in the popular technical analysis literature that Wyckoff did much to foster was a movement away from tape reading as the favored method of analyzing the market and toward the plotting of price changes on a chart ("charting"). Like other early technical analysts, Wyckoff had formerly insisted on the necessity of being able to respond immediately and instinctively to price changes as they appeared on the ticker: this was a central principle of his influential *Studies in Tape Reading*, published under the pseudonym Rollo Tape in 1910.[113] However, by the time of 1925's *How I Trade and Invest in Stocks and Bonds* (as well as in contemporaneous pieces for the *Magazine of Wall Street*),[114] Wyckoff had come to extol the virtues of charting precisely because of the distance, objectivity, and attention to "the facts" that it encouraged, compared to the stupefied over-proximity to the market displayed by many of "the people who . . . hang over the ticker."[115] Leon Wansleben has suggested that a shift away from tape reading (immersive, intuitive, mediumistic) and toward chart reading (detached, reflective, fully analytical) was part of technical analysis's attempt to place itself on a more recognizably "rational" or "scientific" footing in the 1920s and 1930s.[116] While Wansleben (examining only *Studies in Tape Reading*) aligns Wyckoff straightforwardly with tape reading, however, he was in fact a transitional figure, as was one of the other best-known investment authors of the day (whom Wansleben also places squarely in the tape reading camp): William D. Gann.

Gann had been introduced to the investing public as "an operator whose science and ability place him in the front rank" in a profile by Wyckoff published in *The Ticker* in 1909,[117] and his first book, *Truth of the Stock Tape* (1923), established him as a major authority on the stock market—a profile he would capitalize upon over the following decades by publishing a series of further books as well as garnering subscribers to the W. D. Gann Scientific Service's instructional courses and newsletters. As Wansleben notes, Gann begins *Truth of the Stock Tape* with a familiar exhortation for the reader to cultivate the tape reader's sixth sense: "In reading the tape, we are not influenced alone by what we see, but by what we feel or sense, which cannot always be explained or a satisfactory reason given because it is 'intuition.'" Yet the book in fact turns out to be a critique of absorbed tape reading and instead a primer in the advantages of detached and discriminating charting. As Gann puts it, "during the period of accumulation or distribution, the man who tries to read the tape must get fooled dozens of times and make mistakes in trying to follow minor moves which do not mean anything." Instead, "the correct way to read the tape is to keep up a chart showing moves of from three days to one week and the amount of volume. . . . I *emphasize* the *fact* that the *correct way* to *read* the *tape* and *interpret* it *accurately*, is to *stay away from it*."[118]

Gann also complicates a historical narrative in which the valorization of charting over tape reading in investment advice of the 1920s and 1930s follows a logic of disenchantment, as the field strives to establish claims to scientific precision and objectivity. On the contrary, while Gann repeatedly asserts his work's scientific status,[119] his is evidently a "science" of a distinctly hermetic or gnostic kind. In this, Gann was in fact typical of what Jamie L. Pietruska has identified as an early twentieth-century "culture of prediction" in the United States. The period saw efforts to codify, systematize, and professionalize the business of forecasting and prediction. These moves, however, "did not rationalize occult forecasting out of existence"; instead, practices such as clairvoyance, astrology, and dream interpretation emerged as forms "of knowledge production considered systematic,

scientific, and modern by many of [their] practitioners and patrons."[120] Accordingly, Gann's deliberately esoteric style seems to have been key to his
establishment of himself as probably the leading market seer of the period. The extent and sources of the fortune Gann amassed in his lifetime
are matters of some dispute, but it seems probable that while his wealth
was substantial, much (perhaps all) of it derived from sales of his books
and the W. D. Gann Scientific Service's instructional courses and newsletters, rather than his own trading operations.[121] That it would even have
been possible for the economics of an operation like the Gann Scientific
Service to have allowed its proprietor to build a successful career on the
sale of print financial advice (rather than this activity being a mere sideline to another profession) is significant. It signals a shift to an increasingly
familiar twentieth- and twenty-first-century phenomenon: the investment
author who does not necessarily write advice about how they make a living, but may instead make a living by writing advice.

Gann's own writing in *Truth of the Stock Tape* communicates to readers a seductive sense of being in the presence of privileged and profound
knowledge that at the same time remains tantalizingly veiled, enticing ini-
tiates to proceed to a further level of illumination. His practical trading
advice essentially boils down to maxims—variations on "stop your losses
quickly and let your profits run"[122]—that were already received wisdom
when Charles Dow endorsed them more than twenty years earlier.[123] The
book's distinction lies not in the substantive training in financial technique
that it promises, then, but in its cultivation of an oracular air. Readers are
urged, for example, to "read this book carefully several times; study each
chart and subject thoroughly, and a new light and knowledge will come
to you every time you read it." Meanwhile, the Biblical adage that there
is "no new thing under the sun" proves to be Gann's ultimate source of
"authority" for his underlying premise that "history is but a repetition
of the past and . . . charts are the only guide we have of what stocks have
done and by which we may determine what they will do." Similarly, he
alludes to a "cause" that "I could explain to you" but that "many of you
would not believe," and remarks that it "is not my object here to give away
[the] secret" of the all-important "*Time* factor, which I use in making up
my annual forecasts" (which are advertised elsewhere in the book).[124] This
esoteric element would become all the more pronounced in Gann's subsequent work, including the singular stock market almanac-cum-futuristic
novel *The Tunnel thru the Air* (1927) and investment guides including
How to Make Profits in Commodities (1941), in which—belying the prosaic

title—there are strong hints of an affinity for astrology, numerology, sacred geometry, and theories of cosmic laws of "vibration." The impression that Gann's work gives of never quite laying bare the recondite foundations of his system or the precise nature of his own, supposedly highly lucrative, trading practices ("This book . . . is mysterious and contains a valuable secret, clothed in veiled language" runs the foreword to *The Tunnel thru the Air*, for example)[125] has led his adherents to make increasingly arcane efforts at decryption in an outpouring of books, videos, websites, and online forums.[126]

The esoteric aspects of Gann's work and persona have also, though, made him something of a complex and problematic figure in the history of technical analysis. As we discuss below, Gann—like other conspicuously esoteric technical analysts like Ralph Nelson Elliott—was a source of some embarrassment for writers in this tradition who, by midcentury, were intent on stressing the field's rigorously scientific credentials, free of any taint of the superstitious or oracular. The association of occult beliefs and practices with women (occult workers and their clients were predominantly female, and the intuitive qualities of such labor were strongly coded as feminine) and with black communities (caricatured as devoted to dream books and number mysticism) helps to explain this anxiety and suspicion—women and African Americans being insistently marginalized in investment writing of the period.[127]

Today, Gann remains one of only three figures (along with Dow and Elliott) who—in surveys of the technical analysis field—routinely receive chapter-length attention because of their paradigm-setting contributions; and books dedicated to his ideas continue to appear (including from mainstream business publishers like Harriman House, John Wiley, and FT Press, the book-publishing arm of the *Financial Times*). But present-day finance academics aiming to reestablish the legitimacy of the Dow-inspired line of technical analysis typically shy away from the air of quackery and pseudoscience that hangs over his work.[128]

However, while Gann's vatic style and recondite means of determining market "tops" and "bottoms" (involving complex systems of angles and time sequences) are idiosyncratic, many of his basic assumptions clearly derive directly from the mainstream, Dow Theory tradition of technical analysis. In particular, he holds to the proto–efficient market claim (most clearly asserted by William Peter Hamilton) that the stock market is a "business barometer" registering "the dominating force currents from business all over the country" and hence that all relevant news is already "anticipated and discounted" in prices. It follows for Gann (as for many technical analysts) that while "it is all well enough to know the history of a company, whether it is old or new, its earnings over a long period of years, how long it has paid dividends and its future prospects; also whether it is over-capitalized or whether the capitalization is conservative or not," "all of the information that affects the future price of the stock is contained in its fluctuations and you need nothing more than its record of prices."[129]

Similar ideas appear in another of the most perennially popular investment books to appear in the period, Edwin Lefèvre's *Reminiscences of a Stock Operator* (1923). An account of daring financial exploits narrated by a thinly fictionalized version of the Wall Street trading legend Jesse Livermore, the book sits uneasily between fiction, memoir, and advice — though it is as a repository of practical investment lore that it retains its venerated reputation today. Like other technical analysts, the narrator, whom Lefèvre calls Larry Livingstone, discusses "learning to read the tape" for "the repetitions and parallelisms of behavior" and notes the usefulness of charts "for those who can assimilate what they read." He also describes his attempts to approach an ideal of a "mind so machinelike that you can depend upon it to function with equal efficiency at all times" even as he also allows his trading to be shaped by seemingly irrational "feelings" or "irresistible impulses" that he attributes to a subliminal accumulation of faint "warning-signals," or what "old traders" call "ticker-sense." As for Gann and other influential stock market experts of the period, the underlying, "fundamental" reasons why prices change is irrelevant to the cultivation of this sensitivity to the stock market. While "there is always a reason for fluctuations," the tape "does not concern itself with the why and wherefore. It doesn't go into explanations. . . . The reason for what a stock does to-day may not be known for two or three days, or weeks, or months. But what the dickens does that matter? Your business with the tape is now — not to-morrow. The reason can wait."[130]

In such statements we can see one of the key ways in which investment advice contributed to the New Era ideology of the 1920s, according to which the US economy had undergone an epochal shift in its capacity to generate and sustain prosperity, meaning that stock prices could quite reasonably be assumed, by the end of the decade, to have reached a "permanently high plateau" (in the infamous words of the Yale economist Irving Fisher, uttered in mid-October 1929). It's important to note that investment guides largely kept themselves aloof from a wider climate of speculative mania in the period, continuing, instead, to advocate independence of mind, the cool application of proven principles, and the inevitability (even for the most seasoned operator) of frequent loss. There were, though, texts that offered more obvious get-rich-quick blandishments, such as R. W. McNeel's *Beating the Stock Market* (1921), which, beyond its bullish title, was accompanied by an advertising campaign that claimed that one of its users had made profits of $70,000 following its tips. And by 1929, even professors of business organization like Charles Amos Dice, author of *New Levels in the Stock Market*, were arguing that over the previous decade "finally, it began to dawn upon the public that a new day had come in the market; that a marvelous reconstruction was taking place in the economic fundamentals of our time; and that the market was but registering the tremendous changes that were in progress."[131]

And it was (as many commentators at the time and since have suggested) another work of investment advice that did more than any other discursive intervention to establish in the public mind the idea that the US economy had entered a New Era of prosperity in the mid- to late 1920s, and thus to encourage an explosion of popular participation in the stock market. More sober in tone, this book was *Common Stocks as Long Term Investments* (1924) by Edgar Lawrence Smith, a financial adviser at a New York brokerage, who had set out to prove the truism that bonds represented better long-term investments than equities but had found (in studying the period 1866–1922) the opposite to be the case. Smith's findings thus flew in the face of the conventional wisdom that positioned bonds as the safe and prudent choice for the lay investor (leading the overwhelming majority of such investors to invest their money in this way) and identified stocks as inherently speculative and best left either to professionals or a minority of risk-taking amateurs. Ironically, then, given its reputation as the book that fueled the speculative boom, *Common Stocks*, as Smith repeatedly emphasizes, offers rather "conservative" guidance. Indeed, in encouraging investors to assemble a carefully researched and diversified portfolio of common stocks, Smith anticipated the "value investing" brand of fundamental analysis propounded by Benjamin Graham and David Dodd a decade later in *Security Analysis* (1934).

Smith's ideas were, however, liable (albeit inadvertently) to encourage a certain complacency among investors. His central claim was that "directors of conservatively managed corporations . . . will never aim to declare all the company's net earnings in dividends. They will turn back a part of such earnings to surplus account, and invest this increasing surplus in productive operation." As a result, "over a period of years, the principal value of a well diversified holding of common stocks of representative corporations, in essential industries, tends to increase in accordance with the operation of compound interest."[132]

Smith's book was a best seller, and, according to Irving Fisher, writing approvingly in 1929, "threw a bombshell into the investing world. . . . It was only as the public came to realize, largely through the writing of Edgar Lawrence Smith, that stocks were to be preferred to bonds during a period of dollar depreciation, that the bull market began in good earnest to cause a proper valuation of common shares."[133] In their postmortem on the 1929 crash in *Investment and Speculation: Studies of Modern Movements and Basic Principles* (1931), the bond salesmen Lawrence Chamberlain and William Wren Hay similarly attributed changing public attitudes to investment to Smith's book, though with the negative judgment that Smith had inspired "erroneous belief" in the long-term reliability of common stocks.[134] Cedric Cowing comments that the view of investment promulgated by Smith "was undoubtedly a prime factor in the dormancy of the bond market while stocks were in frenzied flux."[135]

The reach and influence of Smith's book is the clearest indication of how the investment advice genre fed the mood of the speculative boom of the 1920s. One factor that has plausibly been cited to help explain the over-escalation of share values in the period is that "investors [had been] misled by exaggerated claims and inadequate disclosure of the true financial position of corporations."[136] Certainly, the architects of the New Deal were convinced that this had been a critical problem, and it led them to mandate company disclosure and reporting requirements for new issues and traded securities as part of regulatory legislation introduced in the early to mid-1930s. One of the reasons that technical analysis predominated in the period prior to the crash is precisely that the kind of detailed information about companies' earnings and book values necessary for thorough "fundamental" analysis was often not publicly available. In insisting that access to such underlying information was in fact unnecessary (since it was always already priced in by a stock market "barometer" that—if not infallible—was very close to it), and thus in advising investors to focus instead on the eddies of asset prices themselves, technical analysis therefore helped to foster the indifference to the actual health of firms in the "real economy" that fueled the boom. Similarly, while Smith was clear that investors must "watch for changes both in the conditions of industries and of individual corporations and be prepared to change the investment to accord with sound analysis of the latest available information," his book, and the digests of its key ideas that he published as op-eds in the *New York Times* and the *Atlantic Monthly* in 1925, were widely taken to

FIGURE 4.2. Illustration by Marshall Frantz, "Paper Profits: A Story of Wall Street by Arthur Train," *Ladies' Home Journal* (January 1930): 5. "Paper Profits" provided courtesy of Meredith Corporation, Ladies' Home Journal®, © 1930. Image published with permission of ProQuest LLC. Further reproduction is prohibited without permission.

imply—like the technical analysis approaches with which Smith was otherwise at odds—that the fundamentals underlying the values of stocks
could be relied upon to take care of themselves, with investors able to
focus their eyes on the stock chart (whose line, over the long haul, should
be expected to tend ever upward in Smith's account).

In early 1930, Smith would appear—thinly fictionalized—in a novel serialized in the *Ladies' Home Journal* (fig. 4.2). *Paper Profits: A Story of Wall
Street* by Arthur Train (well known in the 1920s and 1930s as the author of
popular legal thrillers) portrays an investment expert, closely resembling
Smith, addressing a lunch club in the spring of 1927, when "'the Coolidge
Boom' [is] on" and "multitudes play the stock market," though a few still
"[do] not."[137] The speaker wishes to prod these laggards with a simple message, which was also Smith's: "Buy common stocks!" The rationale is clear
and likewise echoes that of *Common Stocks as Long Term Investments*: "I
cannot foresee—except in a period of panic, or temporary depression—
the time when it will be advantageous to sell common stocks. They should
steadily increase in value." There is a knowing nod, too, to another investment guru, John J. Raskob, in the narrator's exclamation: "Stocks! Stocks!
Was the whole world going into stocks! Was everybody going to be rich?"
(Raskob's by-then-infamous "Everybody Ought to Be Rich" interview
had appeared in the *Ladies' Home Journal* the previous August). All such
boosterish pronouncements take on an unmistakably ironic ring by the
end of the novel, however, which is set in the spring of 1930, after "the
Great Crash—the greatest debacle in the history of speculative finance—
ha[s] occurred" and the "bottom ha[s] at last dropped out of the stock
market" (the setting is exactly synchronous with the installment's publication: it appeared in the *Ladies' Home Journal*'s April 1930 issue).[138] In
this radically transformed context, the investment advice so confidently
issued by men like Smith and Raskob looked very different. Where, just
a few months previously, the leading women's titles had enthusiastically
showcased Smith's and Raskob's optimistic stock market prognoses, now
readers were encouraged to view such claims as deceptive and delusory.

After the Crash

As Janice Traflet has described, the Great Crash that hit the New York
Stock Exchange in the fall of 1929 severely damaged public confidence in
the stock market.[139] The "Shadow of 1929" was long: during the Depression,

Americans showed little sign of willingness to invest whatever savings they had (and few had any at all) in stocks, and, as late as 1952—by which time personal savings rates were relatively high (around 7–8 percent)— only about 9.5 percent of households held any common stock (compared to the 1920s level of around 25 percent).[140] Traflet shows how, from the 1930s on, but more concertedly after the Second World War, the New York Stock Exchange and other Wall Street institutions conducted public relations and advertising campaigns designed to persuade the public of the rectitude and reliability of "the Street"—and, in particular, of the patriotic value of investing in corporate America via the stock market (the marketing campaign "Own Your Share of American Business" ran from 1954 to 1969).

Writers of investment advice faced a similar challenge to reestablish their credibility (and reassure their readership) following a crash whose extent and duration had flown in the face of conventional wisdom— especially that of the technical analysts, whose beloved "mechanical," "support," or "resistance" points (previous lows that would in theory tend to check declining prices) had not curtailed the sell-off in late 1929 and after. The field was also dealt a blow by the post-crash appearance of research that would come to be recognized as a foundational contribution to the development of academic finance theory. First in an investment newsletter published in 1931, then in a lecture delivered in 1932, and finally in a journal article that appeared in 1933, Alfred Cowles III, founder of the Cowles Commission for Research in Economics, presented the results of a study of stock market prediction. The article, "Can Stock Market Forecasters Forecast?" compared predictions from financial newsletters and periodicals, insurance companies, and the Dow theorist William Peter Hamilton's editorials for the *Wall Street Journal* to the results achieved simply by holding a portfolio reflecting the overall composition of the Dow Jones or picking stocks at random. The study concluded that the forecasters tended to underperform relative to holding the "general run of stocks" and that any apparent successes were at least as likely to be attributable to chance as skill. Hamilton—chosen because "several decades of editorials in the country's leading financial newspaper have built up a great popular following for the Dow Theory"—did receive credit for achieving "a result better than what would ordinarily be regarded as a normal investment return," but this outcome was still "poorer than the result of a continuous outright investment in representative common stocks for this period."[141] Defenders of technical analysis would question

Cowles's findings: Hamilton's fellow Dow theorist, Robert Rhea, issued an early critique,[142] and a 1998 paper revisiting the controversy suggests that Hamilton's predictions would have generated superior risk-adjusted returns compared to an index fund strategy.[143] Definitive evaluation of the kinds of forecasts issued by Hamilton and other investment writers of the period remains difficult, since, as Cowles himself noted, "some of the forecasters seem to have taken a page from the book of the Delphic Oracle, expressing their prophecies in terms susceptible of more than one construction."[144]

During the 1930s, Rhea was an exception among such writers in directly responding to Cowles's challenge to their profession: his peers preferred to ignore it entirely as they sought—even as the long bear market continued—to reassert the validity of their field (and of investment in general) in the wake of the Great Crash. Technical analysts were especially active in this period: key publications included Rhea's *The Dow Theory* (1932); Richard W. Schabacker's *Stock Market Theory and Practice* (1930), *Technical Analysis and Stock Market Profits* (1932), and *Stock Market Profits: A Course in Forecasting* (1934); Humphrey B. Neill's *Tape Reading and Market Tactics* (1931); Victor de Villiers and Owen Taylor's *Point and Figure Method of Anticipating Stock Price Movements* (1934); and Harold M. Gartley's *Profits in the Stock Market* (1935). The crash had been damaging to virtually every public figure who presumed to pass judgment on what the stock market would do in the future, but it had been especially ignominious for experts, such as Irving Fisher, who had commanded respect on the basis of their academic credentials and institutional standing. In this context, the appeal of technical analysis—long based in the cultivation of an image of the hardscrabble outsider taking on the elite experts at their own game—was to a certain extent enhanced by the crash. In terms of their basic precepts and rules of thumb, however, the slew of post-1929 technical analysis texts largely hewed to the foundational principles of precrash Dow Theory, elaborating and more thoroughly systematizing the key ideas of the likes of William Peter Hamilton—and of course Charles Dow himself—but not innovating on them in the ways that the crash might seem to demand. Indeed, the *Forbes* financial editor Richard W. Schabacker argued that established forms of technical analysis were perfectly capable of explaining the crash, pointing to various technical features over the course of 1929 that indicated an impending bear market, and noting that he had encouraged investors to get out of the market in September 1929. His attempt to use the same methods to predict where the Dow was heading (he was writing in 1930) would be less helpful to the technical analysis cause, however. He expressed his conviction that the Dow had reached a strong support level (in the region of 170–190 points) that had finally "stopped the Panic of 1929" and in the process proved that "technical study of the stock market is not humbug" but rather of "tremendous practical value, especially when all other factors of market analysis have failed."[145] In fact, though, this "support level" proved to be no such thing, and the market would not bottom out until it hit 41.22 points in mid-1932, having sustained a staggering 89 percent loss from its September 1929 peak.[146]

Perhaps sensing the dangers of rendering themselves hostages to fortune during a period of such acute financial turmoil, other technical analysis authors dealt with the challenge posed by the crash more through shifts in rhetoric than through the substance of their claims and recommendations. Humphrey B. Neill's *Tape Reading and Market Tactics* is especially revealing in this regard. Despite a title that harks back to the turn-of-the-century heyday of tape reading guides, Neill's book reflects the 1920s turn to charting as at least as effective a method of tracking prices as direct observation of the ticker itself.[147] Neill adopts various means to persuade erstwhile or aspiring tape readers or chartists—who may have been deterred from involvement in the market by the crash—that they should not abandon speculation. In opening, he defends speculation as an innate and irresistible impulse, and the very lifeblood of the nation's industrial might:

> The stock market is a great cauldron of the hopes, desires, and despairs of speculators, or traders. . . . If it were not for the speculators, America would not stand where she does, as the leading industrial country in the world. We may deplore speculation, but if it were not for this outpouring of money for stocks, you and I should not enjoy a fraction of the comforts and luxuries which we accept as necessities.[148]

He goes on to reassure readers that losses in the crash should not put them off speculation entirely, since reverses of this kind were almost universal: "Do not be discouraged if you have lost money in the market. Nearly everyone did during 1929 and 1930. Many big traders lost everything and have had to start anew."[149]

Indeed, much of Neill's discussion of the crash is given over to emphasizing its anomalous and exceptional status. The market fell through a supposed "resistance point" without a flicker in late 1930, he tells us, because "the market ... was greatly changed in that year" and "the entire situation was different in all respects, and could not be compared" to conditions the previous year. Similarly, the "great bull market [of 1928–29] was abnormal in its intensity, and it is quite unlikely that we shall witness the like again for some years." We should not be surprised that the boom and bust seemed to contradict some of the prevailing assumptions of technical analysis, Neill implies, because such analysis deals in typical price movements, and—he is at pains to stress—prices between 1928 and 1930 were anything but typical, rising and then falling far further than a technical analysis approach, premised precisely on the power of precedent (old highs and lows) to curb movements, would expect. At the same time, if there is a lesson to be drawn from the mass-participation bull and bear markets that the nation has just lived through, then, for Neill, it is that the emphasis that technical analysis has always placed on market psychology (as the factor that tends to push prices past their true values at the tops or bottoms of trends) needs to be accentuated still further. The "fact that during the past eight or ten years millions of people have bought stocks for the first time, must be considered when we are trying to estimate the ebb and flow of stock prices," he argues, going on to "hazard a forecast": "more attention will be paid in the future to an interpretation of human nature as it is affected by economic factors than to the economic factors themselves." Rather than a turn to fundamental analysis, therefore, the boom and bust years should lead the speculator to double down on a "market philosophy" stressing "market psychology"—a reaffirmation, not a repudiation, of one of the core tenets of technical analysis.[150] Neill here makes evident the influence of psychological theory on technical analysts—and in particular the turn-of-the-century crowd theory of European thinkers such as Gustave Le Bon, Gabriel Tarde, Émile Durkheim, and Georg Simmel (especially as it was filtered through the work of writers in the United States, including the psychologist Boris Sidis, the economist Edward D. Jones, and the sociologist Robert E. Park).[151]

The post-crash period also saw the emergence of the third figure in the technical analysis holy trinity (after Dow and Gann): Ralph Nelson Elliott. Far from a stock market insider (his background was as a writer for restaurant trade magazines), Elliott became fascinated by the movements of stock prices following the 1929 crash. Initially immersing himself in Dow Theory, through the 1930s he developed his own distinctive "Wave Principle" of patterns in the stock market. Elliott was a subscriber to a market letter service published by the Detroit-based Investment Council,

Inc., and in 1934 contacted the service's founder and editor, Charles Collins. Impressed by Elliott's predictions, Collins arranged for the publication of the underlying ideas in book form, and the resulting text—*The Wave Principle*—appeared in 1938. In the first chapter of the book, Elliott remarks that while "there has developed a definite profession with market forecasting as its objective," "1929 came and went, and the turn from the greatest bull market on record to the greatest bear market on record caught almost every investor off guard." Echoing Dow theorists like Neill, Elliott suggests that "attempt[s] to deal with the market's movements have failed to recognize the extent to which the market is a psychological phenomenon." Insisting on a relation between the cosmic and the microcosmic, he argues that "the market has its law, just as is true of other things throughout the universe," and "human emotions . . . are rhythmical. They move in waves of a definite number and direction": truths whose first glimpse he attributes—in the portentously titled follow-up *Nature's Law: The Secret of the Universe* (1946)—to the designers of the Great Pyramid of Giza.[152]

In elaborating the various permutations of the wave principle that he sees as underlying stock market movements, Elliott is at once emphatic and obscure. "A complete wave movement," he states, "consists of five waves" (three "in the direction of the movement," and two "in a contrary direction"). "Why this should be five rather than some other number," however, is "one of the secrets of the universe." "No attempt will be made to explain it," Elliott curtly remarks (though he notes the prominence of the number five in "other basic patterns of nature," such as various features of the human body): it can simply "be accepted without necessity of reasoning the matter out."[153] The remainder of the book is devoted to a detailed taxonomy of the various forms of nested waves and cycles evident, Elliott suggests, in stock market movements stretching back to the mid-nineteenth century—the beginning of a "Grand Super Cycle," whose first wave came to an end in the crisis period of 1928–32. Elliott's, then, is a seductively comprehensive and totalizing vision, in which each minor price fluctuation takes its place in the stock market's rhythmical *longue durée*, itself part of an ordered natural system—first apprehended by the ancients—that is truly universal in scale.

Only around five hundred copies of *The Wave Principle* were printed, but Elliott's ideas sufficiently impressed the editors of one of Wall Street's leading periodicals, *Financial World*, for them to commission a series of articles based on the book, which ran in 1939. On the basis of his rising profile, Elliott was also able to attract subscribers and attendees for his market bulletins and seminars, which he issued and ran during the 1940s, before his death in 1948. Unsurprisingly, given its invocation of cosmic laws and strong hints of numerological influence, Elliott's work has frequently been bracketed with Gann's. Like Gann's, too, Elliott's ideas would spawn mini-industries in the latter half of the twentieth century and into the twenty-first, with a slew of more-or-less respectable-looking books appearing outlining and embellishing his ideas and establishing his status as one of the foremost technical analysis authorities. Yet, despite his prominence, he has attracted the same accusations of crankishness as Gann (though among finance academics sympathetic to technical analysis there have been some attempts to burnish his reputation at the expense of Gann's: Andrew W. Lo and Jasmina Hasanhodzic, for example, sharply distinguish Elliott's work—which they see as rigorous and insightful— from that of his astrologically inclined contemporary).[154]

Elliott's and Gann's postwar status as renowned market visionaries would, however, be in spite of the best efforts of the authors who produced the mid-twentieth century's crowning work of investment advice in the technical analysis tradition: John Magee Jr. and Robert D. Edwards. Magee—a plastics mail-order salesman turned investment expert and trader—teamed up with Edwards—a well-established market analyst and the brother-in-law of Richard W. Schabacker—in the early 1940s, and they collaborated on the writing of *Technical Analysis of Stock Trends*, published in 1948. Their book is very overtly positioned as the culmination and summation of a half-century of investigations into the technical factors affecting the buying and selling of corporate securities, and they freely admit that much of the material in the book is a recapitulation of previous work in the Dow Theory vein. They are equally clear, however, in distinguishing (on the opening page) between "some of the world's most astute accountants, analysts, and researchers"—who have been attracted to the stock market, and on whose shoulders Edward and Magee are proud to stand—and what they describe as "a motley crew of eccentrics, mystics, and 'hunch players.'" While the pioneers of the two major distinctive offshoots from Dow Theory to have appeared in the previous decades— Gann and Elliott—are, tellingly, nowhere mentioned in the book, the targeting of this jibe in their direction is clear (all the more so when Edwards and Magee shortly after refer to the "lunatic fringe" associated with the "cyclical" approach to markets—Elliott's particular specialty).[155] The canonical or textbook version of technical analysis that Edwards and Magee seek to enshrine over their volume's more than 400 pages is, then, decidedly Dow-based and studiously excludes anything that might compromise the Dow Theory's long-standing claim to scientific respectability.

Edwards and Magee are at pains to reassert the idea that, if not quite an "exact science," a technical analysis approach to speculation is nonetheless something more than simply a mere subjective "art." The book also reiterates various key claims of the field that we have encountered in earlier works: that *prices move in trends* and trends tend to continue until something happens to change the supply-demand balance"—such changes being "usually detectable in the action of the market itself"; that the market already discounts both present and future economic conditions in its prices; that, nonetheless, prices are always liable to be swayed from "true" values by the emotions and desires of the investing public, providing lucrative opportunities for those who can keep their heads; that the marking up of charts offers a more objective and reliable method of tracking price movements than "tape reading" or "tape watching"; that all the apparent dislocations of the Great Crash and its aftermath "have not much altered the 'pattern' of the stock market," with the market "in the main . . . go[ing] right on repeating the same old movements in much the same old routine," and "the importance of a knowledge of these phenomena to the trader and investor [being] in no way diminished"; and that "your job, as a speculator," is an honorable and indeed essential one—"to provide liquidity in the market" and "counteract the irrational excesses of a market-in-motion," thereby "performing a useful and necessary service to the general economic welfare."[156]

Edwards and Magee's overt aim of writing the definitive work of technical analysis for their time was undoubtedly successful; indeed, *Technical Analysis of Stock Trends* has outlived its own period, continuing to appear in new, updated editions (the most recent—the eleventh—came out with Routledge in 2019). Yet even as they were writing the book in the mid-1940s they were already fighting something of a rearguard action against a fundamental analysis paradigm that, for a decade, had been gaining greater visibility, legitimacy, and prestige. Thus, alongside the disparagement of the alleged cranks who tarnish the reputation of technical analysis, the book opens by mocking fundamental or "statistical" analysts who naively pore over reams of corporate data without recognizing that (in accordance with one of the key precepts of Dow Theory) such data are already "priced in": "the going price as established by the market itself comprehends all the fundamental information which the statistical analyst can hope to learn (plus some which is perhaps secret from him, known only to a few insiders) and much else besides of equal or even greater importance."[157]

It was vital for Edwards and Magee to put the "statisticians" in their place in this way from the start, because, since the mid-1930s, potential readers of a book like theirs had been given increasingly plausible grounds to believe that it was indeed possible to identify over- or undervalued stocks through close examination of information pertaining to the health and prospects of particular companies. This was thanks in large part to the investment advice written by Benjamin Graham and David Dodd. Graham is probably best known for 1949's *The Intelligent Investor* (its ongoing success helped by the world's most renowned investor, and a former protégé of Graham's, Warren Buffett, praising it as "by far the best book about investing ever written").[158] It was in 1934's *Security Analysis*, however, that Graham, in collaboration with his colleague Dodd, laid out his core philosophy of "value investing." This book, too, has been a perennial success, going through numerous editions (the sixth appeared in 2008) and selling hundreds of thousands of copies. The writers of *Security Analysis* were able to draw on the academic credentials bestowed by teaching posts at Columbia Business School, though for Graham the book was to some extent an exercise in rebuilding a reputation damaged by the ignominious decline of his investment firm the Benjamin Graham Account (a form of early hedge fund) following the crash of 1929. *Security Analysis* is very clearly presented as an attempt to learn the lessons of the speculative hype and excess of the late 1920s and to return to the commonsense basics of determining good value investments. As they put it in their preface, "we have striven throughout to guard the student against overemphasis upon the superficial and the temporary. . . . This overemphasis is at once the delusion and the nemesis of the world of finance."[159]

In the book, Graham and Dodd reserve particular scorn for Edgar Lawrence Smith's *Common Stocks as Long Term Investments*, which they describe as "the small and rather sketchy volume from which the new-era theory may be said to have sprung." Smith's "radical fallacy," as Graham and Dodd put it, was "the assumption that common stocks could be counted on to behave in the future about as they had in the past"—an assumption that the Great Crash and Depression had thoroughly exploded. Instead, Graham and Dodd stress what they refer to as a company's "earning power," which "must imply a fairly confident expectation of certain future results." In determining earning power, "it is not sufficient to know what the past earnings have averaged, or even that they disclose a definite line of growth or decline. There must be plausible grounds for believing that this average or this trend is a dependable guide to the future. Experience has shown only too forcibly that in many instances this is far from true." From earning power can be derived a measure of "intrinsic value"—Graham and Dodd's mantra, though one that they outline pragmatically: rather than seeking to "determine exactly what is the intrinsic value of a given security," the security analyst "needs only to establish either that the value is *adequate* . . . or else that the value is considerably higher or considerably lower than the market price. For such purposes, an indefinite and approximate measure of the intrinsic value may be sufficient." Graham and Dodd's approach leads them, then, to reassert the conceptual and moral distinction between investment and speculation that had so preoccupied nineteenth-century commentators on the stock market, but which technical analysts of the early twentieth century had been content to abandon. "*An investment operation*," they write, "*is one which, upon thorough analysis, promises safety of principal and a satisfactory return. Operations not meeting these requirements are speculative.*"[160]

Viewing the conventional means of determining "value"—earnings per share—as subject to "arbitrary determination and manipulation," Graham and Dodd argue that the "intricacies of corporate accounting and financial policies" provide the security analyst with "unbounded opportunities for shrewd detective work, for critical comparisons, for discovery and pointing out a state of affairs quite different from that indicated by the publicized 'per-share earnings.'"[161] While Graham (the book's lead author) had been working on the material that would make up *Security Analysis* for at least five years, its publication coincided fortuitously with legislative changes that considerably expanded the range and depth of information available to the security analyst. As Timothy Jacobson describes, the New Deal financial regulatory regime mandated the disclosure of an abundance of previously privileged corporate data:

> The cornerstone laws that burned the imperative of "disclosure" onto the psyche of American business and finance were the Securities Act of 1933, which required registration of securities offerings with the Federal Trade Commission and public disclosure of material financial information about issuers; the Glass-Steagall Act of 1933, which erected a fire wall separating investment and commercial banking functions; and the Securities Exchange Act of 1934, which established the Securities and Exchange Commission and required stock

exchanges to get approval of their rules and also required companies to make public detailed information about their financial performance.[162]

By the late 1930s and early 1940s, then, amateur investors had both the potential (if not always the time or resources) to access the kind of information necessary for thorough fundamental analysis as well as systematic guidance to the best means of methodically investigating any profitable discrepancy between price and "intrinsic" value. And they could also work step-by-step through textbook taxonomies of the characteristic technical patterns supposedly displayed by stock prices during their periodic ups and downs. Legislation at this time also clarified the legal status of publications of this kind. The Investment Advisers Act of 1940 (based on a report prepared for Congress by the Securities and Exchange Commission [SEC]) exempted "the publisher of any bona fide newspaper, news magazine, or business or financial publication of general and regular circulation" from a requirement to register with the SEC as an investment adviser and conform to the strict regulations on disclosure and client relations that the act imposed.[163] The act thus permitted writers of guidebooks, columns, and newsletters a freedom of maneuver curtailed for peers who specialized in offering personalized advice to individual clients.[164] Investment counsel firms — as the retailers of specific, tailored investment advice were known — expanded considerably in number during the 1930s. Of the nearly four hundred such firms identified by the SEC as in operation in 1937, over three hundred had been organized after 1929. This sharp increase was likely attributable, the SEC reported, "to the demands of the investing public, which required supervision of its security investments after its experience during the depression years."[165] The growing public demand for investment advice highlighted by the SEC represented a further boon for writers of generic stock market guidance, who presented themselves as the low-cost alternatives for those who desired expert direction but could not afford bespoke services.

Yet internal pressures within the competing methodological fields of investment writing also began to come to a head in this period. The contradiction that technical analysis had always identified in its fundamentalist rival — that it was futile for the amateur investor to try to sniff out new information because "the market" would always have got there first — only seemed to be deepened by the new transparency and availability of business information. Meanwhile, the central contradiction of technical analysis — that if its precepts worked consistently, then all market participants would adopt them, nullifying their efficacy—was more acutely apparent than ever. While proponents of each school delighted in pointing out the flaws in their opponents' approach, they resolutely refused to acknowledge the inherent contradictions in their own. One can see why this silence needed to be maintained by considering a rare exception to it. In his major contribution to the technical analysis canon, *Tape Reading and Market Tactics*, Humphrey B. Neill directly, if fleetingly, acknowledges the issue that strikes at the very heart of this approach:

> If any of the theories we hear about ever did work consistently, they could not do so for long, because too many traders would soon be acting on them, and their effectiveness would thus be ruined. . . . If we all played for a given resistance, there would not be any resistance left when the stock arrived at the expected point, because all of us would have executed our orders ahead of it, in order to take advantage of it.[166]

Neill attempts to minimize the impact of this admission by arguing that recent highs and lows should in any event only ever be treated "as points to watch on the tape and *then* judge," since "they have failed so many times to mark resistance."[167] While this advice is consistent with the genre's tendency to encourage readers to develop their own independence of mind, it quietly surrenders the crucial technical analysis article of faith that prices at which a stock has previously reversed direction possess some particular and predictable significance. As if tacitly acknowledging the irrefutability of the challenge he discusses, while at the same time wishing to minimize its potentially devastating implications for the whole chartist paradigm, Neill simply ends a chapter with this observation and abandons the matter for the remainder of the book. Such moments are so rare in investment advice writing because they bring the basic question of why readers should consume and trust writers' favored systems so sharply and uncomfortably into view. For the most part, as we've seen, writers seek to minimize, disguise, or sideline such challenges to their approaches, lest they cast the whole enterprise of investment advice into doubt. In the 1950s and 1960s university research in financial economics under the rubrics of modern portfolio theory and the efficient market hypothesis would place contradictions of exactly this kind under remorseless focus, presenting challenges—but also new opportunities—for writers seeking to school the public in how they might, if not beat the market, then at least reap the rewards of its supposedly infinite wisdom.

Coda: The Long Road Home from Wall Street

An intriguing career trajectory unites several of the key protagonists in this chapter. After establishing themselves as revered dispensers of investment advice—whether on the chartist or fundamentalist sides of the field's methodological divide—these authors each took a counterintuitive turn toward the ends of their careers. In their later writings, there is a shift in focus away from, or even a complete abandonment of, guidance on securities markets and the stratagems of Wall Street operators in favor of reflection and counsel more in the vein of self-help, spiritual confession, or speculative philosophy.

Roger W. Babson, for example, made the case for the power of faith and positive thinking in the face of the gloom of the Great Depression in *Cheer Up! Better Times Ahead!* (1932), urging readers that "all that is needed today is a determination to live rightly, deal justly, and have faith in the Eternal Spirit."[168] He followed up with his autobiography *Actions and Reactions* (1935), in which he wrote at length about the importance of his devout Christian beliefs to his personal and professional development. Rather similarly, John Moody's autobiography *The Long Road Home* (1933) and its sequel *Fast by the Road* (1942) treat his long and outwardly successful career in business and finance as merely the circuitous route that led him eventually to his true destination: the conversion to Roman Catholicism that he characterized as "coming home" (he would go on to write a biography of Cardinal Newman). "This great Mother Church of the Christian Faith has brought me the inestimable blessing of perfect peace," he wrote in *The Long Road Home*; "where all was doubt before, she gives me faith."[169] William D. Gann also shifted his focus to religious matters in his late writing. Where, in his earlier books, Biblical wisdom had been invoked as a path to enlightenment concerning the mysterious movements of the stock market, in 1950's *The Magic Word* the focus is squarely on understanding the power of "divine law" and the titular "magic word" (i.e., Jehovah) in their own right. And Ralph Nelson Elliott's final book *Nature's Law: The Secret of the Universe* (1946) subordinates the chart analysis that had been the primary concern of his earlier *The Wave Principal* to a full-blown exploration of the author's esoteric interests (including the conjecture that the "law of Nature" he claims to have discovered was known to ancient civilizations whose level of scientific advancement "equalled or exceeded today's development").[170]

If one were not familiar with these canonical investment authors' earlier works, then the shifts in their writings' generic centers of gravity in the final acts of their careers might look, on the face of it, like rather eccentric departures from the core subject matter on which they had built their reputations. These moves might be understood as opportunistic attempts to tap into prevalent Depression-era concerns with self-improvement and personal growth, as successfully channeled by best-selling works like Emmet Fox's *Power through Constructive Thinking* (1932) or—most famously—Dale Carnegie's *How to Win Friends and Influence People* (1936).[171] Another way to interpret this foregrounding of questions of subjective transformation and spiritual and emotional development, however, would be as a *distillation* of what had always been the essential element that made earlier works by these and other authors in the investment field successful. This would not be a departure, then, but (in Moody's phrase) a coming home to what had always been of core significance, even if it had not been superficially apparent. Providing readers with practical tips on playing the stock market would, from this point of view, be only the ostensible purpose of those earlier texts, and the provision of an imaginative space in which to play out fantasies of self-overcoming and psychic enlargement their core underlying function. We continue to explore the thesis that the investment advice genre is ultimately and above all about an investment in the self in the following chapters.

CHAPTER FIVE

Domestic Budgets and Efficient Markets (1950–1990)

T he final chapter of Helen Gurley Brown's self-help primer for the independent woman, *Having It All*, is entitled "Money." In the chapter she tells her readers that acquiring "*keeping* money, share-portfolio money" from a lover actually requires more "talent than learning about the stock market," and she offers detailed investment instructions to women so that they can build their own portfolios without relying on the gifts that may accompany intimacy. Her instructions include a checklist of good investment decisions (choose only the stock of companies that "yield more than 6%," have a "long record of dividend payments," and a "last report of earnings up") and a checklist of bad investment decisions ("not taking the trouble to be informed," "buying on the basis of tips and rumors"). The chapter makes it clear that financial investment advice is the key to the independent life that Gurley Brown became famous for exhorting: "read *The Which Book of Money*" and take advice not from partners or friends but from "*impersonal* advisers and keep checking."[1] The inclusion of this sternly unsentimental chapter would come as no surprise to readers who knew Gurley Brown from her long stint as editor of *Cosmopolitan*, as the magazine regularly reviewed financial investment guides and made the interdependencies of sexual and economic autonomy for the modern woman very clear.

Gurley Brown's writing is suggestive of both the ubiquitous presence of financial investment advice in mainstream culture by the 1980s and the key role that women had come to play in it. It accords with the narrative of overarching and inclusive growth in personal financial investment in the decades following the Second World War in the United States in particular:

an expansion in both the value of investments and in the numbers of investors. The value of the Dow Jones index, starting from a historically low base, rose throughout the four decades following 1945, tripling over the course of the 1950s and surging in the go-go speculative fervor of the early 1960s before cresting in the late 1980s.[2] This growth was reflected in the numbers of individuals who owned stock. The percentage of adults who held stock in the United States steadily grew: from 4 percent in 1945 to nearly 20 percent by 1962; by 1983 well over 30 percent and by 2001 it reached a symbolically significant 51 percent, a peak to which it has to yet return.[3] Yet what this period of apparently sustained growth actually meant for the cultures of personal investment in the United States was much more uneven than either these bald figures or Gurley Brown's confident assertions suggest. The clear contradictions that shaped these decades—the growing disparities in both who held stock and in what stock ownership itself meant and involved—were reflected in its financial advice.

The histories of postwar wealth reveal a notable divergence between the investment practices of the middle and the elite classes. Steve Fraser and Kevin Phillips have both pointed out that the rewards of stock investment were disproportionately concentrated within the elite in the postwar era, even given the already relatively small numbers of people investing. Nearly "half of all dividend income" received from stock market investment was taken by only "one-tenth of 1 percent of the adult population."[4] This asymmetry expanded across this period. Very rich Americans developed vehicles for protecting their wealth from taxation, while middle-class investors moved increasingly toward a variety of collectively managed investment funds. In 1950 individual investors accounted for 80 percent of trades, but by the mid-1970s the situation had almost entirely reversed and institutional investors now accounted for 75 percent of trading, a situation that was largely paralleled in the United Kingdom.[5]

Investing behavior was thus guided for the vast majority of stockholders not by their individual choices but by the nature of their relationship to corporate capital.[6] Buying employer stocks at preferential rates, or being given them as part of a remuneration package, took on increasing significance, as Employee Stock Ownership Plans (ESOPs) and corporate pension plans grew in the immediate postwar decades.[7] These schemes, which flourished in the United States as a result of President Truman's intervention in labor disputes, represented the further privatization of post–New Deal corporatism that had been so effective at providing structures of security for the privileged white male worker in particular.[8] As the individualization of these risks grew, particularly from the late 1970s onward, so did the racial disparities that underpinned them. Studies have consistently demonstrated that African Americans were far less likely throughout the postwar period to be either directly or indirectly invested in the stock market and that, even in instances when the earnings gap has narrowed, the wealth gap—particularly regarding ownership of speculative assets—has not.[9] Analysis by the Office of Economic Opportunity suggested that by the early 1980s African Americans owned only 0.13 percent of the value of stocks in America.[10]

So the narrative of a slow and seemingly imperturbable increase in both the growth of the stock market and the number of participants conceals increasingly significant divisions. On the one hand, we have a largely white elite who have been able to increase their wealth through professional guidance involving estate and tax avoidance planning. On the other, we have those who are either not invested at all or for whom investment is divided between the direct ownership of stocks or bonds and participation in managed funds or pension funds, often in tandem with both state and employer security provision, over which they have little or no control.[11] In the closing decades of the century, in both the United States and Britain, as pensions were either replaced by tax-free shelters such as the 401(k) and Keogh retirement plans or downgraded from defined benefits to defined contributions, the gap between these groups widened dramatically. As social risks were moved from the collective structures of the state and corporation onto the individual, precarity replaced stability and debt became an increasingly central part of family financial planning. Eastman Kodak, for example, once celebrated for its employee support, has recently settled claims on their Employee Stock Ownership Plan and Pension retirement plans.[12] This chapter explores how this shift to individual responsibility was both promoted and negotiated through the genre of personal financial investment advice but, before doing so, it briefly delineates the political, technological, and social changes that framed the genre.

The Financialization of Everyday Life

In the 1950s, especially in the United States, the vocabulary for stock market investment often cleaved to the postwar rhetoric of national growth. The privileged idea of the investor buying into the national economy was supported by politicians and Washington think tanks as well as bodies such as the New York Stock Exchange and large brokerage firms such as Merrill Lynch. This language was also being spoken in the United Kingdom, albeit in a more subdued and politically contested manner. Kieran Heinemann, for example, has detailed the ways in which the "dawning of an 'age of the small investor'" was being proclaimed in late 1950s Britain as Conservative politicians followed the language of the Scottish Unionist politician Noel Skelton and began advocating a paternalist notion of a "property owning democracy." The advocacy of individual ownership, which Margaret Thatcher was to reignite so powerfully in the late 1980s, sought to bridge the gap between capital and labor and mobilize the fantasy of a classless capitalism while encouraging the working class to invest, rather than spend, their disposable income.[13]

Yet the growing genre of financial advice complicates this narrative of liberal economic nationalism by presenting a persistent fear of state growth, intervention, and regulation. By the end of the 1960s, anxieties about an expanding state remained, but earlier fears of socialism or nationalization had been supplanted by concerns about inflation and taxation. For elite investors, these anxieties were defrayed through the use of tax-free municipal bonds and preferential rates of capital gains taxation which, as Phillips notes, flowed mainly to the top 1 percent and "grew like Topsy" until it became the "punchbowl" at the "ball" that the superrich were able to enjoy from the late 1970s onward.[14] For the conservative middle-class investor, these concerns were translated into political resistance to public spending fueled by the growth of neoliberal think tanks. These movements gathered momentum in America with the passing of the property-tax-limiting Proposition 13 in California in 1978, and they spurred the neoconservative tide that carried both Reagan and Thatcher to power and allowed "welfare, public housing and urban services" to become "stigmatized examples of waste."[15]

Although these political and economic changes were clearly profound, the rapid increase in the reach and speed of electronic technology also did much to shape a growing, but increasingly passive, investment culture. The changes occurring in domestic and professional technologies had very different consequences. The ubiquity of the television in American homes allowed for a mass popularization of financial advice. Louis Rukeyser's Friday night *Wall $treet Week* notably first aired in 1970 and ran for thirty-two years. At his peak Rukeyser reached well over four million households every week and popularized the spectacle of investing on a new scale: he went off-air just as entire channels of financial broadcasting were launched. The implications of the development of mass computing for the amateur investor were more ambivalent. The increased availability of computers made the complex statistical analysis demanded by Graham and Dodd's fundamental investing approach theoretically easier to reach—and, indeed, to purchase commercially—by the mid-1970s. Yet the complexity of the computational analyses required by the portfolio management theories that were becoming ascendant in this period actually increased the distance between the professional and amateur investor, despite the rapid growth of home computing. The attention paid to portfolio management in financial advice of the late 1970s either discouraged small investors entirely or demonstrated the necessity of a computational power that was way beyond most of them.

Investing thus became at once both more complex and more passive. The cultural significance of this shift needs to be read against the other social changes taking place in the postwar period, especially women's relative economic emancipation and the growing demands for economic equality made by the civil rights movement. In a superficial sense, the two might be treated in a similar way. We can trace forms of financial advice written specifically for either women or African Americans throughout the period in the periodicals and advice manuals that clearly identified these specific readers as their target audiences. Yet these forms of financial advice also represented something quite different from one another. Disparities between earned and unearned income grew rapidly in the second half of this period and limited the possibilities for social mobility. This enshrining of economic inequality meant that there was a growing, but still very small, African American presence on Wall Street. However, as Janette Rutterford and Dimitris P. Sotiropoulos have argued, the increasing role and visibility of the woman investor was a significant element in the diffusion of stock ownership across the twentieth century. Rutterford quotes, for example, from Elizabeth Kidd's *Women Never Go Broke* (1948) when she notes that women own "80% of the private life insurance, 70% of estates, 50% of the privately owned stock of corporations, 48% of railway and utility holdings, 40% of the nation's homes, 74% of suburban homes, 66% of mutual savings bank accounts, to say nothing of about 104½ billion dollars."[16] Yet the idea that this history of gender and investment is more progressive than that of race is one that this chapter seeks to complicate. We argue that a closer analysis of the gendering of financial advice in this period reveals that the apparent equality of securities ownership is instead due to the expansion of investing cultures and expectations into the domestic realm. The gendered rhetoric that accompanied the expansion of the investment economy, in other words, did not significantly shift in this period, and is therefore better understood as part of the financialization of everyday life rather than of women's economic autonomy. Indeed, as we further show in this chapter, the idea that the presence of the woman investor was emancipatory was something that the genre often in fact railed against—sometimes in subtle ways, but often without apology.

The Great Compression: Wall Street in Washington

The years following the Second World War, as the historian of Wall Street Steve Fraser has made clear, were ones in which "the street no longer served as an effective lightning rod for the gathering in of political energy" in the United States. Instead, this period consolidated the shift in political power from New York to Washington, DC, which had begun with the inauguration of New Deal politics. In practice this meant that the inequalities in the distribution of American wealth shrank in the immediate decades following the war, a tendency attributed to the narrowing of wage inequalities dubbed the "great compression" by economists Claudia Goldin and Robert Margo. During this period, the "greatest share of a rapidly expanding national income went to Middle America, the slimmest gains to the top 5 percent."[17]

This shift was clearly reflected in financial journalism that was more concerned with macroeconomic questions, specifically with the problem of "reconverting" the war economy, than with the microeconomic problems of the individual investor. Wayne Parsons's study of financial journalism, for example, suggests that the American "shareholder class," which had previously required financial journalism to be a source of profit-bearing "information and tips," were replaced by a "managerial class," which demanded "more wide-ranging information on economic conditions, exports, unemployment, international affairs and government economic policies."[18] A. L. Yarrow's account of the expansion of the specialist financial press in this period tells a similar story, describing how relatively low-circulation but elite publications such as the *Wall Street Journal*, *Fortune*, *Business Week*, and *Forbes* increased their readerships. At the same time, broader-based publications, such as *Life*, *Reader's Digest*, the *Saturday Evening Post*, and the *Ladies' Home Journal*, "recognized that the kinds of in-depth stories appearing in *Fortune* and the *Wall Street Journal* could be successfully packaged and told to a vast middle-class audience." The financial writing carried in these mass-circulation magazines, Yarrow suggests, was concerned with domesticating the economy, transforming "economic concepts such as GNP growth and productivity, as well as government policies and business objectives, into housewife-friendly topics such as 'The Fabulous 1950s: America Enters an Age of Everyday Elegance' and instructive tales such as 'If Our Pay Envelopes are Fatter Now, It's Because Workers Produce More.'" This boosterism was also typical of the political motivations that lay behind the dream of a share-owning capitalism as — not for the first or last time — "reporters, columnists, and headline-writers boldly proclaimed that a 'new era' and a 'new economy' had dawned in postwar America." This much-vaunted development was dubbed, with a "wary eye on the nation's Cold War adversary," the "'people's capitalism.'"[19] The move was also starting to occur in the United Kingdom. *The Mirror*, the most influential working-class tabloid in the early 1960s, launched a regular "money page" and declared that "there has been a revolution in the savings habits of Britain. No longer is The City the exclusive domain of Big Money."[20]

The idea, of course, was hardly new in either country. As Julia Ott has demonstrated, the patriotic fantasy of a share-owning society had been embedded in the "New Proprietorship" of the first decades of the twentieth century.[21] Yet it was also an aspiration that was newly suited to these early years of the Cold War. In the United Kingdom, it was supported by Conservative politicians in the late 1950s and 1960s, but it remained in practical terms constrained — until the "Big Bang" of 1986 at least — by the conservativism of the Stock Exchange, which refused to move on the fixed commission system or allow stockbrokers to advertise.[22] In the United States, conversely, the financial investment industries of Wall Street promoted the retail market for small shares with particular alacrity in their marketing. Janice Traflet's account of the promotional campaigns that attended the drives to increase stock ownership, such as the New York Stock Exchange's "Own Your Own Share" and "Monthly Investment Plan," stresses how advertising functioned as "a piece of economic education" that taught "viewers a range of investing lessons, like the wisdom of buying stock only after putting aside money for emergencies." These efforts were often deeply corporatist in structure, as the NYSE collaborated not only with member brokerage firms, such as Merrill Lynch, but also with the "economic education efforts of a host of organizations like the Committee for Economic Development (CED) and the Ad Council, who were working in a similar vein promoting free enterprise."[23]

The aspiration to popularize share ownership through a focus on education, epitomized by the active campaigning of Merrill Lynch and the NYSE, clearly carried through to personal financial investment advice. This phenomenon recalled the blurring of the relationship between financial advice and advertising so prevalent in late nineteenth-century Britain and America. The popularization of share ownership also heralded the expansion of the genre's range of media and its reliance on an increasingly financialized domestic realm. Postwar personal finance writing rehearsed familiar arguments: it identified women as active financial agents (a recurring realization that is continually presented as if it is new), and it offered expanding share ownership as a "practical rebuttal" of the political threat of communism or even a liberal state socialism, apparent in postwar Europe.[24] It also modeled the active consumer as the ideal citizen prepared for the rigors of decision-making demanded by the market, increasingly championed as the most efficient way of organizing society and allocating resources.

We can see the idea that calculation extends across all areas of life and that the knowledgeable investor is the ideal citizen in America's "first personal finance magazine," *Kiplinger Magazine: The Changing Times*, which launched in 1947.[25] In the United Kingdom, the equivalent is the still-running *Investor's Chronicle*, an influential part of this narrative, but one which has retained a much narrower focus on stocks and securities. *Kiplinger*, on the other hand, changed its brand frequently (it was renamed *Changing Times* in 1949, *Changing Times: The Kiplinger Service for Families* in 1960, and then, finally, *Kiplinger's Personal Finance* in 1991) as it sought to carve out a new kind of investing identity. The journal was the brainchild of the financial journalist Willard Monroe Kiplinger, and its aspirations were close to the cultures of postwar business journalism as Yarrow and Parsons describe them. It was published in Washington, DC, rather than New York (Kiplinger's status as a Washington insider was confirmed in the publication of his 1942 guide to the capital, *Washington Is Like That*).[26]

Although the magazine emerged from and sustained "Kiplinger's Washington Letter," a tip sheet of political and business financial advice, its early editions clearly privileged the broader concerns of the managerial rather than the investment class. The first editorial positioned itself *against* the self-marketing ethos of the NYSE and Merrill Lynch, as it proudly proclaimed that it carried no advertising (and "never will"). It also identified itself as "essentially 'economic'" and explained that this did not mean "graphs and five syllable words" but that it would be written in a "nontechnical" language and informed by an awareness that "nothing is purely 'economic' as distinguished from 'social' or 'political' or 'humanitarian.'"[27] Although the journal was embedded in the corporate structures of liberal governance, deferring frequently to the "Economic Committee for Development," for example, its central concern was to articulate the presumed needs of individual households and small businesses against those of both big business and big government. Sometimes this is explicit. For example, an article on trade unions considered the specific difficulties faced by small businesses, while one on a Florida drug store celebrated a "self-contained independent corner merchant developed to full flair."[28] At other times it is implicit. An article retelling the history of the Shays rebellion, for instance, functioned as a warning against postwar inflationary government spending: "the war ended in 1783 and the Revolutionary heroes trudged home to appalling poverty and a tremendous tax load."[29]

The esoteric interests that this range of articles suggests are typical of the early years of the magazine. A single edition from 1950 carries articles on subjects as diverse as alcoholism, the earth worm, work cultures for older men, the relative merits of canned and frozen food, and a citizenship quiz as well as tips on new market trends and "down to earth facts" for purchasers of investment trusts. Indeed, the eclecticism of the magazine evokes the very origins of the genre, in publications such as John Houghton's *Collection for Improvement of Husbandry and Trade* (1692) and *The Ladies Complete Pocket-Book* (1760), with their combination of domestic, investment, and social counsel in one. What has changed is that the tropes of instructional financial advice are now used to frame, rather than simply accompany, domestic advice. *Kiplinger's* esoteric range of interests is united by the assumption that the reader, like the earthworm, is always rationally maximizing opportunities.[30] Publications like *Kiplinger's* promoted the business ledger as a model for organizing the whole of family life, long before Gary Becker started to describe human capital in these terms. The financialization of the domestic sphere is thus decidedly paternalistic. An article in 1949 described the "head of a family" as a "businessman" because the "family has all the elements of a business. It makes and sells something—usually in the form of the services of the breadwinner. It has income, expenses, overhead, invested capital." According to this analogy, the role of the father is to enforce a rational discipline by examining every area of income and expenditure: "The businessman must know exactly where the business stands. Each year his stockholders demand, and get, a straight report. Try making the same kind of report on yourself."[31] The article provides a family balance sheet and models the complex financial evaluations and future planning that the purchase of a new car entails, involving the selling of war bonds and the creation of a new savings account. An article written two years later by General Rampy, the auditor general of the US Air Force, stresses the importance of accounting on a national rather than domestic scale, and he similarly describes it as a good that is not "an end in itself" but rather a "tool" that facilitates transparency and efficiency and maintains "that most necessary end, free competition in America."[32] Indeed, the journal's focus on the everyday economies of the family and small business leads it occasionally to treat investment in the stock market with some suspicion in these early editions. An article about Emil Schram, the president of the NYSE immediately before Keith Funston (who was responsible for the ostensible democratizing of the Monthly Saving Plan), praises him for striving to "keep amateurs out of the speculative markets" because these "economic illiterates want more than their money's worth and usually end up by losing their shirts."[33]

The political implications of this focus on the active consumer are most clearly apparent in the position that the publication took regarding the debates in postwar America, particularly regarding President Truman's attempts to extend the state provision of social services and health insurance in the late 1940s. The magazine included articles that attempted to weigh the pros and cons of these initiatives ("It's not yet cradle to grave but it's heading there. It can be good or bad. How far do we want to go?"), but which consistently lean toward frightening scenarios in which a "Welfare State" is in "full swing." The article worries about the "men who spark plug our economic system—the businessmen, the entrepreneurs, the initiators of things. . . . They work hard. The money that they make is heavily taxed" and if "we take too much from the spark plugs, the few, they might not work so hard."[34] The position is reinforced in an article by Herbert Hoover which starkly denounces "the slogan of a 'welfare state'" as a "disguise for a totalitarian state by the route of spending."[35] Hence when debates about a nationalized health insurance have given way, by the early 1950s, to articles giving consumers "The Truth about Health Insurance" or advice on "A College Fund for Kids: Education Insurance Can Be a Smart Bet IF You Pick a Sound Plan," they are evidence of the healthy functioning of the American democratic free market in the face of the threats to it that the welfare state represented.[36]

Missionary Work: Reeducating Investors

Kiplinger's modeling of the ideal consumer citizen can be traced through the personal investment advice handbooks of the mid-1950s. Most obvious in this context is *Success with Your Money: How to Handle Family Money Matters* (1956; fig. 5.1), edited by John Hazard. The rather literal and bald cover foregrounds the Kiplinger brands over any of its contributors and emphasizes stability and secure domesticity rather than wealth or risk. The book follows the Kiplinger core message: addressing its reader as "the head of a family" and therefore "in fact a businessman" because the "family has all the elements of a business."[37] This use of investing to frame domestic decisions was made most successful in the period by Sylvia Porter, in a long oeuvre that began with *Managing Your Money* (1953). However, other writers in the period, such as Louis Engel (*How to Buy Stocks*, 1953), Hugh A. Johnson (*Making Money with Mutual Funds*, 1955), Philip Fisher (*Common Stocks and Uncommon Methods*, 1958), and Joseph Granville (*New Strategy of Daily Stock Market Timing for Maximum Profit*, 1960), suggest that a wider array of investment techniques were also being explored. Engel's work exemplifies how readers were encouraged to enter the stock market and the blurring of the distinctions between advertisements and advice that this process of education involved; Johnson's work reveals the specific advice that was being developed for mutual funds; Fisher shows the popularization of the techniques of fundamental investment; and Granville demonstrates the continuing power of technical advice. We end this section by returning to Porter to explore how this expanding investing class learned to identify not only its economic judgments but its very sense of self within the languages of the market.

Soon after *Kiplinger's* launched, Merrill Lynch poached the star business reporter, Louis Engel, from the magazine and employed him as its advertising and sales promotion manager. Engel's clear sense that the best form of advertising was actually financial education led him to develop a campaign for Merrill Lynch that included what has been called "the most famous financial ad" in history.[38] The advertisement, "What Everyone Ought to Know about This Stock and Bond Business," first appeared in the *New York Times* in 1948 and is still a remarkable document—a dense, 6,500-word distillation of Engel's study of the securities markets. The ad continued to run until the middle of the 1960s, and responses to the offer for further information that accompanied it nearly overwhelmed Merrill

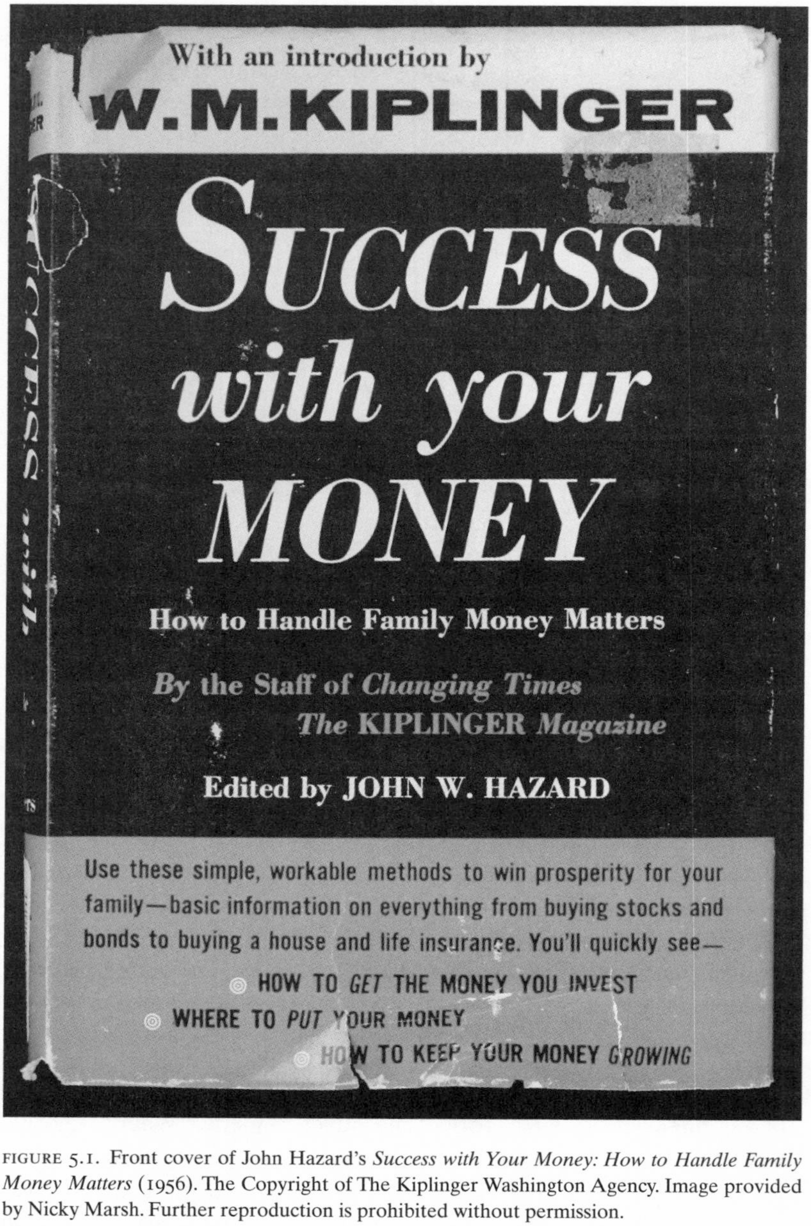

FIGURE 5.1. Front cover of John Hazard's *Success with Your Money: How to Handle Family Money Matters* (1956). The Copyright of The Kiplinger Washington Agency. Image provided by Nicky Marsh. Further reproduction is prohibited without permission.

Lynch: they received four thousand replies in the first week and a total of over three million by the time the ad was finally pulled.[39] Merrill Lynch also distributed educational pamphlets in this period and was emulated in this by the NYSE's Investor Information Department, which went on to distribute an "estimated 8.5 million educational pamphlets."[40]

The advertisement was only one cog in Merrill Lynch's complex promotional machine, which was clearly aware of women's role in making investment decisions. Engel, for example, had written an article for *Vogue* in 1953 entitled "What a Woman Should Know about Investing." Merrill Lynch gave a nod to Engel's article when it ran an advertisement addressed specifically to "Women Who'd Like to Know More about Investments," offering them a series of eight weekly lectures. Instead of the fifty replies that Merrill Lynch expected to receive, it attracted 850 and established a waiting list that grew to a thousand within a week. By the end of the year some thirty thousand women had gone through the eight-week program. The company also organized seminars for married couples, providing child care so husband and wife could attend the seminars together, and produced and screened educational documentary films explaining the work of the stock market. They paid for a small fleet of "stock mobiles," liveried passenger buses that stopped in shopping districts and included a boardroom and a two-way radio to Merrill Lynch offices, allowing prospective clients to open brokerage accounts on the spot. It even ran a contest with the makers of a breakfast cereal, "where the top prize was $25,000 in stocks and bonds of the winner's choice, second prize was $10,000 in securities, and there were sixty other prizes—all paid in stocks. Entrants were judged on twenty-five-word statements beginning, 'I Like Wheaties because . . .'"[41]

Merrill Lynch was not the only company actively widening the demographic pool of potential investors in the postwar period. In the mid-1950s, there were also a number of notable breakthroughs for African American–led brokerage firms. Norman McGhee's McGhee & Co. became the first African American securities firm to obtain a National Association of Securities Dealers (NASD) license in 1952; Lilla St. John became the first African American woman to pass the NYSE exam in 1953; and Philip Jenkin's Specialty Markets, Inc., the first African American–owned securities firm located "in the Wall Street area," opened in 1955. Gregory Bell's history of African Americans on Wall Street attributes the survival of Jenkin's company, especially, to the work of Wilhelmina B. Drake. In 1957, Drake created "Women's Day on Wall Street," an annual event drawing potential African American clients as well as editors and journalists; they received a lecture by Jenkin's Specialty Markets along with lunch and a tour of the New York Stock Exchange. The pitch of the talk domesticated financial investment in a way that was to become familiar, insisting that "investing was an important way to save for children's education, the purchase of a home, travel, retirement, or business" and was successful in bringing accounts such as Alpha Kappa Alpha, a sorority for black women, to the firm.[42]

By the 1960s, African Americans were also working outside of these black-owned companies and were being hired by firms such as Merrill Lynch and Bache and Company (now Prudential Securities). They were employed with a view both to cultivating black investors and—with the passing of the Civil Rights Act in 1964—because these companies "felt that they had to take action before action was taken against them." When Merrill Lynch hired three black stockbrokers in 1965 (out of a possible 2,550 account executives) it became headline news as an "example of a new era of social responsibility." Yet one of these brokers later recollected being told "Since you're black, why don't you go get some black clients?" and spending his "first month going door to door and [getting] nothing, not one account." The men's actual successes, they ruefully noted, were due not to personal meetings or contacts but to the fact that "90 percent of all brokerage business was handled through the U.S. mail and over the phone" and so their racial identities were often not apparent to a largely white clientele.[43] It is a narrative that accords with the longer history of African American finance described by Mehrsa Baradaran, in which the language of individual rights has often served merely to occlude the justice that could only be brought about by addressing structural economic inequalities.[44]

The fullest articulation of Merrill Lynch's promotional education took the form of a financial investment handbook, Louis Engel's best-selling *How to Buy Stocks*. It was published in 1953 and remained in print for the next four decades, selling over four million copies and leading Engel to be named "the man who brought Wall Street to Main Street" by the *New York Times*.[45] The tone of the book is in keeping with the postwar culture that insisted on the connection between the stock market and the general health of the American economy. It offers a simple belief in the rehabilitation of Wall Street after the languor that had prevailed since 1929. The work is based "on a very simple premise: that the stock market is going to go up" because the "market is a measure of the vigor of American business, and unless something drastic happens to America, business is going to go on growing."[46] It focuses on the mechanical practicalities of investing, rather than particular strategies or techniques, and exemplifies the postwar genre of "how to" rather than "get rich" financial advice. It can be read alongside other books of the period that provided such practical overviews, including Don G. Campbell's *Let's Take Stock: An Inside Look at Wall Street* (1959) and George Alvin Cowee's *Ups and Downs of Common Stocks* (1960). The rhetorical questions heading the paragraphs of Engel's ad ("What Are Bonds?"; "How Are Stocks Traded?") become either the extended answers heading the chapters of the latter ("What You Should Know about Government and Municipal Bonds," "How Stocks Are Bought and Sold") or are directly replicated.

The crucial difference, of course, is that *How to Buy Stocks* is *not* presented as an advertisement and might be better read as a gentrified throwback to the self-promoting educational guides offered by the nineteenth-century bucket shops such as Haight & Freese. The first edition, from 1953, for example, simply expands the advice suggested by the ad. Although it encourages its readers toward large brokerage houses that demonstrated how welcoming they were through their use of advertising, it gives Merrill Lynch no explicit billing. Even its opening dedication to Charles Merrill, for forming "a new philosophy of investing to fit a new phase of capitalism," is enigmatically addressed only to "C.E.M." The second edition, published four years later, shows no such delicacy. It contains a pull-out center slip directly advertising the services of the company ("For Investment Help Fill In and Send to Merrill Lynch"), and a full list of the addresses of the brokerage's offices. It spends more space promoting the possibilities of the NYSE's still-new Monthly Investment Plan (Merrill Lynch was responsible for about half of this business) than it does the mutual funds that met a similar set of investing needs much more successfully (and which Charles Merrill infamously, and defiantly, refused to allow the company to become involved in because they "ran afoul of the company credo that investors should make their own decisions"). By the third edition in 1960, however, the changing market meant that the balance between advertising and advice had changed again. Charles Merrill is explicitly named in the dedication, but the company is not, and the dramatically changing fortunes of the Monthly Investment Plan and mutual funds lead Engel to reverse his earlier position. He continues to write approvingly about the Monthly Investment Plan as being "geared to the tempo of life today" but acknowledges that the high numbers of initial investors had now "fallen by the wayside," and blames brokers who were "too busy" to undertake the "missionary work on behalf of M.I.P." rather than its high commission charges.[47] Engel's tone is even more downbeat when he describes the mutual funds that were so at odds with the company's emphasis on individual stock selection. He reminds readers of their failures in the 1920s and wonders "how stable would they prove to be in another period of economic stress," even while noting their exponential growth within the economy and that "if a man can afford to buy only one stock, as he does in the Monthly Investment Plan, he may well take less risk in buying a mutual fund than he does in buying even a 'blue chip' stock" because when "he buys a share in a mutual fund he spreads those eggs over a number of baskets."[48]

Mutual Funds versus Stock Picking

The growth in mutual funds that Engels rather ruefully notes was widespread. These managed funds (also referred to as investment trusts or investment companies in this period) had been a significant part of the investing landscape since their origins in Boston in the 1920s, when the formation of Edward G. Keffler's Massachusetts Investors Trust was quickly followed by Paul Cabot's State Street Investment Trust.[49] Although public confidence in such entities was diminished by their very poor performance in the downturns of the early 1930s, the SEC's regulatory interventions—specifically the Revenue Act of 1936 and the Investment Company Act of 1940—were part of their more general rehabilitation and continued growth. The mutual fund's structures of governance were made more transparent as a result of these interventions, which forced them to diversify their holdings and, most importantly, allowed them the favorable tax treatment that had hitherto only been assigned to direct share ownership.[50] By 1940 mutual funds constituted a significant part of the investing landscape, moving from "5 percent of total managed investment company assets in 1929 to 36 percent in 1940" in a pattern of growth that was to continue. It is hardly surprising that a cover story in 1959 in *Time* magazine declared them to be "the fastest-growing ... phenomenon of the U.S. financial world" and that, by the end of the century they, along—with pension funds—accounted for around half of the value of US stock.[51]

The financial advice that accompanied the emergence of mutual funds in the immediate postwar decades provided data allowing potential investors to compare the performance of different funds. It was a metric-focused approach that was markedly different from the personality-driven advice that was published by fund managers themselves from the 1980s onward. Arthur Wiesenberger provided some of the earliest guidance to mutual funds. Wiesenberger did not sell mutual funds but became convinced that they were the future of American finance and established a brokerage firm that could "advise, nurture and guide mutual funds and investors in them." Wiesenberger began to publish his annual *Investment Companies* survey in the early 1940s. It quickly became the "standard reference work" in the field and developed a classification system that was deemed robust enough to be widely adopted.[52] Wiesenberger's publications combined a general interpretation of the direction of the market with a granular analysis of the performance of individual funds. He wrapped both in the favored proselytizing and nationalist tone of the period: "the idea of the investment trust is sound. The theory of its operation is, however, misunderstood by a large part of the investing public"; and the "popular concept that the investment trust idea has worked well in England and Scotland but has failed miserably here because of inept, dishonest, or selfish management is a delusion. Intelligent diversification of investments originated in Great Britain but the scientific management of funds has received much greater study here."[53]

Wiesenberger did not operate for long without competition. By the mid-1950s his rankings had been joined by those of *Forbes* magazine, which began to publish its own annual survey of mutual funds every August, and by Hugh A. Johnson's *Investment Company Charts*, which offered an "intriguing collection of charts" that included "transparent overlays that permit comparisons of the record of any mutual funds with the performance of the stock market averages."[54] Johnson was the figure who gathered this material into a manual of financial advice and led a subgenre of the field that was soon added to by works such as Joseph Lester's *How to Make More Money from Mutual Funds: A Guide for Conservative Investors* (1965), Amy Booth's *How to Invest in Mutual Funds: Facts You Should Know about This Specialized Form of Investing* (1968), and David Markstein's *How to Make Money with Mutual Funds* (1969).[55] Markstein's book was typical of the subgenre. It steers readers through the terminology of the industry—closed, open, load, and no load—before advocating mutual funds as the solution to all investing predilections and dilemmas. He casts some as the "swift runners of the financial woods who want to gain high profits fast," while others "lumber through the money trees, making haste slowly." Mutual funds can be used for pensions, estate planning, and with investment clubs, Markstein asserts, because they are a kind of panacea for money worries, a form of "insurance for living."[56]

The idea of the mutual fund as the safe place for the small investor—often loaded with a rather patrician attitude to the middle classes, in the United Kingdom especially—did not go uncontested. Some writers, as Matthew Fink has pointed out, perceived mutual funds as threatening the insurance companies that had previously dominated the personal financial marketplace because they offered a more literal form of "insurance for living."[57] Others, notably the muckraker Ralph Lee Smith, were keen to expose the hidden costs and risks that they concealed. The damning critique offered in Smith's *The Grim Truth about Mutual Funds* was to be more fully realized some thirty years later in John Bogle's more motivated uncovering of the inefficiencies of the managed fund.[58]

The growth in mutual funds did not mean that the appetite for individual stock picking had diminished. The prewar techniques of both fundamental and technical analysis continued to thrive in these decades. One of the most frequently cited and enduring works of financial advice from the 1950s, for example, is Philip Fisher's *Common Stocks and Uncommon Profits*. Fisher's book can be set alongside other volumes from this period, including Robert D. Merrit's *Financial Independence through Common Stocks* (1952), Jacob O. Kamm's *Making Profits in the Stock Market* (1954), and Lin Tso's *Sensible Investor's Guide to Growth Stocks* (1962), as key works that simplified the strategies of fundamental analysis for the lay investor. These works sit in the long shadow of Graham and Dodd and share the belief that understanding the long-term prospects of a company, and consequently purchasing it for the lifetime of dividends that it will yield, is a better route to profit than either hedging against risk by diversifying one's stock holdings or churning these holdings according to the business cycle. Fisher's contribution to finding growth stocks lay in the development of the "qualitative equity valuation" model that replaced Graham and Dodd's quantitative emphasis with qualitative analysis.[59] In *Common Stocks and Uncommon Profits*, Fisher describes this approach, which he termed the "scuttlebutt"—the 1950s version of the office watercooler or grapevine—by delineating a series of methodological steps. These included personal and paper-based research into the depth, integrity, and transparency of a company's management cultures as well as its accounting tools, balance sheets, and short- and long-range outputs.

Fisher, who began his career in the late 1920s when he dropped out of the Stanford Graduate School of Business to become a securities analyst, opened his own financial consultancy in the early thirties. The model of investing he describes in *Common Stocks and Uncommon Profits* reveals both the lingering influence of the Depression and his more optimistic sense of the culture of postwar American corporatism. Fisher approves of the increased investment and planning that American companies now boast and acknowledges that they have their origins in the state-sponsored research and defense cultures of the war. Although he laments the "in-built" inflationary bias of the partially planned economy, he nonetheless supports the state regulation it encourages. For Fisher, the "temporary shrinking" of market value caused by a Keynesian dampening of the business cycle is preferable to the "basic threat to the very existence of the investment itself" that the Wall Street crash had brought about. Fisher's representation of the investor as a cog in a healthy manufacturing economy is most apparent in the values that he exhorts investors to adopt. He encourages, for example, positive labor relations and suggests that they can be found not in the company that has no history of strikes but in the company that has proved able to settle "grievances quickly." He also asks investors to seek out companies that are able to make "above average profits" while also giving "above average wages."[60]

Yet it was not only fundamental analysis that continued to thrive in more popular forms in the 1950s and 1960s. Manuals advocating a variety of technical analyses—including even tape reading—also continued to be published in some number. Edwards and Magee's seminal *Technical Analysis of Stock Trends* went into numerous new editions, and its influence was apparent in works that included Joseph Granville's *New Strategy of Daily Stock Market Timing for Maximum Profit* (1960), David Markstein's *How to Chart Your Way to Stock Market Profits* (1966), Orline Foster's *Art of Tape Reading: Ticker Technique* (1965), Harvey Krow's *Stock Market Behavior* (1969), and James Dine's *How the Average Investor Can Use Technical Analysis for Stock Profits* (1972).

Granville's work proved especially enduring, going through numerous editions and providing a full account of the chartist playbook, including descriptions of the "Advance-Decline Line" and "Head and Shoulders" formations as well as climax indicators, volume techniques, and the three phases of "Bear and Bull Swings." The work eschewed the language of the national good deployed by its immediate competitors in favor of a much more individualized register of masculine competition. Granville references the militarized register of Gerald Loeb's classic Depression-era manual, *The Battle for Investment Survival*, as it describes investment as a "battle" against the market. The market becomes a "wily opponent" that is "adept in the use of greys and the subtle art of camouflage in all its forms" and will use "anything it can" to "lay down a smoke screen to mislead the uninitiated." Granville is scathing about the research that fundamental analysis requires, suggesting that it "has little or no part to be played in the successful winning of the market game" and that it is useful only because its adherents are the "'required fall guys' in the market game." Granville's discussion of Graham and Dodd's investing model, for example, is prefaced by the suggestion that their rational approach is insufficiently agile because it doesn't understand "how people *feel*" and it is "mass feelings" that "trample down all the careful but irrelevant work done by the fundamentalist [*sic*] in their misdirected efforts to determine such things as appraised values, estimated earning power, multipliers, and asset values."[61] This gaming model thus required a different kind of temporality from fundamental investing. Granville rejects the deep and slow research of the fundamental investor in favor of a daily analysis that depends on shallower but faster moving streams of data. He was, for example, one of the first writers to popularize Barron's Confidence Index in the early 1960s, using the data that the journal *Barron's National Business and Financial Weekly* provided on the movement between the demand for high-grade (safe) bonds and low-grade (speculative) bonds, in order to suggest that professional traders' appetite for the latter indicated a "confidence in the trading outlook" and thus a good time to buy.[62] Yet this was a strategy that possessed high risks: Barron's Confidence Index was expunged from later editions of Granville's *New Strategy* because measuring volatility proved notably unreliable during the economic crises of the early 1970s.

Cradle to Grave: Sylvia Porter and the Woman Investor

Sylvia Porter was the writer who was more committed than any other to joining financial investment advice with a more general conception of financial literacy in the postwar period. Her financial advice column was syndicated by no less than 333 daily newspapers in the early 1960s and was consequently read by millions.[63] Her appearance on the front cover of *Time* magazine in 1960, a confident assertion of her authority within New York, spoke of the economic power that she had already accrued by the start of the decade (fig. 5.2). The picture also suggests Porter's ability to

FIGURE 5.2. Painting by Henry Koerner, *Sylvia Porter*, on the cover of *Time* magazine (November 28, 1960). Image in public domain.

present herself as a figure who could broker the relationship between the individual consumer and the large institutions of corporatist America. She rendered economic policies and market trends accessible and relevant to the consumer, while representing their specific needs and perspectives to the highest levels of government. Her influence in this latter role, as an economist on the national stage whose advice was actively courted by a succession of politicians and presidents, was significant. Her absence from popular economic history, until the publication of Tracy Lucht's biography of her in 2013, would be puzzling if it were not so predictable.

Porter's identity was rooted in her ability to combine the skills of trained economist with those of the housewife. *Time* magazine described Porter in 1958 as bustling "through the messy, male-contrived world of finance like a housewife cleaning her husband's den—tidying trends, sorting statistics, and issuing no-nonsense judgments as wholesome and tart as mince pie." As Lucht notes, the clear sexism of *Time*'s description is complicated by the ways in which "Porter frequently referred to herself as a housewife in her newspaper column and speeches" and suggested that her financial perspective developed from her experiences as an "individual citizen and wage earner, a consumer, and a housewife."[64] We can see the influence of this combination in the financial investment manuals that Porter published in the 1940s and 1950s, including *How to Live within Your Income* (1939), *How to Make Money in Government Bonds* (1939), *If War Comes to the American Home* (1941), and *Managing Your Money* (1953), which were all dedicated to matching the micro-activities of the domestic household to the macro-needs of the wartime and postwar economies.

Managing Your Money, cowritten with the tax adviser J. K. Lasser, was Porter's first serious attempt to write a popular book of financial advice. It casts the problem of "how to match income to outgoings" as one of the "major personal problems of our generation." The book is innovative, it claims, because it replaces the "'average' family budgets" of other financial handbooks, which are "inconsistent with the spirit of freedom and independence by which most Americans choose to live," with the professional "accrual" skills of the investor: knowing "what money is coming in tomorrow as well as today" and knowing "also what is to be done with tomorrow's as well as today's cash." Porter's use of the tropes of investment to organize family life is described in terms of self-realization: "our primary objective in this book is to stimulate your imagination, to intrigue you into thinking about yourself." Porter's sense of the total family budget also leads her to acknowledge that financial planning is often about a lack rather than a surfeit of choice. She suggests that an income is rarely large enough to "cover all your desires" and that debt, rather than only savings, is a key part of budget planning, because "all your juggling will not get you over these hurdles" and extending the debt into the future may be the only option. The emphasis on the domestic also allows Porter to squarely offer financial investment advice to women. The chapters on annuities, bonds, and securities are headed by a brief aside in which Porter crisply asserts that the "women of America control 70% of our nation's wealth." She also dismisses both those "male pundits" who have chosen to "ridicule the generally respected statistics about the American woman's financial importance" as a "myth, a snare, a delusion, an insidious plot of disordered feminine minds" and those pollsters who have tried to suggest that "women's financial power can't be 'proved.'" Instead, she lists statistics indicating that "women hold a vast percentage of the savings deposits in our country: in New York, they outnumber the men depositors two to one" and that "women represent more than half the stockholders in many of the nation's greatest corporations."[65]

Porter was not alone among writers of the genre in narrating the importance of women's role in the economy through the vocabulary of postwar American exceptionalism. Women's periodicals—racier titles aimed at younger single women, such as Gurley Brown's *Cosmopolitan*, as well as the more domestic and traditional fare of *Women's Own* and *Ladies' Home Journal*—continued to offer women the explicit financial advice that they had done throughout the century. This advice was also bolstered by the continuation of the financial advice manual aimed specifically at women, but which was now often also written by women. The practice of laying out one's life on an accounting sheet, for example, was recommended in texts from across the period, including Edgar Scott's *How to Lay a Nest Egg: Financial Facts of Life for the Average Girl* (1950), Mabel Raef Putnam's *What Every Woman Should Know about Finance* (1955), and Herta Hess Levy's *What Every Woman Should Know about Investing Her Money* (1968). All three books open with what quickly becomes a set of familiarly impressive statistics. In 1950 Scott notes that "women control 70 per cent of this nation's private wealth and own over half the shares of American Telephone and Telegraph and Santa Fe Railroad stocks, and nearly half of the Pennsylvania Railroad, United States Steel, and General Motors companies."[66] In 1955 Putnam notes that "American women are the owners of 70% of the private wealth of the United States" and that they "constitute more than 50% of the stockholders who own the corporations of America" and are the beneficiaries of 71.1% of the life insurance policies.[67] In 1968 Levy opens by noting that women own "almost half of the shares of common stock held by individuals and almost half of the real estate."[68] The premise of all these works is that women investors must adapt, rather than abandon or alter, their feminine skills to better serve the American economy at a time of patriotic need. Scott's argument is that women must learn that the "financial world is not so very different from the home, where the weaker sex has for centuries been the stronger" and that if the "weaker sex does not wake up and make use of its financial strength, the American way of life cannot long endure." Similarly, Putnam's key claim is that "good citizenship requires a knowledge of our country's financial system. For FINANCE is the key, the basis, of our national economy" because we need "good citizenship to buy good government."[69] Putnam, like Porter, exhorts her female readers to extend their existing skills to include financial citizenship: "you learn by reading fashion magazines and observing what others wear, and by feminine instinct . . . Likewise with investments. If you plan to do your own investing you must become qualified in the field." And Putnam encourages the female investor to apply the technologies of finance to the self and to the domestic realm: "make a financial statement of your assets and liabilities and review it every six months" and "keep a budget to facilitate buying." The book combines detailed expositions of Dow Theory with more domestic forms of investment, such as buying and building a home, estate planning, and retirement planning.[70] Levy, writing slightly later and claiming smaller numbers of women investors, is the only figure who notes the obvious caveat overshadowing these numbers, suggesting that women "do *not*, for the most part, control their own wealth—either because they choose to let someone else manage their money or because they have inherited funds but do not control their use. Perhaps half of the wealth owned by women is managed by someone else." Levy's work advocates the development of the woman who can move "knowingly through the investment world" while managing to be "completely feminine and charming." She terms herself an "utter RR girl (and I am not talking about RailRoads rather the ludicrous ease of combining Romanticism and Realism)."[71]

Porter differed from these writers in that she was a clear market maker as well as a market analyst—"directors of U.S. savings bond divisions reported that sales skyrocketed whenever Porter promoted the bonds in her column"—and she was well aware of the ironies of a mass form of investment that she also embodied. She was severely critical of financial journalists who might benefit from their role. She got into acrimonious rows with Walter Winchell, for example, who had spearheaded the use of the radio as a platform for financial advice in his gossip shows of the 1960s, when she suggested that he had been involved in insider training.[72] Yet, at the same time, her advocacy of different forms of securities shows a professional partisanship. Porter remains coolly independent when explaining the different roles that annuities, insurance, savings, and stocks play in personal investment strategies, yet when she describes government bonds her tone changes. She gives them a stirring history and suggests that the "magnitude of the wartime savings bond drives shapes up as even more breath-taking than it seemed then," marveling that "$34,800,000,000 was in the familiar 'E' bonds alone—making it the most widely-held and popular security in all history." Detailed descriptions of the terms attached to each bond are followed by a defense of these securities in the face of the criticism present in most financial advice of the time—both *Kiplinger's* and Fisher advocate selling bonds at this point, for example. Although she acknowledges that these attacks on bonds have a "lot of truth," her reasoning concludes with an emotional appeal that is vested in the patriotism of her wartime writing that she can never quite relinquish: "you are buying and holding the safest, most riskless investment in the world, representing the credit of the greatest financial power in the world. . . . You are disciplining yourself by saving regularly and thus, you are putting aside money that otherwise you might fritter away on goods and pleasures of only temporary value"; and, above all, "you are helping the Treasury to finance the budget and manage debt in the soundest way possible, and by doing so you are helping to fight inflation—you are contributing something toward the defense of America. You are showing your faith in your country which really means you are showing your faith in yourself."[73]

Of course, Porter is also both defending her own historical record (her writing about war bonds in the early 1940s had so impressed Secretary of the Treasury Henry Morgenthau that he had requested her assistance in writing the blueprint for the Series E savings bond) and her conviction that individual investment was a service to the state. Her opinion in this context continued to be sought, especially by Democrats, in the postwar period. John F. Kennedy asked her to serve on his Consumer Advisory Council; Lyndon B. Johnson sought her advice on his federal budgets and offered to make her president of the Export-Import Bank; and Gerald Ford included her in his summit on inflation. It was, indeed, Porter's idea for a "Whip Inflation Now" (WIN) campaign—rather than Milton Fried-man's advocacy of recession or John Kenneth Galbraith's recommenda-tion of a tax increase—that Ford alighted upon as his national strategy.

Porter is a complex figure. Her allegiance, as Lucht suggests, was (de-spite her interest in the woman investor) "clearly with the little guy: the American householder and small business owner. She criticized tax poli-cies that benefited the wealthy at the expense of those less fortunate, and she was not persuaded by the argument that tax breaks for large corpora-tions provided incentives for business investment. 'I don't want to carp. But what about the incentive of the little man? I mean, the incentive to eat?' she wrote."[74] Yet, at the same time, her assumption that the invest-ments of the "little man," properly channeled, could tackle the growing macroeconomic problems of the American economy—the rising inflation that threw the guns-and-butter strategy of successive presidents so dra-matically awry in the late 1960s and early 1970s—now looks not only naive but indicative of the fundamental limitations of the assumption that the financial decisions of individuals were a primary engine for social change and improvement in America.

The beginning of Porter's decline, as Lucht chronicles, coincided with the quiet shelving of the failed WIN campaign and the publication, just one year later, of Porter's most significant book, the 1,100-page *Sylvia Porter's Money Book*.[75] The work was a massive success, a best seller that was followed by dozens of similar titles published by Porter in the next two decades. It came to shape the ways in which personal financial in-vestment would be written about by later writers right up until the end of the twentieth century.[76] The claim on the book's back cover, made by Betty Furness of NBC's *Today Show*, that the volume "should be on every family's book shelf, along with the Bible and the dictionary," provides a neat description of the work, as both proselytizing and encyclopedic. It also recalls the early reviews of Mortimer's *Every Man His Own Bro-ker*. The book provides advice on how and when to buy everything, from the cradle (and obstetrician) to the grave (and mortician), and all that comes in between—day care, schools, colleges, clothes, homes, cars, vaca-tions, doctors, weddings, and divorces. Indeed, the sheer weight of these details, which include strategies for making sure that there is sufficient credit in your "blood bank account" (one can save on "costs of blood" by asking "friends and relatives to donate blood in advance" of planned sur-gery), provides its own testimony to the financialization of every aspect of American life in the early 1970s.[77]

Yet the work marks the decline of Porter's influence as an economist, a decline that Lucht suggests was caused not only by the failure of the WIN campaign but also by her overexposure, reliance on ghostwriters and researchers (with whom she had increasingly vexed relationships), and distance from her middle-class readers. Porter, always sensitive to the multiple platforms through which her journalism could operate, sought to rapidly extend her activities in the 1970s and became involved in new and relatively short-term ventures that included "videotapes, audiotapes, a retirement newsletter, computer software, and even a board game."[78] Yet, as the fate of *Sylvia Porter's Financial Magazine* (which foundered and was eventually bought by *Kiplinger's*) suggests, such innovations were a dilution of her brand. Based on her early investigative journalism, this brand struggled to survive in the changing economic conditions of the late 1970s.

Stagflation: Investing in the 1970s

Porter's attempt to widen her platforms was, in many ways, entirely in keeping with the development of the genre in this moment. The 1970s witnessed radical changes in the technologies and cultures of financial advice as producers of advice responded to the ways in which trading occurred, the ways in which advice could be delivered, and the political contexts in which it operated. It is hardly surprising that Porter's postwar domestic homilies began to look so quickly dated. Despite the fact that investors were becoming less individually active in the investment markets of the 1970s and 1980s, the genre of financial advice was beginning once more to actively and powerfully assert itself as a source of fascination in mass culture, as the baleful memories of the 1930s finally faded from memory. We want briefly to outline the multiple and complex causes of this resurgent interest before identifying the ways in which writers of the genre responded to them.

The advance of workplace technology made buying and selling stocks easier and cheaper from the early 1970s onward. The paper-crush of the late 1960s, in which an increased volume of trading left brokers unable to process daily trades accurately, led to the rapid automation of trading and the implementation of electronic money—transference agreements, including the opening of the Clearing House Interbank Payments System (CHIPS) in 1970 and of the Federal Reserve's Fed Wire in 1971.

The easing of bureaucracy that followed from these innovations contributed to the cause of those campaigning for the deregulation of the

NYSE, a campaign that led in May 1975 to the end of fixed fee brokerage (the same change did not occur in the United Kingdom until the "Big Bang" of 1986). This crucial shift lowered transaction fees and not only contributed to the move from the "buy and hold" culture advocated by Fisher and Graham to the rapid churn of contemporary trading but also led to the first real expansion of a culture of explicit advertising by brokerage services, which saw the practice of personal investing enter the commercial sphere as it had never before.[79]

This commercial interest went hand in hand with a radical expansion in the forms of personal financial investment advice in the 1970s and 1980s. The manuals at the core of the genre entered into popular culture in terms of both their content (as they sought innovative ways of capturing the seesawing moods of the market, from the anxieties of the 1970s to the euphoria of the 1980s) and in terms of their form (as they were increasingly supported by a range of other media forms, including television, film, popular fiction, and memoirs). Indeed, so large and complex did the landscape of these investing books become in this period that a meta-genre of books dedicated to helping readers pick their way through the competing models began to emerge.

Books such as an *Encyclopedia of Stock Market Techniques* (1965), Sheldon Zerden's *Best Books on the Stock Market: An Analytical Bibliography* (1972), and James B. Woy's *Investment Methods: A Bibliographic Guide* (1973) were intended not only to explain the different forms that technical and fundamental analysis were taking in this period but to guide the reader through what was becoming an even more crowded field. Some of the most influential financial advice of the 1970s was given by figures such as Louis Rukeyser, George Goodman (who wrote under the alias of Adam Smith), and Paul Erdman, who had all worked hard to develop a charismatic brand for themselves, one that also relied on their involvement in television, film, and fiction. It is no surprise, then, that the genre carried the influence of these popular forms.

Yet just as some changes in technology were lowering the barriers for individual investors to both access and understand the market, others were raising them. Crucial here was the intellectual revolution on Wall Street that had been brewing in university finance and economics departments since the publication of Harry Markowitz's "Portfolio Selection" in the very early 1950s.[80] This shift, most fully described in Peter Bernstein's *Capital Ideas*, depended on a complex mathematical framework in which a portfolio is constructed by the matching of assets to one another in ways that allow them to hedge the collection's overall risk as well as maximize its returns.[81] As these techniques were increasingly adopted by financial professionals in the 1970s, they radically changed the role of individual investment advice. The complex mathematical models that lay behind the hedging strategies of both modern portfolio theory (MPT) and capital asset pricing models (CAPM) were somewhat unevenly translated into the genre of popular financial advice. Yet these works could not have been further from the commonsense populism of writers such as Louis Rukeyser or the pseudo-psychology of Goodman, both of which we describe below. Writers seeking to translate MPT and CAPM for lay investors often actually underlined the difficulties that the individual investor faced. In the 1970s, this involved providing investors with painstakingly detailed accounts of how the calculations that modern portfolio theory demanded could be managed by the lone investor. In the 1980s, conversely, the genre turned outward, to the importance of selecting the fund managers that were so essential to the operation of MPT.

Finally, and most significantly, the political changes that were taking place in the United States and Britain from the late 1960s onward had a significant role to play in the ascendancy of the financial markets as a key focus for popular culture. The 1970s opened with the first serious postwar financial crisis as the technology-led boom of the go-go 1960s was followed by a "prolonged torpor" in which the percentage of households holding assets in the stock market "shrank from 24.3 percent in 1968 to 8.5 percent in 1978," while the Dow Jones index lost "three-fourths of its value between 1968 and 1982."[82] This collapse of investor confidence was part of a wider economic malaise. OPEC's decision to raise the price of oil, combined with the early effects of deindustrialization, were narrated in both countries through the conservative language of "stagflation." The crisis sharpened the political critique of the postwar financial settlement and an alternative, which had been long prepared for by the neoliberal economists associated with the Mont Pèlerin society, emerged rapidly. In the early 1970s these thinkers were able to draw on the powerful publicity machines of bodies such as the Heritage Foundation and Cato Institute and were also increasingly emboldened by the new alliances between religious and economic conservatives.[83] One of the first indications of what this finance-capital–led politics would look like was when the bond market refused to rollover the debts of the City of New York in 1975. The city, starved of tax revenues by the withdrawal of both small industries and the white suburban middle class, and frustrated in its attempts to provide public services by a string of failing public-private initiatives, was "saved" from bankruptcy by a financial deal that demanded savage cuts in public spending, inaugurating an era of austerity.[84] This was a political shift that profoundly changed the cultural and economic purpose of investing: the transferal of risk, from collectives to individuals, had begun in earnest.

The increasing financialization of daily life in the United States, to use Randy Martin's memorable term, can be also measured by the appearance — the faltering of Porter's financial magazine notwithstanding — of two of the most influential and long-running periodical titles in the industry. The first of these, *Black Enterprise*, was launched by Earl G. Graves in 1970 and was one of a slew of new magazines (*Essence* appeared in 1970 and *Callaloo* in 1976, for example) catering to an African American readership that had been previously primarily served by the Johnson Publishing Company's postwar era periodicals, *Ebony* and *Jet*. The second was *Money*, launched in 1972 by *Time* magazine, which represented a more accessibly middle-class and practical version of the aspirational territory that Henry Luce had done so much to define when he launched *Fortune* some forty years earlier.

Although the two publications had a widely different provenance, they both shared much with the original format of *Kiplinger's*, featuring regular columns (or "departments" in *Black Enterprise*) that included economic and market analysis alongside a wide range of consumer, career, and investment advice. Like *Kiplinger's*, both publications supported financial investment manuals, written by their own staff, which offered the familiar introductory tour of fundamental and technical advice.[85] However, there were also significant editorial differences between the ways in which all three publications broached the politics of finance. *Black Enterprise* offered a broadly national, often international, analysis whereas *Money* and *Kiplinger's* focused on, respectively, the rights of the investor and of the consumer in ways that reflected their much narrower and more conservative stance. The responses each publication gave to the emergence of Reaganomics toward the end of the decade are neatly instructive of these differences. *Money* registered the triumph of this neoliberal economic agenda in the welter of its detail rather than its rhetoric. An article from 1981 offered an early but presciently full account of what Reagan's election would mean for the wealthy middle class, suggesting that the coming years should be "good ones" for those "owning stocks" or seeking to start or expand a business. *Kiplinger's*, conversely, remained aloof from entirely celebrating the era of deregulation and focused its initial concern on how this agenda, and the shrinking of federal agencies such as the Bureau of Consumer Affairs, would limit the consumer rights movement which it had championed for so long.[86] *Black Enterprise* took a very different route and was clearly and persistently articulate about the damage to African American prosperity and opportunity that the political and economic changes that Reagan brought with him would signal for their largely Democratic voting readership. The magazine carried stories almost monthly throughout the early 1980s noting the reduction of African American representation in government, the dangers of Reagan's doublespeak around affirmative action, and the attacks on children and families with the curtailing of the welfare state that was justified through racist and misogynistic logic.

It was not only to race that *Black Enterprise*'s exploration of the political economy was sensitive. *Money* largely ignored the possibility of the woman investor until the mid-1990s, and *Kiplinger's* patriarchal tone led it to only occasionally decry feminism's threat to the traditional family unit, quoting Betty Friedan in asking "feminists to make family problems a central issue" in the early 1980s.[87] By contrast, *Black Enterprise* foregrounded the economic importance of the African American woman and ran articles in this period detailing the importance and successes of the African American businesswoman, the role of young black women leading the entry into the stock market, and the relative successes of women-led investment clubs.[88] This emphasis was supported by the demographic research of brokers such as Brimmer and Company and, later, Ariel Investments, as well as by the anecdotal observations of historians such as Gregory Bell, which indicated that African American women were more likely to organize the family's financial affairs than men.[89]

Yet articles about the African American woman investor that were appearing in women-centered periodicals such as *Essence* in the mid-1970s went further than this, associating the female investor with personal autonomy and fulfillment rather than a matriarchal control of the household. An article called "Miss Moneybags," for example, presents its careful financial advice through the form of a detailed biography of Jean Gibson, a hospital technician who spends two hours a day reading the *Wall Street Journal* "with a dictionary by her side" and understands stock picking, bookkeeping, and compound interest. The result, the article stresses, is not luxury or family security but freedom. When Jean's marriage ended she was able to support herself, and, although she hopes that her ex-husband is happy, she also tartly notes that she is "very happy [. . .] especially sexually" and keeps her "divorce decree next to her will bequeathing her fortune to her parents and brothers."[90]

Other genres of financial advice coded the tumultuous political changes that were taking place in the 1970s through the dramatic tropes and narratives of popular culture rather than the biographies of the careful investor. The increasing popularity of books such as Adam Smith's *Money Game* (1968), Harry Schultz's *Panics and Crashes and How You Can Make Money out of Them* (1972), and Howard Ruff's *How to Prosper during the Coming Bad Years* (1979) offered an apocalyptic reading of the economy. In these texts, economic crises were consistently clothed in a militarized language, by both their critics and their celebrants. Here, we explore what this language suggested, and the way in which it frequently contrasted the disciplined rhetoric of war with the ludic or libidinal vocabularies of play and desire—precisely at the moment when the need for arithmetic rationality in financial investment was being championed as never before.

In the most apocalyptic of these best-selling works, such as that written by the libertarian Howard Ruff, for example, it is very clear that the crisis in the economy is a political one and that the appropriate response is a radically individualized one. Ruff argues, in a move not unfamiliar to the genre in the 1970s, that inflation is a form of taxation that "transfers your spending power to government as surely as if the government had taken the dollars away from you." However, he departs from this standard line when he presents a diagnosis of this laxness that spreads far beyond mere fiscal responsibility. The "changing value" that "concerns" Ruff most as an "economic factor" is the "sexual revolution" and the expensive "assault upon the basic nurturing unit of society" that it has wrought. Ruff devotes an entire chapter to explaining the detrimental effects of women's liberation upon the financial investor.[91]

The financial advice that the book gives is as deeply uneven as this insight suggests. Ruff combines some of the fairly predictable advice being offered in the context of the inflation and economic uncertainty of the 1970s (to buy the right kind of real estate because inflation will reduce the real cost of the mortgage, to buy gold, to go into money market funds, to diversify one's assets in a credible portfolio) with extremely apocalyptic scenarios than seem to annul this advice entirely (to store food and ammunition, to keep gold in a security deposit box at home, to prepare to escape the urban riots that will engulf cities as the banking system entirely collapses). The book's veering between political anger, practical advice, and apocalypse frequently seeks coherence in the scenarios of fiction.

Ruff not only provides a series of imaginary vignettes—like the "moral" of the "restless girl" that teaches us that if every family can "become solvent, self-sufficient and panic-proof" then the world will be a better place— but also draws explicitly on the financial fiction that other financial professionals had recently published. He warns against the dangers of hyperinflation by retelling the dystopian debt jubilee described by Benjamin Stein's novel *On the Brink*, which depicts a "not unlikely future" in which the White House radically accelerates inflation in order to allow "millions of Americans with mortgages and debts" to pay them off "with a few days salary" but destroys the economy in the process. Similarly, his advice on what to do if war is threatened in the "Mid-East" borrows from the actions of the hero of Paul Erdman's novel *The Crash of '79* who "immediately liquidated all of his paper holdings and bought nothing but gold and that is precisely what you should do under these conditions."[92]

Ruff's movement between these genres was not unusual for this period, and it suggests something of the role that fantasy played in future modeling, even on the brink of finance's quantitative revolution. A review of *How to Prosper during the Coming Bad Years* in the *Financial Analysts Journal*, for example, compares Ruff's writing to the novels of Paul Erdman but suggests that the latter is actually preferable because it is at least "better written."[93] The use of Erdman's fiction, rather than his financial advice (which often involved getting out of the dollar and buying gold or other currencies), as a plausible way of representing the future of the economy was not limited to these examples. An interview with Erdman suggests that the "awareness—or should I say wariness—of future problems" that his fiction presents has made it "required reading for classes at Harvard, Stanford, and Princeton," while "his fiction has been lauded by economists as notable as Susan Strange for the verisimilitude of an analysis that is 'firmly based on the reality of financial markets.'"[94] The plot of Erdman's novel *The Crash of '79* was used not only by Ruff but by other journalists and academics seeking to discuss the security implications of international monetary policy: "since the publication of Paul Erdman's popular book *The Crash of '79*," one newspaper article begins, "the general public has become more aware of the risk to the floating exchange rate system of a sudden and large-scale liquidation of the U.S. dollar assets" held by OPEC; similarly, Erdman himself has described how his testimony to a congressional hearing regarding such a crisis was eventually implemented.[95]

Erdman and Ruff both used the genre of financial advice to rehearse strategies for dealing with crisis. This is also apparent in *The Money Game* by Adam Smith (the pseudonym of George Goodman), which remains one of the most influential and well-read books of popular financial advice. The work was published in 1968 and it is remarkably prescient about what was to come, specifically the ending of the Bretton Woods agreement, the inflationary crises of the 1970s, and the speculative cultures of the 1980s. Although the book is primarily concerned with the art of stock picking rather than the alternative securities that both Erdman and Ruff are advocating in the 1970s, it cheerfully rejects both the hand-wringing debates between the various forms of technical and fundamental analysis and the emergence of efficient market portfolio theories. In their place it produces a New Age analysis of the relationships among "image and reality and identity and anxiety and money." Money, Goodman insists, "which can preoccupy so much of our consciousness is an abstraction and a symbol." "The game we play with it," he continues, "is an irrational one, and we play better with it when we realize that, even as we try to bring rationality to it."[96]

Goodman's recognition that the "discipline" that finance brings has been militarized (he calls traders "gunslingers" and describes financial crises as "mushroom clouds") is consistently cut through with his recognition that finance's abstractions lend themselves better to the language of play and desire than to the cooler languages of calculation and analysis. For Goodman the financial marketplace is one of irrationality and illusions, which the investor can be taught to understand and manipulate. *The Money Game* is rooted in popular psychology, referencing the predictably misogynistic thinking of Gustave Le Bon ("'crowds,' says the good Dr. Le Bon, 'are everywhere distinguished by feminine characteristics'") and the Freudianism of Norman O. Brown (the "whole money complex is rooted in the psychology of guilt" and gold is the "absolute symbol of sublimation"). Although Goodman admires both thinkers, he is also clear that the contemporary stock market is distinguished by a sense of money not as "condensed, useless, and guilty" but as "sport, frolic, fun and play." This sense of play is contrasted positively to a sense of work: "we slave one hour, we get one white chip for the Game. But three of us form a little company, create stock (paper), earn $50,000, and our public liquid market will give us not $50,000 but a million. . . . That really is effortless, and we live in one of the only countries that this can be done." We can read his language as marking the move from industrial to financial capitalism in the most approving ways. As he says: the "Federal Reserve creates money all the time. It just waves its wand of bill purchases and sales, and presto, there is money where there was none before."[97] Hence, the financial marketplace is excitingly irrational and ephemeral for Goodman not because of the collective pressures of the crowd, nor because of the individual's guilt about their "condensed wealth," but rather by dint of its increasing abstraction and accelerated expansion.

Goodman's work can be compared with Louis Rukeyser's financial advice manual *How to Make Money in Wall $treet* and the long-running television program *Wall $treet Week* that it accompanied. The latter had a set format. It included an interview with a leading economist or financier about the broad financial issues of the day (the names of its one thousand guests was as impressive in quality as it was quantity, featuring not only key economists such as John Kenneth Galbraith, Milton Friedman, Paul Samuelson, and Alan Greenspan but also famous financial advisers, including Louis Engel, Sylvia Porter, and Gerald Loeb), followed by a series of stock tips that self-consciously nodded to the debates between fundamental and chartist approaches. The program occupied the same coveted mid-Friday night slot for over three decades, was carried by over three hundred television stations, and weekly reached over 4.2 million homes. Rukeyser was heralded, shortly before the show's rather acrimonious ending, as the "ballsy, shaggy-haired prankster" who had made a show with the "premise that money is sexy." *People* magazine described him as the "dismal science's only sex symbol."[98]

The positioning of Rukeyser as a hyper-masculinized showman was also implicit in the format of the program, which preserved the sexist tropes of 1970s popular culture until its twenty-first-century conclusion. The single female presence on the show, apart from rare figures like Porter, were the glamorously dressed but entirely silent women who escorted the male guests from the stage and who were *all* simply known as "Miss Smythe" (becoming "Ms." Smythe in 1991, in the same year, perhaps not coincidentally, that Rukeyser began writing a regular column for the journal *Working Women*). Demographic research into the program seems to confirm the conservative male viewer that such a practice implicitly assumes: a report into the reach of public broadcasting completed in the late 1970s indicated that *Wall $treet Week* had one of the most "distinctive" audiences of any public affairs broadcast, an audience that was not only overwhelmingly white but was also largely male, middle class, and Republican.[99] The homogeneity of this audience was extended to its behavior, as a series of economists revealed that the prices of the common stocks that were tipped on the show consistently demonstrated a short-term rise, as the market moved in the direction Rukeyser pointed, whereas the long-term benefit of this advice has been much more difficult to prove.[100]

The androcentric assumptions coding the register if not the content of Rukeyser's show also underpin his book, *How to Make Money in Wall $treet*. The work addresses itself to the "Little Man" who, Rukeyser predicts, is about to come into his own once more with the deregulation of the NYSE: Rukeyser notes that "as recently as 1952, only one in sixteen American adults owned stock. By 1970, the figure was one in four."[101] When this same set of statistics forces Rukeyser to acknowledge that his "little man" is very likely to be a woman—that 1970 was the first time since the NYSE census began that male stockholders outnumbered women, and even then only by a "statistically skinny 50,000"—he still retains a patrician tone. He coyly suggests that he will pass on the news that men now outrank women as investors to "the Women's Liberation Movement," presumably implying that feminists' social and political successes are actually rather pyrrhic ones.[102]

More generally, Rukeyser's catholic approach to covering the broad spectrum of investment advice leads him to share opinions with writers as different from one another as Philip Fisher and George Goodman's Adam Smith. He takes from the latter the need to cultivate a gaming attitude toward investing and the understanding that "Wall Street is about as scientific and logical as the most incurable manic-depressive at your local asylum. In the long run it still responds to forces more powerful than itself, such as a truly expanding economy, but in the short run it is difficult to predict precisely because its behavior is so unscientific and illogical." From Fisher, he takes the conviction that common stocks are preferable to the "exotic" securities of the income seekers, who look to "municipal bonds, convertible bonds, preferred stocks, utilities and real estate investment trusts." He accompanies the guide to qualitative and quantitative fundamental analysis that underpins the book with somewhat arch descriptions of both technical analysis (which he enjoys as he enjoys all "religious fanatics. They are stimulating and provocative") and the emerging modern portfolio theory (the "vogue for the beta coefficient," which he warns is particularly "perilous for an ordinary investor with only a small number of issues in his portfolio. For him there has got to be a beta mousetrap").[103] Where Rukeyser most clearly differs from Fisher is in his account of the relationship between investing and the economy. We can, for example, see the withdrawal from industries that are dependent on either labor or expensive R&D investment—a strategy that Warren Buffet came to perfect in the 1980s and 1990s—emerging as Rukeyser counsels the investor to "favor companies whose enlightened labor policies promote harmony and stability" but to find them in "areas where labor is a relatively small portion of a company's total costs." He is explicit that this means avoiding heavy industry and transport infrastructure. In their stead, he advocates the service industries—leisure, retailing, airlines, or cable television—that came to the fore in the deindustrialized 1980s.[104] For Rukeyser, as for Porter, the manual and even the television program were only a small part of a widely diversified media portfolio, and it was to the service industry that he himself also turned to sustain his own value. By the late 1990s, he was not only publishing a successful tip sheet but was also running huge financial trade fairs in Las Vegas hotels, attended by over eleven thousand people at a time, at which, both ironically and entirely obviously, fund managers would ply their business.[105]

The Random Walk and the Celebrity Money Manager

What this final example neatly indicates, of course, is that Rukeyser's advice was already somewhat obsolete by the time he achieved such notoriety and short-term influence on the stock market. He was obsolete, most obviously, because offering financial news for an hour on a Friday night show no longer captured the networked possibilities of knowledge. Cable television was beginning to experiment with broadcasting constant market data in the early 1970s in a project that was to come to fruition with the launch of the Merrill Lynch–supported Financial News Network in 1981.

It was not only the form but also the content of Rukeyser's advice that risked being outdated. *How to Make Money in Wall Street* was published the year *after* Burton Malkiel's *A Random Walk Down Wall Street*. Malkiel's work did more than any other to popularize the insights of contemporary academic financial theory and to systematically debunk the rationale that supported the selection of stocks as an investment strategy. The cover of the book's first edition, which compares Malkiel to the famous pediatrician Benjamin Spock, aligns the work with a tradition in which professional advice is translated into a model of self-help which transformed a generation (fig. 5.3). In some ways this was not too far-fetched. Malkiel's work was positioned against the cultures of individual investment that Rukeyser embodied, and it critiqued at length what it described

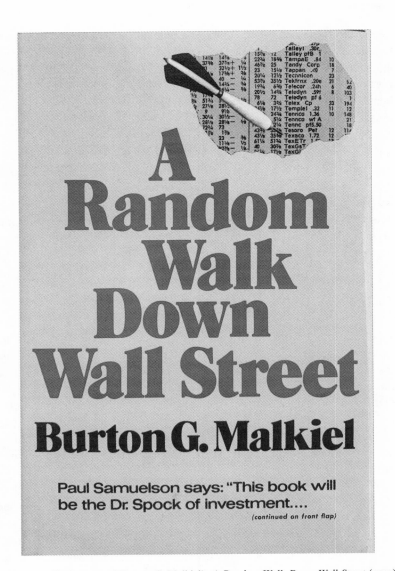

FIGURE 5.3. Front cover of Burton G. Malkiel's *A Random Walk Down Wall Street* (1973). Copyright Burton Malkiel. Image provided by W. W. Norton, with permission for reproduction from Burton Malkiel and W. W. Norton. Further reproduction is prohibited without permission.

as the "firm foundation" theory of Graham and Fisher or the "castles in air" theory of George Goodman (which he rightly aligned with Keynes's beauty competition—in which investors pick stocks by trying to second-guess the decisions that *other* investors are likely to make). Malkiel's work thus marks a significant transition in the genre of personal financial advice as the pendulum swings from picking the right individual stocks and bonds to either balancing the right portfolios or picking the right funds and fund managers who can do this work for you. We want to trace the ways in which both tendencies, which had very different implications for the individual investor, were played out through the genre.

First, understanding the academic work of the 1950s, including Eugene Fama's work on the efficient market hypothesis (EMH) and Harry Markowitz's analysis of matching risk against return, proved a significant challenge for the individual investor. It was a challenge that popularizing books such as Robert Hagin's *Guide to Modern Portfolio Theory* (1979) and Jerry Felsen's *Cybernetic Approach to Stock Market Analysis versus Efficient Market Theory* (1975), as well as the works by academics such as Fama and future Nobel Prize in Economics winners Merton Miller and William F. Sharpe, tried to meet. These books provided earnest attempts to make the implications of modern portfolio theory available to the investor. But they actually often only underlined the ways in which the enormity of the task overwhelms the individual investor. Felsen, for example, carefully explains why the theories of both the efficient market and of hedged portfolios threaten the validity of the fundamental, technical, and psychological modes that preceded them. He rejects the limitations that efficient market theory places on the individual investor—who will never be able to beat the all-knowing market—and outlines an ambitious computational model that can meet the challenge of reacting to an information-saturated market. Felsen's model aims to "capture analytically the decision behavior of a superior analyst (whose intellect may be further amplified by a computer)" and involves studying "directly the dynamic information processes which take place in the market." Yet the account is largely abstract and Felsen "deliberately omits" the practical details because they are too lengthy, too "difficult to comprehend," and are evolving too quickly to be useful for the general reader. Instead, the work combines a "bare skeleton of the required mathematical apparatus" that this approach requires with a much more familiar account of "playing the market" that is "easy and fun." Think of "a share of stock as a burning match," he advises. "The game consists in passing it rapidly from hand to hand. The last hand to grab it gets burned. All those burned howl in pain. And that's why the stock market is so noisy."[106] Where Felsen tries to make sense of the implications of Fama's view of the efficient market, Hagin does the same with Markowitz's conceptualization of an efficient portfolio, which analyses the *"expected return* for each security" and the *"variance of the expected return* for each security" in order to determine the "possibly offsetting, or possibly complementary, interaction or *covariance*, of returns with every other security consideration." Hagin uses William Sharpe's work to develop a theory of an asset allocation line but, like Felsen, makes the enormity of the task for the individual investor sharply apparent, as he notes that the "evaluation of the covariance between 100 pairs of securities necessitates the estimation and processing of 4,550 estimates of covariance."[107]

The second response to the magnitude of the challenge that portfolio theory represented for the individual investor were those books written by, or sometimes about, the successful money managers that had moved firmly to the center of investing culture. These were financial money managers turned authors, men such as Peter Lynch, John Templeton, and John Train, who presented their works as sharing the secrets that their successful careers had revealed to them.

The cult of the financial adviser who promulgates a lifestyle, rather than practical money management, was best characterized in John Templeton's *Templeton Plan: 21 Steps to Personal Success and Real Happiness*. The book connects financial success to spiritual thinking and offers a template for molding a successful personality that can be at once thrifty, generous, ambitious and, above all, hardworking. Templeton's work describes in some detail the labor that his journey has involved—from a childhood of austerity in Tennessee to global offshore philanthropy (founding Oxford University's Templeton College from his home in the Bahamas). The work is entirely focused on cultivating the independent financial spiritual self of the individual fund manager and provides very little in the way of actual financial advice. Templeton's pioneering role in something as prosaic as the financial industry, for example, is presented as part of a personality that "was not afraid of new frontiers: he welcomed them. Whether it was the frontier of Yale, or travelling to England on his Rhodes scholarship, or touring far-flung and exotic places in the world on a few hundred dollars or making the decision to enter a field—mutual fund investing—almost before such a field existed, John Templeton was convinced that there were new frontiers to discover." The lesson that is to be learned from Templeton's experience with mutual funds is that "success-bound people have to believe in themselves because the frontier exists inside of them."[108]

The vast majority of financial advice that appeared in the context of the rise of the managed funds was less esoteric than Templeton's. These works sought to sculpt the financial self while recognizing that the landscape for the individual investor had radically and paradoxically changed. Malkiel's own handbook is exemplary of this trend. The financial advice that Malkiel delivers would have been quite familiar to the reader steeped in the genre at this point, despite the revolutionary implications of the efficient market hypothesis that are described in the first half of his book. It combines some of the fundamental principles that had characterized the genre since the domestic turn of *Kiplinger's* in the 1950s (have appropriate life and medical insurance; keep some money liquid; know your objectives and risk appetite; use tax-free municipal bonds to minimize your tax exposure) with a guide to the "Mutual Fund Mire" (Malkiel recommends closed end mutual funds only), in addition to four rules for "successful stock selection" (seeking above average earnings; correlating the price with a firm foundation of value; identifying stocks with an "anticipated growth" that other investors believe in; trade as little as possible). Malkiel's work did not, in other words, follow the two obvious choices that EMH and MPT suggested for financial investment, which were either to arduously learn how to enact portfolio theory by understanding the correlations between investment risks (a strategy suggested in Hagin's *Modern Portfolio Theory*) or to offer the individual investor efficient ways of working with diversified portfolio or tracker index funds (a strategy that was consolidated so effectively by Bogle). Rather, Malkiel suggested what was to become the more well-trodden path in the genre as he acknowledged the "fundamental paradox" involved in the very production of mass financial advice, noting that if the "advice reaches enough people and they act on it, knowledge of the advice destroys its usefulness. If everyone knows about a 'good buy' and they all rush in to buy, the price of the 'good buy' will rise until it is no longer particularly attractive for investment."[109] At the same time, however, he also insists that there is still investment activity that can be pursued.

When Malkiel reveals the paradox of individual investment decisions in the wake of EMH and MPT, a paradox exponentially multiplied by financial advice, he also reveals how the genre was often imagined in this otherwise somewhat counterintuitive moment. It is not only that he believes that "anomalies" in pricing will continue temporarily to exist, and that the shrewd investor can identify them ahead of the market, it is that he recognizes—like so many of the books in the genre—that investment is an activity whose rewards are not necessarily only, or perhaps even primarily, financial. For Malkiel, more specifically, "telling an investor that there is no hope of beating the averages is like telling a six-year-old that there is no Santa Claus. It takes the zing out of life."[110] In his conclusion he suggests that the "zing" that financial investment provides is a more adult one than the six-year-old might recognize. Investing, he suggests, is a "bit like lovemaking" because "ultimately it really is an art requiring a certain talent and the presence of a mysterious force called luck" and because it is simply "too much fun to give up." If Templeton's bible for self-help was, literally, the Bible, then Malkiel's, it seems, may have been Alex Comfort's *Joy of Sex* published just one year earlier. The purpose of Malkiel's investment advice, then, appears to be prophylactic. Its aim is to allow the investor to "play the game with more satisfaction" because they know they will either "win or at least not lose too much." His parting hope is that he has imparted a confidence to the reader that will make playing all the "more enjoyable."[111]

Malkiel was certainly not the only writer who was stressing the libidinal pleasures of investing that emerged once it was openly acknowledged that the possibility of the individual investor beating either the market or the financial professional were so very low. Indeed, this sense of investing as a site of erotic and primarily male heterosexual pleasure, one tinged with danger, became widespread in cultural representations of finance in both Britain and America during the 1980s. The apocalyptic freight of individual investing that had appeared with such regularity in the 1970s was now being ameliorated by writers who were offering equivocal critiques of the libidinous pleasures written into this competition, alternately satirical and admiring. The "sexygreedy" register of 1980s popular culture, to borrow the playwright Caryl Churchill's phrase, which was shared with writers such as Martin Amis, Tom Wolfe, and Don DeLillo, offers an often lurid counterpart to Malkiel's writing. The idea that "greed is good," the apparently satirical line issued by Michael Douglas's Gordon Gekko in Oliver Stone's *Wall Street* in 1987, had become itself integral to the way in which finance was imagined.[112]

Malkiel's coding of investing as a form of self-realization in quite normatively masculine ways continued to characterize the genre in the wake of the EMH revolution. It also made sense of a genre that was dominated in this period by advice from the money managers whose very professions embodied the paradox of individual investment advice. These works differed from those concerned with educating readers about the practicalities of placing their money in what was clearly still seen as a secure, if niche, corner of the market, in that they were written by fund managers but were dedicated to the ideal of the investor who *did not* want simply to park their money in a fund.[113] Something of the varied nuances of this language are apparent in the ways in which these authors return to the use of individual biography that was seen in much earlier works. They often narrate their financial maturation, introducing what they have learned through a financial biography and drawing retrospective conclusions from their own successful selections of individual stocks—an act that both their careers and the theoretical field suggest is largely irrelevant to financial success. That some of the stocks that they reference are shared across these texts allows us to identify the similarities and differences in their narrative techniques.

Investing in the Domestic: The Recurring Story of Tampax

One such example is Tampax, which Malkiel, Train, and Lynch all identify as a stock that could make the individual investor very rich. In many ways it is an excellent example to use. The price of the stock rose steadily through the 1960s, when these men were first entering the market, and the company had litigiously and successfully guarded its brand and possessed a clear market dominance, at least until the toxic-shock health scares of the mid-1970s. It is also a brand that, especially compared to the more obviously glamorous attractions of the IBM and Motorola tech shares of the go-go decade, would have been easy for the male investor to overlook or shy away from. It is mentioned, despite its clear growth, surprisingly rarely in the financial press. The single article that covered the stock in the 1960s was entitled "Telling Their Secrets," and it noted that Tampax was one of a few sizable but still unlisted stocks for which the SEC had asked Congress to approve new reporting requirements.[114] Yet the scant attention the brand received in the financial press was belied by its presence in popular culture. It was the first sanitary product to be advertised on television, in the early 1970s, and the poster campaign that ran from the 1960s, including images of women astronauts and the strapline "Why Be Earth Bound," clearly identified the product with a popularized new frontier for women's liberation.

Yet the description of the stock that these men give, charged as it so obviously is with what they feel to be the social unease or illicitness of discussing women's reproductive bodies in public, is actually suggestive of the connections between cultures of investing and the changes that were occurring in gender politics in America in the 1970s. These were changes to which figures such as Rukeyser, Ruff, Goodman, and Erdman were all responding in more direct and explicit ways. Their writing, we want to suggest, responds not only to the problem of the imagined absence of women from the market—an absence that the empirical evidence refutes—but also the problem of their actual *presence*.

For some investors the uncomfortable social charge that was associated with Tampax was integral to its value. The financial advice writer John Train, for example, recollects telling Warren Buffet about his own contrarian success with Tampax and recalls an interview with John Templeton in which they share memories of buying the stock. The conversations suggest that it was the intimate nature of the product that made it so financially attractive, as it was not only other investors but the state—feared much more than professional competitors in the financial advice writing of the 1960s and 1970s—that would stay clear of it. Train notes that "Templeton was entertained by his observation that Tampax seemed an unlikely subject of regulation: one could scarcely conceive of Teddy Kennedy rising on the Senate floor to excoriate the profits made from this humble device: 'I have here in my hand . . .'" He uses the example to gently chide the comparatively active British regulatory culture at this time, as he notes that in the United Kingdom "even Tampax" has been the "subject of an attempt at price regulation."[115]

Other writers use the example to construct the male investor in more elaborate ways. Peter Lynch was the manager of the Fidelity Magellan Fund and the author of the promisingly titled *One Up on Wall Street*. Like Malkiel, Lynch recognizes that the genre risks contradiction—he opens by giving the reader "three good reasons to ignore" him. He represents investment as a kind of sport, comparing it to poker and suggesting that "betting on seven-card stud can provide a very consistent long-term return to people who know how to manage their cards" because, like Wall Street, "there's a lot of information in the open hands, if you know how to look for it."[116] The advocacy of "common knowledge" is central to Lynch's advice and this knowledge is primarily gained in the domestic realm. Lynch contends that his wife is "one of his best sources" and details the investment successes that followed from her somewhat artless observations about the changes in women's shopping habits. These stories form the center of Lynch's advice as he suggests that it is in the experience of the everyday consumer economy, one implicitly registered first by women, that growth stocks can be found. He recounts how he bought stock in a hosiery company whose product his wife admires. The deal earned him a "six-bagger"—the language of the mountaineer translating the language of the domestic shopper into the more rugged and heroic language of the speculator.

Lynch hangs this notion of "common knowledge" on the "famous story" of "a fireman from New England" who noticed that the local Tampax plant "was expanding at a furious pace." On the evidence of this growth he invested $2,000 and carried on doing so "every year for the next five years" until he was a "millionaire" by the early 1970s. It was an investment, Lynch assures his readers, that flew in the face of the advice that would have been given by brokers who would have told him to "stick with the blue chips" or the "hot electronics," but "luckily the fireman kept his own counsel."[117] The fireman's success is unlikely to the point of serendipity. The average family income was below $7,000 in 1960 and had not yet quite reached $10,000 by the end of the decade. In order to make his million the fireman, assuming his wages were equivalent to the national average (which, using contemporary US parallels as our guide, can only be assumed if he is at the *very* top of the fireman's pay scale) would need to be investing around 30 percent of his entire income, every year, in the stock. So the story of the fireman, which Lynch continued to repeat in amended versions in speeches into the first decade of the 2000s, is one that may well do cultural rather than economic work. It positions investing as a masculine blue-collar activity, one still rooted in a local manufacturing economy, even, or perhaps *especially*, in the moment in which this economy was coming under threat. This is a threat, moreover, that is identified less with the all too self-evident facts of deindustrialization than with the growing economic power and liberation of women (the "furious pace" of commodities that cater only to them) that both the brand, and Lynch's own wife's advice, suggest.

It is a narrative that is made even clearer in the concluding chapters to the early editions of Malkiel's *A Random Walk Down Wall Street*. Malkiel also frames himself as an individual stock selector, and this biographical narrative foreshadows the libidinal charge that the work's conclusion assigns to investing:

Back in 1959, during my days in the investment business, I used to spend many a pleasant lunch hour strolling randomly along Wall Street and gazing upon the bevy of young women passing by. In those chauvinistic days I must admit to thinking of most of the women I saw simply as sex objects. And the thought that with each passing year, as the baby boom matured, there would be more and more of these delightful creatures for me to admire warmed my soul.

Unfortunately, my intellect got into the act and I began to think what a market these young women were forming. Almost before I could fully comprehend what I was doing, I had ceased my luncheon walks and found myself poring through the census statistics instead. [...]

Lively, better educated, ever more numerous—these young women formed a potent market. But for what? Because I was entertaining all sorts of libidinous thoughts I reacted immediately when an annual report for Tampax passed my desk.[118]

The passage stages Malkiel's investment decisions as an internal drama of financial and social maturation, and the meaning of the reiterated description of the women as a "market" changes across the passage. In the first instance women are being evaluated as investments: he notices them, he wryly jokes, taking a "random walk down Wall Street." Yet after his "intellect" intervenes he realizes that women are the subjects, rather than the objects, of the market and that their real worth is in their growing numbers and gradual emancipation: they are "lively, better educated" than ever before, and it is this more sober recognition that leads him to invest in a lucrative but overlooked stock. Yet this narrative of cool reflection is also one that undermines itself in its very presentation. The rational thoughts are presented by Malkiel as the "unfortunate" ones and it is his calculations, rather than his desires, that run ahead of his comprehension: he begins them before realizing what he is doing. Indeed, it is actually the persistence of the "libidinous thoughts," rather than the evidence from the census research, that leads him to "immediately react" when an "annual report on Tampax" reaches his desk. Hence, Malkiel uses the example of this stock not to narrate a young man's emergence into a self-controlled adulthood but to do quite the opposite: to suggest that it is these visceral thoughts and impulses, coded in deeply masculine ways, that are the core to his identity as an investor. By attending closely to these seemingly incidental aspects of key works of 1970s and 1980s financial advice writing (the starkly gendered languages, and examples that they all "happen" to use), it becomes clear that, in such texts, to be invested—both financially and emotionally—in the stock market is to be invested in a particular conception of subjectivity that is conspicuously and assertively masculine.

The assertion of this active and clearly masculine identity in these texts can, perhaps, be read as a response to the challenge that the success of passively managed index funds posed to the genre's ability to sculpt the agency of the individual financial self. The leading figure in developing the index fund was John Bogle. Bogle's Vanguard Group of Investment Companies began in the early 1970s and launched what he was to call "the index revolution," in which passively managed low-cost tracker funds were to rival the managed portfolio funds that figures such as Lynch and Templeton had made their names in. Although Bogle's contribution to the genre of financial advice was relatively belated (his first book, for example, wasn't published until 1992), it drew on a critique that he had initially elaborated in his Princeton thesis in the early 1950s and that had informed his entire professional career. Bogle is lucid and consistent in arguing that low-cost passive tracker funds, of the kinds that Vanguard so successfully established, were superior in nearly every way to both amateur individual stock picking and to the managed portfolio funds of his contemporaries. His first book, *Bogle on Mutual Funds: New Perspectives for the Intelligent Investor*, styled itself in the slow and cool tradition of Benjamin Graham. It assumed that picking funds, rather than picking stocks, was the primary activity of the investor and explained the significance of the varied differences between funds and how potential investors should learn to match them against their own financial needs and risk appetites. Although learned in style (quoting Tennyson, Shakespeare, Hugo, Horace, and Wilde, and siding with the "intellectual-philosopher" over the "scientist technician" in his referencing of C. P. Snow's *Two Cultures and the Scientific Revolution*), the work is profoundly practical. One of its central premises is that analyzing the prior performance of funds and investor managers should be regarded as a trap rather than as a bait; the work advocates the use of paid analytical services such as Morningstar that offer a "full understanding of the structure of a mutual fund, of its risks, returns, and costs" in order to make decisions about how to allocate the management of one's money to others.[119]

In his later work, Bogle becomes more explicit about how his principles position him against the very cultures of financialization that the genre was steeped in. In *The Battle for the Soul of Capitalism* Bogle critiques the short-term aims of finance capital and angrily mourns the move from "owners' capitalism," which provided the "lion's share of the rewards of investment to those who put up the money and risk their own capital," to an "extreme version of managers' capitalism" which provides "vastly disproportionate rewards" to money managers and has replaced the ethos of stewardship with that of self-interest and short-term sales.[120] Bogle translates this critique of finance capital into the genre of financial advice, and *The Little Book of Commonsense Investing* critically compares mutual funds with index tracker funds, lambasting the former for their transaction and commission costs as well as the tax inefficiencies of incurring capital gains, all of which are avoided by the index fund. The book reiterates Bogle's commitment to long-term investing (not simply for one's retirement but for one's children and their children) and the magic of compound interest that extends across decades. It also celebrates the personal triumph that the success of low-cost index funds in the first decade of the 2000s represents to its author, citing the approving words not only of economists such as Paul Samuelson but also those of managed fund investors including Warren Buffet, Peter Lynch, and Burton Malkiel.

The critique of contemporary finance capital that is somewhat ironically embedded into Bogle's advocacy of the index fund has continued to reverberate. For some financial writers the predictability of the index fund promised to release investors from money itself. In 1992, the same year as Bogle's first work was published, Vicki Robin and Joe Dominguez published *Your Money or Your Life*. The work, with its nine steps to financial freedom, was an unashamedly motivational self-help guide to "financially independent" thinking that aimed to persuade its readers to reevaluate the dominance of money and in order to resist the pointless exchange of "life energy" for either work or consumerism. Robin and Dominguez advocated the extreme saving—up to 70 percent of one's income—that only the middle classes could ever afford in order to quicken the possibility of early retirement. The book was a forerunner of the FIRE movement (Financial Independence Retire Early) that gained momentum in the early 2010s and was given impetus with the publication of Jacob Lund Fisker's *Early Retirement Extreme*. The movement combined the possibilities of secure passive investment that Bogle had outlined, the ability to safely withdraw 3–4 percent of one's capital via an index fund, with a critique of debt-fueled consumer culture.

Yet for advocates of the free market, the increasing dominance of passive investment approaches and the prioritization of already large and established companies simply because they are large and established were seen to discourage the entrepreneurial spirit and the efficient allocation of capital. Financial fund managers and academic economists alike have suggested that, although passive investing offers retail investors the better deal, it "might not be good for the financial markets, public companies, or the American economy writ large," and for some its effects are "worse than Marxism."[121] The rise of index funds influences how the market behaves in various ways. First, it has led to a decline in the fundamental analysis of company performance and balance sheets which risks "worse production decisions" because "index investing distorts the price signal thereby generating a negative externality that impedes firms' ability to make production decisions."[122] Second, it leads to a convergence of market behavior, as stocks move increasingly in concert with one another, and the herding increases the possibility for market volatility and sudden swings.[123] Finally, and most worryingly, it concentrates corporate ownership, leading to a decline in competition and the potential for a monopolistic rise in prices—the very thing that index funds sought to resist.[124]

* * *

In the second half of the twentieth century the genre of the personal investment advice manual was supported by an industry which reached across radio, television, and especially periodicals. The broad-brush picture of the period is one that we might expect: thinking about the market, and imagining oneself as invested in it, became represented as a mass cultural activity, first in the United States but eventually in the United Kingdom as well. It is hardly surprising, for example, that the penultimate year of this period saw the launch of CNBC, the Consumer News and Business Channel, which indicated the almost insatiable market for financial information that the online providers we explore next were able to more fully realize. Yet, as we have suggested, this apparent fascination with financial data did not accord with either an increasingly active or increasingly egalitarian financial class. The wealth disparity in both the United States and the United Kingdom continued unchecked through the 1970s and the 1980s, and the middle classes who were invested in the stock market became increasingly passive as the complexities of managing modern portfolios were turned over to the money managers of pension fund capitalism.

This narrative is one that we can clearly trace through the changes that took place in the financial investment advice manual, which remained a core and steady presence throughout this period. Initially we see the tenor of these books is one of motivated reeducation, as investors are given not only the mechanistic skills but also the nationalistic rationale to reenter the arena of financial speculation in the wake of the long downturn of the 1930s. We also see, beyond these practices of pedagogical instruction and encouragement, that the methods of speculation itself—including the tension between fundamental and technical analysis—continue in a variety of only subtly nuanced forms. By the early 1970s, in the face of both financial crisis and the radical changes signaled by the widespread assumption of the efficient market hypothesis and modern portfolio theory, the tensions between those who are guided by facts about stocks and those who are guided by feelings about markets start to take on a different shape. The former clustered around the possibilities that portfolio analysis offers to the lay investor and the latter around an often deeply visceral and embodied language of gaming, gambling, battle, or seduction. What emerges as new across the period is the genre's ability to absorb the contradictions that the move toward these large funds involved. We can trace this tendency through the appearance of books guiding investors through the options of choosing between managed funds and, later, through the biographical guides of those who have done this most successfully and who—despite their own careers—continue to advocate for the pleasures and dangers of individual stock picking despite the growing success of passively managed index funds.

Yet, beyond this historical narrative, our close readings of these texts have also revealed the social and cultural changes that were occurring across this period, especially regarding how participation in investing was ostensibly widening—if not in terms of class or wealth, then at least in terms of race and gender. Women were, indeed, invested in significant numbers in a wide range of speculative securities throughout this period, and an increase in the number of African American individuals and companies within the predominately white cultures of Wall Street also occurs. However, both of these developments, in different ways, are deeply ambivalent. Although a genre of financial advice that acknowledged the different experiences and political identifications of African Americans thrived in this period, it did not correspond to a shift in the profound structural inequalities that underpin the racial distribution of unearned wealth. Similarly, the language of the financial advice manuals themselves suggests that the significance of women's ownership of assets is more complex than the quantitative data suggest. First, we found that the interpellation of women as financial agents was often intertwined, especially in the early part of this period, with the extension of the processes of financialization into the domestic realm, and that any progressive meaning that we may imagine assigning to these developments is undercut by the conservative insistence on the heteronormative family that accompanied them. The "risk shift" that took place in both the United Kingdom and the United States, we have seen, was enabled not only by the financialization of health, housing, and education, but also by the privileging of what neo-liberal economist Gary Becker was to later call the "natural insurance function" of the family.[125] Indeed, as we have seen in our final analysis in this chapter, the uncomfortable representations of women who might in some way disrupt this pattern—representations which might speak of even the most limited and literal kind of feminist awareness—suggest that it was not the absence but rather the presence of women in the financial marketplace that actually concerned many of our authors.

CHAPTER SIX

Gurus and Robots (1990–2020)

"**M**y idea was that someone needed to start a website that gave financial news and advice . . . in verse." So runs the rueful confession of Matt Prior, the protagonist of *The Financial Lives of the Poets*, a 2009 novel by the American author Jess Walter. Matt's brain child, poetfolio.com, which he quit his job as a financial journalist to establish, is envisaged as publishing "all sorts of *literary* writing about the financial world," not only "fiscal poetry" but also "creative essays, profiles of brokers, short fiction about business, and investment memoirs." Matt acknowledges the quixotic nature of his "dream of writing stock news and tips in pedestrian, amateurish verse"; and the site's planned launch turns out to be disastrously timed, coinciding with the onset of the global financial crisis in 2007. The story is manifestly absurd, but part of the joke is that this fictional form of investment advice is at heart no more fanciful than many of the other works of financial writing we have been examining in this book. Walter's portrayal of poetfolio.com is on the money: in its attempted exploitation of the power of the internet as a vehicle for disseminating financial advice on a mass scale; in its underlying premise that there is a virtually inexhaustible market for such advice because "people spend so much time thinking about business and finance, about their mortgages, about investing, about retirement and college funds"; and in its showcasing of a brand of "money-lit" that blurs the boundaries between financial commentary and guidance and more imaginative or expressive forms of writing.[1] This chapter traces the multimedia and multi-genre proliferation of financial advice over the past thirty years, an array of texts and products that take themselves seriously (and which in turn are taken seriously by their audience) but which are every bit as bizarre as the idea of "fiscal poetry."

The crisis that forms the backdrop to Walters's work of "crunch lit" is just one of a succession of financial upheavals that punctuated the closing decades of the twentieth century and the early decades of the twenty-first.[2]

With the unraveling in the 1970s of the postwar Bretton Woods agreement that had governed the world's economic system, the cycle of boom and bust that had long been a feature of the stock market returned. But financial crashes have now become more frequent, and more globally contagious. The 1970s saw a damaging period of high inflation and recession, and the monetarist policy used to cure it (the so-called Volcker shock) subsequently helped trigger the Latin American debt crisis of the 1980s. This was followed by the stock market crash of 1987 (known as Black Monday in the United Kingdom) and the Lost Decade of unrelenting economic recession in Japan following its stock market and real estate crash in 1989. In addition to the major savings-and-loan banking crisis in the United States, the 1990s saw the banking system in many Scandinavian countries collapse. In 1994 Mexico needed to be bailed out by the International Monetary Fund following reckless investment in the country, while in 1997–98 speculation in emerging economies in Asia hit the buffers when foreign investors pulled out their money amid fears that the local currencies were overvalued and the governments unable to prop them up. The Russian ruble collapsed in 1998 and the government defaulted on its debt, an action that in turn caused the collapse of the US-based hedge fund Long-Term Capital Management, whose Nobel Prize–winning economists were left with egg on their faces. In the late 1990s and early 2000s crises hit Ecuador, Pakistan, Brazil, Ukraine, Turkey, Uruguay and—most devastatingly—Argentina. In addition the dotcom bubble burst in the United States in 2000. Although a recession was averted that time, the crash of 2007–8 led to a global financial recession, and, at the time of this writing, the world has been plunged into economic chaos because of the coronavirus pandemic. Despite—or perhaps precisely because of—this roller-coaster ride of shocks and corrections, stock market investment advice has not only continued to be produced but has become the paradigm for a wider culture of self-help, led by high-profile personal advice gurus. In addition to the obvious lure of making money, the fantasy sold by this genre is increasingly that private investment can replace collective provision of welfare. And, despite the emergence of new media forms in which guidance is distributed, the printed financial advice manual has not only survived but thrived.

Financial Advice in the Digital Age

The development of the internet as an increasingly pervasive medium of communication in the 1990s promised a revolution in both financial advice and access to stock markets. In theory the "disruptive" nature of the internet should have signaled the final demise of the printed popular financial advice manual, consigning it to the scrap heap with other supposedly outmoded technologies such as the printed newspaper, network television, and the vinyl LP. But the story is more complicated. Far from being replaced, books by celebrity financial advice gurus have, if anything, reached new levels of popularity. These authors indeed often present themselves as gurus, encouraging a cult following among their devotees, as they promise salvation through financial enrichment for those who follow their prescriptions religiously. The focus is increasingly on the lifestyle and charismatic personality of the multimedia entrepreneur, rather than the minutiae of individual stock picks.

The longer history of financial advice we have been tracing in this study demonstrates that new communication media do not inevitably replace earlier forms. Instead, they are often integrated into a mixed-media economy, which aims to target different consumers and which does not map easily onto a simple story of technological progress. Dave Ramsey, for instance, combines his website with his deliberately folksy syndicated radio show along with a string of books. As we have seen, stock market advice on television dates back to the 1970s in programs such as Louis Rukeyser's Friday night *Wall $treet Week*. Yet, in the late 1990s, at the height of the dotcom boom—at the very moment when the internet had begun to move from academia to the wider public—the most prominent outlet for financial news was not online but on television, with CNBC and CNNfn, albeit now more as endless attention-grabbing entertainment by proxy than worthy instructional advice. Jim Cramer's career captures the complex interplay between different media: he jumped from managing a hedge fund to being one of the early providers of financial advice and information via the web, but he then moved instead to a magazine, and then onto TV, all the while keeping up a regular churn of new books. These multimedia synergies help increase the overall profile of financial advice gurus like Cramer, but they also enable them to reach different audiences (retired people, for example, are more likely to turn to books than blogs). In some cases, high-profile books lead to gigs on radio, television, and websites, but the direction can also go the other way: the readership for the books is driven by the media visibility in other modes. In very few cases—the Zero Hedge website would be one example—are there no spin-off books from a successful website or television program.

Although it is clear that the internet—like other, disruptive forms of new media before it—has not yet killed off the book-length financial advice manual, it is still worth considering the claims that have been made about the radical possibilities it affords. Many commentators breathlessly championed the power of the internet to make stock markets friction-less and democratic, in effect producing a more perfect market—claims which, as we have seen, were also made in their time about the newspaper, the telegraph, and the stock ticker. The internet introduced the possibility of customers buying and selling their own shares directly with discount e-brokers such as TD Ameritrade, E-Trade, and Fidelity. The disintermedi-ation of finance brought lower trading costs, improved execution speed, and gave greater ease of access for ordinary investors who in the past would have conducted their business through a professional, licensed (and com-mensurately expensive) broker. The internet did not only make it easier to trade stocks in a DIY fashion, but also—in theory at least—for retail investors to access a seemingly unlimited trove of information and advice. As David Denby put it in his memoir of getting suckered into the dot-com bubble around the turn of the millennium, the internet held out the heady hope of a brave new world of financial immediacy and self-reliance, albeit one that directly connects back to Thomas Mortimer's pioneering introduction to the stock market: "Everyone his own financial adviser!"[3] The online revolution would in theory allow round-the-clock, up-to-the-minute access to information and the markets, intensifying the relentless attention economy based on a sense of immediacy and virtual presence that the stock ticker had introduced a century before, but this time en-abling everyone to have their own souped-up private ticker. With a fa-miliarly exaggerated claim to the unprecedented nature of the situation, the creators of the financial website the Motley Fool insisted in their 2001 book extolling the virtues of "getting online" that the opportunity "to stay informed about your investments, while at the same time learning more and more about investing in general, so far surpasses anything previously available that it's not unlike comparing our current picture of the universe with those days when everyone was sure the sun circled the earth."[4] The implied message, of course, is that such an unparalleled situation requires market neophytes to shell out on new modes of financial information and advice, of exactly the kind that the Motley Fool is purveying. In addition to the ease of buying and selling stocks, and the easy access to and endless flow of information, in the eyes of its apologists the internet also had the potential to overturn the hierarchy of expertise and to end the gatekeep-ing role of professionals. In short, the internet promised to level up the information asymmetry between insiders and outsiders, professionals and amateurs, finally bringing about a truly frictionless stock market—although, as we have seen, this was *always* the promise made in popular financial advice literature.

Such was the hype in the heady years of the dotcom boom in the last decade of the twentieth century, but did it match the reality? There is no denying that it is now much easier for ordinary investors to trade, and the average cost of buying and selling shares has fallen dramatically since the emergence of online discount brokerages in the 1990s: from a high point of 0.9 percent commission per transaction in 1974 to 0.1 percent in the 2010s.[5] However, the ease of access and reduction in transaction costs have led to their own problems. For example, one study of the consequences of clients in the late 1990s moving from telephone orders via their broker to direct transactions online found that on average they went from beating the market by 2 percent annually to trailing the market by 3 percent.[6] The authors hypothesized that the decline in customers' success was the result of a dangerous combination of overconfidence on the part of the clients and the newfound possibilities for overtrading—in part because trading online was now so cheap and convenient, but also because they had bypassed any note of caution that a responsible broker might have offered. Precisely because online firms cut back on brokers in order to reduce costs, there was now a lack of personal, professional advice, creating an information void that the new forms of citizen-advice enabled by the internet turned into a virtue. The rise of discount brokers and e-trading platforms also made it possible for amateur investors to engage in day-trading (rapid buying and selling intraday in order to make speculative profits from temporary price movements), who often referenced discredited forms of technical analysis, including (as we'll see below) reprinted "classics." Yet, as one study notes, as many as 99 percent of day traders make a loss, even though many convince themselves that the technology allows them to compete as equals with Wall Street professionals.[7] Although electronic trading in theory creates a level playing field where all orders are instantaneous and anonymous, the reality of High Frequency Trading (HFT) is that individual humans can no longer hope to compete against algorithmic trading that now happens at the speed of nanoseconds; moreover, it has been revealed that the big Wall Street firms such as Goldman Sachs game the system by getting their computer servers physically closer to the computer running the market, coupled with the increased use of so-called dark pools (that allow institutional investors, quite legally, to sell large blocks of stock without revealing their order book in advance).[8] As Michael Lewis explains in his account of High Frequency Trading, when a slower competitor or amateur outsider places an order to buy shares, the computer of the HFT firm manages to detect it and speeds ahead to buy up the shares being offered. It then sells them to the clueless broker at a slight hike, making a small profit from the difference. In this way the market that mom-and-pop brokers see on their screens is not the one that they actually end up buying into. The fantasy of electronic trading producing perfect markets and a level playing field thus remains elusive.[9]

The revolution in access to financial information and advice on the internet has likewise produced mixed results. Financial blogs emerged out of the discussion boards of platforms such as Yahoo! Finance in the late 1990s, a virtual space for day traders and armchair speculators to "argue investment ideas and vent little-guy frustrations about the Wall Street power structure."[10] At first the blogs (and then more fully developed websites) were written by renegade financial industry professionals, and part of their appeal was to give amateurs a sense of immediate connection with savvy, insider talk. Their contrarian, anti-elitist stance attracted a wider audience after the global financial crisis of 2008, speaking to a more widespread distrust about financial expertise. They cultivated an underground, "hacker" ethic that vaunted the power of the internet to overturn traditional knowledge hierarchies in favor of more participatory forms of media. Already by 2008, nearly a quarter of Americans relied on investment advice transmitted via peers on social media rather than more orthodox forms of expert advice from certified advisers, with some of the most prominent blogs regularly attracting 3 million page views per day.[11] The crowd-sourced wisdom of financial blogs spoke to the wider populist rejection of elites that was beginning to reshape the political landscape in many countries in the first decade of the 2000s, but they also served to create a sense of community among the anonymous and dispersed amateur investors, despite their frequently individualist message (you can be one of the clever few to outsmart those so-called experts!). Although, like other forms of internet culture, online financial blogs emphasized their disruptive power, they have similarities with the investment clubs that were popular in both the United States and the United Kingdom from the 1950s on—albeit now connecting strangers into a virtual community.[12] There is, however, some evidence that these participatory forms of financial advice can manage to level the playing field, by providing data and insights that were previously hard for outsiders to access. A study in 2013, for example, found that investment advice blogs can indeed be effective in reducing the information asymmetry that, as we have seen, has long been a central feature of the stock market.[13] Yet, as we discuss later, episodes like the GameStop saga indicate that populist forms of financial activism create as many problems as they solve.

As we've seen in cases such as that of the stock promoter and journalist Thomas Lawson in the early 1900s, the circulation of financial advice in the mass media can create a self-fulfilling prophecy. As early as 2000, academic studies found that stock recommendations on websites such as the Motley Fool moved the market as much as television and other electronic media.[14] Perhaps more significant are findings that discussion forums and comment sections can themselves predict market movements and even earnings surprises (when corporate reports are above or below expectations). More than the pronouncements of the financial gurus running the websites, the wisdom of crowds—enabled by the participatory structure of web 2.0—can indeed sometimes level up the information asymmetry between insiders and outsiders.[15] Although some investors have been able to take advantage of the easier access to data that was once reserved for insiders, and collectively this virtual crowd can at times outsmart the professional market seers, the democratization of financial advice on the web has not been an unqualified success. As Brad Barber and Terrance Odean note in their summary of academic research on this topic, amateur investors

> trade frequently and have perverse stock selection ability, incurring unnecessary investment costs and return losses. They tend to sell their winners and hold their losers, generating unnecessary tax liabilities. Many hold poorly diversified portfolios, resulting in unnecessarily high levels of diversifiable risk, and many are unduly influenced by media and past experience. Individual investors who ignore the prescriptive advice to buy and hold low-fee, well-diversified portfolios, generally do so to their detriment.[16]

Research has found that amateurs often get in above their heads, driven by an overconfidence that comes from having seemingly unlimited access to vast quantities of data and free advice.[17] The rise of DIY investing and financial advice by social media coincided with—and indeed helped to inflate—the dotcom boom in the late 1990s, creating a perfect storm in which novice investors felt empowered to speculate on tech start-ups that were virtually impossible to value accurately.

Many of the personal finance gurus profiled in this chapter claim to be on the side of the ordinary investor, providing money advice based more on the authority of experience than credentialed knowledge, and to be resolutely independent of any financial institution. Yet often they are in reality promoting their own financial products and services, and, ultimately, their business model is making money from selling advice, whether in print, on television, or through in-person seminars. As Helaine Olen points out, even Harvey Houtkin, the pioneer of day-trading, "made his millions not from successful stock picks, but from convincing others that they had the ability to make such picks themselves, racking up millions in commissions from customers of his day-trading firm while losing hundreds of thousands of dollars on his own investments."[18] In contrast, blogs and websites, especially in the early years of the internet, held out the promise of free and impartial financial advice, making a virtue out of their crowd-sourced knowledge and community spirit. However, financial advice on the web has also suffered from a lack of transparency about its sources of funding and its economic incentives, especially with the use of undisclosed affiliate marketing that undermined the claims to impartiality. The early entrepreneurs of online advice tried out different funding models. Some began as subscription newsletters with very small audiences before transitioning to become free websites, albeit funded initially by start-up cash but increasingly by advertising. In an echo of late nineteenth-century magazines such as *Town Topics* offering the simulation of personal advice in their mass-circulated money columns and newsletters but supplementing it with a full-service personal investment advice bureau, many websites (such as the Motley Fool) have now developed a hybrid economic model that combines free content with premium services. Financial advice online might be cheap and easy to access, but it is not necessarily produced with the best interests of its consumers in mind, especially those with limited means who are likely already to be leading financially precarious lives, the victims of an economic environment in which health care and education costs have soared while incomes for all but the wealthiest have stagnated since the 1970s. Unsurprisingly, researchers have found that free online financial advice has not led to a general improvement of financial literacy. On the contrary, "personal finance blogs are preaching to the choir, since the consumers who are most likely to use personal finance blogs seem to need them the least given their higher levels of financial literacy and lower levels of perceived financial uncertainty."[19] The democratization of financial advice enabled by the internet has thus not produced the utopian revolution suggested by its early promoters. As the economist Robert Shiller scathingly notes, "the entire gabby system of market advice—the magazines, newspaper columns, and books, the appearances on CNBC and CNNfn—is fatuous and worthless, a contemptible scam that foists absurd delusions on a gullible public."[20] There is little we would disagree with in Shiller's assessment—except that the "entire gabby system of market advice" is not simply a product of the digital age but has been part of the genre from the start.

Having assessed the general claims made about the radical potential of the internet to transform the genre of financial advice, we now turn to consider in more detail two prominent examples, one that sets itself up as the voice of the amateur (the Motley Fool), and the other a website whose libertarian stance makes appeal to both professionals and outsiders (Zero Hedge). The Motley Fool was founded by the brothers David and Tom Gardner, parlaying the knowledge they had gleaned from trading the stocks that they had inherited early in life. They first tried an investment newsletter in 1993 ("Ye Olde Printed Fool") but only managed to secure thirty-eight subscribers. In the following year, they partnered with AOL to provide a similar diet of opinion pieces and stock picks, and, with help from a *New Yorker* profile that cemented their brand-name recognition, became the most visited financial service on AOL. Over the years they have diversified their channels of communication, producing a number of books and podcasts as well as offering a full-blown wealth management service, real estate advice, a crowd-sourced ratings system for stock picks (that ranks and weights by success from both their 50,000 ordinary members and 100 professional stock market analysts), and, coming full circle, paid subscription newsletters (see fig. 6.1).

Their brand name is based on the idea that only the Fool can speak truth to power, and in both their website and the books distilling their advice they set themselves up in opposition to the "conventional wisdom" of Wall Street professionals—not so different from Mortimer, who presented himself as a reliable guide precisely because he was a market renegade who had tasted failure.[21] In their early years they touted an elaborate system for picking stocks to create a portfolio. Choosing the "Foolish Four" involved an iterative process of taking each company's dividend yield and dividing it by the square root of its share price, but it soon became clear that their methodology did not stand up to rigorous scrutiny.[22] They soon simplified their system for beating the market. Starting from the assumption that stocks outperform all other asset classes if held for the long term, they recommended picking a mixture of blue-chip companies and more risky stocks, coupled with advice to avoid day-trading and penny stocks. Their books turned the piecemeal advice on the website into a more de-

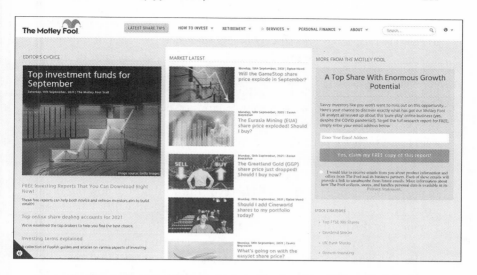

FIGURE 6.1. Homepage of the Motley Fool website. The Copyright of The Motley Fool. Image published with permission of The Motley Fool. Further reproduction is prohibited without permission.

tailed and programmatic instruction on the basics of financial knowledge, such as how to read corporate reports and balance sheets to determine whether a stock is undervalued and represents a sensible investment. The Motley Fool's appeal is to amateur investors, but their claim—as we have seen so often before—is that, equipped with the right education, the "fool" can outsmart Wall Street and beat the market, all with fifteen minutes' effort per year. It turns out, however, that it probably requires more than a quarter of an hour to master the market.[23] Although less abstruse than the Foolish Four system, they still recommend using a basket of metrics (such as a company's rate of profit and growth, the proportion of its revenue spent on R&D) to determine whether a particular stock is a good long-term prospect. As much as they promote a stock-picking formula, they also hedge their bets by emphasizing—like their investment advice forebears in the nineteenth and early twentieth century—that at the end of the day cultivating the right attitude is more important than learning particular techniques of analysis: "The greatest investors are often paragons of self-discipline and temperament, exhibiting admirable and useful characteristics such as patience, diligence, perceptiveness, and common sense."[24]

Their claim in effect is that with a modicum of research it is possible to reliably pick long-term stock winners, and thereby beat not only passive index funds but also managed funds—in large part because by doing one's own research paying professional fees and expenses can be avoided, but also because individuals are not constrained by the rules governing investment funds (which, for example, are not permitted to hold more than 5 percent of the portfolio in a single company and are not allowed to own more than a 5 percent stake in an individual firm). Independent research has confirmed that their long-term "Stock Adviser" recommendations outperformed various benchmarks in both the short and long term in the period studied (2002–11).[25] However, the Motley Fool now offers an array of different subscription advice services, some of which have been renamed or discontinued, which can make it hard to verify the claims of success. Moreover, the subscription services undermine the main message of the site, which is that only DIY research can combat the damage to return caused by fees, and only by maintaining an independent stance can the adviser remain a wise fool.

The Zero Hedge website was set up in 2009 by Daniel Ivandjiiski, a former hedge fund trader who in 2008 had been caught insider trading and was banned from any future employment in the securities industry. The articles (now written by several contributors) on the website appear under the pseudonym Tyler Durden, the character in the Chuck Palahniuk novel *Fight Club* (played by Brad Pitt in the film version) who leaves his corporate job to set up a revolutionary underground organization, the ultimate goal of which is to destroy financial capitalism through acts of terrorism. Like the Durden character, Zero Hedge adopts an edgy, angry, outsider stance of supposedly imperiled white masculinity, coupled with a strong sense of the authenticity of its insider knowledge. Established in the wake of the 2008 crash, it has remained resolutely bearish in its outlook, convinced that a far greater crash is not merely inevitable but desirable—because only by razing the current Wall Street system to the ground can a new, purer market emerge in its wake. It formed part of a wave of websites that offered a far more cynical form of investment advice than the personal financial gurus we examine later in this chapter. Sites like Seeking Alpha, the Big Picture, Infectious Greed, and Angry Bear created online communities who saw themselves as Davids battling the Goliath of Wall Street banks and hedge funds, creating a financial equivalent of the populist, anti-elitist rise of groups like the Tea Party and Trump supporters. Zero Hedge's pessimistic tagline, taken from *Fight Club*, is that "on a long enough timeline the survival rate for everyone drops to zero." (The irony, of course, is that Zero Hedge's relentlessly nihilistic commentary unfolded against the backdrop of a sustained bull market—at least until the temporary collapse of stock market prices in the spring of 2020 with the COVID-19 pandemic.)

The worldview of Zero Hedge mixes cyber-libertarian utopianism (its stated mission is "to liberate oppressed knowledge") and alt-right conspiracy theory. It repeatedly suggests that Wall Street is irredeemably corrupt, with the big players constituting a conspiracy against ordinary investors. Nothing can be trusted. All markets are corrupt. As the journalist Joe Hagan noted in an article that revealed the identity of Ivandjiiski in 2009, "the darker [Ivandjiiski's] vision the more popular he became. . . . The blog's inscrutability was part of its appeal. It had the feel of a financial insider leaking forbidden information."[26] Zero Hedge encouraged those contributing to its discussion threads to think of themselves as smarter than the "naïve, easily-manipulated, small-time mom-and-pop investors."[27] It attacked what it considered ham-fisted government attempts at regulation and reform, on the one hand, and the secretive practices of Wall Street's top firms, on the other. It scored a reporting coup in 2009 when it broke the story of how Goldman Sachs was skewing the market with its high-frequency trading strategies, which it then developed into a more overarching conspiracy theory that Goldman Sachs had been manipulating the entire market and the regulatory framework for decades.[28] Although there are no reliable figures, the site generates healthy advertising revenue based on its (claimed) 2 million page views per day. Despite its vehement stance against financial corruption, the site relies on "sponsored financial content" that at times is little more than clickbait.

Although there have been several accusations that the site is—both metaphorically and quite literally—in the pay of Putin's Russia, it seems more likely that its political positions (e.g., anti-Obama, pro-Assad, pro-Trump) are in keeping with its deliberately contrarian and nihilistic stance toward all establishments. (Albeit from a seemingly fringe part of the political spectrum, Zero Hedge's alt-right stance is reminiscent of a more mainstream strand of apocalyptic financial writing that emerged in the 1970s, and which continues in forms of "disaster capitalism" financial prophecy, such as *The Sovereign Individual* by British writer and former broadsheet editor William Rees-Mogg.[29]) Zero Hedge has courted many conspiracy theories, including the #Pizzagate and QAnon "deep state" theories amplified on alt-right anti–political correctness message boards

such as 4chan. In March 2020 Twitter deplatformed Zero Hedge for vio-
lating the platform's "rules against abuse and harassment" by promoting
conspiracy theories claiming that the Chinese had created the COVID-19
virus in a biolab and doxing one of the lab workers, only to then rein-
state the site later in the year.[30] The line Zero Hedge takes repeatedly is
that the global elite are duping the masses, from the claim that the white
supremacist Charlottesville shootings were staged by crisis actors to the
pro-Kremlin claim that the United States was planning to use the crash of
flight MH17 as a pretext for a NATO invasion of Ukraine. The comment
sections regularly attract anti-Semitic and alt-right racist diatribes, and,
since 2013, social and political topics have replaced finance as the site's
most-read articles.

Since the 1970s personal finance has increasingly focused on investment advice, as the stock market has become the central instrument
but also the dominant metaphor for self-realization. In effect, self-help
has come to take the form of financial advice and vice versa. The advice
guides of Dave Ramsey, Suze Orman, and Jim Cramer sell the illusion
of an individual solution to the structural problems of current economic
life. Zero Hedge (and other, similar websites) offers a different—but also
equally illusory—fantasy of control. It holds out to its readers the promise
of all conspiracy theory: that those special few who have managed to see
through establishment lies (taking the "red pill," in alt-right parlance), and
who have the determination to sift through the endless clues hidden in
plain sight, can understand what is really going on. And, the delusion continues, if enough misfits and renegades join the cause and defeat the all-
powerful conspiracy, a utopian future awaits. This is financial advice not
as practical guidance but as armchair revolution and messianic fantasy.

Robo-Advising

Producers of financial advice have continued to adapt to the changing
technological affordances of the internet, as social media platforms—as
well as emerging assets such as cryptocurrencies—create both new possibilities and new dangers for speculation. Twitter, for example, has led to
both a surge in "pump-and-dump" hot tip posts and also to ventures such
as StockTwits, a social network for investors and traders that claims 3 million registered members.[31] The microtargeting capabilities of Facebook
have contributed to the rise of fraudulent stock advertising online, while

YouTube provides the perfect platform for self-declared financial experts to directly reach an audience without needing television or book fame first. Searching for "financial advice" on YouTube, for example, brings up the channels of people like Kris Krohn, whose videos chart his progress from champion of real estate hypothecation as the easiest way to riches to full-blown lifestyle guru, as his accompanying website explains: "Limitless Belief Breakthrough, Kris helps people bridge the gap between where they are and the results they want—the results their potential demands."[32]

Perhaps the most significant new development in "fintech" (the now ubiquitous shorthand for a cluster of emerging digitally mediated forms of financial technology), however, is not a new medium for the promotion of personal finance gurus but the use of sophisticated algorithms by financial service companies to provide automated financial advice that is supposedly tailored to the needs of individual clients. "Robo-advising," as it has come to be called, uses algorithms on online platforms to automatically build and manage clients' portfolios.[33] A typical robo-adviser collects information from clients about their financial situation and future goals through an online survey and then uses the data both to offer advice and to automatically invest clients' assets. The formula of most robo-advising firms is quite simple: they buy low-cost index funds (usually exchange-traded funds [ETFs]), allocated between stocks and bonds, at a risk level that a client finds tolerable. In addition to portfolio allocations, the services provided often include automatic rebalancing and tax management. This process greatly reduces the costs of these facilities as they have been offered by traditional financial management companies. Start-up firms such as Betterment and Wealthfront (which began in 2008) offer investors automated portfolio management for as little as 0.25 percent annually, in comparison with the standard 1 percent charged by traditional financial planners.

A Gallup opinion poll in 2016 found that 70 percent of Americans insisted that human advisers are better than robo-advisers. Nevertheless, robo-advising is taking off rapidly—no doubt in part due to its significant cost reductions and ease of use. As of 2020, robo-advising accounts in the United States have $1.4 trillion in assets under management (currently increasing by 20 percent per year), with 70 million clients, who have an average of $20,000 invested.[34] The growth of robo-advising comes as little surprise, given that by 2019 the total invested in the United States in passive index-tracking funds exceeded the amount under active management. Robo-advising is popular because it seems to offer the best of both worlds:

individually tailored advice and portfolio management (usually out of the reach of lower-income clients), coupled with low fees. The simulation of personal advice that it creates taps into the desire for individual attention we have seen repeatedly in this study, yet it couples that "trust in people" with "trust in numbers," a reassuring sense (for some) that they can take advantage of the most sophisticated investment and portfolio allocation algorithms. Some robo-advising firms have begun to advertise services that combine robot and human elements: Moneyfarm, for example, offers a "robo advisor with a human touch," while Betterment's Premium Plan offers "Unlimited access to our CFP [Certified Financial Planner] professionals for guidance to life events."[35] On the one hand, then, robo-advising taps into the contradictory desire that has always been the selling point for mass-produced financial advice, namely for the recipients to feel unique and exclusive: only the chosen few can benefit from this wisdom. On the other hand, robo-advising speaks to the recurrent populist appeal of the democratization of investment, perhaps finally achieving the desire that the consumer breaks free of all advice and professional interference, so that finally "Every Man [Is] His Own Broker."

Some preliminary studies by financial economists have suggested that robo-advising is reasonably successful in providing adequate financial advice (within the current paradigms of investment) for its clients at an affordable price, especially for those without much prior knowledge or experience. These studies note that robo-advising reduces management fees, produces a better diversification of portfolios, and automates processes such as portfolio rebalancing and tax-loss harvesting.[36] Research has also shown that robo-advising can serve to reduce the harmful effects of the behavioral biases of both clients and (human) advisers, because machines are less prone to emotion.[37] Needless to say, professional bodies representing traditional financial advisers have countered that there is still a need for a good financial adviser, with whom clients have a long relationship built on trust: "an advisor can provide insight that a robo can't. Emotions can cloud the judgment of even the most battle-tested investor. The urge to sell during a downturn or chase after underperforming stocks is human nature and can be hard to fight on your own. A human advisor can help clients balance emotions with practical advice and judgment."[38] Ironically, the claim here is that a human adviser can make you more machine-like than the robots.

It is also unclear to what extent the advice is genuinely "personalized" to individual clients or is largely formulaic. It can begin to seem that clients are merely paying an unnecessary extra fee (albeit a small one compared to traditional in-person advice) for some fancy advertising rhetoric and a slick interface, because in most cases the robo recommendation is to invest in a basket of low-cost index funds, an outcome which—armed with a copy of Burton Malkiel—clients could easily reach themselves. Some critics have also noted that—like much financial advice—robo-advice is rarely impartial or based on a fiduciary responsibility to provide advice that is genuinely in the best interest of clients. Ultimately the incentive structure is based on getting clients to invest more in order to increase the firm's revenue from fees. There is always a price to pay for advice that seems free or low cost. Furthermore, although part of the appeal of robo-advising is that it allows seemingly democratic access to some quite sophisticated algorithms and automated portfolio rebalancing processes, there is still a suspicion that the wealthy elite—as they have always done—will not make do with this off-the-peg advice, however much it looks like you're buying a custom-made suit. Robo-advising is unlikely to replace "wealth management," which is advertised as a more personal form of all-round financial planning reserved for clients with at least $1 million in liquid assets, targeted at those who are willing to pay for a sense of exclusive treatment. Advertisements for wealth managers emphasize both the personal attention and the fantasy of using esoteric asset management and tax-minimizing techniques to achieve "alpha," that is, beating the market. As is clear from the long history of financial advice, the rhetorical appeal is often to a sense of specialness, of being better than the masses—even if the advice increasingly comes in the mass-mediated form of simulated personal advice from a robot.

Managing the Contradictions of Financial Advice

Part of the advertised appeal of robo-advising is that it cuts out human biases, encouraging clients to place their faith in the emotionless impartiality of the algorithms (while downplaying the fact that the algorithms are themselves constructed according to received wisdom, with all its inevitable bias). Celebrity financial self-help gurus effectively make the opposite claim. Even more than their predecessors, these best-selling writers—household names who have often become wealthy through their advice rather than their investing—rely on the strength of their charismatic personalities and the generalized attitudes toward investing that they project rather than on any detailed or specific advice. The invested self that these writers model can be read against two of the more persistent features of the genre that we have traced through the work. First, this writing has been sculpted by a set of gendered languages and assumptions, as a feminized notion of the secure home is often implicitly contrasted against a masculinized notion of risk and enterprise. Second, the genre itself, as it has become an increasingly significant part of mass culture, has begun to inevitably register the contradictions that mass financial advice necessarily involves. It is its ability to self-consciously deflect and absorb these paradoxes that we want to focus upon in these final sections.

Suze Orman has become one of the most powerful financial gurus of the early twenty-first century. She made the move from being a Merrill Lynch broker to a successful financial guru when her first book, *You've Earned It, Don't Lose It: Mistakes You Can't Afford to Make When You Retire* (1995), entered the best-seller list after she promoted it on the QVC shopping channel. Orman became a leading figure of financial investment advice, publishing ten best-selling books, hosting a long-running CNBC television program, and marketing a wide range of commercial CD-ROM kits, covering everything from will writing to protecting against identity theft. She was, as she candidly admitted when she married her brand manager, very aware that her success relied on the status of her brand.[39] And it was a brand with a reach both domestic and dazzling. Her *Money Minded Moms* website recalled Merrill Lynch's postwar domestic campaigns as it was sponsored by General Cereal, whereas her book talks, supported by the $600,000 tour bus that was normally reserved for Shakira and Ozzy Osbourne, spoke to her firm position in celebrity culture.[40]

Orman's first book, as its title suggests, was concerned with protecting retirees' wealth, and it combined cautious words on investment with the more general money management advice (on care, estate, taxation, and probate costs) of the kind explored by writers such as Sylvia Porter in her first work, *Managing Your Money*, some half-century earlier. It was in her second book, *The 9 Steps to Financial Freedom: Practical and Spiritual Steps So You Can Stop Worrying* (published two years later), that Orman began in earnest to hone the new age self-help mantra of the woman who carried a crystal ball to work with her on her first day at Merrill Lynch. Orman's work is gendered in ways that were quite different from those of Porter, to whom she is most often compared. First, her work is couched in the individualized postfeminist language in which women's emancipation is framed through "knowing their worth" rather than through a critique of the particular kinds of commodification that valuing women's "worth" involved.[41] This was, of course, a widespread and familiar move in American popular culture from the 1970s onward, as highlighted by feminist critics such as Nancy Fraser.[42] Second, Orman's writing, like much of the conservative financial advice that started to appear in the nineties, reverses the primary assumption of the implicitly male *homo economicus*—that our economic self is our most rational self, unencumbered by bodies or desires—by invoking the importance of our emotional connections to money. Orman does not consider the emotional dimensions of finance explored by economic anthropologists and sociologists but instead merely suggests instead that it is our "fears" that prevent us from realizing our true financial potential. The book adapts a crude Freudianism that conflates the paternal injunction with money itself: because "we are all powerless as children" and because "money looms so powerfully," we have to understand our childish memories of money, "riddled with self-doubt, unworthiness, insecurity," in order to do "what must be done to put the fears to rest."[43] Orman urges her readers to write out their most powerful but disabling childhood memories of money in order that they can be replaced with "a financial mantra, a new truth, a new belief in yourself" that comes down to three rules: "I have more money than I will ever need," "I am in control of all my affairs," and "I am putting at least $200 a month into savings."[44] Orman's work, as this headily contradictory mixture of belief, agency, and pragmatism suggests, consolidated the combination of self-help and financial investment advice in the most literal of ways.

The marketing of Orman's personality was so important to her success because her advice itself, as commentators frequently noted, is actually decidedly uncontroversial: invest early and often; get out of credit-card debt; use discount brokers. Moreover, it was also being frequently echoed elsewhere. Orman's bearish shift in the early 2000s, when she began aggressively prioritizing paying off debt, including home mortgages, was affirmed by the Democratic politician Elizabeth Warren when she suggested that "Orman is right to advise families to prepare for the worst. [...] Middle-class families are in trouble like never before. The dangers facing families are rising fast—faster than families can keep up, no matter how hard they work."[45] Yet Warren's support of Orman's advice actually deepens the ironies that attended the genre's now hegemonic hold on Americans' understanding of financial risk and individual responsibility. Warren endorses Orman's advice, despite the fact that her own book, *The Two-Income Trap* (cowritten with her daughter, Amelia Warren Tyagi), sought to position itself *against* the perniciousness of the fantasy that good personal money management alone was enough to stave off the precarity faced by an increasing number of Americans. Indeed, Warren's background as a champion of consumer rights was one that was often at direct loggerheads with the financial advice industry which, as Helaine Olen has noted, was able to grow so dramatically in the 1990s precisely because it was "viewed by publishers and broadcasters" as offering content to their readers that "would not offend the car dealers, supermarkets, and real estate brokers who were their main advertisers," and who had previously been stung by the criticisms of the consumer movement.[46]

Warren and Tyagi's work punctures the familiar myths of the financial advice industry, that debt is caused by careless overconsumption — the demonized latte, later replaced by avocado toast — or that home ownership is an automatic route to financial autonomy and freedom.[47] Instead they note that the "basic premise" of most money management books can "be misleading or even dangerous. They show how to draw up a budget or choose a mutual fund but in most cases their advice is aimed only at those lucky families for whom work is steady, everyone is healthy, and there are no emergencies."[48] Yet Warren and Tyagi can only muster threadbare resources in response to the knowledge that financial disaster is only ever one crisis away for most Americans. The policy changes that they advocate are rooted in the normative language of "family rights": "economics are nestled at the core of family values. Any group that is serious about lowering divorce rates should focus on reducing the economic stress that strains a marriage." As Melinda Cooper has demonstrated, however, it was precisely this rhetoric of the nuclear family, and its ability to privatize the risks that had previously been publicly shared, that had been so effectively mobilized by neoliberals such as Gary Becker as a key to unraveling the postwar liberal consensus.[49] Warren and Tyagi's alternative strategy invokes what they call the "Financial Fire Drill," which they then expanded into their *own* financial advice manual, *All Your Worth: The Ultimate Lifetime Money Plan*. This book, with chapters such as "Escape from the Thinking Traps" and "Build Your Dreams a Little at a Time," risks circling back to Orman's self-help therapy, as it suggests that "getting straight with your money happens in your head" and that it's time to "identify" and "eliminate" your "negative thinking traps."[50]

The couching of money management in the language of the home found its paternalistic counterparts in the works of Dave Ramsey (America's most prominent evangelical Christian financial adviser) and Robert Kiyosaki (the originator of the "Rich Dad Poor Dad" series). The homespun domestic analogies of both men, and their focus on "traditional family values," spawned multimedia franchises in which the financial advice manual was again the jewel in the crown of a complex structure of services and products. Yet the actual advice that the two men gave could not be more different. Ramsey's religious and moral advocacy of financial "peace" started in the debt counseling he gave in his local church. He came to prominence through a Nashville radio show in the early 1990s which eventually claimed an audience of 7.7 million—in the pecking order of other leading right-wing mass-media figures, just behind Rush Limbaugh and Sean Hannity. Ramsey's advice is predicated, as Orman's came to be, on a stringent critique of debt. He identifies the "borrower" as a "slave to the lender." Ramsey is also sensitive to the centrality of and emotional relationship to money in his listeners' lives. He advocates a "snowball" relationship to debt, for example, in which small sums are repaid before large sums because of the self-belief that repaying a loan brings. He warns against long-term mortgages, recommends buying houses in cash wherever possible, and advocates investing only in the kinds of low-cost mutual funds that John Bogle had made accessible. Ramsey's shows, books, counseling classes, courses, and workshops were consolidated in his Financial Peace University which claims "a biblically based curriculum that teaches people how to handle money God's ways."[51] Like other personal finance proselytizers, Ramsey has a loyal following, with his book *The Total Money Makeover: A Proven Plan for Financial Fitness* (2013) receiving an average rating of 4.9 out of 5 stars, along with gushing testimonials of how it has helped happy purchasers on their way to being "debt free."[52]

In a similar vein, Kiyosaki evangelizes about the connections between the family and the formal teaching of financial literacy, and he too offers a range of products including wealth seminars, classes, workshops, books, and board games. The rich dad/poor dad vignettes that structure his first book are rooted in his childhood in Hawaii. They contrast the advice of his own well-educated but poor father with the advice of his best friend's richer but uneducated father. They form a series of memories—later revealed to be fictitious, like much supposedly true autobiographical financial advice—that link good fatherhood to a domestication of the "greed is good" mantra of Oliver Stone's *Wall Street*.[53] Kiyosaki's actual advice could not be further from Ramsey's. Kiyosaki knows what Marx knew, that nobody can achieve prosperity solely through their own labor.

Instead he advocates an asset-heavy mode of speculation, led primarily by real estate speculation, because his key lesson is "Have money work for you. Don't work for money."[54]

However, this blurring of domestic money management and investment advice was one steadfastly rejected by Jim Cramer, the figure who looms largest in twenty-first century popular financial culture in the United States. Cramer, who began as a financial journalist, went from managing his own hedge fund to purveying personal financial investment advice when he launched TheStreet.com in 1996. The site, providing both financial analysis and subscription investor services, went public in 1999 and the expansion of Cramer's brand followed. His "RealMoney" radio show was replaced by CNBC's "Mad Money," which Cramer wanted to be "a *Wall $treet Week* for the new generation of investors, one that talked about today's market in terms that the baby boomers would find more compelling than the world Louis Rukeyser exposed them to on Friday nights."[55] Both the radio and the TV show were supported by manuals, including *Jim Cramer's Real Money: Sane Investing in an Insane World* (2005) and *Jim Cramer's Mad Money: Watch TV, Get Rich* (2006), which are presented as meta-guides to the Cramer franchise, providing the educational counterpart to the entertainment delivered by the television program. The advice that he gives in his manuals, a blueprint to the quick-win tenor of his programs, is familiar. Cramer wants his readers to understand their own risk, which he measures largely in terms of proximity to retirement, and to use only money that they can afford to lose (thereby discounting the many who struggle to get by and never have money they can afford to lose). From there on he advocates a dynamic and speculative attitude to the market. Echoing a long tradition, his advice is to buy slowly (he provides a weak form of Graham and Dodd's fundamental approach, warning readers that they will have to do "homework" because "owning stocks isn't all booyahs and excitement") but to sell quickly (he counsels his readers to "take profits while a stock is on the way up" rather than "watch their profits erode on the way down").[56]

Cramer is also clear that this advice involves fashioning the right kind of self. He describes his first book as "a financial-diet-for-life book, not a money book" and claims that he has "written the first diet book of investing!"[57] This is a form of self-idealization, however, that is more masculine than the comparison at first suggests. His diet is the steak-and-butter of the Atkins regime rather than one of self-denial or restraint. He quickly, and self-consciously, combines it with more masculine analogies, "to sports, to movies, to battles, to anything I can find that makes the stock market more simple."[58] Indeed, his second book actively disavows the potentially feminized language of self-help as he notes that he *does not* "want this to be a self-help book. The last thing in the world I want is to turn into the Dr. Phil of investment advice." Cramer's identification with sports extends through the ways in which he shapes his financial advice, and the focus on sport erects clear masculine boundaries around this activity, encouraging an ideal of aggressive speculation. The format of MadMoney's "Lightning Round," for example, in which viewers call in for advice on specific stocks and Cramer performs his exhaustive knowledge, requires callers to identify themselves with their favorite football team as a mode of introduction. It is an act which, as discourse analysts have argued, effectively functions as a shibboleth to deter and delegitimize the very small number of female participants on the show.[59]

Yet Cramer's most revered popular culture avatar was actually from Fox Television rather than from sport. He frequently refers on both the show and in his books to Jack Bauer, the maverick, inexhaustible counterterrorist agent in the real-time thriller *24* that was airing at about the same time as *Mad Money*'s launch. It is a move that links Cramer to the identification of the financier as a modern secret agent who, like money itself, never stops moving and is able to transcend the merely physical boundaries of time and space. It is a trope that was becoming increasingly widespread in the popular culture of the mid-1990s, evident in the best-selling fiction of ex-traders-turned-novelists Michael Ridpath and Stephen Frey, who were themselves building on the earlier traditions of writers such as Paul Erdman.[60]

Cramer's sensitivity to the different registers that the masculine celebration of financial culture was employing in the United States at this moment was also apparent in the publication of his biographical *Confessions of a Street Addict* in 2002. It was widely compared to Michael Lewis's 1989 *Liar's Poker*, and it likewise narrates the extremes of professional trading through an autobiographical bildungsroman in which the narrator depicts himself as the dazzled outsider fighting for acceptance. Yet Cramer replaces Lewis's wry ambivalence toward the profession with an intense commitment to it, and the book's recurring narrative is of a man whose 24/7 addiction to the adrenaline of his own work (first trading and then building his financial advice empire) results in the neglect of all domestic fealties. In Cramer's account, his mother's death, his daughter's birth, as well as the more mundane realities of marriage, fatherhood, and

missed vacations, are occluded. He represents himself, before the caesura
in which he breaks the addictive pattern at the text's end, as "a true king,
no, a Stalinist, a colossal fixture at the office . . . making partners move up
on the Forbes 400 list of the wealthiest solely by his own trading prowess.
And a total fraud at home, who knew he really didn't matter anymore
to those whom he had routinely and faithfully disappointed because he
always made money for his partners."[61]

What is striking about all of these financial investment celebrities is
the way in which their limitations—the interestedness and often frank
failures of their advice—were both so clearly apparent and yet also irrelevant to their continued success. Orman stands at the heart of Helaine
Olen's scathing critique of the financial industry in which she notes that
the independence of Orman's advice has been compromised through "so
many deals over the years it's impossible to count them all." In particular,
Olen offers detailed accounts of two scandals: Orman's "approved" pre-
paid debit card (which Orman promoted for improving credit scores and
lowering fees, neither of which it clearly did) and "navigator newsletter"
(which sent domestic investors toward the rocky ground of highly speculative vehicles that Orman herself avoided).[62] The fault lines of Kiyosaki's
urging of aggressive real estate speculation also became all too visible in
the 2008 subprime housing crisis but did little to remove him from the
best-seller list or fundamentally change his advice. Similarly, the financial
investment industry has pointed out that Ramsey's sweepingly moral critique of debt was both blunt regarding the different kinds of investment
debt it facilitated and at odds with his own use early in his career of the
very bankruptcy laws about which he now fervently warns others. Critics also pointed to the disparity between his conservative advice and the
claim that following his program can deliver an annual return of well over
10 percent.[63] True to form, Cramer includes a reflection on his own ethically compromised actions in his writing. He spends much of *Confessions
of a Street Addict* describing the legal scrutiny resulting from his decision
to write about stocks and run his own positions on these stocks. He notes
that "although the government's inquiry" eventually "just went away, people I meet in business now remember the scandal as a generic 'insider trading' rap even though the outcome produced no indictments."[64]

The clear shadows on the legitimacy of the advice provided by personal finance gurus did not hinder their ability to thrive, indicating that
the genre provided its audience with something other than straightforward guidance. It is entertainment and spectacle masquerading as prag-

matic advice, and, despite encouraging its audience to take active control of their money and their lives, it lends itself to a passive mode of consumption. This is most obviously true of Cramer's *Mad Money,* a program that shared a producer with the daytime television phenomenon *Jerry Springer.* In the words of one financial journalist, *Mad Money* similarly functioned for its audience as "an addictive guilty pleasure," because "frenzied 5-second analysis on hundreds of stocks never ceases to amuse. But we won't turn to him for investment advice . . . as most of what he says simply describes the previous day's market action."[65] Indeed, Cramer's own commentary on his work often suggested a deeply ambivalent relationship to what he was actually advocating. Gerald Sim, for example, has noted that Cramer's jokes often exceeded "perfunctory stock market wisdom by taking leftist political positions. He highlights the ideological contradiction between capitalism and competition with demonstrable cynicism," and even appropriates a "Marxist language to maintain a critical distance to rapacious ideology but stops well short of revolution or of undoing bourgeois domination since the point of it all is still to make 'mad money.'"[66] These financial writers, then, came to occupy a curious position in American cultural life in the opening decades of the twenty-first century. They were powerful and ubiquitous, and yet their cultural function seemed often to be in excess of the actual financial investment advice they peddled. They sold a fantasy, "a dream that personal finance had almost magical abilities," all the while glossing over the larger structural issues of stagnating wages, increasing precarity and inequality, and the dismantling of the welfare state.[67]

The ambiguity of their position, as gurus who clearly offered something more than practical financial advice, is nowhere more apparent than in the ways in which these figures were represented elsewhere in popular culture. Recalling the satirical imitations of the founding work of the genre, Thomas Mortimer's *Every Man His Own Broker* (1761), some of the most popular recent works of financial advice have inspired parodies that were critical of the simplicity of the message that the original text promulgated. Kiyosaki's *Rich Dad Poor Dad,* for example, was directly mocked by Robin Burchett's *Smart Dad, Dumb Dad* for being "smug, cruel, and condescending," in the same ways in which Thomas J. Stanley and William D. Danko's guide to effective saving, *The Millionaire Next Door: The Surprising Secrets of America's Wealthy,* was lampooned in Andy Borowitz's *Trillionaire Next Door: The Greedy Investor's Guide to Day Trading.*[68] Other satirical representations worked in more ambivalent ways. Kristen Wiig's impression of Suze Orman, for example, became a regular skit on *Saturday Night Live* as Wiig sent up Orman's claims to save money through extreme forms of feminine domesticity (such as making maxipads from baby socks). Yet Orman, who sat in to watch the show in its subsequent outings, was delighted by this impression. In an interview for the Television Academy Foundation, she suggested that it made her an "icon" in America and was "the greatest honor" of her life—alongside, she takes the opportunity to note, being nominated among the "100 most influential people in the world by *Time* magazine."[69] In another interview, one of her many appearances with Larry King, Orman was similarly adulatory of Wiig but also gestured to her own postmodern alertness to the artifice of performance that the sketch brings with it, suggesting that, on her own show every Saturday night on CNBC, she is now "playing me, playing Kristen Wiig, playing me."[70]

These ironies are at their most acute in the ways in which Jim Cramer has become such a ubiquitous popular cultural icon in America. Versions of *Mad Money*'s frenetic and prop-filled segments have appeared in a number of sitcoms (*Arrested Development* and *30 Rock*) and films (*Iron Man* and *Wall Street: Money Never Sleeps*) in the 2000s and 2010s. Cramer himself starred in cameo performances in these films, and his commentary was used to add drama to the crisis of falling stocks. In the sitcoms, however, the references were more clearly satirical and were part of both series' more general, if often also ironically self-conscious, critique of the increasing visibility of corporate culture in mainstream American television. It was a critique that was made explicit by Jon Stewart in *The Daily Show*. Stewart began by mocking Cramer's advice to buy Bear Stearns shortly ahead of its 2008 crash. Cramer's rejection of the claim led to a series of hostile exchanges between the two, which concluded with Cramer appearing on Stewart's show in March 2009. The subsequent conversation allowed Stewart to mount an attack on the broader purpose of the entire CNBC remit, as a channel carrying solely business and investment news, but concluded with the qualification that this intervention was a joke and that if Cramer could stick with accurate facts then he would stick with comedy.[71]

Such ambivalently critical parodies of *Mad Money* reached a climax in the 2016 film *Money Monster*, directed by Jodie Foster and starring George Clooney and Julia Roberts. Clooney is a financial adviser on a show with a format remarkably similar to *Mad Money*, although Foster has claimed that it wasn't based on Cramer because "there are a lot of financial hosts, he's just the most famous."[72] In the film Clooney's character is taken hostage by a furious viewer, wearing explosives: a viewer who had followed the show's advice, thus losing the small amount of money left to him after his mother's death. Yet this satirical spectacle, which unites a condemnation of the corrupt marketization of financial investment advice with the anger of the working-class white man "left behind" by both technology and corporations, turns out to be at odds with the film's narrative conclusion. In its final third the Clooney and Roberts characters unravel the causes of the company's stock price crash, discovering it was corruption and strikes in an exoticized South African mine, rather than a glitch in a High Frequency Trading algorithm, that was to blame. Thus, at the end of the film, the threatening figure of the disaffected angry white man is dead, shot by the police who mistakenly assume he is going to detonate his vest, whereas the genre of financial advice is actually alive and well—real value and meaning have been returned to it. As is so common in contemporary culture, then, *Money Monster* incorporates satire and critique of the figure of the financial guru into a package that ultimately affirms that figure's charismatic authority. Like the film, the true guru does not reject contradiction but rather finds a means at once to internalize and transcend it.

The Power of the "Classic"

The double movement we've just discussed has many precedents. As we've seen in this book, the investment advice genre has, since its inception, been riven by paradoxes and contradictions. It sells the fantasy of getting something for nothing, the thrill of speculation, the promise of self-transformation, and, above all, the need for people to consume this advice. A key question is why, if none of this vast outpouring of advice reliably works, have people continued to write and consume it for three centuries? One secret of its longevity, we've argued, lies in its capacity to manage these conceptual challenges and conflicting desires at a rhetorical level, often by laying claim simultaneously to supposedly timeless wisdom and to pressing novelty—after all, there has to be a justification, whether advertised on the cover or merely implied, for readers to buy yet another book of financial advice. A measure of the ongoing success of such strategies might be that—as discussed in the next section—a 600-page work of investment advice can become a #1 *New York Times* best seller (as Tony Robbins's *Money: Master the Game* [2014] did) while offering, as its central and most readily practical guidance, a message that boils down to: 1) buy a set of index funds; 2) do nothing. One of the key paradoxes of contemporary investment advice writing, then, is that, even forty years on from the publication of *A Random Walk Down Wall Street*, an author with the requisite public profile and ability to command readers' hopes and aspirations may still achieve major commercial success with a doorstopper investment manual whose core take-home message is that, to get the best out of the stock market, readers should have as little active involvement in it as possible. By the same token, a further puzzle is that increasingly elaborate stock-picking or market-beating guides (primarily in the technical analysis tradition) continue to pour forth from the presses of major publishers, in the face of many decades' worth of evidence of the profound difficulties of outperforming the market overall. The Wiley Trading Series from John Wiley has been particularly active in this field. Indicative titles include Al Brooks's *Trading Price Action Trends: Technical Analysis of Price Charts Bar by Bar for the Serious Trader* (2012), Thomas N. Bulkowski's *Encyclopedia of Chart Patterns* (second edition, 2007) and *Chart Patterns after the Buy* (2016), Greg Capra's *Trading Tools and Tactics: Reading the Mind of the Market* (2011), Michael W. Covel's *Trend Following: How to Make a Fortune in Bull, Bear, and Black Swan Markets* (2017), Adam Grimes's *Art and Science of Technical Analysis* (2012), Robert C. Miner's *High Probability Trading Strategies: Entry to Exit Tactics for the Forex, Futures, and Stock Markets* (2008), Larry Pesavento and Leslie Jouflas's *Trade What You See: How to Profit from Pattern Recognition* (2009), and Courtney Smith's *How to Make a Living Trading Foreign Exchange: A Guaranteed Income for Life* (2010). The efficient market hypothesis may no longer hold the authority that it enjoyed prior to the 2008 crash, but the well-documented difficulties faced by professional fund managers in delivering consistently above-market returns would—one might think—be enough to persuade amateurs that their own chances are, as we've seen, slim indeed. Yet ever more recondite refinements of analytical methods targeted at the retail trader continue to proliferate and to be widely consumed. The nonprofessional's fantasy of succeeding in securities trading where so many others have failed still holds the appeal that has sustained the investment advice manual throughout its history.

Perhaps the most perplexing phenomenon of all in the field of contemporary investment advice writing, however, is the status afforded to the perennial "classic." Books that are now anything up to a century old—and were therefore written in ignorance of the myriad legal, regulatory, institutional, and technological changes that have transformed the face of investment in the intervening decades—are held up as the go-to sources for readers seeking insight into the stock market today. Recognizing how profoundly outdated such volumes now are, however, their present-day editors cannot allow them simply to speak for themselves but must hedge them round with increasingly verbose commentaries and glosses, which verge on crowding out the original text itself. Yet these accompanying materials are, at the same time, deeply invested in demonstrating the "enduring" or "timeless" nature of the wisdom enshrined in such books—the authors' capacity to communicate sage principles across the ages. In this way, these texts' very anachronism—their very distance from the contemporary financial sectors' frenetic search for novelty and innovation—is held to be the ultimate source of their strength. As the reviews on Amazon and the discussion in day-trader online forums attest, for their admirers these books represent "timeless" wisdom as an antidote to the relentless churn of both financial markets and financial advice in a wired world. At the same time, they bestow the legitimating aura of "heritage" or "tradition" on the investment advice genre as a whole. And their proliferation testifies, again, to the remarkable longevity of the stock market manual in an age whose technological advances might have been expected to usher in the form's obsolescence.

Perhaps unsurprisingly, the most enduring and venerable "classics" in the field date back to the early to mid-twentieth century, the period in which investment writers—primarily in the United States—devised, elaborated, and codified an array of distinct analytical systems for evaluating securities prices and making profitable trades. Among the select volumes of this era that have made the grade are William Peter Hamilton's *Stock Market Barometer* (1922) and Edwin Lefèvre's fictionalized account of the life of the speculator Jesse Livermore, *Reminiscences of a Stock Operator* (1923), both of which feature in John Wiley's renowned "Investment Classics" series. The foreword to the series' edition of Hamilton's text, written by the investment adviser and author Charles B. Carlson, is typical of the rhetorical framing of such revered but historically remote writings. Carlson acknowledges the obvious objection to the continued utility of a work like Hamilton's: "surely a simple theory that focuses exclusively on the movements of the Dow Jones Industrial and Transportation Averages ... would have little forecasting ability in today's complex and fast-moving stock market." But Carlson insists that "what will strike you is how fresh many of [Hamilton's] views are today despite having been written many decades ago." The Dow Theory that Hamilton expounds "has passed the most important test of all—the test of time," Carlson suggests, and "if you are a serious student of investing, you owe it to yourself to go 'back to the future' and read this book."[73] Reflecting the peculiarly celebrated status of Lefèvre's *Reminiscences* (it is one of the few popular investment books widely endorsed by professional traders),[74] Wiley singled the book out for publication in a lavish large-format edition in 2010, offering readers an extensively illustrated text with voluminous editorial commentary. In an interview at the end of the book, the Wall Street asset manager Paul Tudor Jones (who describes "hand[ing] a copy to every new trader we have, regardless of his or her considerable experience")[75] offers the requisite tribute to the book's timelessness:

> As the book states very early on, there is nothing new under the sun in the art of speculation, and everything that was said then completely applies to the markets today. My guess is that the same will hold true for time eternal as long as man's basic emotions remain intact—fear, greed, happiness, sorrow, elation, dejection, excitement, and apathy.[76]

As we saw in chapter 4, the technical analysis methods that Hamilton and Livermore (via Lefèvre) espoused were exhaustively and meticulously systematized at midcentury by John Magee Jr. and Robert D. Edwards in their *Technical Analysis of Stock Trends* (1948). This book was the chartists' answer to the definitive early text in the "statistical" or "fundamental" analysis tradition, Benjamin Graham and David Dodd's *Security Analysis*, which had popularized the authors' philosophy of value investing upon its publication in 1934. Since their appearance, both texts have continued to be held up not only as sources of eternally applicable maxims concerning the immutable underlying factors affecting the markets but also as compendiums of specific and practical directives on the day-to-day conduct of trading activity in stocks and other securities. Inevitably facing an increasing risk of obsolescence, as the institutions and practices of investment have moved on, however, the texts have required regular and extensive updating and revision, and the deployment of some especially agile rhetorical gymnastics in order to persuade readers of their continued usefulness and reliability.

Both texts' current custodians are forced to acknowledge the works' apparent outmodedness. As Seth A. Klarman notes in his preface to the latest edition of *Security Analysis* (the sixth, published by McGraw-Hill in 2009), "companies today sell products that Graham and Dodd could not have imagined. Indeed, there are companies and entire industries that they could not have envisioned."[77] Consequently, Graham and Dodd's text comes laden with extensive introductory materials and lengthy framing chapters setting up each section of the text, as well as an accompanying CD. Collectively, the additions to the book by other hands make up around a quarter of its 800 pages. Similarly, W. H. C. Bassetti, the longtime editor and reviser of *Technical Analysis of Stock Trends* (whose eleventh edition appeared from Routledge in 2019), concedes in the preface to the first edition to appear under his stewardship (the eighth, 2001) that there are places in which "the passage of time has made the text obsolete." In these instances, Bassetti advises the reader, "I have either footnoted the anachronism and/or provided a chapter-ending annotation"; yet so extensive are the necessary glosses and revisions in some cases that, by Bassetti's own admission, "these annotations amount to new chapters." Despite their potentially forbidding length, however, Bassetti insists that "it is absolutely essential to read these annotations. Failure to do so will leave the reader stranded in the 20th century."[78] Though often identified as sources of near-scriptural authority, neither *Security Analysis* nor *Technical Analysis* is today to be consumed unadorned by the laity but must rather be mediated via a cohort of priestly interpreters.

The versions of these foundational, classic texts being touted to the public today, then, are unwieldy, hybrid creatures, stitched together from markedly heterogeneous parts, some of which invoke the 1920s as familiarly as others reference the 2000s or 2010s. The books' presenters insist, however, that their interpolations serve only to allow the original authors' perennially valuable message to be heard clearly. Klarman, for example, prefaces Graham and Dodd's tome by asserting that "*Security Analysis* remains an invaluable roadmap for investors as they navigate through unpredictable, often volatile, and sometimes treacherous financial markets. Frequently referred to as the 'bible of value investing,' *Security Analysis* is extremely thorough and detailed, teeming with wisdom for the ages. Although many of the examples are obviously dated, their lessons are timeless." The book's insights are sufficiently profound and far-reaching, Klarman suggests, that they may be readily adapted to trading in the most advanced or "exotic" financial innovations: "The same principles [Graham and Dodd] applied to the U.S. stock and bond markets of the 1920s and 1930s apply to the global capital markets of the early twenty-first century . . . and even to derivative instruments that hardly existed when *Security Analysis* was written."[79] Likewise, for Bassetti, in the preface to the tenth edition of Edwards and Magee, *Technical Analysis of Stock Trends* remains the one indispensable text in its field: it "still towers over the discipline of technical analysis like a mighty redwood."[80] Indeed, Bassetti argues that it is precisely the book's ostensible weaknesses—its "apparent anachronisms"—that are in fact its most valuable features. As he puts it in the preface to the eighth edition: "Critics with limited understanding of long-term trading success may think that discussions of 'what happened in 1929' or 'charts of ancient history from 1946' have no relevance to the markets of the present millennium. They will point out that . . . many charts are records of long-buried skeletons." Yet such an attitude "ignores the significance of the past to trading in the present." He quotes the commodity trading adviser Al Weiss's observation that "recognizing these repeating and shifting long-term patterns requires lots of history. Identifying where you are in an economic cycle . . . is critical to interpreting the chart patterns evolving at that time."[81] For Bassetti, then, it is the very antediluvian nature of Edwards and Magee's text, its fossilized recording of trading patterns and cycles long past, that makes it such a repository of investment guidance in the present. Bassetti echoes the belief, first developed in the nineteenth century, that studying past trends unlocks possibilities of prediction. Awareness of the past is presented as (yet) another way of gaining an edge on your competitors.

Investing in the Self

This book has explored how, in the eighteenth century, stock market investment advice writing emerged from a culture of printed aids to household management and financial and commercial conduct. It has traced the mounting visibility and influence of this genre of writing—and its various subgenres—as the stock market itself has gained an increasingly central place in the everyday economic life of Britain and the United States. One key index of the growing importance of this genre is the way in which its principles, assumptions, and strategies have increasingly shaped personal financial advice writing in general. As we've seen, much of the popular appeal of the stock market investment manual lies in its promise to unveil a field of financial activity viewed as uniquely exciting, dynamic, risky—and potentially rewarding. Writers of more general personal financial guidance have sought to annex some of this glamour in instructing readers on how best to approach the more prosaic matters of their day jobs, pensions, mortgages, savings, or insurance policies: evidently, such topics are liable to assume a new piquancy when one is encouraged to view them with the mindset of a Wall Street hotshot. Indeed, in major strands of contemporary self-help writing, the reader is urged to cultivate a stock market investment mentality that is not even limited to financial activity in the broadest sense but extends to the very understanding of the self and its relation to others. In fact, as an understanding of just how difficult it is to beat the market has penetrated popular consciousness, readers of personal financial advice and self-help writing are increasingly encouraged to adopt an active, decisive persona—modeled on the archetypal stock market operator—in their wider financial and personal activities, while ironically being ushered toward a passive, hands-off approach to stock ownership itself. The ultimate—if paradoxical—triumph of the model of the heroic, risk-taking subject codified in stock market investment advice may be its shaping of contemporary advice writing as such, as it pertains to everything other than—precisely—the stock market.

The idea of the financialization of the self and of everyday life has been much discussed among social scientists over the past two decades.[82] Such work is invariably informed by Michel Foucault's foundational analysis of neo-liberalism in lectures delivered in the late 1970s. According to Foucault, "in neo-liberalism . . . there is a theory of *homo economicus* . . . as an entrepreneur, an entrepreneur of himself . . . being for himself his own producer, being for himself the source of [his] earnings."[83] In the work of the Chicago school "human capital" theorists—principally Gary Becker—to which Foucault responds, the self is a kind of firm or enterprise in which the subject itself invests capital in order to gain a dividend or return. For more recent scholars in economic sociology and related fields, Foucault's account is remarkably prescient, describing a model of subjectivity that has become hegemonic in economic theory, management discourse, and popular culture. One study summarizes this idea of "Me Incorporated"— the self as a firm in which to invest—in these terms:

> The notion of one's own person as a joint-stock company . . . People regard themselves increasingly as entrepreneurs of their own lives, electing to assume responsibility for themselves rather than making others responsible for them. . . . A core component, as in a real joint-stock company, is the importance of working on one's own person: "I must increase the market value of my Me-shares."[84]

Rhetoric of this kind is ubiquitous in contemporary personal finance guidebooks, reflecting both the "responsibilization" of the self—the obligation to ensure one's own security in the face of the neoliberal erosion of the social safety net—and its financialization: the configuring of subjectivity as a nexus of investments, transactions, and returns.

Two prominent recent books from one of the leading global business and finance publishers, Harvard Business Review Press (HBRP), exemplify this extension of the language of stock investment to all aspects of money (and self-) management. In *How to Invest Your Time Like Money* (2015), Elizabeth Grace Saunders recasts Benjamin Franklin's old saw that "time is money" specifically in terms of allocating capital in the stock market. For Saunders, time management is to be modeled on how, "with your finances, putting more money into investment opportunities . . . like stocks . . . can lead to an exponential return on investment. For every dollar that you put in, you could end up with two or three in return." Embracing the opportunities offered by the stock market, then, is Saunders's template for the optimal apportioning of one's time: individuals invest time in the appropriate activities in order to maximize profits and dividends of all kinds. In Saunders's model, the stock market concept of return on investment (ROI)—the ratio of profit or loss to capital invested—is reconfigured as a program to "maximize your time ROI."[85]

Another recent high-profile HBRP title adopts the notion of the "entrepreneur of the self" especially directly. *Entrepreneurial You: Monetize Your Expertise, Create Multiple Income Streams, and Thrive* (2017), by the highly acclaimed American business coach and consultant Dorrie Clark, places particular emphasis on the idea of the "portfolio career." Clark's argument for the desirability of a multifaceted, multi-income stream professional life derives directly from the classic piece of stock market advice to the effect that investors shouldn't put all of their eggs in one basket but instead assemble a properly diversified portfolio of securities. As Clark puts it: "Common wisdom tells us that we should diversify our investment portfolios because it's foolish to put all our money in one stock. But we're far less careful on the other end. Too many of us rely on one employer for our entire sustenance, just as I once did." Clark also borrows the notion of "leverage" from stock market parlance: just as stock investors may attempt to scale up returns by leveraging a pool of capital already in their possession, Clark writes approvingly of an acquaintance who "had an asset—his finely honed intellectual property—that he could leverage" in order to advance his career and expand his earnings potential.[86]

A very similar philosophy shapes one of the best-selling personal finance books of recent years, *The Start-Up of You: Adapt to the Future, Invest in Yourself, and Transform Your Career* (2012) by Reid Hoffman, cofounder and chair of LinkedIn, and his fellow tech entrepreneur Ben Casnocha. A #1 *New York Times* best seller, which comes garlanded with endorsements from the likes of Michael Bloomberg, Sheryl Sandberg, and Jack Dorsey (cofounder of Twitter), the book finds its particular model for the self in the fledgling Silicon Valley company, as it demands the financial and affective devotion of its founders, strives to attract venture capital, and aspires to be the object of a lucrative acquisition or IPO. For Hoffman and Casnocha, investing in one's self through education is equivalent—or indeed superior to—investing in the stock market: as they put it, "for far too many, focused learning ends at college graduation. They read about stocks and bonds instead of reading books that improve their minds. . . . They invest in the stock market and neglect investing in themselves. They focus, in short, on hard assets instead of soft assets."[87] The authors also urge their readers to reflect on their appetite for risk in ways modeled on risk tolerance approaches to securities investment:

> Just as financial advisors counsel young people to invest in stocks more than bonds, it's important to be especially aggressive accepting career risk when you are young. This is a main reason many young people start companies, travel around the world, and do other relatively "high-risk" career moves: the downside is lower. If something worthwhile will be riskier in five years than it is now, be more aggressive about taking it on now. As you age and build more assets, your risk tolerance shifts.[88]

Just as younger people, with fewer responsibilities, have the potential to be more risk-hungry or aggressive in securities markets, Hoffman and Casnocha suggest, so they are in a position to assume relatively greater risk in their careers and lives generally.

A similar modeling of personality and lifestyle on approaches to securities investment is evident in probably the most revered self-improvement book of recent years, *Principles: Life and Work* (2017) by Ray Dalio, the founder and co–chief investment officer of the world's largest hedge fund, Bridgewater Associates. Another #1 *New York Times* best seller (also #1 Amazon business book of the year), whose list of endorsers is even more stellar than Hoffman and Casnocha's (Bill Gates, Sean "P. Diddy" Coombs, Arianna Huffington, etc.), Dalio's book details the principles underlying Bridgewaters' legendarily exacting business culture. It expands on Dalio's earlier statement of his fund's ethos, whose online release in 2011 attracted more than three million downloads.[89] *Principles* blends an autobiographical account of Dalio's life and career with articulations of his business philosophy. While Dalio is apparently reserving a detailed account of his "economics and investing" principles for a promised second volume, the appeal of *Principles: Life and Work* of course rests on its author's status as one of the most admired and successful equities investors of recent decades, and he does not fail to cast life and relationships advice in terms of the wise investor's approach to the stock market. In a key passage, for example, he likens keeping faith with one's proven investment strategy to maintaining fidelity in one's personal relationships:

> All great investors and investment approaches have bad patches; losing faith in them at such times is as common a mistake as getting too enamored of them when they do well. Because most people are more emotional than logical, they tend to overreact to short-term results; they give up and sell low when times are bad and buy too high when times are good. I find this is just as true for relationships as it is for investments—wise people stick with sound fundamentals through the ups and downs, while flighty people react emotionally to how things feel, jumping into things when they're hot and abandoning them when they're not.[90]

Dalio's celebrated contribution to the advice guide canon exemplifies, then, the way in which contemporary career and business guidance and self-help writing understand the self and its relationships through the prism of stock investment strategies, techniques, and approaches.

One of *Principles*' most high-profile and enthusiastic endorsers ("I found it to be truly extraordinary") is a longtime admirer: the world-renowned self-help guru Tony Robbins. This admiration is consistent with Robbins's long-standing focus on investment success as a template for understanding success in any walk of life. The conclusions that Robbins draws from his considerations of expert stock investors, though, are paradoxical and revealing, in ways that repay sustained examination. Robbins has a strong claim to the title of "the world's most famous self-help entrepreneur" (*Inc.* magazine) or "most successful life coach on the planet" (*Business Insider*). The books branch of the Robbins Research International empire has achieved worldwide sales of some 15 million volumes, while its founder boasts the likes of Bill Clinton, Oprah Winfrey, and

Serena Williams among his clients.[91] Robbins's breakthrough into popular consciousness came with his book *Awaken the Giant Within*, published in 1991 and reissued in multiple editions since. In contrast with Robbins's later writings, this paean to *"the unlimited power that lies sleeping within you"*[92] contains only a brief direct discussion of the stock market, though this section proves to be key to the message of the book as a whole.

In this section, Robbins reports a conversation with the renowned mutual fund manager John Templeton. He recalls the exchange in these terms:

> What has made Templeton one of the greatest investment advisors of all time? When I asked him this question, he didn't hesitate a moment. He said, "My ability to evaluate the *true value* of an investment." He's been able to do this despite the vagaries of trends and short-term market fluctuations.[93]

In addition to Templeton, Robbins also commends other investment managers and authors in the "value investing" tradition: Peter Lynch, Warren Buffet, and the field's foundational figure, Benjamin Graham. Robbins advises readers to seek out "books by the masters"—the likes of Lynch and Buffet—and follow the stock-picking tips contained therein in order to construct "a clear-cut investment plan." Robbins's interest in such figures extends far beyond their ability to dispense investment wisdom, however. He quotes Buffet paraphrasing Graham's famous account (from *The Intelligent Investor*) of "Mr. Market," whose manic-depressive fluctuations the value investor must appraise dispassionately: "If you aren't certain that you understand and can value your business better than Mr. Market, you don't belong in the game."[94] Robbins comments:

> Clearly, Buffet evaluates his investment decisions quite differently from those who are extremely worried when the market crashes or euphoric when it soars. And because he evaluates differently, he produces a different quality of result. **If someone is doing better than we are in any area of life, it's simply because they have a better way of evaluating what things mean and what they should do about it. . . .**
>
> The goal . . . is to be able to evaluate everything in your life in a way that consistently guides you to make choices that produce the results you desire.[95]

For Robbins, then, the value-investing approach—with its emphasis on the careful determination of a security's "fundamental" or "intrinsic" value—provides him with his core paradigm for the project of self-actualization in all aspects of an individual's life. As he puts it elsewhere in the book, "if there's one thing I've learned in seeking out the core beliefs and strategies of today's leading minds, it's that **superior evaluations create a superior life**. We *all* have the capacity to evaluate life at a level that produces outstanding results." In Robbins's philosophy, one must follow the likes of Buffet in basing decisions on optimal evaluations: "we must remember that all decision-making comes down to values clarification." Indeed, Robbins describes himself as having "written this book to challenge you to **awaken the giant power of decision** and to **claim the birthright of unlimited power, radiant vitality, and joyous passion that is yours!**"[96] Robbins's breakthrough text centers, then, around a psychological model—embodied, for him, by investor-authors like Templeton, Lynch, Buffet, and Graham—in which better evaluations lead to better decisions and a better life. Like the value-investing stock picker, who coolly assesses the condition of a company in light of its current price before making a surgical intervention in the market, this is a model that casts the subject in a highly active, assertive, and dynamic role.

Such ideas play out markedly differently, however, when Robbins offers his own full-length investment guidebook in the shape of 2014's *Money: Master the Game*. Expanding on *Awaken the Giant Within*, this later book contains profiles of various investment "masters," including Templeton and Buffet, as well as other major gurus, such as John C. Bogle and Ray Dalio. The key lesson that Robbins takes from the world's expert investors in this book, however, is that the average person should simply invest in a low-cost, broad market index fund, such as an S&P 500 index fund, and passively hold it. This perspective reflects the fact that Robbins's primary authority in *Money* (a figure unmentioned in *Awaken the Giant Within*) is Burton Malkiel, whose *A Random Walk Down Wall Street* both popularized the efficient market hypothesis's skepticism about the capacity of individual investors consistently to beat the market and presented investment in an index fund as the only sensible way to approach the stock market. As we saw in the previous chapter, even investment writers, such as Malkiel, who accepted the essential soundness of the efficient market hypothesis, nonetheless recognized the irresistibility of venting one's impulses and desires by playing at stock picking. Despite echoing such ideas in his titular promise to equip the reader with "mastery" of a "game," Robbins—in contrast—is adamant that stock picking can be nothing other than a futile, worthless exercise. As he puts it in this distillation of the book's key message:

You don't have to waste your time trying to pick stocks yourself or pick the best mutual fund. A portfolio of low-cost index funds is the best approach for a percentage of your investments because we don't know what stocks will be "best" going forward. And how cool to know that by "passively" holding the market, you are beating 96% of the world's "expert" mutual fund managers and nearly as many hedge fund managers. It's time to free yourself from the burden of trying to pick the winner at the race. As Jack Bogle told me, in investing it feels counterintuitive. The secret: "Don't do something, just stand there." And by becoming the market and not trying to beat it, you are on the side of progress, growth, and expansion.[97]

Though it goes unacknowledged in the book, Robbins thus presents the reader with a striking paradox, whereby the model of evaluation and decisive action that he derives from stock market investment and continues to propound in his writings and seminars is abandoned when he addresses the stock market directly, the emphasis here being on passivity rather than activity, letting things run their course rather than intervening in them directly. By this point in his career, then, Robbins is urging his followers to act like an expert stock picker—confident, strategic, decisive—in any area of activity *other than* stock investment itself. But he squares this circle by urging readers precisely to merge with the source of endless dynamism and growth that is the market. In this sense, far from presenting a deviation from a stock market model of subjectivity, Robbins's philosophy can be understood as its ultimate expression, for in his account the expansion of the stock market and the individual's own self-expansion are thoroughly coterminous: one "becomes" the market. Robbins's recent work thus provides an instructive example of how the financial advice genre—and the wider self-help genre from which it is increasingly indistinguishable—constructs understandings of agency and subjectivity that blend the active and the passive in complex ways. One's sense of self can be enhanced and enlarged by imagining mastery of the market, but also by imagining submission to and identification with the market. In Robbins's writing, we see the culmination of trajectories we have traced throughout this book: not only the thoroughgoing merger of the financial advice and self-help genres but also a vision of the individual's total investment in the market.

Investing through the Crisis

The genre of written financial investment advice has grown expansively across the past three centuries. The financial advice manual, the guide promising to offer the amateur investor a privileged path to insider success, has become a genre anchoring a diverse range of financial advice writing forms and platforms. It is, we have argued, a genre that can be best understood as a form of self-help and it has played an important role in shaping the attributes and attitudes of the financialized self. The broadest arc of this book, from the ambivalence of Thomas Mortimer to the ubiquitous ebullience of Jim Cramer, narrates the increasing centrality of this self to mainstream cultural life. Its legitimacy was secured as the individual was increasingly freighted with the responsibility for managing what were previously understood to be cultural and shared risks. This fantasy of the individual, shorn of partiality and possessing limitless agency and knowledge, occupies a privileged role in the contemporary political imaginary. The ability to measure meaning through the management of self-capital has been extended as human, cultural, social, and natural capital have become widespread and frequently used social and political concepts. Indeed, these calculating skills are both so central and so transferable that, as we saw in our final chapter, they are adopted for every realm *but* stock picking, an activity which has now been ironically usurped for many amateur investors by the certainties of passive investment.

The book has recounted the various ways in which the genre of financial investment advice seized the publishing opportunities that the growth of the stock market offered to create and sculpt a financial self that slowly shaped the paradigms of self-help itself. It begins in earnest in the early nineteenth century, as Mortimer's work finally finds its competitors and a raft of recognizably similar titles starts to appear. One of the first tasks of these authors, as we traced in chapter 2, was to construct the market as a legible entity. These works allowed the reader to engage with making decisions about a market presented as knowable, as able to recover from recurrent crises, and as socially respectable. This reassuring confidence went alongside texts that encouraged a move toward the diversification of assets in this period, notably to foreign loans and joint-stock companies. The writers of these texts encouraged the reader to participate in the colonial project, and the language of adventure that attended their writing ameliorated both the financial risks and the extractive violence that this undertaking necessarily involved. By the second half of the century, especially in the United States, where the ticker tape widened the possibilities for reading the domestic market, a fascination with the stock market's uncertain movements and the prizing of the masculine sovereign self who could control them (even when not directly invested in the market) became a primary register for the genre. More formal techniques for training this self were honed in the first half of the twentieth century. The division between the elaborate languages of technical and fundamental modes of analysis—of reading charts or reading company balance sheets—started to shape the genre as it responded to the twin dynamics of first crisis and then regulation. By the middle of the century, long before Gary Becker had elucidated the neoliberal idea of human capital, the triumph of the market as a mode of organizing all aspects of human life was becoming evident in self-help manuals that celebrated the risk-taking pleasures of the market while also applying the instructive tropes of financial advice to all areas of domestic and intimate life.

Yet this fantasy of the financial self is, of course, always revealed as an impossible ideal: an ideal that functions as an alibi for the radical inequalities over which the financial sector continues to preside. Just as not *everyone* can beat the market—as a mass genre, these texts contain their own obvious contradictions—so too is it the case that not *everyone* can summon the capital and calculative resources to withstand the increasingly urgent crises of twenty-first-century life. We want to, briefly, recap the ways in which our study has emphasized the contradictory nature of what it means to create this financial self before exploring the ways in which these tensions played out in the crises that have opened the second decade of the twenty-first century.

Our study reveals a history in which guides to inculcating self-maximizing rational behavior—the ability to master one's own desires in order coolly to perform market calculations—are beset with recurring contradictions. One of the primary tasks for many early writers of the genre, for example, was to legitimize investing as a respectable activity, to render it distinct from speculation or, worse, gambling. However, the goal was consistently interrupted by writers who themselves proved *too* invested in the market, undermining their claim to offer impartial and objective advice. This is a history in which the boundaries between financial advice, education, sales, marketing, and outright fraud have been frequently and easily blurred—extending from the motivated "education" given by respectable but proselytizing firms such as Merrill Lynch to the creation of fake brokerage offices to the sheer audacity of George MacGregor's sale of the imaginary Poyais. The writers of financial advice, it seems, were often made richer through the sales of their work, carefully branded and marketed by the most successful purveyors of the genre, than through their investing alone. The manuals' role in representing knowable data, so crucial to rendering the market legible and for allowing the role of good judgment to be distinguished from that of luck or chance, was also continually undermined by the actual practices they advocated. The activities that are associated with the reading of stock market data in these works are frequently presented as relying on far more than untrammeled calculations. The emergence of the stock ticker in the nineteenth-century United States, for example, enabled a practice so viscerally engaging that it was felt to risk addiction; the technical analysis of longitudinal charts that proved so influential in the first half of the twentieth century depended upon superstitious languages of luck, faith, and belief; the individual stock picking that continued, somewhat anachronistically given the rise of passive and managed funds, into the late twentieth century was often accompanied by masculine discourses of play, sport, battle, and erotic fulfillment. The veil of professional neutrality was differently torn when the authors of this advice turned to the social rather than financial drama of investing. The genre consistently drew on imaginary scenarios to populate its dramas of heroes and villains—even the very skeptical Thomas Mortimer couldn't help but present the market as a place of energy and intrigue—and it is clear that the market has long been a site of emotional and social rather than purely rational decisions. The representations that foregrounded the excitement of the market, the need for the investor to tame or conquer its exuberance, also often reinforced the primacy of the masculine self that persists throughout this history in implicit and explicit ways. The actively competing self being trained by the genre consistently relies on the hegemonic assertion of white middle-class masculinity and largely, if increasingly querulously, addresses a male interlocutor—even as it acknowledges that at many points in this history over half the stock market is held by women investors.

One of the central questions remaining is how the genre, and the emphasis on the active financial self that it sustained against often countervailing market dynamics, has responded to the crises that have characterized the start of the 2020s. The most obvious of these are, of course, the crises that the COVID-19 pandemic has brought with it. Through the spring and early summer of 2020—as infection rates surged out of control in many places, mass lockdown measures were imposed, and fatality numbers around the world mounted—a steady stream of books reached the market. Their titles were at once familiar and insistently topical: *Investing during Coronavirus: A Guide to Making Money through a Financial Crisis; How to Profit from the Coronavirus Recession: 50 Actionable Investment Ideas; How to Make Money from the 2020 Financial Crisis: Pandemic Edition; Best Ways to Invest Money during COVID-19: Investing Tips during the Pandemic While You Are at Home; Investing in Stock Market during COVID-19 Period: Perfect Guide on How to Invest in Stocks or Real Estate during COVID-19; Ultimate Guide to Investing, COVID-19 Edition: Create Wealth in Quarantine.*

While most such books were hastily self-published efforts, with all the hallmarks of that style of production in their design and content, the mainstream publishing industry was not oblivious to the opportunities posed by the novel coronavirus's financial and economic impact. At the beginning of April 2020, the prominent Canadian press Nimbus Publishing released *Don't Panic! How to Manage Your Finances and Financial Anxieties during and after Coronavirus* by Christine Ibbotson, a financial adviser and author of the widely syndicated newspaper column "Ask the Money Lady." Having noted the terrible human toll of the pandemic, as well as economists' dire forecasts, the text shifts to adopt an emphatically upbeat tone. Ibbotson partly presents the pandemic as an opportunity for the kind of investment in one's own "human capital" that is such a key feature of the contemporary nexus of financial advice and self-help writing. She encourages the reader to invest in "yourself. Yes—*you*!" "This pandemic has us all in a flutter, but it also has us all now thinking about our lives, our families, our jobs, and our futures as we adapt to the new 'normal,'" she continues. "Why not leverage yourself? You are a sure-fired exceptional risk to bet on, guaranteed. Use this new low-rate environment to help fund your dreams." Ibbotson primarily focuses, however, on the more narrowly financial investment opportunities presented by the pandemic—and indeed successful navigation of the securities markets once again provides the master metaphor for an individual's positive life trajectory: "Recognize that life, just like the financial market, has its highs and lows and we must always learn from the past in order to become more resilient, stronger, and ultimately more successful in every aspect of our lives." "Is this an environment you can still make money in?" Ibbotson asks; "The answer is YES!" Working on the basis that financial markets have "always reached significantly newer highs than before each crisis— often highs we never thought possible," she insists that "the markets will get through this, too, and—to put it bluntly—there may be a lot of money to be made if you invest when the market is down." "This is the time," she urges, "to buy stocks that are at record low prices and a great value."[1]

During the early phase of the pandemic, the message that declining stock prices (the major global indexes saw falls on the order of 25–30 percent during March 2020) meant that there were bargains to be had was widely repeated across the international media. As markets recovered a significant portion of their losses over subsequent months—supported by massive central bank stimulus measures—a chorus of voices encouraged investors to jump on the rising escalator while the opportunity remained open. Against the backdrop of such coverage, and amid the empty days of lockdown, retail trading boomed, with the leading online brokerages reporting huge growth in new users. The leading e-broker Robinhood—renowned for its vibrant, dynamic interface redolent of video game design and a huge social media presence—saw an especially marked rise, attracting three million new users in the first quarter of 2020, and increasing its overall numbers to more than 13 million. One of the millions of Robinhood users who whiled away time during the coronavirus closures was a twenty-year-old American student named Alex Kearns. In June 2020, Kearns took his own life, apparently in the mistaken belief that he had accrued losses of almost $750,000 in an options trade gone wrong (his account in fact showed a balance of $16,000).[2] This horrifying case highlights the dangers of encouraging ordinary members of the public to engage in active securities trading, especially of the opaque, high-risk kinds now commonplace on internet trading platforms, where derivatives instruments are increasingly popular. It is now easier than at any time in the past for individuals to sign up for investment services that allow them to act out fantasies of market success. Sadly, though, it is no more likely than it has ever been that such neophyte investors will be equipped properly to understand the systems they seek to navigate, or that they will enjoy any financial reward in doing so.

In the wake of Kearns's death, Robinhood stressed that it was expanding its provision of learning resources, especially relating to options. Such enhanced guidance—providing a clearer understanding of a user's financial position—might have helped to avert the end to Kearns's young life. As we've seen, however, studies suggest that retail traders—even those who have immersed themselves in specialized instructional guides and manuals—are highly unlikely to achieve meaningful returns on their trades. As we've further seen, many authors of investment advice over recent decades would concede that it is futile to attempt the kind of precise market timing needed to be a successful day trader; but they would insist (as Ibbotson does in her COVID-19 book) that one should nonetheless hold a broad-based portfolio and wait for the reliably upward trajectory of the stock market over the long haul to take its course.

But even if the stock market were the dependable source of long-term financial security that so many investment gurus assume, breezy encouragements to get in the market while the going's good belie how vastly out of reach such a move is for much of the population, whose incomes may barely cover the most basic essentials, let alone leave money for assembling a stock portfolio. It was of course such low-income and insecurely employed individuals who were most at risk of intensified hardship when COVID-19 brought economies to a virtual standstill in early 2020. And as was tacitly implicit in the measures introduced even by conspicuously rightwing governments—furlough and income support schemes, mortgage and rent relief—a form of financial security that is truly "democratized" must also be socialized, a common resource rather than a private possession. It was a sign of the magnitude of the crisis that proposals for shifting the balance of responsibility for economic security from the individual to the collective that had previously been confined to the fringes of policy debate in the United States and United Kingdom—most obviously the idea of a Universal Basic Income—began to gain unprecedented mainstream attention.[3] For the great majority of people, the stock market is not and never will be a viable buffer against the vicissitudes of economic fortune. The financial advice genre has done much to foster the long-prevalent view that the surest means to financial well-being is to invest oneself and one's money in the market. An additional lesson that we can learn from this genre, however, is that societies will not mitigate the economic risks of our age unless they invest once more—both ideologically and financially—in a collective future.

This political claim on a foundational or democratized model for finance, which has been gathering increasing momentum since the 2008 crisis and has been briefly energized in the mainstream by the COVID-19 crisis, takes on a very particular and peculiar form within the genre of financial advice itself.[4] COVID-19's exacerbation of existing inequalities, particularly the generational asymmetry of precarity and the clear need for collective forms of social insurance, heightened a millennial malaise that appeared to reject the favored clichés of the contemporary financial advice manual. Suze Orman's suggestion that it was the purchase of brunch that was preventing a generation from accessing the housing market (those who bought lattes or avocado toast could not "finish rich" in David Bach's ubiquitous phrase) became a widely mocked metonym for generational and class privilege during the early months of the lockdown—when, of course, nobody was eating out.[5]

Yet what we also see in this most recent crisis, as we do in other twenty-first-century countercultural financial movements (notably the fiercely libertarian advocates of cryptocurrency and, more recently, nonfungible tokens) is that attacks on the inequality and elitism of the financial market often find it very hard to prize themselves away from its assumptions. Our opening example of the GameStop phenomenon, for example, offers a neat example of this as its apparent critique of the stock market was enabled by a renewed attachment to its very promises.

In January 2021, only days after Trump encouraged his MAGA supporters to disrupt the confirmation of the Democratic president-elect by storming the Capitol, another kind of political protest emanating from the "left behind" men of Main Street grabbed American headlines.[6] The news story involved the rapid increase in the stock price of the electronic games retailer, GameStop. The bubble was fueled by amateur investors, networked through the Reddit forum r/wallstreetbets and active on the Robinhood platform, acting collectively upon shared information. The investors initially appeared to buy GameStop in the belief that Ryan Cohen, its new activist investor CEO, could repeat his previous success with the pet food company Chewy and reverse the company's fortunes. The possibility, for the young, male, and relatively disadvantaged gamer community that inhabited WallStreetBets, suggested a symbolically powerful reversal of a long historical trend. The rapid rise in stock prices created its own momentum as investors realized that they had the collective ability to thwart the hedge funds that assumed the company could not compete against streaming services and had been aggressively short-selling it. The "David and Goliath" drama of the moment was heightened as the community represented itself as avengers seeking justice, or disruption, rather than wealth, most obviously in the widely circulated trope from Christopher Nolan's *Dark Knight*—"it's not about the money, it's about sending a message."[7] The drama became a populist scandal when Robinhood froze trading of the stock, and figures as different as Nigel Farage and Alexandra Ocasio-Cortez took to social media to berate it for abandoning its constituency and ostensible commitment to "democratizing finance for all."The ensuing wave of hostility toward Wall Street was compared to the start of the 2011 Occupy movement by some commentators, and in some respects the moment appeared to be coded very differently to the alt-right libertarianism of either Trump's supporters or Zero Hedge acolytes.[8]

The moment was absorbed uneasily by the writers of financial advice. For the advisers at *Forbes*, for example, the story was a flash in the pan of outsider activity that should not deter established middle-class investors from their commitment to a "slow, tortoise-like enterprise best served by buying low-cost diversified index funds that you know will help you retire securely."[9] Bloomberg journalists such as Matt Levine, conversely, initially read the phenomenon through the forms of more active individual investment that have remained central to the genre. First, the rise in GameStop shares was a "fundamental story" about analysts recognizing undervalued stocks: "GameStop, which was bad, is becoming good. It was a money-losing mall retailer in a dying business during a pandemic, and traded like it, but now it will be a dynamic e-commerce leader in the rapidly growing gaming segment, and should trade like it." Second, the rise in GameStop shares was a "technical story" about the ways in which financial charts inevitably move:"a short squeeze and a gamma trap, if you like—combined to push the stock up rapidly on Friday. . . . stock going up forced short sellers and options market makers to buy stock, which caused it to go up more, which caused them to buy more." Finally, the rise in GameStop shares was evidence of the competitive pleasures and collective fantasies that the stock market also harbors: "if pure collective will can create a valuable financial asset, without any reference to cash flows or fundamentals, then all you need is a collective and some will. Just hop on Reddit and create value out of nothing. If it works for Bitcoin, why not . . . anything? Why not Dogecoin? Why not Signal Advance? Tesla Inc.? GameStop?"[10] It was only when Levine returned to the story, a few days later, that he proposed the explanation that pundits who were *not* dispensing financial advice had been quicker to see: this was a narrative of "anti-establishment anger: People are tired of feeling like the stock market is controlled by big evil institutions, and it is satisfying when a band of misfits on Reddit can stick it to the hedge funds." The possibility propels the Bloomberg journalist anxiously back to defend the fundamentals—"shouldn't there be some connection between the fun gambling that is going on in Game-Stop's stock, and the actual company GameStop?"—but it nevertheless indicates how the conventional tropes of financial investment advice were deeply embedded in this apparent rejection of them.[11]

The GameStop saga's ostensible critique of the asymmetrical and generational privileges of Wall Street, for example, often extended, rather than challenged, the assumptions of the genre. The language of the male outsider embarked in battle, for whom winning was rooted in more elaborate libidinal pleasures than money alone, has been a recurring trope—familiar from at least Gerald Loeb's 1930s classic *The Battle for Investment Survival*. What seemed potentially new about the moment—the millennial attack on the structural privileges of the "boomers"—was often loaded with an oedipal revenge narrative that undermined this as a critique. Social media analysis of the self-presentations of GameStop investors, for example, suggests that the "boomers are at once the abject aging parent and the reviled hedge fund investor" and are thus "a shifting index that refers variously to the millennial's own ancestor who must be avenged and to the corrupt financier against whom the revenge will be exacted. The resulting Oedipal complex exceeds the representational capacity of the term 'boomer.'"[12] As an attack on Wall Street, then, the GameStop phenomenon of January 2021 encapsulates the terrible irony underpinning the always endlessly deferred promise of the self-help genre that makes any kind of critique or self-reflection from within it impossible. The moment was steeped in what Lauren Berlant so powerfully termed the "cruel optimism" of the contemporary, when "the thing you desire is actually an obstacle to your flourishing," as popular writing about the market holds out the hope for a form of agency that it simultaneously renders impossible.[13]

At the start of the twenty-first century, advice exhorting the amateur to become invested in the stock market as a way of coping with contemporary crises has persisted and proven itself capable, once more, of absorbing contradictions. The claim that financial advice gives the amateur investor a privileged route to escape financial precarity remains buoyant, even as the role of the financial sector in creating these systemic and structural inequalities is being explicitly, and antagonistically, acknowledged by the advice itself. Similarly, the twin impossibilities of mass financial self-help—the partiality of authors selling the idea that *everyone* can beat the market existing alongside the increasing dominance of passive funds suggesting that *nobody* can beat the market—have done little to dent its spectacular pleasures. The cultural work of the genre, its belief in the subject who can exploit the individualization of risk for personal gain, continues outside of the logic of the marketplace itself: *homo economicus* thrives beyond the rationality that was once "his" single defining characteristic.

Acknowledgments

This book has emerged from an extended and interdisciplinary project, and we are privileged to be able thank a wide number of colleagues and collaborators who have made it possible.

First and foremost, we would like to thank the Arts and Humanities Research Council (AHRC) in the United Kingdom for awarding us a Standard Grant (2016–19) to research the history of financial advice. This grant provided us with the support, time, and resources necessary to undertake both the research and the collaborative activities that contributed to this final manuscript. In the context of our wider activities, we would like to thank the industry professionals who generously gave us their time and access to insights, archives, and contacts. Their contributions made our research richer and also enabled it to valuably exist beyond the pages of this current book. We would like to thank Hilary Cooper of the Finance Foundation, Braden Clamp of Young Enterprise, and Didasko Financial Education Company. We are particularly grateful to Russell Napier, Helen Williams, and Anna Girling for their collaborative work in developing and hosting a permanent archive of the History of Financial Advice at the Library of Mistakes, a specialist financial reference library in Edinburgh.

We would also like to thank the University of Manchester's Research Support Fund from the School of Arts, Languages, and Cultures for enabling us to host a workshop in 2014 that provided the initial impetus for the project. In addition, we are indebted to two teams within the University of Southampton that enabled us to extend the educational outreach of our research. First, we would like to thank the University of Southampton's Economic and Social Research Council Impact Acceleration Account for supporting our work with secondary school teachers and enabling us to run a teacher-scholar program, from which emerged a set of lesson plans that widened the technocratic emphasis of financial literacy education in the United Kingdom to include a historical and cultural account of money and finance. We would like to thank Samantha Shave for organizing this program, the time-pressed teachers who attended it and offered such valuable collaborations, and Amy Bride for her contributions to the lesson plans. We would also like to thank Melanie Smith, of Smith&Wonder, for her work in designing the finished lesson plans. Second, we are grateful for Southampton's digital learning and scholarship team, especially Tamsyn Smith and Sofy Bazzini, who worked with us to develop an online course with FutureLearn, "Understanding Money: The History of Finance, Speculation and the Stock Market." This allowed us to creatively engage with many thousands of learners from across the world. We have also been supported in running this course by Chris Clarke and Lian Patston, two very energetic and patient Early Career Researchers, and we thank them for their contributions.

The task of completing the research for the manuscript itself, of course, has not been insignificant. We would especially like to thank Samantha Shave, who was also our research associate on the AHRC project, for her patient and careful work in compiling the database of financial advice manuals from which our historical narratives and readings were able to emerge. Sam was a key part of the team for the early years of this project, and we appreciated the insights, expertise, and experience that she shared with us. Our debt to her is a large one. If Sam was central to the success of the start of the project, then Emily Harless has been key to the success at its end, and we would like to thank her for her professional and thorough editorial assistance in compiling the final manuscript and acquiring the images. At the University of Chicago Press, we are grateful to Timothy Mennel for making a speculative investment in this project; the two reviewers who gave thorough and helpful advice on revising the manuscript; Susannah Engstrom for shepherding the book through production; and Susan Olin for attentive copyediting.

We were also privileged enough to have some colleagues who were able to guide us throughout the life of the entire project. We would like to warmly thank our formal board of advisers who shared their time, energy, and inspirational insights. We have been humbled, again and again, by the generosity of Emma Clery, Joyce Goggin, Chris McKenna, Russell Napier, and Janette Rutterford. The book has been greatly improved by their readings, comments, and thoughts, and we also thank them for modeling the ideal academic and intellectual community for us.

We have also shared our thoughts with a community of peers throughout the development of this project, and we would also like to thank the organizers and contributors of a number of conferences and seminars at which we have been able to share our ideas as they developed. These include "Cultural Finance," Queen Mary University of London; "Intersections of Finance and Society," City University London; "The Transmission of Financial Knowledge in Historical Perspective," German Historical Institute, Washington, DC; "Women's Committee of the Economic History Society," University of Southampton; "Finance and Society," University of Edinburgh; "Economic Lives: Histories of Money, Finance and Capitalism," University of Manchester; and conferences of the Modern Language Association and American Historical Association, Chicago. In this context we would also like to thank Oxford University Press and the editors of *American Literary History* for allowing us to reuse material from an article that sketched out some of the main ideas in this book: Paul Crosthwaite, Peter Knight, and Nicky Marsh, "The Economic Humanities and the History of Financial Advice," *American Literary History* 31, no. 4 (2019), 661–86, by permission of Oxford University Press.

We are a team of five and our ability to dedicate the time to complete this project has often also depended upon the generosity and understanding of our separate professional and private networks. These are too large to mention individually, but we would like to thank colleagues in the Department of English and Department of Economics (University of Southampton), Department of History (Lancaster University), Department of English, American Studies and Creative Writing (University of Manchester), and Department of English Literature (University of Edinburgh).

Notes

Introduction

1. "Are 'Meme Stocks' Harmless Fun, or a Threat to the Financial Old Guard?" *Economist*, July 6, 2021, https://www.economist.com/the-economist-explains/2021/07/06/are-meme-stocks-harmless-fun-or-a-threat-to-the-financial-old-guard.

2. Yun Li, "Melvin Capital, Hedge Fund Targeted by Reddit Board, Closes Out of GameStop Short Position," CNBC, January 27, 2021, https://www.cnbc.com/2021/01/27/hedge-fund-targeted-by-reddit-board-melvin-capital-closed-out-of-gamestop-short-position-tuesday.html.

3. The slogan is taken from the movie *Rise of the Planet of the Apes* and also, wittingly or not, references Burton Malkiel's idea that blindfolded monkeys throwing darts at stock listings would do just as well as expert stock pickers.

4. Katie Martin, Richard Henderson, and Eric Platt, "The 'Retail Bros' Betting on a Quick Recovery from the Pandemic," *Financial Times*, June 12, 2020, https://wuww.ft.com/content/dd6c7674-d0ed-4865-82ed-48ee169bc6cc; George Schultze, "Are the Apes Now Running Wall Street?" *Forbes*, June 15, 2021, https://www.forbes.com/sites/georgeschultze/2021/06/15/are-the-apes-now-running-wall-street/.

5. "Bears" contract to sell stocks they do not possess in the expectation that prices will fall, allowing them to make a profit: the term derives from the adage "to sell the bearskin before one has caught the bear." The term "bull" was coined as the optimistic counterpart of the bear, both terms being used in a financial context beginning in the 1710s. "Lame ducks" were brokers who could not meet their commitments, a term first committed to print by Thomas Mortimer in the 1760s. Emerging later, in the railway boom of the 1840s, "stags" are speculators who buy up new share issues in the hope of selling for a quick profit. Geoff P. Smith, "How High Can a Dead Cat Bounce? Metaphor and the Hong Kong Stock Market," *Hong Kong Papers in Linguistics and Language Teaching* 18 (1995): 47–49; Laura Favero Carraro, "The Language of the Emerging Financial Market and Early Eighteenth-Century English Plays," *Essays in Economic and Business History* 37 (2019): 222.

6. Dan Mangan, "GameStop, Cryptocurrency and Bubbles: Market Lessons from My Son—and Dad," CNBC, January 29, 2021, https://www.cnbc.com/2021 /01/29/gamestop-cryptocurrency-and-market-bubbles-mone.html; Michael Mackenzie, "Beware the Madness of Markets," *Financial Times*, February 5, 2021, https://www .ft.com/content/cdf7b2a1-1a45-4fad-afa5-667a5d0e38be; Marco Quiroz-Gutierrez, "Is GameStop a Bubble? History's Spectacular Crashes, from Tulips to Beanie Babies," *Wall Street Journal*, February 6, 2021, https://www.wsj.com/articles/is-gamestop -a-bubble-historys-spectacular-crashes-from-tulips-to-beanie-babies-11612607400.

7. "Investing for Hotties: Megan Thee Stallion x Cash App," YouTube, June 30, 2021, https://www.youtube.com/watch?v=NGr_MMZ8_hQ.

8. Niall Ferguson, "GameStop, Robinhood and the Return of the Wind Trade," *Bloomberg Opinion*, February 7, 2021, https://www.bloomberg.com/opinion/articles /2021-02-07/niall-ferguson-gamestop-robinhood-reddit-and-the-wind-trade.

9. Advertisement for George Gregory and Company in *The Standard*, April 2, 1889, 1.

10. The words are Dave Portnoy's: cited in Martin, Henderson, and Platt, "Retail Bros."

11. Dave Portnoy (@stoolpresidente), Twitter, June 7, 2020, https://twitter.com /stoolpresidente/status/1269706445299335171.

12. Dave Portnoy (@stoolpresidente), Twitter, https://twitter.com/stoolpresidente ?ref_src=twsrc%5Egoogle%7Ctwcamp%5Eserp%7Ctwgr%5Eauthor.

13. Sunniva Kolostyak, "Why You Should Stop Taking Investment Advice from Social Media," Halifax UK, June 11, 2021, https://www.investments.halifax.co.uk /research-centre/news-centre/article/?id=212989&type=apiMS.

14. Jean-Baptiste Andrieux, "GameStop Gets Gen Z to Want Financial Advice," *Money Marketing*, May 17, 2021, https://www.moneymarketing.co.uk/news/research -shows-that-gen-zs-want-professional-financial-advice/.

15. Lendol Calder, "Saving and Spending," in *The Oxford Handbook of the History of Consumption*, ed. Frank Trentmann (Oxford: Oxford University Press, 2012), 349.

16. James Vernon, *Distant Strangers: How Britain Became Modern* (Berkeley: University of California Press, 2014), 110.

17. Elaine Freedgood, "Banishing Panic: Harriet Martineau and the Popularization of Political Economy," *Victorian Studies* 39, no. 1 (1995): 33–53; Hilda Hollis, "The Rhetoric of Jane Marcet's Popularizing Political Economy," *Nineteenth-Century Contexts* 24, no. 4 (2002): 379–96; Evelyn L. Forget, "Jane Marcet as Knowledge Broker," *History of Economics Review* 65, no. 1 (2016): 15–26; Willie Henderson, "Millicent Garrett Fawcett's *Political Economy for Beginners*: An Evaluation," *Paedagogica Historica* 40, no. 4 (2004): 435.

18. The book is the result of research conducted for the AHRC-funded project "The History of Financial Advice." The approximately three hundred volumes cited were selected from a larger set of texts identified by means of a thorough bibliographic trawl of library catalogs. Some of these additional texts are discussed in Paul

Crosthwaite, Peter Knight, Nicky Marsh, Helen Paul, and James Taylor, *The History of Financial Advice: A Finder's Guide to the Collection at the Library of Mistakes* (2018), available at: https://historyoffinancialadvice.wordpress.com/finders-guide/.

19. John J. McCusker, "The Demise of Distance: The Business Press and the Origins of the Information Revolution in the Early Modern Atlantic World," *American Historical Review* 110, no. 2 (2005): 295–321; Anne Murphy, *The Origins of English Financial Markets: Investment and Speculation before the South Sea Bubble* (Cambridge: Cambridge University Press, 2009), 97–106.

20. Mary Poovey, *The Financial System in Nineteenth-Century Britain* (Oxford: Oxford University Press, 2003); Mary Poovey, *Genres of the Credit Economy: Mediating Value in Eighteenth- and Nineteenth-Century Britain* (Chicago: University of Chicago Press, 2008); Alex Preda, *Framing Finance: The Boundaries of Markets and Modern Capitalism* (Chicago: University of Chicago Press, 2009); Wayne Parsons, *The Power of the Financial Press: Journalism and Economic Opinion in Britain and America* (Aldershot, UK: Edward Elgar, 1989).

21. Edward J. Balleisen, *Fraud: An American History from Barnum to Madoff* (Princeton, NJ: Princeton University Press, 2017).

22. Walter A. Friedman, *Fortune Tellers: The Story of America's First Economic Forecasters* (Princeton, NJ: Princeton University Press, 2014).

23. G. K. Chesterton makes the distinction in an essay on success literature: G. K. Chesterton, "The Fallacy of Success," in *All Things Considered* (North Charleston, SC: Createspace, n.d. [1908]), 8–12.

24. Burton G. Malkiel, *A Random Walk Down Wall Street* (1973; New York: W. W. Norton, 2007), 24.

25. See, e.g., Mohnish Prabrai, *The Dandho Investor: The Low-Risk Value Method to High Returns* (Hoboken, NJ: Wiley, 2007); Olivier Seban, *Tout le monde mérite d'être riche* (Paris: Maxima, 2011); Francisco García Paramés, *Invirtiendo a largo plaza: Mi experencia como inversor* (Barcelona: Deusto, 2016).

26. Henry Roseveare, *The Financial Revolution, 1660–1760* (Harlow, UK: Longman, 1991).

27. For more on this, see Paul Crosthwaite, Peter Knight, and Nicky Marsh, "The Economic Humanities and the History of Financial Advice," *American Literary History* 31, no. 4 (2019): 661–86.

Chapter One

1. Letter from Jane Ashe to the Hon. Richard Hill, April 22, 1720, Shropshire Archives, 112/1/1775, Shrewsbury.

2. Letter from Sir Ralph Gore to the Hon. Richard Hill, February 13, 1720, Shropshire Archives, 112/1/1772. The letter is dated 1719, but before 1752, following the Julian calendar, the new year began on March 25.

3. Letter from Sir Ralph Gore to the Hon. Richard Hill, September 7, 1720, Shropshire Archives, 112/1/1784.

4. Randolph Vigne, "Hill, Richard," *Oxford Dictionary of National Biography*.

5. Aaron Graham, *Corruption, Party, and Government in Britain, 1702–1713* (Oxford: Oxford University Press, 2015), 42; Henry Roseveare, *The Financial Revolution, 1660–1760* (Harlow, UK: Longman, 1991), 2–32.

6. Graham, *Corruption*, 43.

7. Patrick Walsh, *The South Sea Bubble and Ireland: Money, Banking and Investment, 1690–1721* (Woodbridge, UK: Boydell, 2014), 65–66.

8. Letter from Gore to Hill, February 13, 1720.

9. Hill scribbled on the bottom of the letter: "NB I did not venture six pence of my own money into ye S. S. but kept my Banque & Lottery annuityes."

10. Letter from Sir Ralph Gore to the Hon. Richard Hill, July 20, 1720, Shropshire Archives, 112/1/1781.

11. Account of St. George Ashe late Lord Bishop of Derry, 1721, Shropshire Archives, 112/1/1798.

12. Letter from Gore to Hill, September 7, 1720.

13. Holders of government annuities who converted into South Sea stock were among the biggest losers: Anne Laurence, "Women Investors, 'That Nasty South Sea Affair' and the Rage to Speculate in Early Eighteenth-Century England," *Accounting, Business and Financial History* 16, no. 2 (2006): 259–60.

14. Edmond Smith, "The Social Networks of Investment in Early Modern England," *Historical Journal* 64, no. 4 (2021): 912–39.

15. John Francis, *Chronicles and Characters of the Stock Exchange* (Boston: Wm. Crosby and H. P. Nichols, 1850), 10.

16. The idea that women were excluded from coffeehouses seems to have taken hold in some economic history circles, yet no one seems to know where it originated. See Emma J. Clery, "Women, Publicity and the Coffee-House Myth," *Women: A Cultural Review* 2, no. 2 (1991): 168. Amy Froide provides two examples of women in the coffeehouses: Hester Pinney conducted business for her brother in a "coffeehouse about the Exchange" in 1701, and Mary Bailey went in pursuit of a male broker who owed her money and had "been at severall coffee houses after him." Amy Froide, *Silent Partners: Women as Public Investors during Britain's Financial Revolution, 1690–1750* (Oxford: Oxford University Press, 2017), 15, 80.

17. S. R. Cope, "The Stock Exchange Revisited: A New Look at the Market in Securities in London in the Eighteenth Century," *Economica* 45, no. 177 (1978): 3–4.

18. Bankers would often perform this service, the partners of Hoare's Bank buying and selling shares on their own account and on behalf of their clients: Laurence, "Women Investors," 246.

19. Shropshire Archives hold a substantial correspondence between the two. For more on Hart, see Ann M. Carlos, Karen Maguire, and Larry Neal, "'A Knavish

People . . .': London Jewry and the Stock Market during the South Sea Bubble," *Business History* 50, no. 6 (2008): 728–48.

20. Ellen T. Harris, "Handel the Investor," *Music & Letters* 85, no. 4 (2004): 525.

21. Miles Ogborn, *Indian Ink: Script and Print in the Making of the English East India Company* (Chicago: University of Chicago Press, 2007), 162.

22. Ranald C. Michie, *The London Stock Exchange: A History* (Oxford: Oxford University Press, 2001), 16. Limited liability means that investors are not personally responsible for the company's debts. They can lose the money they have invested in the company but cannot be pursued for any further sums by the company's creditors.

23. Anne L. Murphy, *The Origins of English Financial Markets: Investment and Speculation before the South Sea Bubble* (Cambridge: Cambridge University Press, 2009), 20.

24. Murphy, *Origins of English Financial Markets*, 15; Ann M. Carlos and Larry Neal, "The Micro-Foundations of the Early London Capital Market: Bank of England Shareholders during and after the South Sea Bubble," *Economic History Review* 59, no. 3 (2006): 521.

25. Carlos and Neal, "Micro-Foundations," 509, 525.

26. John Carswell, *The South Sea Bubble* (Thrupp, UK: Sutton, 2001), 77.

27. P. G. M. Dickson, *The Financial Revolution in England: A Study in the Development of Public Credit, 1688–1756* (London: Macmillan, 1967), 273, 285–86.

28. James Raven, "The Abolition of the English State Lotteries," *Historical Journal* 34, no. 2 (1991): 371–89; Anne L. Murphy, "Lotteries in the 1690s: Investment or Gamble?" *Financial History Review* 12, no. 2 (2005): 227–46.

29. Roseveare, *Financial Revolution*, 51; Colin Nicholson, *Writing and the Rise of Finance: Capital Satires of the Early Eighteenth Century* (Cambridge: Cambridge University Press, 1994), 58.

30. E. Warren, *Stock-Broker, at His State Lottery and Public Register Office* (London, 1757); J. Maddison, *Stock-Broker, Removed from His Late Dwelling-House* (London, 1777); *Hornsby and Co. Stock-Brokers, Removed from No. 19, Corner of Pope's-Head Alley, Cornhill* (London, 1779).

31. Froide, *Silent Partners*, 68–69.

32. Amy Louise Erickson, *Women and Property in Early Modern England* (Abingdon, UK: Routledge, 1995), 104–5.

33. Christopher W. Brooks, *Law, Politics and Society in Early Modern England* (Cambridge: Cambridge University Press, 2008), 371.

34. Murphy, *Origins of English Financial Markets*, 15.

35. Michie, *London Stock Exchange*, 18–25.

36. Mary Poovey, *Genres of the Credit Economy: Mediating Value in Eighteenth- and Nineteenth-Century Britain* (Chicago: University of Chicago Press, 2008), 25.

37. [Daniel Defoe], *An Essay upon Projects* (London: R. R. for Tho. Cockerill, 1697).

38. Valerie Hamilton and Martin Parker, *Daniel Defoe and the Bank of England: The Dark Arts of Projectors* (Winchester, UK: Zero Books, 2016), 8–9.

39. J. G. A. Pocock, *Virtue, Commerce, and History: Essays on Political Thought and History* (Cambridge: Cambridge University Press, 1985), 112.

40. See, e.g., Sandra Sherman, *Finance and Fictionality in the Early Eighteenth Century: Accounting for Defoe* (Cambridge: Cambridge University Press, 1996); Catherine Ingrassia, *Authorship, Commerce and Gender in Early Eighteenth-Century England* (Cambridge: Cambridge: University Press, 1998); and Natalie Roxburgh, *Representing Public Credit: Credible Commitment, Fiction, and the Rise of the Financial Subject* (London: Routledge, 2015).

41. Roxburgh, *Representing Public Credit*, 3. On character and credit, see Catherine Gallagher, *Nobody's Story: The Vanishing Acts of Women Writers in the Marketplace, 1670–1920* (Berkeley: University of California Press, 1995); and Deidre S. Lynch, *The Economy of Character: Novels, Market Culture, and the Business of Inner Meaning* (Chicago: University of Chicago Press, 1998).

42. Nicholson, *Writing and the Rise of Finance*, chap. 2.

43. [Daniel Defoe], *The Villainy of Stock-Jobbers Detected, and the Causes of the Late Run upon the Bank and Bankers Discovered and Considered* (London, 1701), 22.

44. Laura Favero Carraro, "The Language of the Emerging Financial Market and Early Eighteenth-Century English Plays," *Essays in Economic and Business History* 37 (2019): 211–14.

45. Stuart Banner, *Anglo-American Securities Regulation: Cultural and Political Roots, 1690–1860* (Cambridge: Cambridge University Press, 2002), 25–26.

46. For early criticisms of time-bargaining, see Banner, 79–87.

47. [Thomas Gordon], *An Essay on the Practice of Stock-Jobbing, and Some Remarks on the Right Use, and Regular Improvement of Money* (London: J. Peele, 1724), 3, 2.

48. Defoe, *Villainy of Stock-Jobbers Detected*, 26.

49. A Gideonite, *The Art of Stock-Jobbing: A Poem, in Imitation of Horace's "Art of Poetry"* (London: R. Baldwin and J. Jefferys, 1746), 46.

50. Carlos, Maguire, and Neal, "'A Knavish People,'" 730.

51. J. A. Giuseppi, "Sephardi Jews and the Early Years of the Bank of England," *Transactions* (Jewish Historical Society of England) 15 (1955): 53.

52. Lucy Stuart Sutherland, "Samson Gideon: Eighteenth Century Jewish Financier," *Transactions* (Jewish Historical Society) 17 (1951–52): 79; punctuation per original.

53. Todd M. Endleman, *The Jews of Georgian England, 1714–1830: Tradition and Change in a Liberal Society* (Ann Arbor: University of Michigan Press, 1999), 29.

54. Endleman, 31.

55. The classic example is Shylock in *The Merchant of Venice*. Unusually, Shylock is given the opportunity to denounce his Gentile opponents.

56. [Edward Ward], *The Picture of a Coffee-House: or, the Humour of the Stock-Jobbers* (London, 1700), 5.

57. Julian Hoppit, "Attitudes to Credit in Britain, 1680–1790," *Historical Journal* 33, no. 2 (1990): 309; Matthew David Mitchell, "'The Extravagant Humour of Stock-Jobbing' and the Members of the English Body Politic, 1690–1720," *Essays in Economic and Business History* 30, no. 1 (2012): 49.

58. Anon., *Exchange-Alley: or, the Stock-Jobber Turn'd Gentleman; with the Humours of Our Modern Projectors* (London: T. Bickerton, 1720), preface.

59. Carraro, "Language of the Emerging Financial Market," 231.

60. Defoe, *Villainy of Stock-Jobbers Detected*, 24–25; Anon., *A Proposal for Putting Some Stop to the Extravagant Humour of Stock-Jobbing* [no publication details, 1697?].

61. Murphy, *Origins of English Financial Markets*, 83–84.

62. 8 & 9 Will. III, c. 32. For discussion, Murphy, *Origins of English Financial Markets*, 86–87.

63. E. Victor Morgan and W. A. Thomas, *The Stock Exchange: Its History and Functions* (London: Elek Books, 1969), 65; Cope, "Stock Exchange Revisited," 3.

64. Jackson Tait, "Speculation and the English Common Law Courts, 1697–1845," *Libertarian Papers* 10, no. 1 (2018): 10–11; Dickson, *Financial Revolution*, 494–96. A later act of 1708 repealed the 1697 measure, removing the limit on the number of brokers but maintaining the licensing system: 6 Anne, c. 16, ss. 4–5. The City authorities subsequently limited the number of Jewish brokers to twelve: Cope, "Stock Exchange Revisited," 2.

65. Officially, the Bubble Act of 1720 was "An Act for better securing certain Powers and Privileges intended to be granted by His Majesty by Two Charters for Assurance of Ships and Merchandizes at Sea, and for lending Money on Bottomry; and for restraining several extravagant and unwarrantable Practices therein mentioned," 6 Geo I, c. 18.

66. Ron Harris, "The Bubble Act: Its Passage and Effects on Business Organization," *Journal of Economic History* 54, no. 3 (1994): 610–27.

67. Cited in Banner, *Anglo-American Securities Regulation*, 102.

68. For discussion of Barnard's Act, see Banner, 101–5.

69. Cope, "Stock Exchange Revisited," 9–11.

70. H. V. Bowen, "'The Pests of Human Society': Stockbrokers, Jobbers and Speculation in Mid-Eighteenth-Century Britain," *History* 78, no. 252 (1993): 46. Opponents of regulation also ventured into print to defend the market: see, e.g., Anon., *Reasons Humbly Offered: Against a Clause in the Bill for Regulating Brokers* (London, 1700?); Anon., *Considerations on a Bill Now Depending in Parliament* (London, 1756).

71. A Jobber [Daniel Defoe], *The Anatomy of Exchange-Alley: or, A System of Stock-Jobbing* (London: E. Smith, 1719), 35–37.

72. Carraro, "Language of the Emerging Financial Market," 221–22.

73. Gordon, *Essay on the Practice of Stock-Jobbing*, 6. Earlier, Defoe had criticized market manipulators in the same language: "the Price shall dance attendance on their designs, and rise and fall as they please, without any regard to the Instrinsick worth of the Stock." Defoe, *Villainy of Stock-Jobbers Detected*, 5.

74. *Appendix to the London Magazine*, December 2, 1733, 655.

75. The word "speculation" was only rarely used in a financial context before the 1770s: Banner, *Anglo-American Securities Regulation*, 88–89.

76. John J. McCusker, "The Demise of Distance: The Business Press and the Origins of the Information Revolution in the Early Modern Atlantic World," *American Historical Review* 110, no. 2 (2005): 295–321.

77. Murphy, *Origins of English Financial Markets*, 98–101.

78. Larry Neal, *The Rise of Financial Capitalism: International Capital Markets in the Age of Reason* (1990; Cambridge: University of Cambridge Press, 1993), 23. The *Collection* was a revival of Houghton's earlier *Collection of Letters for the Improvement of Husbandry and Trade* (1681–83), which had not published stock prices.

79. *A Collection for Improvement of Husbandry and Trade*, April 6, 1692 (1727 edition).

80. John Houghton, *A Proposal for Improvement of Husbandry and Trade* (London, 1691), 1.

81. Ogborn, *Indian Ink*, 176–80.

82. Natasha Glaisyer, "Readers, Correspondents and Communities: John Houghton's *A Collection for Improvement of Husbandry and Trade* (1692–1703)," in *Communities in Early Modern England: Networks, Place, Rhetoric*, ed. Alexandra Shepherd and Phil Withington (Manchester: Manchester University Press, 2000), 236.

83. *Collection*, June 8, 1694 (1727 edition).

84. *Collection*, April 6, 1692 (1727 edition).

85. The articles appeared between June 8 and July 20, 1694. A call option gives the holder the right to buy shares at a certain price on a certain date, while the put option gives the holder the right to sell shares at a certain price on a certain date.

86. Ogborn, *Indian Ink*, 185.

87. Ogborn, 183. Originally sold for 2d, the price was halved to 1d in 1693: Neal, *Rise of Financial Capitalism*, 23.

88. Cited in Ogborn, *Indian Ink*, 193.

89. Glaisyer, "Readers," 246; Natasha Glaisyer, *The Culture of Commerce in England, 1660–1720* (Woodbridge, UK: Boydell, 2006), 154–55.

90. Philip Mirowski, "The Rise (and Retreat) of a Market: English Joint Stock Shares in the Eighteenth Century," *Journal of Economic History* 41, no. 3 (1981): 564.

91. Murphy, *Origins of English Financial Markets*, 100.

92. Neal, *Rise of Financial Capitalism*, 26.

93. Froide, *Silent Partners*, 15.

94. John Freke, *Prices of the Several Stocks, Annuities, and other Publick Securities, &c*, March 26, 1714–March 25, 1715.

95. Froide, *Silent Partners*, 15.

96. Richard Dale, *The First Crash: Lessons from the South Sea Bubble* (Princeton, NJ: Princeton University Press, 2004), 16.

97. Lindsay O'Neill, "Dealing with Newsmongers: News, Trust, and Letters in the British World, ca. 1670–1730," *Huntington Library Quarterly* 76, no. 2 (2013): 224.

98. Laurence, "Women Investors," 255.

99. Natasha Glaisyer, "Calculating Credibility: Print Culture, Trust and Economic Figures in Early Eighteenth-Century England," *Economic History Review* 60, no. 4 (2007): 688. By the late seventeenth century, it was legal to charge interest (although only up to a certain maximum which changed over time). Roseveare, *Financial Revolution*, 110. Usury can be any lending of money for interest or it can be defined as charging interest above a specific rate. For more on opposition to usury, see Eric Roll, *A History of Economic Thought*, new and rev. ed. (London: Faber and Faber, 1992), 22–40.

100. Glaisyer, "Calculating Credibility," 690.

101. E. Hatton, *The Merchant's Magazine: or, Trades-man's Treasury*, 2nd ed. (London: J. Heptinstall, 1697), title page.

102. Froide, *Silent Partners*, 20–21.

103. [Richard North], *The Gentleman Accomptant: or, An Essay to Unfold the Mystery of Accompts* (London: E. Curll, 1714), glossary.

104. Froide, *Silent Partners*, 20.

105. Glaisyer, "Calculating Credibility," 699.

106. G. Clerke, *The Dealers in Stock's Assistant*, 2nd ed. (London: J. Read, 1725), title page.

107. Richard Hayes, *The Money'd Man's Guide: or, the Purchaser's Pocket-Companion* (London: W. Meadows, 1726), title page, iii.

108. Hayes, *Money'd Man's Guide*, iv–v.

109. Hayes, iv.

110. Froide, *Silent Partners*, 23.

111. Stephen Colclough, "Pocket Books and Portable Writing: The Pocket Memorandum Book in Eighteenth-Century England and Wales," *Yearbook of English Studies* 45 (2015): 159–60.

112. Anon., *The Liverpool Memorandum-Book* (Liverpool: R. Williamson, 1753), 1.

113. Colclough, "Pocket Books," 161.

114. Amanda J. Flather, "Space, Place, and Gender: The Sexual and Spatial Division of Labor in the Early Modern Household," *History and Theory* 52, no. 3 (2013): 348.

115. Anon., *The Ladies Complete Pocket-Book for the Year 1760* (London: John Newbery, 1760), 1–12.

116. Anon., *The Ladies Complete Pocket Book for the Year 1762* (London: John Newbery, 1762), 1–34.

117. William Lane, *Lane's Ladies Museum* (London: William Lane, 1792), 1.

118. Anon., *The Ladies Most Elegant and Convenient Pocket Book, for the Year 1790* (London: E. Newbery, 1790), 1.

119. Anon., *The Court and Royal Lady's Pocket-Book for the Year 1797* (London: Minerva-Press, 1797).

120. B. Crosby, *Crosby's Royal Fortune-Telling Almanack* (London: B. Crosby, 1796), 1.

121. Jennie Batchelor, "Fashion and Frugality: Eighteenth-Century Pocket Books for Women," *Studies in Eighteenth-Century Culture* 32 (2003): 14.

122. Hayes, *Money'd Man's Guide*, v.

123. Kathleen Ashley and Robert L. A. Clark, "Medieval Conduct: Texts, Theories, Practices," in *Medieval Conduct*, ed. Kathleen Ashley and Robert L. A. Clark (Minneapolis: University of Minnesota Press, 2001), x; Stephen Greenblatt, *Renaissance Self-Fashioning: From More to Shakespeare* (1980; Chicago: University of Chicago Press, 2005).

124. Jacques Carré, introduction to *The Crisis of Courtesy: Studies in the Conduct-Book in Britain, 1600–1900*, ed. Jacques Carré (Leiden: Brill, 1994), 3.

125. Nancy Armstrong, *Desire and Domestic Fiction: A Political History of the Novel* (Oxford: Oxford University Press, 1987); Kevin J. Hayes, *A Colonial Woman's Bookshelf* (Knoxville: University of Tennessee Press, 1996), 64.

126. Samuel Richardson's *The Apprentice's Vade Mecum* (1734) and Eliza Haywood's *A Present for a Servant-Maid* (1743) are discussed in Naomi Tadmor, *Family and Friends in Eighteenth-Century England: Household, Kinship, and Patronage* (Cambridge: Cambridge University Press, 2001), chap. 2.

127. For a discussion of this genre, see Edward Cahill, "The English Origins of American Upward Mobility; Or, the Invention of Benjamin Franklin," *ELH* 83, no. 2 (2016): 543–71.

128. Anon., *The Art of Thriving, or, The Way to Get and Keep Money* (London: J. Coniers, 1674), 1.

129. N. H., *The Pleasant Art of Money-Catching, Newly and Fully Discovered* (London: J. Dunton, 1684), title page.

130. Elizabeth Anne Rothenberg, "'The Diligent Hand Maketh Rich': Commercial Advice for Retailers in Late Seventeenth- and Early Eighteenth-Century England," in *Cultures of Selling: Perspectives on Consumption and Society since 1700*, ed. John Benson and Laura Ugolini (Aldershot, UK: Ashgate, 2006), 224–25.

131. James Raven, *Publishing Business in Eighteenth-Century England* (Woodbridge, UK: Boydell, 2014), 191.

132. [Daniel Defoe], *The Complete English Tradesman, in Familiar Letters; Di-*

recting Him in All the Several Parts and Progressions of Trade (London: Charles Rivington, 1726), 72.

133. Richard Steele, *The Spectator*, no. 428, July 11, [1712], 180.

134. Ogborn, *Indian Ink*, 195. Though Houghton's *Collection* had included a "History of the Stocks," its overall coverage of the stock market does not tally with Steele's description here.

135. Steele, *The Spectator*, no. 428, July 11, [1712], 183.

136. *Public Ledger*, May 23, 1761, 491; *Public Advertiser*, May 28, 1761, 1.

137. Philanthropos, *Every Man His Own Broker: or, A Guide to Exchange-Alley* (London: S. Hooper, 1761), iv, xiii, 102. All subsequent references are to this first edition unless otherwise specified.

138. Philanthropos, xi.

139. John Bunyan, *A Pilgrim's Progress from This World, to That Which Is to Come* (London: Nath. Ponder, 1678).

140. This section was extended from the second edition: Anon., *Every Man His Own Broker: or, A Guide to Exchange-Alley*, 2nd ed. (London: S. Hooper, 1761), 80–88.

141. For the Dutch, financial speculation is known as the Wind Trade, hence Windbuil is both a windbag and a "windtrader" or jobber. See Joyce Goggin and Frans de Bruyn, eds., *Comedy and Crisis: Pieter Langendijk, the Dutch, and the Speculative Bubbles of 1720* (Liverpool: Liverpool University Press, 2020), 1–20; R. L. Hayley, "The Scriblerians and the South Sea Bubble: A Hit by Cibber," *Review of English Studies* 24, no. 96 (1973): 452–53.

142. Philanthropos, *Every Man*, 76, 78.

143. Lawrence E. Klein, ed., *Shaftesbury: Characteristics of Men, Manners, Opinions, Times* (Cambridge: Cambridge University Press, 2000), viii–ix.

144. Philanthropos, *Every Man*, 79–80.

145. Philanthropos, 82–83.

146. Philanthropos, vii, xvi.

147. Philanthropos, vi.

148. T. Mortimer, *Every Man His Own Broker: or, A Guide to Exchange-Alley*, 3rd ed. (London: S. Hooper, 1761), xviii–xxii.

149. Philanthropos, *Every Man*, vii.

150. Philanthropos, xv.

151. Mortimer, *Every Man*, 3rd ed., xxiii.

152. Philanthropos, *Every Man*, 103–4.

153. Philanthropos, xi–xiv.

154. Thomas Mortimer, *Every Man His Own Broker: or, A Guide to Exchange-Alley*, 9th ed. (London: G. Robinson, 1782), xx.

155. Philanthropos, *Every Man*, 102–3.

156. Philanthropos, *Every Man*, 19–21, x, 22, 32, 131.

157. *Monthly Review*, June 1, 1761, 442.

158. Anon., *Every Man*, 2nd ed., 134–35.

159. *Critical Review*, July 1761, 27.

160. Mortimer, *Every Man*, 3rd ed., title page.

161. Mortimer, xxii–xxiii. After 1762, further editions appeared in 1765, 1769, 1775, 1782, 1785, 1791, 1798, 1801, and 1807.

162. The book was reviewed and advertised at the time, but few copies seem to have survived: *Monthly Review*, April 1, 1763, 327; *St. James's Chronicle*, February 8–10, 1763, 4.

163. Catherine Ingrassia, "The Pleasure of Business and the Business of Pleasure: Gender, Credit, and the South Sea Bubble," *Studies in Eighteenth-Century Culture* 24 (1995): 191–210.

164. Anon., "Every Man His Own Novelist," *Westminster Magazine*, June 1, 1785, 301.

165. *Monthly Ledger: or, Literary Repository* 2, April 1774, 208.

166. Thomas Mortimer, *Every Man His Own Broker; or, A Guide to the Stock-Exchange*, 12th ed. (London: W. J. and J. Richardson, 1798), v–vi.

167. J. R. McCulloch, *The Literature of Political Economy: A Classified Catalogue* (London: Longman, Brown, Green, and Longmans, 1845), 53. Intriguingly, Adam Smith had a 1761 copy of *Every Man* in his library, but Mortimer's work does not seem to have influenced Smith in any obvious way—or vice versa. There is a copy held in the University of Edinburgh's *Adam Smith Collection* with the shelf mark "Smith. 1141 (old shelf mark JA 2902)."

168. The title page of his *Elements of Commerce* identified himself as the author of *Every Man*: Thomas Mortimer, *Elements of Commerce, Politics and Finances, in Three Treatises on Those Important Subjects* (London: S. Hooper and others, 1774).

169. Thomas Mortimer, *Every Man His Own Broker: or, A Guide to the Stock Exchange*, 14th ed. (London: W. J. and J. Richardson, 1807), xxiii.

170. Anon., *The Lottery Pamphlet, or, The Wheel of Fortune Laid Open to the Public; or, Thoughts on State Lotteries* (London: Messrs. Smith, 1776), 10.

171. Anon., *Lottery Pamphlet*, 27.

172. A Gentleman of the Bank, *The Bank of England's Vade Mecum; or, Sure Guide* (London: M. Becket, 1782), title page.

173. J. Phillips, *A General History of Inland Navigation, Foreign and Domestic* (London: I. and J. Taylor, 1792), xiii.

174. Michie, *London Stock Exchange*, 31–32.

175. Thomas Mortimer, *Every Man His Own Broker: or, A Guide to the Stock-Exchange*, 9th ed. (London: G. G. J. and J. Robinson, 1791), 90.

176. Mortimer, *Every Man*, 9th ed., xxi, iv.

177. Mortimer does not mention Adam Smith at all. In the 1798 edition of *Every Man*, Mortimer makes a brief reference to Sir James Steuart's book *An Enquiry into the Principles of Political Oeconomy* (1767), but he does not engage with Steuart's ideas, merely using Steuart's name to bolster his own view on the national debt. Mortimer, *Every Man* (1798), 46.

178. Ingrassia, *Authorship, Commerce and Gender*, ix.

179. [Daniel Defoe], *An Essay upon Publick Credit*, 3rd ed. (London, 1710), 6.

180. Anon., "Every Man His Own Novelist," 301.

181. The ". . . for Dummies" series began in 1991, with *Investing for Dummies* first published in 1996.

182. *Reading Mercury*, October 8, 1787, 4.

183. Mortimer, *Every Man*, 14th ed., v–vi.

184. Philanthropos, *Every Man*, 78–79.

185. Philanthropos, 23, iv.

Chapter Two

1. *Marx and Engels Collected Works*, vol. 41, *Letters, 1860–64* (London: Lawrence and Wishart, 2010), 543.

2. Gregory Claeys, *Marx and Marxism* (London: Pelican, 2018), 146.

3. Around nine-tenths of the national debt was held by British investors: Boyd Hilton, *A Mad, Bad, and Dangerous People? England 1783–1846* (Oxford: Clarendon Press, 2006), 130; Ranald C. Michie, *The London Stock Exchange: A History* (Oxford: Oxford University Press, 1999), 34.

4. Michie, *London Stock Exchange*, 34.

5. Stockbrokers could continue to operate without being members of the Stock Exchange: James Taylor, "Inside and Outside the London Stock Exchange: Stockbrokers and Speculation in Late Victorian Britain," *Enterprise and Society* 22, no. 3 (2021): 842–77.

6. Paul Johnson, *Making the Market: The Victorian Origins of Corporate Capitalism* (Cambridge: Cambridge University Press, 2010), chap. 7; Ian Klaus, *Forging Capitalism: Rogues, Swindlers, Frauds, and the Rise of Modern Finance* (New Haven, CT: Yale University Press, 2014), chap. 2.

7. Gentleman of the Exchange, *Tricks of the Stock-Exchange Exposed: The Cause of the Rise and Fall of the Public Funds Explained, with Observations on . . . Time Bargains . . . Abolishing the Present Stock-Exchange, and Establishing an Open Public Market* (London: C. Chapple, 1814); A Practical Jobber, *The Art of Stock Jobbing Explained; Exposing the Secret Manoeuvres, Tricks, and Contrivances, and the Cause of the Rise and Fall of the Funds: With Useful Hints on the Proper Time to Buy and Sell*, 7th ed. (London: W. Clarke, [1820]). These two pamphlets were by the same author. See also Anon., *The Bank—The Stock Exchange—The Bankers—The Bankers' Clearing House—The Minister, and the Public: An Exposé, Touching Their Various Mysteries* (London: Effingham Wilson, 1821).

8. Charles Hales, *The Bank Mirror; or, A Guide to the Funds* (London: J. Adlard, [1796]), 17–24.

9. George G. Carey, *Every Man His Own Stock-Broker; or, A Complete Guide to the Public Funds* (London: J. Johnston, 1820), 69.

10. T. Fortune, *An Epitome of the Stocks and Publick Funds; Containing Every Thing Necessary to Be Known for Perfectly Understanding the Nature of Those Securities, and the Mode of Doing Business Therein*, 3rd ed. (London: T. Boosey, 1797), 17–21.

11. Carey, as a mathematics teacher, was the exception.

12. Thomas Mortimer, *Every Man His Own Broker; or, A Guide to the Stock-Exchange*, 12th ed. (London: W. J. and J. Richardson, 1798), errata; T. Fortune, *An Epitome of the Stocks & Public Funds*, 5th ed. (London: T. Boosey, 1800), 19; T. Fortune, *An Epitome of the Stocks & Public Funds*, 8th ed. (London: T. Boosey, 1810), 20; E. F. T. Fortune, *National Life Annuities: Comprizing All the Tables, and Every Necessary Information Contained in the Act of Parliament for Granting the Same* (London: T. Boosey, 1808).

13. Fortune, *Epitome of the Stocks*, 3rd ed., 5; William Fairman, *The Stocks Examined and Compared: or, A Guide to Purchasers in the Public Funds*, 2nd ed. (London: H. L. Galabin, 1796), v.

14. Stuart Banner, *Anglo-American Securities Regulation: Cultural and Political Roots, 1690–1860* (Cambridge: Cambridge University Press, 2002), 99–121.

15. Fairman, *Stocks Examined*, iii.

16. The relationship was deepened by a spate of books of calculating tables, many compiled by stockbrokers: John Hemming, *Tables Shewing the Amount of Any Quantity of Omnium, Or of the Several Scrips of which Omnium is Composed, at Different Prices* (London: H. D. Steel, 1797); William Blewert, *Tables, Formed on a New and Easy Principle, for Calculating the Value of Stocks and Annuities, and for a Ready Dispatch of Business in the Public Funds*, 2nd ed. (London: W. J. and J. Richardson, 1804); Robert Watson Wade, *The Stock-Holder's Assistant* (London: H. D. Steel, 1806).

17. Fairman, *Stocks Examined*, iii.

18. Carey, *Every Man*, iv.

19. Robert E. Wright, *The Wealth of Nations Rediscovered: Integration and Expansion in American Financial Markets, 1780–1850* (Cambridge: Cambridge University Press, 2002).

20. Fortune, *Epitome of the Stocks*, 3rd ed., 67.

21. For more on the background to the creation of consols in the 1750s, see L. S. Sutherland, "Samson Gideon and the Reduction of Interest, 1749–50," *Economic History Review* 16, no. 1 (1946): 15–29.

22. Klaus, *Forging Capitalism*, 77–78; Frank Griffith Dawson, *The First Latin American Debt Crisis: The City of London and the 1822–25 Loan Bubble* (New Haven, CT: Yale University Press, 1990), 21; Hilton, *A Mad, Bad, and Dangerous People?*, 300–301.

23. Timothy L. Alborn, *Conceiving Companies: Joint-Stock Politics in Victorian England* (London: Routledge, 1998), 191; Joseph Lowe, *The Present State of England in Regard to Agriculture, Trade, and Finance; with a Comparison of the Prospects of England and France*, 2nd ed. (London: Longman, 1823), 366.

24. Michie, *London Stock Exchange*, 53.

25. Peter E. Austin, *Baring Brothers and the Birth of Modern Finance* (Abingdon, UK: Routledge, 2016), 20.

26. Ron Harris, *Industrializing English Law: Entrepreneurship and Business Organization, 1720–1844* (Cambridge: Cambridge University Press, 2000), 217–18.

27. Ron Harris, "Political Economy, Interest Groups, Legal Institutions, and the Repeal of the Bubble Act in 1825," *Economic History Review* 50, no. 4 (1997): 675–96.

28. A Member of the Stock Exchange, *Fortune's Epitome of the Stocks and Public Funds*, 11th ed. (London: Boosey and Sons, 1824), 94, 107. By now the guide was edited by J. G. Dessoulavy, a London Stock Exchange broker.

29. Fairman's manual was now edited by Bernard Cohen, a broker on the London Stock Exchange, whose decision to omit them was no doubt influenced by the fact that he was the author of a rival guide which offered an exhaustive survey of public debts: Bernard Cohen, *Compendium of Finance: Containing an Account of the Origin, Progress, and Present State, of the Public Debts, Revenue, Expenditure, National Banks and Currencies . . . Shewing the Nature of the Different Public Securities, with the Manner of Making Investments Therein* (London: W. Phillips, 1822).

30. Robert W. Dimand, "Ricardo and International Trade Theory," *History of Economic Ideas* 8, no. 3 (2000): 7–24. Of course, Britain's newfound love of free trade disguised the unfair trading relationships imposed on colonies and less developed countries such as China which had to accept trade on British terms, including allowing imports of opium. For an overview of how the situation was reported in the British radical press, see Shijie Guan, "Chartism and the First Opium War," *History Workshop* 24, no. 1 (1987): 17–31.

31. An Old Merchant, *Remarks on Joint Stock Companies* (London: John Murray, 1825), 64–65. For more, see James Taylor, *Creating Capitalism: Joint-Stock Enterprise in British Politics and Culture, 1800–1870* (Woodbridge, UK: Boydell, 2006), 110–11.

32. Marc Flandreau and Juan H. Flores, "Bonds and Brands: Foundations of Sovereign Debt Markets, 1820–1830," *Journal of Economic History* 69, no. 3 (2009): 646–84.

33. J. Fred Rippy, "Latin America and the British Investment 'Boom' of the 1820s," *Journal of Modern History* 19, no. 2 (1947): 127.

34. Helen J. Paul, *The South Sea Bubble: An Economic History of Its Origins and Consequences* (London: Routledge, 2011), 57.

35. Calvin P. Jones, "The Spanish-American Works of Alexander von Humboldt as Viewed by Leading British Periodicals, 1800–1830," *The Americas* 29, no. 4 (1973): 442–48; Michael P. Costeloe, *Bonds and Bondholders: British Investors and Mexico's Foreign Debt, 1824–1888* (Westport, CT: Praeger, 2003), 270; Klaus, *Forging Capitalism*, 66–67.

36. Often claimed to be a pseudonym of MacGregor, Strangeways was in fact a military contemporary of his: Alfred Hasbrouck, "Gregor McGregor and the Colonization of Poyais, between 1820 and 1824," *Hispanic American Historical Review*

7, no. 4 (1927): 444n14; Damian Clavel, "What's in a Fraud? The Many Worlds of Gregor MacGregor, 1817–1824," *Enterprise & Society* 22, no. 4 (2021): 1017.

37. Robert W. Randall, *Real del Monte: A British Silver Mining Venture in Mexico* (Austin: University of Texas Press, 1972).

38. John Woodland, *Money Pits: British Mining Companies in the Californian and Australian Gold Rushes of the 1850s* (Farnham, UK: Ashgate, 2014), 17–18. Disraeli went on to author another two pamphlets on the same topic: Anon., *Lawyers and Legislators: or, Notes on the American Mining Companies* (London: John Murray, 1825); Anon., *The Present State of Mexico* (London: John Murray, 1825).

39. Roger Burt, "The London Mining Exchange, 1850–1900," *Business History* 14, no. 2 (1972): 128.

40. Thomas Strangeways, *Sketch of the Mosquito Shore, Including the Territory of Poyais, Descriptive of the Country; With Some Information as to Its Production, the Best Mode of Culture, and Chiefly Intended for the Use of Settlers* (Edinburgh: William Blackwood, 1822), v–vi.

41. *Selections from the Works of the Baron De Humboldt, Relating to the Climate, Inhabitants, Productions, and Mines of Mexico, with Notes by John Taylor* (London: Longman, 1824), vi, viii, xxviii.

42. Henry English, *A General Guide to the Companies Formed for Working Foreign Mines* (London: Boosey & Sons, 1825), 1.

43. Writing of the Bolivar Mining Association, for example, English noted that "we have been informed the Company have received advices from their Agents at La Gerayra, which are of a very favourable nature. The contents have not yet been made public." English, *General Guide*, 78.

44. Angela Esterhammer, "Speculation in the Late-Romantic Literary Marketplace," *Victoriographies* 7, no. 1 (2017): 17.

45. Strangeways, *Sketch*, 349.

46. *Selections from the Works of the Baron De Humboldt*, vi, viii; see also Sir William Rawson, *The Present Operations and Future Prospects of the Mexican Mine Associations Analysed* (London: J. Hatchard and Son, 1825).

47. For a recent account challenging the orthodox view that MacGregor was simply a fraudster, see Clavel, "What's in a Fraud?"

48. Randall, *Real del Monte*, 67, 87.

49. Woodland, *Money Pits*, 19.

50. Henry English, *A Compendium of Useful Information Relating to the Companies Formed for Working British Mines* (London: Boosey & Sons, 1826).

51. English published a third volume, effectively a postmortem of the boom, in 1827: Henry English, *A Complete View of the Joint Stock Companies Formed during the Years 1824 and 1825* (London: Boosey & Sons, 1827).

52. Dilwyn Porter, "Thomas Massa Alsager," *Oxford Dictionary of National Biography*. For examples of these reports, see *The Times*, April 1, 1818, 2; April 17, 1818, 3; April 23, 1818, 3.

53. D. M. Griffiths, "William Innell Clement," *Oxford Dictionary of National Biography*.

54. See, e.g., *Morning Chronicle*, April 4, 1822, 3; June 18, 1822, 3; August 7, 1822, 2.

55. Six company stocks were listed at the end of November: *Morning Chronicle*, November 30, 1824, 2. The number of stocks covered rapidly extended early the following year: see *Morning Chronicle*, January 24, 1825, 2.

56. London dailies copied the *Morning Chronicle*'s regular titled money column from late 1825: *Morning Post*, November 3, 1825, 3; *The Times*, November 12, 1825, 2.

57. Dawson, *Latin American Debt Crisis*, 12–14.

58. Costeloe, *Bonds and Bondholders*, 267.

59. For more on the idea of the stock market representing "the pulse of the people," see Audrey Jaffe, *The Affective Life of the Average Man: The Victorian Novel and the Stock-Market Graph* (Columbus: Ohio State University Press, 2010), 53–54.

60. *Morning Chronicle*, October 29, 1822, 2.

61. *Morning Chronicle*, August 18, 1824, 2.

62. Cited in Costeloe, *Bonds and Bondholders*, 269.

63. James Taylor, "Watchdogs or Apologists? Financial Journalism and Company Fraud in Early Victorian Britain," *Historical Research* 85, no. 230 (2012): 632–50.

64. By the end of 1827, all the Latin American republics had defaulted on their loans: P. L. Cottrell, *British Overseas Investment in the Nineteenth Century* (London: Macmillan, 1975), 19.

65. Anon., "The Morning and Evening Papers," *Fraser's Magazine* 13 (May 1836): 620–21. See also "Politics and Politicians," *London Saturday Journal*, January 18, 1840, 33–35.

66. For more on prospectuses, see Wade E. Shilts, "Accounting, Engineering, or Advertising? Limited Liability, the Company Prospectus, and the Language of Uncertainty in Victorian Britain," *Essays in Economic and Business History* 22, no. 1 (2004): 47–62; Janette Rutterford, "'Propositions Put Forward by Quite Honest Men': Company Prospectuses and Their Contents, 1856 to 1940," *Business History* 53, no. 6 (2011): 866–99.

67. Taylor, *Creating Capitalism*, 130–31.

68. Michie, *London Stock Exchange*, 59.

69. Michie, 60.

70. E. Victor Morgan and W. A. Thomas, *The Stock Exchange: Its History and Functions* (London: Elek Books, 1969), 281.

71. Taylor, *Creating Capitalism*, chap. 4.

72. W. A. Thomas, *The Provincial Stock Exchanges* (Abingdon, UK: Routledge, 2016).

73. Goulven Guilcher, "The Press Mania during the Railway Mania, 1844–45," *Journal of the Railway and Canal Historical Society* 35 (2005): 26.

74. Harold Pollins, "The Marketing of Railway Shares in the First Half of the Nineteenth Century," *Economic History Review* 7, no. 2 (1954): 233.

75. Frank Dobbin and Timothy J. Dowd, "How Policy Shapes Competition: Early Railroad Foundings in Massachusetts," *Administrative Science Quarterly* 42, no. 3 (1997): 506.

76. Robert E. Wright, *Corporation Nation* (Philadelphia: University of Pennsylvania Press, 2014), 4. See also Andrew M. Schocket, *Founding Corporate Power in Early National Philadelphia* (DeKalb: Northern Illinois University Press, 2007).

77. R. C. Michie, *The London and New York Stock Exchanges: 1850–1914* (London: Allen & Unwin, 1987), 167, 170, 171.

78. Joel E. Thompson, "Early Books on Investing at the Dawn of Modern Business in America," *Accounting Historians Journal* 35, no. 1 (2008): 88.

79. New York permitted general incorporation for manufacturing companies as early as 1811 and passed general incorporation statutes for most other organizations between 1847 and 1855: Colleen A. Dunlavy, "From Citizens to Plutocrats: Nineteenth-Century Shareholder Voting Rights and Theories of the Corporation," in *Constructing Corporate America: History, Politics, Culture*, ed. Kenneth Lipartito and David B. Sicilia (Oxford: Oxford University Press, 2004), 79–80; Wright, *Corporation Nation*, 15–16.

80. Douglas Steeples, *Advocate for American Enterprise: William Buck Dana and the "Commercial and Financial Chronicle," 1865–1910* (Westport, CT: Greenwood Press, 2002).

81. Michael J. Cullen, *The Statistical Movement in Early Victorian Britain: The Foundation of Empirical Social Research* (Hassocks, UK: Harvester Press, 1975); Mary Poovey, *A History of the Modern Fact: Problems of Knowledge in the Sciences of Wealth and Society* (Chicago: University of Chicago Press, 1998).

82. Theodore M. Porter, *The Rise of Statistical Thinking, 1820–1900* (1986; Princeton, NJ: Princeton University Press, 2020), xiii.

83. Ruth Dudley Edwards, *The Pursuit of Reason: "The Economist," 1843–1993* (London: Hamish Hamilton, 1993), 1, 273; Wayne Parsons, *The Power of the Financial Press: Journalism and Economic Opinion in Britain and America* (New Brunswick, NJ: Rutgers University Press, 1990), 25–27.

84. Laurie Dennett, *Slaughter and May: A Century in the City* (Cambridge: Granta, 1989), 7–8.

85. *John Bull*, October 18, 1845, 676.

86. Andrew Odlyzko, "The Collapse of the Railway Mania, the Development of Capital Markets, and the Forgotten Role of Robert Lucas Nash," *Accounting History Review* 21, no. 3 (2011): 326.

87. Thompson, "Early Books on Investing," 94.

88. Thompson, 95; Alfred D. Chandler, *Henry Varnum Poor, Business Editor, Analyst, and Reformer* (Cambridge, MA: Harvard University Press, 1956); David P. Forsyth, *The Business Press in America, 1750–1865* (Philadelphia: Chilton, 1964).

89. *Age and Argus*, March 22, 1845, 11.

90. William Frederick Spackman, *An Analysis of the Railway Interest of the United Kingdom* (London: Longman, 1845).

91. Mihill Slaughter, *Railway Intelligence*, no. 9 (London: W. H. Smith and Son, 1857), v.

92. *Birmingham Daily Post*, February 17, 1869, 5. See also *The Times*, January 19, 1857, 4.

93. Dorothy R. Adler, *British Investment in American Railways, 1834–1898* (Charlottesville: University Press of Virginia, 1970), 17.

94. Thompson, "Early Books on Investing," 97.

95. Benjamin Homans, *The United States Railroad Directory, for 1856* (New York: B. Homans, 1856), iii–iv.

96. Thompson, "Early Books on Investing," 99–100.

97. Charles R. Geisst, *Wall Street: A History*, 4th ed. (Oxford: Oxford University Press, 2018), 40.

98. *Economist*, November 25, 1848, 1325.

99. Tamara Plakins Thornton, *Nathaniel Bowditch and the Power of Numbers: How a Nineteenth-Century Man of Business, Science, and the Sea Changed American Life* (Chapel Hill: University of North Carolina Press, 2016), 185.

100. Alex Preda, "The Rise of the Popular Investor: Financial Knowledge and Investing in England and France, 1840–1880," *Sociological Quarterly* 42, no. 2 (2001): 227. An early example of such data is James Vansommer, *Tables, Exhibiting the Various Fluctuations in Three Per Cent. Consols, In Every Month during Each Year from 1789 to 1833 Inclusive* (London: A. H. Baily, 1834). Vansommer was secretary to the Committee of the London Stock Exchange.

101. Elaine Freedgood, *Victorian Writing about Risk: Imagining a Safe England in a Dangerous World* (Cambridge: Cambridge University Press, 2000), 14.

102. Henry Tuck, *The Railway Shareholder's Manual: or, Practical Guide to All the Railways in the World, Completed, in Progress, and Projected*, 8th ed. (London: Effingham Wilson, 1847), xi.

103. See, e.g., *Morning Chronicle*, April 13, 1848, 1; *The Times*, October 27, 1848, 1; *The Times*, November 14, 1848, 4. A bear trader predicts that the market will fall and trades accordingly.

104. Alborn, *Conceiving Capitalism*, 193. Spackman denied this: *The Times*, November 20, 1845, 2. See also Gareth Campbell, John D. Turner, and Clive B. Walker, "The Role of the Media in a Bubble," *Explorations in Economic History* 49, no. 4 (2012): 461–81.

105. *Daily News*, October 13, 1848, 4; Odlyzko, "Collapse of the Railway Mania," 330–32. Undeterred, in 1848 Nash established the *Money Market Examiner and Railway Review* as a vehicle for his railway analyses.

106. Sir Henry Burdett, *Burdett's Official Intelligence for 1898* (London: Spottiswoode, 1898), 7.

107. The nineteenth-century market for "practical knowledge" was a lucrative one: Aileen Fyfe, "The Information Revolution," in *The Cambridge History of the Book in Britain*, vol. vi, *1830–1914*, ed. David McKitterick (Cambridge: Cambridge University Press, 2009), 585.

108. Stephen Greenblatt, *Renaissance Self-Fashioning: From More to Shakespeare* (1980; Chicago: University of Chicago Press, 2005), 2.

109. Jeremy Daniel Kaye, "Between Self-Improvement and Self-Destruction: The Male Conduct Manual in the Consumer Society" (PhD diss., University of California, Riverside, 2008), 5–6.

110. James Vernon, *Distant Strangers: How Britain Became Modern* (Berkeley: University of California Press, 2014), 22.

111. Maria Damkjær, *Time, Domesticity and Print Culture in Nineteenth-Century Britain* (Basingstoke: Palgrave Macmillan, 2016), 120–21.

112. For a British equivalent, see Anon., *Success in Life: A Book for Young Men* (London: T. Nelson and Sons, 1851).

113. Malcolm Chase, "'An Overpowering "Itch for Writing"': R. K. Philp, John Denman and the Culture of Self-Improvement," *English Historical Review* 133, no. 561 (2018): 380.

114. J. F. C. Harrison, "The Victorian Gospel of Success," *Victorian Studies* 1, no. 2 (1957): 160. This was a technique used particularly frequently by the authors of primers on the emerging "science" of political economy, like Jane Marcet, to present inequalities between rich and poor as incontestable and inevitable: Hilda Hollis, "The Rhetoric of Jane Marcet's Popularizing Political Economy," *Nineteenth-Century Contexts* 24, no. 4 (2002): 391–92.

115. Michael Zakim, *Accounting for Capitalism: The World the Clerk Made* (Chicago: University of Chicago Press, 2018), 86.

116. Edwin T. Freedley, *A Practical Treatise on Business: or, How to Get, Save, Spend, Give, Lend, and Bequeath Money: With an Inquiry into the Chances of Success and Causes of Failure in Business* (Philadelphia: Lippincott, Grambo, 1853), 165–71.

117. Freeman Hunt, *Worth and Wealth: A Collection of Maxims, Morals and Miscellanies for Merchants and Men of Business* (New York: Stringer & Townsend, 1856), xii, 73.

118. *Open Sesame! Or, The Way to Get Money, By A Rich Man Who Was Once Poor* (London: Thomas Griffiths, 1832), 14–15.

119. *Glasgow Citizen*, June 14, 1845, 2; William Quinn and John D. Turner, *Boom and Bust: A Global History of Financial Bubbles* (Cambridge: Cambridge University Press, 2020), 69.

120. Early editions of the former retailed at 6d, increasing to 1s for the eighth, expanded edition of 1846.

121. Extracts from *A Short and Sure Guide* appeared in, among others, the *Leicester Journal and Midland Counties General Advertiser*, the *York Herald*,

Woolmer's Exeter and Plymouth Gazette, and the *Fife Advertiser* in September 1845.

122. Henry Wilson, *Hints to Railroad Speculators, Together with the Influence Railroads Will Have upon Society in Promoting Agriculture, Commerce, and Manufacturers* (London: Henry Wilson, 1845), 5; see also An Observer, *Ten Minutes' Advice to Speculators in Railway Shares* (London: W. Strange, n.d.), 4–5.

123. One of the Initiated, *The Railway Investment Guide: How to Make Money by Railway Shares; Being a Series of Hints and Advice to Parties Speculating in the Shares of British, Colonial, and Foreign Railways* (London: G. Mann, 1845), 3.

124. One of the Initiated, *Railway Investment Guide*, 4.

125. *The Railway Shareholder's Pocket Book and Almanack for 1846* (London: D. Bogue, [1845]), 56; One of the Initiated, *Railway Investment Guide*, 8. See also Successful Operator, *Short and Sure Guide to Railway Speculation: A Few Plain Rules How to Speculate with Safety and Profit in Railway Shares*, 7th ed. (London: Effingham Wilson, 1845), 9. Wilson, by contrast, warned readers that impressive-sounding names alone were no protection: Wilson, *Hints to Railroad Speculators*, 4.

126. One of the Initiated, *Railway Investment Guide*, 5–7.

127. Successful Operator, *Short and Sure Guide to Railway Speculation*.

128. Successful Operator, *Short and Sure Guide to Railway Speculation*, 6–12.

129. *Railway Shareholder's Pocket Book*, 57.

130. Unus Post Scenum, *The Railway Speculator's Memorandum Book, Ledger, and General Guide to Secure Share Dealing* (London: Simpkins & Marshall, 1845), 3–5.

131. Gareth Campbell, "Deriving the Railway Mania," *Financial History Review* 20, no. 1 (2013): 6.

132. A Successful Operator, *A Short and Sure Guide to Permanent Investments in Railways: A Few Plain Rules How to Invest and Speculate with Safety and Profit in Railway Shares* (London: Effingham Wilson, 1846), 8th ed., 8.

133. James Taylor, *Boardroom Scandal: The Criminalization of Company Fraud in Nineteenth-Century Britain* (Oxford: Oxford University Press, 2013), 84–89.

134. Robert Frank Cleveland, *Are Railways a Good Investment? The Question Considered by an Examination of the Last Half-Yearly Statements of the Six Leading Companies* (London: Effingham Wilson, 1848), 3.

135. John Blackham and A. Hickey, *Advice to Promoters, Subscribers, Scripholders, and Shareholders, of Joint-Stock and Railway Companies* (Dublin: Edward J. Milliken, 1846), 2.

136. George Cochrane, *The Way to Make Railroad Shares Popular* (London: Longman, Brown, Green, and Longmans, 1846).

137. Prices only bottomed out at the end of 1849: Odlyzko, "Collapse of the Railway Mania," 310–11.

138. R. W. Kostal, *Law and English Railway Capitalism, 1825–1875* (Oxford: Clarendon Press, 1997), 53.

139. Michie, *London Stock Exchange*, 64.

140. Ranald C. Michie, "Gamblers, Fools, Victims, or Wizards? The British Investor in the Public Mind, 1850–1930," in *Men, Women, and Money: Perspectives on Gender, Wealth, and Investment, 1850–1930,* ed. David R. Green, Alastair Owens, Josephine Maltby, and Janette Rutterford (Oxford: Oxford University Press, 2011), 156.

141. *Bury and Norwich Post*, January 19, 1858, 2.

142. Well-publicized cases of fraud by such personal advisers may also have discouraged some from approaching them: George Robb, *White-Collar Crime in Modern England: Financial Fraud and Business Morality, 1845–1929* (Cambridge: Cambridge University Press, 1992), 91–92.

143. "Dot," *The Stock Exchange and Its Victims* (London: G. Cox, 1851); Anon., *Exposure of the Stock Exchange and Bubble Companies: Dedicated to the Victims of Time Bargains and the Public Generally* (London: Piper, Stephenson, and Spence, 1854).

144. *Daily News*, January 21, 1846, 7. In 1846, Mitchell began publishing the *Newspaper Press Directory*, for which he would become best known: Laurel Brake, "Nineteenth-Century Newspaper Press Directories: The National Gallery of the British Press," *Victorian Periodicals Review* 48, no. 4 (2015): 569–90.

145. Eric W. Nye, "Effingham Wilson: The Radical Publisher of the Royal Exchange," *Publishing History* 36 (1994): 92. The first edition of Fenn was published by Sherwood, Gilbert, and Piper, but all subsequent editions were published by Effingham Wilson.

146. G. M. Bell, *Guide to the Investment of Capital; or, How to Lay out Money with Safety and Profit* (London: C. Mitchell, 1846), 8.

147. T. S. Harvey, *What Shall I Do with My Money? Or, Thoughts about Safe Investments* (London, D. Steel, 1849), 5.

148. For more on corporate fraud in the 1840s, see Taylor, *Boardroom Scandal*, chap. 4.

149. Financial journalists played a similar game: Taylor, "Watchdogs or Apologists?"

150. Bell, *Guide to the Investment of Capital*, 45.

151. T. S. Harvey, *What Shall I Do with My Money? Or, Thoughts about Safe Investments*, 4th ed. (London, D. Steel, 1852), 36, 26.

152. Jasper Schelstraete, *Incorporation, Authorship, and Anglo-American Literature (1815–1918)* (New York: Routledge, 2020), 62. By contrast, private firms were thought to be more easily "read," inhabiting a sphere of greater "representational stability": Aeron Hunt, "Open Accounts: Harriet Martineau and the Problem of Privacy in Early-Victorian Culture," *Nineteenth-Century Literature* 62, no. 1 (2007): 10–11.

153. Charles Dickens, *Martin Chuzzlewit* (1844; Ware, Herts: Wordsworth, 1994), 397; Robert Arthur Ward, *A Treatise on Investments: Being a Popular Exposition of*

the Advantages and Disadvantages of Each Kind of Investment, and of Its Liability to Depreciation and Loss, 2nd ed. (London: Effingham Wilson, 1852), 92–93.

154. Ward's guide was different in that its focus, particularly in the first edition, was less on the stock market than investments in land and property, and with an emphasis throughout on legal liabilities. However, the sections on stocks and shares broadly followed the sector-by-sector structure.

155. Ward, Treatise on Investments, 2nd ed., 184–85.

156. Ward, Treatise on Investments, 2nd ed., 6. The usury laws were repealed in 1854: Boyd Hilton, The Age of Atonement: The Influence of Evangelicalism on Social and Economic Thought, 1785–1865 (Oxford: Clarendon Press, 1986), 144.

157. Harvey, What Shall I Do with My Money?, 4th ed., 16.

158. Bell, Guide to the Investment of Capital, 100–101.

159. Ward, Treatise on Investments, 1. See also Harvey, What Shall I Do with My Money?, 4th ed., 33–36.

160. Ward, Treatise on Investments, 2.

161. Bell, Guide to the Investment of Capital, 39–40.

162. Harvey, What Shall I Do with My Money?, 4th ed., 27–28.

163. Mark Freeman, Robin Pearson, and James Taylor, Shareholder Democracies? Corporate Governance in Britain and Ireland before 1850 (Chicago: University of Chicago Press, 2012).

164. Harvey, What Shall I Do with My Money?, 4th ed., 36–37.

165. T. S. Harvey, What Shall I Do with My Money? Or, Thoughts about Safe Investments, 7th ed. (London: Washbourne, 1858), 71. Here Harvey is quoting from Herapath's Journal.

166. Harvey, What Shall I Do with My Money?, 4th ed., 39.

167. Harvey, What Shall I Do with My Money?, 7th ed., 71.

168. In this respect, it is perhaps significant that, unlike the anonymous authors of the railway mania guides, Bell, Harvey, and Ward were much more upfront about their credentials.

169. Stamford Mercury, November 12, 1852, 2.

170. Ward, Treatise on Investments, 2–3.

171. Newcastle Guardian, November 20, 1852, 3. See also Railway Record, September 11, 1852, 593.

172. Sunday Times, August 29, 1852, 2.

173. A belated third edition appeared in 1871.

174. The Times, June 4, 1846, 7.

175. Royal Cornwall Gazette, Falmouth Packet, and General Advertiser, November 9, 1858, 6; Cheltenham Chronicle and Parish Register and General Advertiser for Gloucester, December 7, 1858, 6.

176. Nancy Henry, "'Ladies Do It?': Victorian Women Investors in Fact and Fiction," in Victorian Literature and Finance, ed. Francis O'Gorman (Oxford: Oxford University Press, 2008), 119.

177. Wright, *Corporation Nation*, 59; Taylor, *Creating Capitalism*, chap. 4.

178. H. A. Shannon, "The First Five Thousand Limited Companies and Their Duration," *Economic History* 3 (1932): 421; P. L. Cottrell, *Industrial Finance, 1830–1914: The Finance and Organization of English Manufacturing Industry* (London: Methuen, 1980), 80.

179. Robert Bell, *The Ladder of Gold* (London: Richard Bentley, 1850); Emma Robinson, *The Gold-Worshippers: or, The Days We Live In* (London: Parry, 1851); A. MacFarlane, *Railway Scrip; or, The Evils of Speculation: A Tale of the Railway Mania* (London: Ward & Lock, 1856).

180. John R. Reed, *Victorian Conventions* (Athens: Ohio University Press, 1985), 181–86; Jonathan Rose, "Was Capitalism Good for Victorian Literature?" *Victorian Studies* 46, no. 3 (2004): 489–501.

181. Monroe Lippman, "The American Playwright Looks at Business," *Educational Theatre Journal* 12, no. 2 (1960): 98–99. The latter play was inspired by the rise and fall of the Life and Fire Insurance Company: Eric Hilt, "Rogue Finance: The Life and Fire Insurance Company and the Panic of 1826," *Business History Review* 83, no. 1 (2009): 89n9.

182. [Frederick Jackson], *A Week in Wall Street. By One Who Knows* (New York, 1841), 43–45. For more on Jackson, see María Carla Sánchez, *Social Activism and the Problem of Fiction in Nineteenth-Century America* (Iowa City: University of Iowa Press, 2008), chap. 2.

183. Several examples are discussed in George Robb, *Ladies of the Ticker: Women and Wall Street from the Gilded Age to the Great Depression* (Urbana: University of Illinois Press, 2017), chap. 1.

184. A Reformed Stock Gambler, *Stocks and Stock-Jobbing in Wall-Street, with Sketches of the Brokers, and Fancy Stocks* (New York: New-York Publishing, 1848), preface (n.p.), 6, 7, 12, 17–18. "Intrinsic value," as we have seen in the previous chapter, was a term occasionally used in the eighteenth century which was becoming more widely discussed by the mid-nineteenth century: Nash in his *Money Market Examiner* was also using it: see, e.g., December 16, 1848, 25; December 23, 1848, 37; February 17, 1849, 133.

185. A Reformed Stock Gambler, *Stocks and Stock-Jobbing*, 23.

186. A Reformed Stock Gambler, 16. For more on the "reformed gambler" confessional trope, see Ann Fabian, *Card Sharps and Bucket Shops: Gambling in Nineteenth-Century America* (Abingdon, UK: Routledge, 2013), chap. 2.

187. A Reformed Stock Gambler, *Stocks and Stock-Jobbing*, preface.

188. D. Morier Evans, *Fortune's Epitome of the Stocks and Public Funds, English, Foreign & American: Containing Every Necessary Information for Understanding the Nature of Those Securities, and the Manner of Transacting Business Therein*, 16th ed. (London: Letts, Son and Steer, 1851), 289.

189. *National Magazine* 11, no. 62 (December 1861): 56–57.

190. Sir Thomas Gresham founded the Royal Exchange in the sixteenth century,

while "Omnium" was the name for new issues of government debt. Other guides from the time include Anthony Madders, *A Practical Guide for Conducting Transactions in the Government Funds and Other Securities* (London: Groombridge & Sons, 1855) and Anon., *The Hand-Book of Investments: Being a Complete Account of Government Stocks, Railway Shares, Foreign Stocks, and Miscellaneous Securities* (London: Cassell, Petter & Galpin, 1861).

191. Rosemary Mims Fisk, "The *Marble Faun* and the English Copyright: The Smith, Elder Contract," *Studies in the American Renaissance* (1995): 267–68; B. E. Maidment, *Reading Popular Prints: 1790–1870*, 2nd ed. (Manchester: Manchester University Press, 2001), 109.

192. *The Critic*, February 1, 1856, 72. See also *Reading Mercury*, January 26, 1856, 2; *Western Times*, January 26, 1856, 8; *Morning Post*, February 7, 1856, 2; *Morning Chronicle*, March 24, 1856, 3. Capel Court was where the entrance to the London Stock Exchange was located, and was often used as shorthand for the Exchange itself.

193. Francis Playford, *Practical Hints for Investing Money: With an Explanation of the Mode of Transacting Business on the Stock Exchange* (London: Smith, Elder, 1855), v–vi, 58, iii–iv. Omnium was somewhat more critical of time-bargains: Gresham Omnium, *A Handy Guide to Safe Investments* (London: Groombridge & Sons, 1858), 40.

194. Omnium, *Handy Guide*, iv. Omnium's status as member is not spelled out, but he gives his address as Capel Court in the preface.

195. Playford, *Practical Hints*, 10, 60–61.

196. Omnium, *Handy Guide*, 113–14.

197. David C. Itzkowitz, "Fair Enterprise or Extravagant Speculation: Investment, Speculation, and Gambling in Victorian England," *Victorian Studies* 45, no. 1 (2002): 121–47; Taylor, "Inside and Outside."

198. Old Chatty Cheerful, *What Shall I Do with My Money?* (London: Jarrold and Sons, [1864]).

199. Mining investment literature had an earlier history but was circulating much more extensively by the 1850s. Earlier examples include George Abbott Jr., *An Essay on the Mines of England; Their Importance as a Source of National Wealth, and as a Channel for the Advantageous Employment of Private Capital* (London: privately printed, 1833); Anon., *A Brief Address on Mining in Cornwall, Demonstrating Some of the Advantages Resulting to Commerce, and the Profit to Capitalists by Investment in These National Undertakings* (London: F. Waller, 1835); Joseph Yelloly Watson, *A Compendium of British Mining, with Statistical Notices of the Principal Mines in Cornwall* (London: privately printed, 1843).

200. For the bank failures, see James Taylor, "Commercial Fraud and Public Men in Victorian Britain," *Historical Research* 78, no. 200 (2005): 230–52.

201. For these arguments, see J. H. Murchison, *British Mines Considered as a Means of Investment*, 2nd ed. (London: Mann, Nephews, 1855); R. Tredinnick, *A

Review of Cornish and Devon Mining Enterprise, 1850 to 1856 Inclusive (London: Thompson & Vincent, 1857); Richard Tredinnick, *A Review of Cornish Copper Mining Enterprise*, 2nd ed. (London: Thompson & Vincent, 1858).

202. Murchison, *British Mines Considered*, 22.

203. Henry Gould Sharp, *Investments for Capital (To Pay from 15 to 25 Per Cent. Per Annum): A Useful Guide for Small and Large Capitalists* (London, 1858), 1; Henry Gould Sharp, *The Capitalist's Guide; or, Cornish and Devon Mining Investments* (London, 1859), 3.

204. The pamphlet is undated but was advertised in the press in 1857: *Weekly Dispatch*, August 23, 1857, 13. The title page bears an alternative title: *How to Make Money in the Stock Exchange, Bank and Mining Shares, Land Lots, &c.; or, Hints to Speculators*.

205. A Late M.P., *How to Make Money, and Plenty of It; or, Hints on Speculation*, 21st ed. (Birmingham: William Cornish [1857]), cover, 3, 9.

206. A Late M.P., 14, 35, 39-42.

207. Cornish ran a "cheap book establishment" on New Street: *Birmingham Journal*, December 5, 1857, 4.

208. A City Man, *The Bubbles of Finance: Joint-Stock Companies, Promoting of Companies, Modern Commerce, Money Lending, and Life Insuring* (London: Sampson Low, 1865); Anon., *The Profits of Panics; Showing How Financial Storms Arise, Who Makes Money by Them, Who Are the Losers, and Other Revelations of a City Man* (London: Sampson Low, 1866). For more on Meason, see Daniel P. Scoggin, "A Speculative Resurrection: Death, Money, and the Vampiric Economy of *Our Mutual Friend*," *Victorian Literature and Culture* 30, no. 1 (2002): 99-125.

209. Overend & Gurney was a "discount house," discounting bills of exchange and taking deposits, rather than a bank. Its straitened finances were not mentioned in its prospectus: Taylor, *Boardroom Scandal*, 143-44, 150-51.

210. Anon., *Profits of Panics*, preface.

211. "The Stock Exchange," *Chambers's Journal*, June 10, 1865, 366-68.

212. Urs Stäheli, *Spectacular Speculation: Thrills, the Economy, and Popular Discourse* (Stanford, CA: Stanford University Press, 2013), 176. See also Marieke de Goede, *Virtue, Fortune, and Faith: A Genealogy of Finance* (Minneapolis: University of Minnesota Press, 2005), chap. 2.

213. George Robb, "Women and White-Collar Crime," *British Journal of Criminology* 46, no. 6 (2006): 1060. For the 1870 act, see Mary Beth Combs, "*Cui Bono?* The 1870 British Married Women's Property Act, Bargaining Power, and the Distribution of Resources within Marriage," *Feminist Economics* 12, no. 1-2 (2006): 51-83.

214. Dena Attar, *A Bibliography of Household Books Published in Britain, 1800-1914* (London: Prospect Books, 1987), 34.

215. Attar, *Bibliography of Household Books*, 13-14. Though it should be noted that women's self-help literature did not solely target married women: Melissa

Walker, "On Their Own: The Single Woman, Feminism, and Self-Help in British Women's Print Culture (1850–1900)" (PhD diss., University of Guelph, 2012).

216. S. P. Walker, "How to Secure Your Husband's Esteem: Accounting and Private Patriarchy in the British Middle Class Household during the Nineteenth Century," *Accounting, Organizations and Society* 23, no. 5–6 (1998): 485–514.

217. [Maria Rundell], *A New System of Domestic Cookery; Formed upon Principles of Economy: And Adapted to the Use of Private Families*, new ed. (London: John Murray, 1810), vii–x; Isabella Beeton, *The Book of Household Management* (London: S. O. Beeton, 1861), 6.

218. Beeton, *Book of Household Management*, 1; Walker, "How to Secure," 509.

219. David R. Green and Alastair Owens, "Gentlewomanly Capitalism? Spinsters, Widows, and Wealth Holding in England and Wales, c. 1800–1860," *Economic History Review* 56, no. 3 (2003): 524–25. Though their holdings were smaller than men's, they were still significant, at 32.1 percent by 1840.

220. Sarah J. Hudson, "Attitudes to Investment Risk amongst West Midland Canal and Railway Company Investors, 1760–1850" (PhD diss., University of Warwick, 2001), 152.

221. Janette Rutterford and Josephine Maltby, "'The Widow, the Clergyman and the Reckless': Women Investors in England, 1830–1914," *Feminist Economics* 12, no. 1–2 (2006): 124–25.

222. Robb, "Women and White-Collar Crime."

223. Nancy Henry, *Women, Literature and Finance in Victorian Britain: Cultures of Investment* (Cham: Palgrave Macmillan, 2018), 43; Freeman, Pearson, and Taylor, *Shareholder Democracies*, 125–27.

224. Janette Rutterford and Josephine Maltby, "'The Nesting Instinct': Women and Investment Risk in a Historical Context," *Accounting History* 12, no. 3 (2007): 318; Robb, *Ladies of the Ticker*, chap. 2.

225. *La Belle Assemblée*, December 1, 1822, 509.

226. Kathryn Ledbetter, "Bonnets and Rebellions: Imperialism in *The Lady's Newspaper*," *Victorian Periodicals Review* 37, no. 3 (2004): 252–72. For an example of its money-market report, see *Lady's Newspaper*, December 8, 1855, 359.

227. *Ladies' Treasury*, January 1, 1858, 8.

228. *Englishwoman's Domestic Magazine*, March 1, 1863, 229–31; Robb, "Women and White-Collar Crime," 1064–65; Robb, *Ladies of the Ticker*, 27.

229. "The Railway Queen," *Bentley's Miscellany* 18 (July 1845): 387.

230. Jennifer Phegley, *Educating the Proper Woman Reader: Victorian Family Literary Magazines and the Cultural Health of the Nation* (Columbus: Ohio State University Press, 2004), 1–2.

231. *The Letters of Charlotte Brontë: With a Selection of Letters by Family and Friends*, vol. 1: *1829–1847*, edited by Margaret Smith (Oxford: Clarendon, 1995), 390.

232. Taylor, "Watchdogs or Apologists?"; "Who Starved Kars?" *Saturday Review*, April 26, 1856, 516–17.

233. Teresa Gerrard, "New Methods in the History of Reading: 'Answers to Correspondents' in the *Family Herald*, 1860–1900," *Publishing History* 43 (1998): 53–69.

234. *Lloyd's Weekly Newspaper*, May 19, 1861, 6. For other examples, see *Birmingham Daily Post*, December 7, 1863, 3; *Liverpool Mercury*, April 19, 1865, 6.

235. Karl Pearson, *The Life, Letters and Labours of Francis Galton* (Cambridge: Cambridge University Press, 1914), i, 162.

236. A Banker's Daughter, *A Guide to the Unprotected in Every-Day Matters Relating to Property and Income* (London: Macmillan, 1863), vi.

237. A Banker's Daughter, 10–11. In British terminology, a debenture is a type of company debt instrument which pays a fixed rate of interest and secured against an asset. In the United States, it is an unsecured loan. A preference share pays a fixed dividend which is paid before dividends are paid to ordinary shareholders. Therefore, British debentures and preference shares are lower risk than unsecured debt and ordinary shares in the same company.

238. A Banker's Daughter, 10, 13.

239. Typescript extracts from Galton's diary give only a terse outline of her life's activities, but the entry "July 13th, Unprotected came out!!" betrays much pride in her achievement. Typescript Extracts from Miss Galton's Diary, 12: UCL Special Collections, GALTON/1/1/9/3, https://wellcomelibrary.org/item/b20629217#?c=0&m=0&s=0&cv=12&z=-0.8004%2C0%2C2.6008%2C1.2513.

240. A Banker's Daughter, *Guide to the Unprotected*, 13–14.

241. *John Bull*, August 15, 1863, 523. See also *London Review*, August 15, 1863, 179.

242. Rutterford and Maltby, "The Widow, the Clergyman and the Reckless," 120; Robb, *White-Collar Crime*, 185, 190.

243. A Banker's Daughter, *First Lessons in Business Matters* (London: Macmillan, 1875).

244. "Ladies and Their Money," *Englishwoman's Domestic Magazine*, January 1, 1864, 112–17.

245. *Beeton's Guide to Investing Money with Safety and Profit* (London: Ward, Lock, and Tyler, 1870), 53–54.

246. Beeton, by now a widower, continued to write prodigiously for Ward, Lock, and Tyler: Margaret Beetham, "Samuel Orchart Beeton," *Oxford Dictionary of National Biography*.

247. Robert Arthur Ward, *Notes on Joint-Stock Companies* (London: Effingham Wilson, 1865), 4–5.

248. Geisst, *Wall Street*, 36–39.

249. Lance E. Davis and Robert A. Huttenback, *Mammon and the Pursuit of Empire: The Political Economy of British Imperialism, 1860–1912* (Cambridge: Cambridge University Press, 1986), chap. 2; Benjamin R. Chabot and Christopher J. Kurz, "That's Where the Money Was: Foreign Bias and English Investment Abroad, 1866–1907," *Economic Journal* 120, no. 547 (2010): 1056–79.

250. *Western Flying Post*, September 13, 1864, 5.

251. *Economist*, May 7, 1864, 575–76. That said, many investors preferred to stick with local investments, traded on provincial stock exchanges, over which they could exercise a greater degree of oversight. One recent study has shown that in the 1870s, nearly 70 percent of investors sampled lived within fifteen miles of firms' registered headquarters: Janette Rutterford, Dimitris P. Sotiropoulos, and Carry Van Lieshout, "Individual Investors and Local Bias in the UK, 1870–1935," *Economic History Review* 70, no. 4 (2017): 1316. This declined to 35 percent by the 1930s.

252. *The Standard*, January 24, 1865, 2. Ebbw Vale and Rhymney are both located in south Wales.

253. The contrasting positions on the imperial-mindedness of British investors are summarized in Andrew Smith, "Patriotism, Self-Interest and the "Empire Effect": Britishness and British Decisions to Invest in Canada, 1867–1914," *Journal of Imperial and Commonwealth History* 41, no. 1 (2013): 59–80. See also Gary B. Magee and Andrew S. Thompson, *Empire and Globalisation: Networks of People, Goods and Capital in the British World, c. 1850–1914* (Cambridge: Cambridge University Press, 2010), chap. 5.

254. Smith, "Patriotism," 66–71; David Sunderland, *Financing the Raj: The City of London and Colonial India, 1858–1940* (Cambridge: Cambridge University Press, 2013), 30–31. The government guarantee of a 5 percent return on Indian railways made them a particularly attractive investment, easy to recommend to risk-averse capitalists: *The Government Guarantee on Indian Railways* (London: William H. Allen, 1861); John Whitehead, *Indian Railways Described; The Government Contract Explained: With a Map, and the Contract in Full* (London: Messrs. J. & J. Whitehead's, 1862); W. J. Macpherson, "Investment in Indian Railways, 1845–1875," *Economic History Review* 8, no. 2 (1955): 177–86.

255. Smith, "Patriotism," 61. For an example, see William Bartlett and Henry Chapman, *A Handy-Book for Investors; Comprising a Sketch of the Rise, Progress, and Present Character of Every Species of Investment, British, Colonial, and Foreign; Including an Estimate of Their Comparative Safety and Profit* (London: Effingham Wilson, 1869), 79.

256. This resulted in a language of what Marc Flandreau terms "financial racism," drawing on national and racial stereotypes to create moral hierarchies of risk. Marc Flandreau, *Anthropologists in the Stock Exchange: A Financial History of Victorian Science* (Chicago: University of Chicago Press, 2016), 79.

257. *The Investors' Guardian Almanack for 1869. Containing a Classified Arrangement of Securities and Investments, According to Their Relative Value* (London: James Y. Jackson, [1869]), 7–11. For an example of overtly racist language to describe Latin American loans, see *The World*, March 3, 1875, 8.

258. E. G. Squier, *Notes on Central America; Particularly the States of Honduras and San Salvador* (London: Sampson Low, Son, 1856), 135, 72. See also E. G.

Squier, *Honduras Interoceanic Railway: With Maps of the Line and Ports* (London: Trübner, 1857).

259. Charles L. Stansifer, "E. George Squier and the Honduras Interoceanic Railroad Project," *Hispanic American Historical Review* 46, no. 1 (1966): 1–27.

260. *Select Committee on Making of Contracts for Loans to Foreign States*, Parliamentary Papers, 1875, XI. 1; 95. The book, *Honduras, Descriptive, Historical, and Statistical*, secured positive reviews in the press: *Examiner*, October 29, 1870, 694–95; *Athenaeum*, October 29, 1870, 558. The latter review did query some of Squier's statistics.

261. A Manchester Man, *A Guide to Indian Investments* (London: Trübner, 1861), 3.

262. An Anglo-American, *American Securities: Practical Hints on the Tests of Stability and Profit for the Guidance and Warning of British Investors* (London: Mann Nephews, 1860), 3. For postbellum literature encouraging investment in the United States, see Belding, Keith & Co., *United States Bonds and Securities: What They Are—Their Cost—and the Interest They Pay* (London: Cassell, Petter & Galpin, 1867); Robert Giffen, *American Railways as Investments* (London: Edward Stanford, 1872).

263. The Californian and Australian gold rushes of the late 1840s and early 1850s also generated a substantial promotional literature. For examples, see: William H. Hall, *Practical Experience at the Diggings of the Gold Fields of Victoria* (London: Effingham Wilson, 1852); R. M. Thomas, *The Present State of Melbourne: And the Gold Fields of Victoria* (London: W. Kent, 1853).

264. Though no British banks were willing to promote the sale of Union bonds, 1863 saw the successful flotation of a loan for the Confederate cause on the London and Liverpool markets, which was more than five times oversubscribed: Jay Sexton, "Transatlantic Financiers and the Civil War," *American Nineteenth Century History* 2, no. 3 (2001): 39–40; John D. Bennett, *The Officials, Clergy, Businessmen and Journalists Who Backed the American South during the Civil War* (Jefferson, NC: McFarland, 2008), 87–94; Judith Fenner Gentry, "A Confederate Success in Europe: The Erlanger Loan," *Journal of Southern History* 36, no. 2 (1970): 157–88.

265. Clarke C. Spence, "When the Pound Sterling Went West: British Investments and the American Mineral Frontier," *Journal of Economic History* 16, no. 4 (1956): 484.

266. Donald Nerbas, "Empire, Colonial Enterprise, and Speculation: Cape Breton's Coal Boom of the 1860s," *Journal of Imperial and Commonwealth History* 46, no. 6 (2018): 1083–85.

267. José Augusto Ribas Miranda, "Small Money, Big Problems: How an Investigation on Small Latin American Republics Shaped the Financial Market for Sovereign Debt in the 19th Century," *Estudos Históricos* 30, no. 60 (2017): 64; Flandreau, *Anthropologists*, 85–86.

268. Charles Edward Lewis, *Select Committee on Making of Contracts for Loans to Foreign States*, 211.

269. *Economist*, August 14, 1875, 959.

270. Harrison argues that in the hands of authors like Smiles, self-help, initially a radical principle, was increasingly "integrated into the dominant individualist philosophy of the middle class": Harrison, "Victorian Gospel of Success," 163.

271. *The Times*, January 21, 1856, 7.

272. "Numbingly repetitive" advice was a feature of other types of self-help literature: Dara Rossman Regaignon, "Anxious Uptakes: Nineteenth-Century Advice Literature as a Rhetorical Genre," *College English* 78, no. 2 (2015): 148–49, 156.

273. A Banker's Daughter, *Guide to the Unprotected*, 108.

Chapter Three

1. *Daily Telegraph*, July 15, 1907, 3; *The Times*, July 17, 1907, 4; *Daily Mail*, July 27, 1907, 3.

2. *Old Bailey Proceedings Online* (www.oldbaileyonline.org, version 8.0, August 14, 2020), July 1907, trial of LESLIE, Marie Josephine (39) (t19070722–52).

3. For just a few examples of press coverage, see *Daily Mail*, February 5, 1898, 3; *Courier and Argus*, March 2, 1901, 5; *Devon and Exeter Daily Gazette*, May 6, 1905, 5.

4. *Daily Mail*, February 22, 1901, 7.

5. There has been considerable debate about the precise figures, but all agree that both the absolute numbers and the percentage of each population holding securities was still comparatively low in this period, with the real surge coming after the First World War. For good summaries of previous estimates and a consideration of the methodologies used to calculate the numbers, see Julia C. Ott, *When Wall Street Met Main Street: The Quest for an Investors' Democracy* (Cambridge, MA: Harvard University Press, 2011), 2; and Janette Rutterford and Dimitris P. Sotiropoulos, "The Rise of the Small Investor in the United States and United Kingdom, 1895 to 1970," *Enterprise & Society* 18, no. 3 (2017): 495–501. Ott suggests that only 0.5 percent of Americans owned stocks or bonds in 1900, while Rutterford and Sotiropoulos estimate that in 1907 in the United Kingdom there were approximately 1.1 million shareholders (2.4% of the population), while in the United States there were 0.8 million (0.9% of the population).

6. George Gregory and Company, *Hints to Speculators and Investors in Stocks and Shares*, 5th ed. (London: George Gregory, 1889), 5.

7. On the changes to the international investing culture resulting from the panic of 1873, see Hannah Catherine Davies, *Transatlantic Speculations: Globalization and the Panics of 1873* (New York: Columbia University Press, 2018).

8. The story of the changing legal regime of incorporation is documented by William G. Roy, *Socializing Capital: The Rise of the Large Industrial Corporation in America* (Princeton, NJ: Princeton University Press, 1999); and Charles Perrow, *Organizing America: Wealth, Power, and the Origins of Corporate Capitalism* (Princeton, NJ: Princeton University Press, 2002).

9. Joel E. Thompson, "Early Books on Investing at the Dawn of Modern Business in America," *Accounting Historians Journal* 35, no. 1 (2008): 83–110.

10. Robert Sobel, *The Big Board: A History of the New York Stock Market* (New York: Free Press, 1965), 103; Norton Reamer and Jesse Downing, *Investment: A History* (New York: Columbia University Press, 2016), 89.

11. Ranald C. Michie, *The London Stock Exchange: A History* (Oxford: Oxford University Press, 2001), 95.

12. Mary A. O'Sullivan, *Dividends of Development: Securities Markets in the History of U.S. Capitalism, 1866–1922* (Oxford: Oxford University Press, 2016).

13. Janette Rutterford, David R. Green, Josephine Maltby, and Alastair Owens, "Who Comprised the Nation of Shareholders? Gender and Investment in Great Britain, c. 1870–1935," *Economic History Review* 64, no. 1 (2011): 157–87.

14. Janice M. Traflet and Michael P. Coyne, "Ending a NYSE Tradition: The 1975 Unraveling of Brokers' Fixed Commissions and Its Long Term Impact on Financial Advertising," *Essays in Economic and Business History* 25 (2007), 136–37, 140n25.

15. "The Golden Calf: High-Class Bunco Steering," *Town Topics*, February 24, 1887, 14.

16. David Kynaston, "The London Stock Exchange, 1870–1914: An Institutional History" (PhD diss., University of London, 1983), 325–26.

17. See, e.g., Ernest B. Wallis, *Hints to Small Investors: A Practical Handbook and Guide for Their Use* (London: The Money-Maker, 1901), 5; and G. Bartrick-Baker, *Sound Investments for Small Savings* (London: J. S. Virtue, 1889), v.

18. *On the Stock Exchange: An Explanation of Stocks and Stock-Jobbing and A Complete Manual of Stock Exchange Practice and Customs* (London: Charles and Edwin Layton, 1877), iii.

19. William Relton, *Saving and Growing Money* (London: John Heywood, 1887); R. Denny Urlin, *Hints on Business, Financial and Legal* (London: Suttaby, 1884); William Harman Black, *The Real Wall Street: An Understandable Description of a Purchase, A Sale, A "Short Sale," with Forms, Definitions, Rules Etc.* (New York: Corporations Organization, 1908).

20. Robert Giffen, *Stock Exchange Securities: An Essay on the General Causes of Fluctuations in Their Price* (London: G. Bell and Sons, 1877); Robert Lucas Nash, *A Short Inquiry into the Probable Nature of Our Investments* (London: Effingham Wilson, 1880); Arthur Crump, *The Theory of Stock Exchange Speculation* (London: Longmans, Green, Reader and Dyer, 1874); Arthur Crump, *The Theory of Stock Exchange Speculation* (New York: H. W. Rosenbaum, 1887).

21. Charles Duguid, *How to Read the Money Article* (London: Effingham Wilson, 1901); Henry Lowenfeld, *All About Investment* (London: Financial Review of Reviews, 1909); Hartley Withers, *Stocks and Shares* (London: Smith, Elder, 1910); Francis W. Hirst, *The Stock Exchange: A Short Study of Investment and Speculation* (London: Williams & Norgate, 1911); *The Financial Times Investor's Guide* (London, 1913).

22. David Hochfelder, "'Where the Common People Could Speculate': The Ticker, Bucket Shops, and the Origins of Popular Participation in Financial Markets, 1880–1920," *Journal of American History* 93, no. 2 (2006): 335–58; Ann Fabian, *Card Sharps and Bucket Shops: Gambling in Nineteenth-Century America* (New York: Cornell University Press, 1990); Jonathan Ira Levy, "Contemplating Delivery: Futures Trading and the Problem of Commodity Exchange in the United States, 1875–1905," *American Historical Review* 111 (2006): 307–35; Dilwyn Porter, "'Speciousness Is the Bucketeer's Watchword and Outrageous Effrontery His Capital': Financial Bucket Shops in the City of London, c. 1880–1939," in *Cultures of Selling: Perspectives on Consumption and Society since 1700*, ed. John Benson and Laura Ugolini (Aldershot, UK: Ashgate, 2006), 103–25; James Taylor, "Inside and Outside the London Stock Exchange: Stockbrokers and Speculation in Late Victorian Britain," *Enterprise & Society* 22, no. 3 (2021): 842–77.

23. Universal Stock Exchange, *Stock Exchange Investments: Their History; Practice; and Results*, 4th ed. (London: Simpkin, Marshall, Hamilton, Kent, 1897), 3.

24. Tumbridge & Co., *Secrets of Success in Wall Street* (New York: printed by author, 1875), 3. In addition to the annual guide, Tumbridge & Co. also put out a weekly newsletter, touting Russell Sage's share promotions; see Paul Sarnoff, *Russell Sage: The Money King* (New York: Obolensky, 1965), 242.

25. Haight & Freese went into receivership in 1905, accused (like many bucket shops) of never executing their customers' orders and of cooking their books. See "Haight & Freese Co. in Receiver's Hands," *New York Times*, May 10, 1905, 1. The subsequent court case found that the transactions were "fictitious sales and bogus purchases, and mere bookkeeping entries" (Haight v. Haight Freese Co., 46 Misc. 501, 505 [N.Y. Sup. Ct. 1905]).

26. Haight & Freese, *Guide to Investors* (New York: printed by author, 1898), 24–25.

27. In Britain, David Morier Evans, deputy city editor at *The Times* before going on to direct *The Standard*'s city column, argued that financial journalists had public duties, in particular, the "fearless exposure of anything like fraud or foul dealing." [David Morier Evans], *The City; or, the Physiology of London Business; With Sketches on 'Change and at the Coffee Houses* (London: Baily Brothers, 1845), 134.

28. Dilwyn Porter, "'A Trusted Guide of the Investing Public': Harry Marks and the *Financial News*, 1884–1916," *Business History* 28, no. 1 (1986), 1.

29. Mary Poovey, *Genres of the Credit Economy: Mediating Value in Eighteenth-and Nineteenth-Century Britain* (Chicago: University of Chicago Press, 2008), 243–75; Mary Poovey, "Writing about Finance in Victorian England: Disclosure and Secrecy in the Culture of Investment," in *Victorian Investments: New Perspectives on Finance and Culture*, ed. Nancy Henry (Bloomington: Indiana University Press, 2009), 30–57.

30. *Financial Truth*, February 28, 1889, 4.

31. *Financial Answers*, August 17, 1895, 8.

32. On the redrawing of the boundaries between investment, speculation, and gambling, see David C. Itzkowitz, "Fair Enterprise or Extravagant Speculation: Investment, Speculation, and Gambling in Victorian England," in *Victorian Investments*, 98–119; Fabian, *Card Sharps and Bucket Shops*; Marieke de Goede, *Virtue, Fortune, and Faith: A Genealogy of Finance* (Minneapolis: University of Minnesota Press, 2005), 47–86; Urs Stäheli, *Spectacular Speculation: Thrills, the Economy, and Popular Discourse*, trans. Eric Savoth (Stanford, CA: Stanford University Press, 2013), 19–92; Stuart Banner, *Speculation: A History of the Fine Line between Gambling and Investing* (Oxford: Oxford University Press, 2017).

33. Jackson Lears, *Something for Nothing: Luck in America* (New York: Viking, 2003).

34. Thomas A. Davies, *How to Make Money, and How to Keep It* (New York: Carleton, 1867), 234.

35. Davies, 235, 238, 237 (emphasis in original), 239, 249, 250. For other conservative advice, see, e.g., William Relton, *Saving and Growing Money; With Practical Instructions for Judging Some Investment Accounts* (London: John Heywood, 1887), 17; A. J. Wilson, *Practical Hints to Small Investors* (London: Longmans, Green, 1893), 3–4.

36. Crump, *Theory of Stock Exchange Speculation*, 1.

37. *Pump Court*, October 31, 1888, vi; *Cosmopolitan Financier*, January 1908, 250.

38. Moses Smith, *Plain Truths about Speculation: How to Avoid Losses in Wall Street* (Brooklyn, NY: E. V. Smith, 1887), preface (n.p.), 92, 24, preface (n.p.), 212.

39. H. M. Williams, *The Key to Wall Street Mysteries and Methods* (New York: M. W. Hazen, 1904).

40. On the trope of the reformed gambler, see Fabian, *Card Sharps and Bucket Shops*, 59–107.

41. George Adam & Co., *Stock Exchange Investments, Fluctuations of Prices and How to Benefit Thereby* (London: George Adam, 1886), 11; Senex, *Counsel to Ladies and Easy-Going Men on Their Business Investments and Cautions against the Lures of Wily Financiers & Unprincipled Promoters* (London: Leadenhall Press, 1892), 27; Plus Minus, *The Tricks of Stocks and the Mysteries of Money* (Brighton: Cuthbert, [1903]), 7.

42. Universal Stock Exchange, *Stock Exchange Investments*, 217.

43. W. W. Duncan and Company, *Duncan on Investment and Speculation in Stocks and Shares*, 3rd ed. (London: Effingham Wilson, 1895), 5, 7.

44. Lewis C. Van Riper, *The Ins and Outs of Wall Street* (New York: printed by author, 1898), 7–8.

45. J. Overton Paine, *Speculating in Wall Street on Margins: A Simple and Complete Treatise on the Buying and Selling of Bonds, Stocks, Grain and Cotton on a Margin* (New York: printed by author, n.d. [c. 1900]), 7.

46. Van Riper had previously been implicated in a "racing information bureau" scam and was "keenly sought" by detectives in 1900, along with other discretionary-account traders, after customers claimed that although they had been informed that their investment had made a profit, they had been unable to get their money. In 1920, Van Riper was finally imprisoned for five years for using the mails to sell fraudulent stock promotions as well as for running a bucket shop. Paine's bucket shop operation fell foul of the law in 1901. Continuing in his trade of fraud, he was again convicted in 1937 for suspect land deals, at the age of sixty-nine. "Broker Charles W. Morgan Assigns," *New York Times*, December 7, 1900; "Oil Fraud Suspect Faces New Charge," *New York Times*, June 26, 1920; "J. Overton Paine in Court," *New York Times*, September 1, 1901.

47. Rutterford et al., "Who Comprised," 159–60.

48. Global Financial Data, Federal Reserve Board, Haver Analytics, Goldman Sachs Global Investment Research, https://www.nber.org/feldstein/BondBubble _130422–2.pdf, 3.

49. Susan Strasser, *Satisfaction Guaranteed: The Making of the American Mass Market* (New York: Pantheon, 1989); William Leach, *Land of Desire: Merchants, Power, and the Rise of a New American Culture* (New York: Pantheon, 1993).

50. The problem was sometimes addressed directly in investment guides. See, e.g., E. Hay, *Double Your Income; or, Resources of the Money Market* (London: Omnium Investment Agency, [1869]), 7–8.

51. On the fantasy of self-made success for young men, see Richard Weiss, *The American Myth of Success: From Horatio Alger to Norman Vincent Peale* (New York: Basic Books, 1969); and Judith Hilkey, *Character Is Capital: Success Manuals and Manhood in Gilded Age America* (Chapel Hill: University of North Carolina Press, 1997).

52. *Pit and Post*, September 1903, 194. See also Angus McNeill [T. W. H. Crosland], *The Egregious English* (London: Grant Richards, 1903), 185.

53. On the role of the stock ticker in cultivating a popular culture of speculation, see Alex Preda, *Framing Finance: The Boundaries of Markets and Modern Capitalism* (Chicago: University of Chicago Press, 2009), chap. 4; Peter Knight, *Reading the Market: Genres of Financial Capitalism in Gilded Age America* (Baltimore: Johns Hopkins University Press, 2016), chap. 2; and Hochfelder, "'Where the Common People Could Speculate.'"

54. Michie, *London Stock Exchange*, 80–81; Taylor, "Inside and Outside," 6–7.

55. See, e.g., Edwin Lefèvre, *Sampson Rock of Wall Street: A Novel* (New York: Harper & Bros., 1907) and Edwin Lefèvre, "James Robert Keene," *Cosmopolitan*, November 1902, 91. Though less common, these scenes also feature in British writing. In "The Hypochondriac; or, A Cure for the Blues," for example, the previously jaded Sir William Benson watches "the tape as it rolled out into the basket, being as pleased as a child with a new toy." He forgets his troubles and he experiences the thrill of speculation: "His icy demeanour was melting beneath the genial influence of the tape." Bracebridge Hemyng, "The Hypochondriac; or, A Cure for the Blues," in *The Stockbroker's Wife and Other Sensational Tales of the Stock Exchange* (London: John and Robert Maxwell, 1885), 152–53.

56. It was a slogan employed by a variety of investment firms on both sides of the Atlantic, including Messrs. Simpson & Co., Jordan and Jordan, Percy Barclay & Co., the American Investment and Security Co., and Charles Coventry & Co. See *Evening Star* [Washington, DC], November 11, 1879, 4; *Morning Post*, July 12, 1886, 1; *Morning Post*, October 6, 1890, 4; *New Haven Morning Journal and Courier*, September 29, 1896, 7; Charles Coventry & Co., *Prudent Speculation the Secret of Success: A Guide to Operators in Stock Exchange Securities* (London: n.p., 1905).

57. The condemnation of futures trading as gambling continued in some quarters. In Britain, see, e.g., David George Hoey, *"Bulling and Bearing" or "Operating," Otherwise Betting or Gambling on the Stock Exchange* (Glasgow: Robert Maclehose, 1885); and H. M., *On the Analogy between the Stock Exchange and the Turf* (London: Effingham Wilson, 1885). On the agrarian populist attacks on futures trading in the United States, see Cedric B. Cowing, *Populists, Plungers, and Progressives: A Social History of Stock and Commodity Speculation, 1890–1936* (Princeton, NJ: Princeton University Press, 1965), 27–38.

58. Charles Castelli, *The Theory of "Options" in Stocks and Shares* (London: Frederic C. Mathieson, 1877), 3.

59. In Britain, see, e.g., Anon., *Speculation and Investment in Stocks and Shares*, 7; and George Gregory and Company, *Hints to Speculators*, 9–11; and in the United States, Paine, *Speculating in Wall Street*.

60. Messrs Finch Ellis & Co., *Safety and Profit*, 3rd ed. (London, [1888]), 2.

61. In the United States it was only with the formation of the Consolidated Stock Exchange in 1886 that "odd lots" became available; see Sobel, *Big Board*, 131.

62. David Hochfelder, *The Telegraph in America, 1832–1920* (Baltimore: Johns Hopkins University Press, 2012), 127.

63. See Rutterford and Sotiropoulos, "The Rise of the Small Investor"; and W. Elliot Brownlee, *Federal Taxation in America: A Short History* (Cambridge: Cambridge University Press, 2016), 56–57.

64. Nash, *Short Inquiry*, 108. In the context of government stocks, this meant rejecting both the safest stocks paying under 5 percent, and the riskiest foreign loans, and opting for those paying between 5 and 7 percent.

65. William Barker, *Sound Advice for Investors* (London, 1885), 3–6.

66. *African Critic*, January 23, 1897, 125.

67. James K. Medbery, *Men and Mysteries of Wall Street* (Boston: Fields, Osgood, 1870); William Worthington Fowler, *Ten Years on Wall Street* (New York: Burt Franklin, 1870); Matthew Hale Smith, *Twenty Years among the Bulls and Bears of Wall Street* (Hartford, CT: J. B. Burr & Hyde, 1871); Henry Clews, *Twenty-Eight Years on Wall Street* (New York: J. S. Ogilvie, 1887).

68. Smith, *Twenty Years*, iv.

69. Henry Clews, *Fifty Years in Wall Street* (New York: Irving, 1908).

70. Medbery, *Men and Mysteries of Wall Street*, 25.

71. The London Stock Exchange had no gallery and excluded all visitors, yet the press contained similar imaginative evocations of the trading floor. See, e.g., Godefroi Drew Ingall, "The London Stock Exchange," in *Living London*, ed. George R. Sims (London: Cassell, 1901), vol. 1, sec. 2, 261–66; Henry Norman and G. C. Ashton Jonson, "The London Stock Exchange," *Century Illustrated Monthly Magazine* 66 (June 1903), 177–94.

72. Medbery, *Men and Mysteries*, 38.

73. John F. Muirhead, *The United States, with an Excursion into Mexico: Handbook for Travelers*, ed. Karl Baedeker (Leipzig: Karl Baedeker, 1893), 27.

74. Historians have argued that in turn-of-the-century Britain, though weak by modern standards, corporate disclosure was comparatively good, and that Britons enjoyed "the best information possessed by any investors anywhere": Richard Sylla and George David Smith, "Information and Capital Market Regulation in Anglo-American Finance," in *Anglo-American Financial Systems: Institutions and Markets in the Twentieth Century*, ed. Michael D. Bordo and Richard Sylla (Burr Ridge, IL: Irwin Professional Publishing, 1995): 190. See also Leslie Hannah, "Pioneering Modern Corporate Governance: A View from London in 1900," *Enterprise & Society* 8, no. 3 (2007): 653–62.

75. *Pit and Post*, September 1903, 193.

76. David F. Hawkins, "The Development of Modern Financial Reporting Practices among American Manufacturing Corporations," *Business History Review* 37, no. 3 (1963): 135–68.

77. Sobel, *Big Board*, 131–32. The alternative exchanges dealt, for example, in Amalgamated Copper and American Sugar, which in effect operated as "blind pools," that is, with outsiders having no knowledge of the true state of affairs of the company, meaning that manipulators could take advantage of their inside information; see O'Sullivan, *Dividends of Development*, 194–96; and Jerry W. Markham, *A Financial History of the United States: From J. P. Morgan to the Institutional Investor (1900–1970)*, vol. 2 (New York: Sharpe, 2002), 4.

78. See James H. Bridge, ed., *The Trust: Its Book (Being a Presentation of the Several Aspects of the Latest Form of Industrial Evolution)* (New York: Doubleday, Page, 1910).

79. US Congress, House of Representatives, *Report of the Committee Pursuant to House Resolutions 429 and 504 to Investigate the Concentration of Control of Money and Credit*, 62nd Cong., 3rd sess., 1913, H. Rep 1593, 115. On the history of the political struggles over the democratization and regulation of shareholding, see Cowing, *Populists*, 25–74, and Ott, *When Wall Street*, 9–54.

80. Thompson, "Early Books on Investing"; Kevin R. Brine and Mary Poovey, *Finance in America: An Unfinished Story* (Chicago: University of Chicago Press, 2017).

81. State of New York, *Report of the Governor's Committee on Speculation in Securities and Commodities* (Hughes Committee, June 7, 1909), 4. Supreme Court case, *Board of Trade v. Christie Grain & Stock Co.*, 198 US 236 (1905). The story of Justice Holmes's decision is told in Hochfelder, "'Where the Common People Could Speculate,'" 351–52.

82. For the emergence of this genre in the United Kingdom, see Jakob Gaardbo Nielsen, "Poets of Promotion: Corporate Personality and Crowd Psychology in Guy Thorne and Leo Custance's *Sharks*," *Journal of Victorian Culture* 26, no. 1 (2021): 103–18.

83. Edwin Lefèvre, "The Newspaper and Wall Street," *Bookman* (April 1904), 139.

84. For more detailed accounts of each, see James Taylor, "'Distrust all Advice . . . and Make No Exception in Favour of Our Advice': Popular Financial Journalism in Late Victorian Britain," *English Historical Review* 136, no. 580 (2021): 619–50; and Knight, *Reading the Market*, 44–58.

85. *The World*, August 9, 1876, 5–7; *Truth*, April 12, 1877, 468.

86. *Town Topics*, January 6, 1887, 14.

87. Edwin Post Jr., *Truly Emily Post* (New York: Funk & Wagnalls, 1961), 143. In Edith Wharton's *The Custom of the Country* (New York: Scribner's, 1913), parvenu Undine Spragg is instructed in the ways of society by Mrs. Heeny, the society manicurist and masseuse, who brings in clippings from *Town Talk*, Wharton's thinly disguised version of *Town Topics*. The same title also appears in Wharton's *The House of Mirth* (New York: Scribner's, 1905).

88. *Truth*, August 15, 1878, 193.

89. *Town Topics*, February 3, 1887, 19.

90. *Town Topics*, January 2, 1890, 20. By the 1900s, even the *Wall Street Journal* had begun to include a column offering conservative investment advice, in the forum "Answers to Inquirers."

91. On the use of financial advice to manipulate the market, see Knight, *Reading the Market*, 144–90.

92. *African Critic*, July 31, 1897, reprinted in *Supplement to "The African Critic": The Stock-Jobbing of Henry Labouchere* (London, 1897), v–ix. The story was more complicated than it seemed, however. Labouchere claimed (with some justification) that he had written the letters in order to deliberately sow false information to his correspondent.

93. *African Critic*, August 7, 1897, reprinted in *The Stock-Jobbing of Henry Labouchere*, ix–xv.

94. For details of the court case, see Andy Logan, *The Man Who Robbed the Robber Barons* (London: Victor Gollancz, 1966), chaps. 2–3, 8–10; and Maureen E. Montgomery, *Displaying Women: Spectacles of Leisure in Edith Wharton's New York* (New York: Routledge, 2016), 145–47.

95. See Montgomery, *Displaying Women*, 191n12.

96. *Harper's Weekly*, October 7, 1899, 1023.

97. G. Herbert Stutfield, "Modern Gambling and Gambling Laws," *Nineteenth Century* 26 (November 1889): 853–54.

98. David Zimmerman, *Panic!: Markets, Crises, and Crowds in American Fiction* (Chapel Hill: University of North Carolina Press, 2006), 81–122.

99. "Hoyle" [William E. Forrest], *The Game in Wall Street, and How to Play it Successfully* (New York: J. S. Ogilvie, 1898), iii.

100. George Bliss to Mr. Grenfell, September 18, 1877, Letter Books of George Bliss (1877), Morton, Bliss & Company, Stockbrokers, New York Historical Society.

101. George Bliss to Theodore [Bliss], January 13, 1882, Letter Books of George Bliss (1882).

102. On the concerted public relations campaigns aimed at presenting the corporation as having a "soul," see Roland Marchand, *Creating the Corporate Soul: The Rise of Public Relations and Corporate Imagery in American Big Business* (Berkeley: University of California Press, 1998).

103. Unsurprisingly, Ostrander's business was far from sound: see "'W. M. Ostrander' in Receiver's Hands," *New York Times*, April 11, 1909, 3.

104. See James Taylor, *Boardroom Scandal: The Criminalization of Company Fraud in Nineteenth-Century Britain* (Oxford: Oxford University Press, 2013); and, on sucker lists, see Sobel, *Big Board*, 180–81.

105. Karen Halttunen, *Confidence Men and Painted Women: A Study of Middle-Class Culture in America, 1830–1870* (New Haven, CT: Yale University Press, 1982), 6. For more on "personalization amid bureaucratization" in fraud, see Edward J. Balleisen, *Fraud: An American History from Barnum to Madoff* (Princeton, NJ: Princeton University Press, 2018), 26–33.

106. Anthony Comstock, *Frauds Exposed; or, How the People Are Deceived and Robbed, and Youth Corrupted* (New York: J. Howard Brown, 1880), 15.

107. John Hill, *Gold Bricks of Speculation* (Chicago: Lincoln Book Concern, 1904), 140.

108. George S. McWatters, *Forgers and Confidence Men*, Pinkerton Detective Series 3 (Chicago: Laird & Lee, 1891), 254.

109. Hill, *Gold Bricks of Speculation*, 72.

110. Comstock, *Frauds Exposed*, 17.

111. Hill, *Gold Bricks of Speculation*, 141.

112. *Harper's Weekly*, December 19, 1900, 1275; December 7, 1901, 1214.

113. William Stafford Young, *Safe Methods in Stock Speculation* (Chicago: Frederick J. Drake, 1902), 5, 7, 9, 10–11.

114. Young, *Safe Methods*, 22, 23, 21, 16.

115. Young, *Safe Methods*, insert between 30 and 31, 52, 51.

116. Michael Barkun, *A Culture of Conspiracy* (Berkeley: University of California Press, 2003), 3–4.

117. Young, *Safe Methods*, 51.

118. Young, *Safe Methods*, 67, 68.

119. Universal Stock Exchange, *Stock Exchange Investments*, 149. For similar sentiments, see Ursa Minor, *On the Science and Practice of Stock Exchange Speculation* (London: W. W. Gibbings, 1891), 5.

120. W. W. Duncan and Company, *Duncan on Investment and Speculation*, 2.

121. Preda, *Framing Finance*, 99–100; Erasmus Pinto, *Ye Outside Fools! Glimpses Inside the Stock Exchange* (London: Samuel Tinsley, 1876), 382–83.

122. Universal Stock Exchange, *Stock Exchange Investments*, 217. See also [E. C. Maddison], *On the Stock Exchange: An Explanation of Stocks and Stock-Jobbing, and a Complete Manual of Stock Exchange Practice and Customs* (London: Charles and Edwin Layton, 1877), 171.

123. Preda, *Framing Finance*, 94–105.

124. An early example was E. B. Sutton, *Highest and Lowest Prices of the English and Foreign Funds, from 1825 to 1838* (London, 1839). The publisher Frederic Mathieson specialized in such works, beginning with railway lists in 1855 and covering the wider economy from the mid-1870s with *Mathieson's Highest and Lowest Prices and Dividends Paid during 1872, 1873, 1874, and 1875* (London: Frederic C. Mathieson, 1876).

125. Anon., *Speculation and Investment in Stocks and Shares with a Minimum Risk* (London: W. Gutteridge, 1882), 7. See also Maddison, *On the Stock Exchange*, 150–51; Senex, *Counsel to Ladies*, 33; LLB, *Money-Making on the Stock Exchange and Racecourse. A Slight Explanation of the Theory That Losses May Be Averted and Profits May Be Secured in Speculations Conducted According to the Law of Averages* (Blackburn: George Haynes, 1894).

126. Samuel Benner, *Benner's Prophecies of Future Ups and Downs in Prices: What Years to Make Money on Pig-Iron, Hogs, Corn, and Provisions* (Cincinnati: printed by author, 1876), 121. Benner's theories anticipate the Soviet economist Nikolai Kondratiev's theories (developed in the 1920s) about forty-to-sixty-year economic cycles, driven by technological changes.

127. Benner, *Benner's Prophecies*, 16–17. Preda, in *Framing Finance*, outlines how, in the early decades of the twentieth century, the emerging profession of market analysis endeavored to create a tradition for the "science" of market forecasting by harking back to Benner and others (158–60).

128. Benner, *Benner's Prophecies*, 28.

129. Benner, *Benner's Prophecies*, 131. On the shifting relationship between

prophecy and prediction in the late nineteenth century, see Jamie L. Pietruska, *Looking Forward: Prediction and Uncertainty in Modern America* (Chicago: University of Chicago Press, 2017).

130. Van Riper, *Ins and Outs*, 11.

131. H. M. Williams, *The Key to Wall Street Mysteries and Methods* (New York: M. W. Hazen, 1904). "H. M. Williams" was the pseudonym of New York lawyer Marshman Williams Hazen.

132. "Hoyle," *The Game in Wall Street*, 34–35 (emphasis in original).

133. "Hoyle," 33.

134. A. N. Ridgely, *The Study and Science of Stock Speculation* (New York: printed by author, 1901), 1, 19.

135. *Pit and Post*, September 1903, 193, 194.

136. *Pit and Post*, September 1903, 204–5, 205–6.

137. This form of analysis was supported by guides instructing readers how to read the money article, balance sheets, and prospectuses: from the United Kingdom, see, e.g., Duguid, *How to Read the Money Article*; T. H. Gough, *Balance-Sheets and How to Read Them* (London: Simpkin, Marshall, Hamilton, Kent, 1906); Philip Tovey, *Balance Sheets: How to Read and Understand Them* (London: Sir Isaac Pitman & Sons, 1911); and Philip Tovey, *Prospectuses: How to Read and Understand Them* (London: Sir Isaac Pitman & Sons, 1912).

138. *Pit and Post*, September 1903, 197, 265, 233–34.

139. For more on this theme, see Janette Rutterford and Dimitris P. Sotiropoulos, "Financial Diversification before Modern Portfolio Theory: UK Financial Advice Documents in the Late Nineteenth and the Beginning of the Twentieth Century," *European Journal of the History of Economic Thought* 23, no. 6 (2016): 919–45.

140. *Beeton's Guide to Investing Money with Safety and Profit* (London: Ward, Lock, and Tyler, [1870]), 54. See also *The Investors' Note Book for 1871: How to Invest Money Profitably and Safely* (Bristol: G. H. Bowyer, 1871), 2; [Maddison], *On the Stock Exchange*, 226–29; Thomas Crumplen, *Practical Advice on Stocks and Shares, Addressed to Investors of All Classes* (London: Harding, 1878), 36; Barker, *Sound Advice for Investors*, 6. For a US example, Fowler, *Ten Years on Wall Street*, 463.

141. Janette Rutterford, "Learning from One Another's Mistakes: Investment Trusts in the UK and the US, 1868–1940," *Financial History Review* 16, no. 2 (2009): 157–81.

142. Bartrick-Baker, *Sound Investments for Small Savings*, 75–76. For further discussion, see Urlin, *Hints on Business*, 33–34. For criticisms of trusts, see E. M., *A Word to Investors of Fifty Pounds to Fifty Thousand Pounds* (Edinburgh: Bell & Bradfute, 1889), 7–9; and J. D. Walker and Watson, *Investor's and Shareholder's Guide* (Edinburgh: E. & S. Livingstone, 1894), 264.

143. W. W. Duncan and Company, *Duncan on Investment and Speculation*, 164–69.

144. *Advice on Investments* (London: printed by author, [1913]), 2.

145. Henry Lowenfeld, *How to Manage Capital Invested in Stock Exchange Securities* (London: Investment Registry and Stock Exchange, [1904?]), 5.

146. Advertising leaflet in rear of Lowenfeld, *How to Manage Capital*, n.p.

147. For more on Lowenfeld, see Barbara Evans, *Freedom to Choose: The Life and Work of Dr Helena Wright, Pioneer of Contraception* (London: Bodley Head, 1984).

148. Clews, *Twenty-Eight Years in Wall Street*, 437.

149. John B. McKenzie, *Bulls and Bears of Wall Street*, 3rd ed. (New York: printed by author, 1899), 66.

150. For a summary of the popular and literary culture of regarding women's place in business in the Gilded Age, see George Robb, *Ladies of the Ticker: Women and Wall Street from the Gilded Age to the Great Depression* (Urbana: University of Illinois Press, 2017), chaps. 1–2.

151. Edwin Lefèvre, "A Woman and Her Bonds," in *Wall Street Stories* (New York: S. S. McClure, 1901).

152. *The Sayings of Uncle Rufus* (New York: Jesse Haney, 1881), 15.

153. By the mid-1870s, most of the states in the North had passed a version of the Married Women's Property Act, allowing women (to varying degrees) to own property, keep their own income, and engage in business. See Nancy Marie Robertson and Susan M. Yohn, "Women and Money: The United States," in *Women and Their Money 1700–1950: Essays on Women and Finance*, ed. Anne Laurence, Josephine Maltby, and Janette Rutterford (London: Routledge, 2009), 218–25; and R. Richard Geddes and Sharon Tennyson, "Passage of the Married Women's Property Acts and Earnings Acts in the United States: 1850 to 1920," *Research in Economic History* 29, no. 1 (2013): 145–89.

154. Robb, *Ladies of the Ticker*, 2.

155. Janette Rutterford, "The Shareholder Voice: British and American Accents, 1890–1965," *Enterprise & Society* 13, no. 1 (2012): 120–53.

156. Barton Cheyney, "Buying a House without Cash," *Ladies' Home Journal* (April 1898): 28.

157. See, e.g., Ruth Hall, "How to Make Money," chap. 3, *Good Housekeeping* (March 1898): 97–98; and Ruth Ashmore, "Girls and the Use of Money," *Ladies' Home Journal* (September 1893): 21.

158. An example of an article that does try to give stock market advice to the female readership is Walter H. Barrett, "Investment in Stocks and Bonds," *Ladies' Home Journal* (March 1893): 10. However, it begins with advice about advice, rather than the actual advice itself: it implies that women often naively ask for advice on a small, sure investment with large returns.

159. Caroline Haddon, *Where Does Your Interest Come from? A Word to Lady Investors* (Manchester: John Heywood, 1886), 3, 4, 6, 13–14.

160. Josephine Maltby and Janette Rutterford, "Investing in Charities in the Nineteenth Century: The Financialization of Philanthropy," *Accounting History*

21, no. 2–3 (2016), 263–80; Eugenie Ladner Birch and Deborah S. Gardner, "The Seven-Percent Solution: A Review of Philanthropic Housing, 1870–1910," *Journal of Urban History* 7, no. 4 (1981): 403–38.

161. Maltby and Rutterford, "Investing in Charities," 265.

162. A. S. Wohl, "Octavia Hill and the Homes of the London Poor," *Journal of British Studies* 10, no. 2 (1971): 118–19. See also Sarah Roddy, Julie-Marie Strange, and Bertrand Taithe, *The Charity Market and Humanitarianism in Britain, 1870–1912* (London: Bloomsbury Academic, 2019).

163. Jonathan Levy, *Freaks of Fortune: The Emerging World of Capitalism and Risk in America* (Cambridge, MA: Harvard University Press, 2012), 104–49.

164. Shennette Garrett-Scott, *Banking on Freedom: Black Women in U.S. Finance Before the New Deal* (New York: Columbia University Press, 2019), 24–40.

165. See Garrett-Scott, *Banking on Freedom*, 207n45.

166. Ann Fabian, *Card Sharps and Bucket Shops: Gambling in Nineteenth-Century America* (Ithaca, NY: Cornell University Press, 1990), 112, 116.

167. See Michael Zakim, *Accounting for Capitalism: The World the Clerk Made* (Chicago: University of Chicago Press, 2018).

168. Universal Stock Exchange, *Stock Exchange Investments*, 150.

169. Nash, *Short Inquiry*, 5.

170. Wilson, *Practical Hints to Small Investors*, 18–19.

171. Senex, *Counsel to Ladies*, 103. For more on contrarian approaches, see Kristian Bondo Hansen, "Crowds and Speculation: A Study of Crowd Phenomena in the U.S. Financial Markets, 1890 to 1940" (PhD diss., Copenhagen Business School, 2017).

172. Crump, *Theory of Stock Exchange Speculation* [1874], 41.

173. Crump, *Theory of Stock Exchange Speculation* [1874], 41; 58–59, 46–47.

174. Plus Minus, *Tricks of Stocks*, 57.

175. On the role of self-help in American life, see Steven Starker, *Oracle at the Supermarket: The American Preoccupation with Self-Help Books* (New Brunswick, NJ: Transaction, 1989), and Micki McGee, *Self-Help, Inc.: Makeover Culture in American Life* (Oxford: Oxford University Press, 2005); and in British culture, Anne Baltz Rodrick, "The Importance of Being an Earnest Improver: Class, Caste, and *Self-Help* in Mid-Victorian England," *Victorian Literature and Culture* 29, no. 1 (2001): 39–50, and R. J. Morris, "Samuel Smiles and the Genesis of *Self-Help*; The Retreat to a Petit Bourgeois Utopia," *Historical Journal* 24, no. 1 (1981): 89–109.

176. Gregory, *Hints to Speculators & Investors*, 6; Haight & Freese, *Guide to Investors*, 24–25. Gregory's booklet was published in 1889, and Haight & Freese was established in 1890, suggesting that the direction of influence may have been toward the United States in this case. For Haight & Freese, see John J. Dillon, *Hind-Sights or Looking Backwards at Swindles* (New York: Rural Publishing Company, 1911), 57.

177. Van Riper, *Ins and Outs*, 16.

178. Senex, *Counsel to Ladies*, 99.

179. Crumplen, *Practical Advice on Stocks and Shares*, 36.

180. Young, *Safe Methods*, 8.

181. Plus Minus, *Tricks of Stocks*, 79.

182. Samuel Smiles, *Self-Help; With Illustrations of Character, Conduct, and Perseverance* (London: John Murray, 1868), v.

183. T. H. E. Travers, "Samuel Smiles and the Origins of 'Self-Help': Reform and the New Enlightenment," *Albion* 9, no. 2 (1977): 172.

184. Lowenfeld, *How to Manage Capital*, 109.

185. Richard D. Wyckoff, *Studies in Tape Reading* (New York: Ticker, 1910), 18.

186. On the development of crowd theory in accounts of market panics in the late nineteenth century, see Zimmerman, *Panic!*, 123–50.

187. This was a common trope in fictional accounts; see, e.g., Lefèvre, *Sampson Rock of Wall Street*.

188. Wyckoff, *Studies*, 16, 6–7. In a similar vein, Van Riper urged readers to "drop all sentiment, pay no attention to news gossip, points or tips, but merely become a machine with sufficient power to execute your orders according to market movements." Van Riper, *Ins and Outs*, 16.

189. Lefèvre, "James Robert Keene," 91.

190. Labouchere, who advocated the careful and dispassionate calculation of "intrinsic value," later admitted that he did not always practice what he preached. "I did not make much by my theory of parity of value and price, and what I did make—with more, too—I lost by investing in mines. Copper, gold, silver, lead, it was all the same to me." *Truth*, October 7, 1897, 889.

191. Audrey Jaffe, *The Affective Life of the Average Man: The Victorian Novel and the Stock-Market Graph* (Columbus: Ohio State University Press, 2010), 43.

192. In the first academic study of speculation (submitted as a PhD in 1896), Henry Crosby Emery argued that the democratization of finance—in the sense of speculation no longer being confined to a small clique of insiders, but opened up to the masses—would diminish the possibility of manipulating the market through inside information and perhaps even make it impossible. Henry Crosby Emery, *Speculation on the Stock and Produce Exchanges in the United States* (New York: Macmillan, 1904).

193. Daniel Souleles and Kristian Bondo Hansen, "Can They All Be 'Shit-Heads'?: Learning to be a Contrarian Investor," *Journal of Cultural Economy* 12, no. 6 (2019), 491–507.

Chapter Four

1. F. Scott Fitzgerald, *The Great Gatsby*, ed. Matthew J. Bruccoli, Cambridge Edition of the Works of F. Scott Fitzgerald (Cambridge: Cambridge University Press, 1991), 7, 46, 134–35.

2. Maury Klein, *Rainbow's End: The Crash of 1929* (Oxford: Oxford University Press, 2001), chap. 1.

3. Janette Rutterford and Dimitris Sotiropoulos, "The Rise of the Small Investor in the United States and United Kingdom, 1895 to 1970," *Enterprise & Society* 18, no. 1 (2017): 498, 501.

4. Adolf A. Berle and Gardiner C. Means, *The Modern Corporation and Private Property* (New York: Macmillan, 1932), 60.

5. Rutterford and Sotiropoulos, "Rise of the Small Investor," 501.

6. Kieran Heinemann, "Investment, Speculation, and Popular Stock Market Engagement in 20th-Century Britain," *Archiv für Sozialgeschichte* 56 (2016): 254.

7. Ranald Michie, "Gamblers, Fools, Victims, or Wizards? The British Investor in the Public Mind, 1850–1930," in *Men, Women, and Money: Perspectives on Gender, Wealth, and Investment 1850–1930*, ed. David R. Green, Alastair Owens, Josephine Maltby, and Janette Rutterford (Oxford: Oxford University Press, 2011), 181.

8. F. E. Armstrong, *The Book of the Stock Exchange: A Comprehensive Guide to the Theory and Practice of Stock and Share Transactions and to the Business of Members of the London and Provincial Stock Exchanges*, 3rd ed. (London: Sir Isaac Pitman & Sons, 1939), 137.

9. Liaquat Ahamed, *Lords of Finance: 1929, the Great Depression, and the Bankers Who Broke the World* (London: Windmill, 2010), 370.

10. Rutterford and Sotiropoulos, "Rise of the Small Investor," 516.

11. Heinemann, "Investment, Speculation," 255.

12. Rutterford and Sotiropoulos, "Rise of the Small Investor," 521, 488.

13. Phillip G. Payne, *Crash! How the Economic Boom and Bust of the 1920s Worked* (Baltimore: Johns Hopkins University Press, 2015), 50.

14. Rutterford and Sotiropoulos, "Rise of the Small Investor," 528.

15. Alex Preda, "Where Do Analysts Come from? The Case of Financial Chartism," in *Market Devices*, ed. Michel Callon, Yuval Millo, and Fabian Muniesa (Oxford: Blackwell, 2007), 48.

16. G. C. Selden, *The Machinery of Wall Street: Why It Exists, How It Works, and What It Accomplishes* (New York: Magazine of Wall Street, 1919), 157.

17. David Kynaston, *City of London: The History* (London: Vintage, 2012), 354.

18. See P. J. Cain and A. G. Hopkins, *British Imperialism: Innovation and Expansion, 1688–1914* (London: Longman, 1993).

19. Victor de Villiers and Owen Taylor, *The Point and Figure Method of Anticipating Stock Price Movements: Complete Theory and Practice*, 2nd ed. (New York: Stock Market Publications, 1934), 27.

20. Kynaston, *City of London*, 355–57.

21. On such boundary-drawing, see Alex Preda, *Framing Finance: The Boundaries of Markets and Modern Capitalism* (Chicago: University of Chicago Press, 2009).

22. A. T. K. Grant, *A Study of the Capital Market in Post-War Britain* (London: Macmillan, 1937), 137, 141, 170–71.

23. Orline D. Foster, *Making Money in the Stock Market* (Garden City, NY: Doubleday, 1930), 74.

24. Marc Flandreau, *Anthropologists in the Stock Exchange: A Financial History of Victorian Science* (Chicago: University of Chicago Press, 2016), 79, 96, 100, 277–78.

25. Hartley Withers, *The Business of Finance* (New York: E. P. Dutton, 1918), 168.

26. Herbert H. Bassett, *The Shareholder's Manual: An Elementary and Non-Technical Treatise on the Investment of Capital in Stocks and Shares* (London: Sir Isaac Pitman & Sons, 1922), 1–2.

27. Hon. Lord Hardinge, *Investment and Investors* (London: Investment Registry, 1935), 10–11, v, x, 81, ii, 12, 13, 66.

28. See, e.g., Bassett, *Shareholder's Manual*, 89; Armstrong, *Book of the Stock Exchange*, 136.

29. Bassett, *Shareholder's Manual*, 90.

30. Withers, *Business of Finance*, 268.

31. Armstrong, *Book of the Stock Exchange*, 136, 138.

32. Francis W. Hirst, *The Stock Exchange: A Short Study of Investment and Speculation*, 4th ed. (London: Oxford University Press, 1948), 21.

33. Alexander Zevin, *Liberalism at Large: The World According to the Economist* (London: Verso, 2019), 155.

34. Hirst, *Stock Exchange*, 21.

35. Hargreaves Parkinson, *Scientific Investment: A Manual for Company Share and Debenture Holders*, 2nd ed. (Sir Isaac Pitman & Sons, 1933), 216 (emphasis in original).

36. Ibid., 216–17.

37. Flandreau, *Anthropologists*, 100.

38. See John M. MacKenzie, ed., *Imperialism and Popular Culture* (Manchester: Manchester University Press, 1986).

39. For an extensive review of attempts to gauge the increase, see Rutterford and Sotiropoulos, "Rise of the Small Investor," 495–501.

40. Kevin R. Brine and Mary Poovey, *Finance in America: An Unfinished Story* (Chicago: University of Chicago Press, 2017), 128–29.

41. Julia C. Ott, *When Wall Street Met Main Street: The Quest for an Investors' Democracy* (Cambridge, MA: Harvard University Press, 2011), 230n3, 2.

42. Janice M. Traflet, *A Nation of Small Shareholders: Marketing Wall Street after World War II* (Baltimore: Johns Hopkins University Press, 2013), 179n15; Steve Fraser, *Wall Street: A Cultural History* (London: Faber and Faber, 2005), 347.

43. Klein, *Rainbow's End*, 15.

44. Fraser, *Wall Street*, 346; Klein, *Rainbow's End*, 15.

45. Cedric B. Cowing, *Populists, Plungers, and Progressives: A Social History of Stock and Commodity Speculation* (Princeton, NJ: Princeton University Press, 1965), 184; Fraser, *Wall Street*, 346; Klein, *Rainbow's End*, 15.

46. Cowing, *Populists*, 184.

47. Martin S. Fridson, *It Was a Very Good Year: Extraordinary Moments in Stock Market History* (New York: John Wiley, 1998), 81; Theodore Peterson, *Magazines in the Twentieth Century* (Urbana: University of Illinois Press, 1956), 56.

48. Ott, *When Wall Street*, 56.

49. Lizabeth Cohen, *Making a New Deal: Industrial Workers in Chicago, 1919–1939*, 2nd ed. (Cambridge: Cambridge University Press, 2008), 76–79; Cowing, *Populists*, 95; Fraser, *Wall Street*, 309–10; Ott, *When Wall Street*, 56–59. It's important to note that, while the extent of public participation in securities ownership via the purchase of Liberty Bonds was new, such campaigns were not unprecedented in the United States: during the Civil War, the Union made particular efforts to finance its effort through the sale of bonds. See David K. Thomson, "Financing the War," in *The Cambridge History of the American Civil War*, ed. Aaron Sheehan-Dean (Cambridge: Cambridge University Press, 2019), 174–92.

50. Ott, *When Wall Street*, 56, 57, 55.

51. Vincent P. Carosso, *Investment Banking in America: A History* (Cambridge, MA: Harvard University Press, 1970), 250; Klein, *Rainbow's End*, 22.

52. James Grant, *Money of the Mind: Borrowing and Lending in America from the Civil War to Michael Milken* (New York: Farrar, Straus, and Giroux, 1994), 150; quoted in Brine and Poovey, *Finance in America*, 129. See also Mary A. O'Sullivan, *Dividends of Development: Securities Markets in the History of US Capitalism, 1866–1922* (Oxford: Oxford University Press, 2016), 351.

53. Rutterford and Sotiropoulos, "Rise of the Small Investor," 488; Ott, *When Wall Street*, 170–73, 182–83.

54. See Ott, *When Wall Street*.

55. David Hochfelder, "'Where the Common People Could Speculate': The Ticker, Bucket Shops, and the Origins of Popular Participation in Financial Markets, 1880–1920," *Journal of American History* 93, no. 2 (2006): 345–46, 349–53, 355. Some such establishments lingered on, in diminished and more clandestine forms, only to face a further campaign of investigations and closures following the passage of the 1921 anti–securities fraud Martin Act, which all but ended the industry. See Ott, *When Wall Street*, 210–11.

56. "Trading in Odd Lots New Market Force," *New York Times*, April 30, 1916, 21; quoted in Hochfelder, "'Where the Common People,'" 357.

57. Harold J. Aldrich, *The Stock Market Investor* (Boston: Four Seas, 1923), 76.

58. Klein, *Rainbow's End*, 160. "Hoover Market" was the term applied to the culminating phase of the 1920s stock market boom, which played out against the backdrop of Herbert Hoover's successful bid for the presidency (in the election of November 1928) and the early months of his administration.

59. Peter Wyckoff, *Wall Street and the Stock Markets: A Chronology (1644–1971)* (Philadelphia: Chilton, 1972), 40, 46; quoted in Preda, *Framing Finance*, 127.

60. Gerald M. Loeb, *The Battle for Investment Survival* (Burlington, VT: Fraser, 1988), 281.

61. Preda, *Framing Finance*, 267n9; Fraser, *Wall Street*, 347.

62. David F. Jordan, *Managing Personal Finances: How to Use Money Intelligently* (New York: Prentice Hall, 1936), 6.

63. Jordan, 6.

64. Jordan, 8.

65. John A. Leavitt and Carl O. Hanson, *Personal Finance* (New York: McGraw-Hill, 1950), 183.

66. See Charles R. Geisst, *Encyclopedia of American Business History* (New York: Facts on File, 2006), 48.

67. See Klein, *Rainbow's End*, 150–51; Fraser, *Wall Street*, 349.

68. See Cowing, *Populists*, 96–98.

69. Walter A. Friedman, *Fortune Tellers: The Story of America's First Economic Forecasters* (Princeton, NJ: Princeton University Press, 2014), 4.

70. Enoch Burton Gowin, *Developing Financial Skill* (Boston: American Institute of Finance, 1922), 59–60.

71. Paul F. Wendt, "The Classification and Financial Experience of the Customers of a Typical New York Stock Exchange Firm from 1933 to 1938" (PhD diss., Columbia University, 1941), 210; cited in Cowing, *Populists*, 125.

72. Cowing, *Populists*, 125.

73. Henry Howard Harper, *The Psychology of Speculation: The Human Element in Stock Market Transactions* (Boston: privately printed, 1926), 93, 106.

74. "B." [John T. Brand], *The Business of Trading in Stocks*, 2nd ed. (New York: Magazine of Wall Street, 1917), 112.

75. Thomas Temple Hoyne, *Speculation: Its Sound Principles and Rules for Its Practice* (Chicago: Economic Feature Service, 1922), 154.

76. See Ott, *When Wall Street*, 75–76, 80–82; Shennette Garrett-Scott, *Banking on Freedom: Black Women in U.S. Finance before the New Deal* (New York: Columbia University Press, 2019), 154.

77. "B.," *Business of Trading in Stocks*, 106.

78. Gregory S. Bell, *In the Black: A History of African Americans on Wall Street* (New York: Wiley, 2002), 23.

79. Bell, *In the Black*, 27, 24–26; Garrett-Scott, *Banking on Freedom*, chap. 5.

80. Bell, *In the Black*, 24, 26, 28.

81. George Robb, *Ladies of the Ticker: Women and Wall Street from the Gilded Age to the Great Depression* (Urbana: University of Illinois Press, 2017), chap. 2, n. 57, e-book.

82. J. George Frederick, *Common Stocks and the Average Man* (New York: Business Bourse, 1930), 285–92; see Cowing, *Populists*, 120.

83. *Investing for a Widow* (New York: Barron's, 1940).

84. Cowing, *Populists*, 121–24.

85. Robb, *Ladies of the Ticker*, chap. 2; Ott, *When Wall Street*, 284n37.

86. Ott, *When Wall Street*, 187; Cowing, *Populists*, 121–23; Klein, *Rainbow's End*, 148; Robb, *Ladies of the Ticker*, chaps. 1–2.

87. See, e.g., J. Greig and M. Gibson, "Women and Investment," *Financial Review of Reviews* (June 1917): 174–82; L. S. Helen, "The Business Woman's Investments," *Magazine of Wall Street* (October 24, 1925): 1199, 1246.

88. See, e.g., Mrs. William Gibbs McAdoo, "What a Liberty Bond Means: Questions That Are Asked about United States War Bonds," *Ladies' Home Journal* (October 1917): 1; Herbert Quick, "Be an Investor: Why Not, When Uncle Sam Makes You This Proposition?" *Ladies' Home Journal* (March 1917): 1; Edith J. R. Isaacs, "What the Liberty Bond Has Done for All of Us," *Ladies' Home Journal* (October 1918): 36; Carter Glass, "Why Another Liberty Loan?" *Ladies' Home Journal* (April 1919): 33.

89. Samuel Crowther, "The Management of Money," *Ladies' Home Journal* (November 1928): 33. See also, e.g., Christine Frederick, "Getting 100% Out of Your Income," *Ladies' Home Journal* (September 1919): 59; Alice Ames Winter, "The Family Purse" *Ladies' Home Journal* (May 1925): 35; Ernest Poole, "Women in Wall Street," *Ladies' Home Journal* (August 1928): 9, 130; Samuel Crowther, "A Woman and Her Money," *Ladies' Home Journal* (October 1928): 18–19, 138, 141.

90. Ruth Boyle, "A Business Girl's Investments," *Good Housekeeping* (July 1929): 108.

91. Ruth Boyle, "The ABC of Investments," *Good Housekeeping* (October 1929): 100.

92. Ruth Boyle, "Common Stocks and Common Sense," *Good Housekeeping* (May 1930): 106.

93. Samuel Crowther, "Everybody Ought to Be Rich: An Interview with John J. Raskob," *Ladies' Home Journal* (August 1929): 9.

94. Klein, *Rainbow's End*, 193; Ahamed, *Lords of Finance*, 342.

95. Crowther, "Everybody," 9.

96. Elizabeth Frazer, *A Woman and Her Money* (New York: George H. Doran, 1926). A comparable volume from the period is Hazel Zimmerman's *Do's and Dont's for the Woman Investor* ([*sic*]; San Francisco: printed by author, 1931), though this self-published work appears to have had very limited visibility and circulation (for a discussion, see Urs Stäheli, *Spectacular Speculation: Thrills, the Economy, and Popular Discourse*, trans. Eric Savoth [Stanford, CA: Stanford University Press, 2013], 191, 193–94).

97. "When Woman Holds the Purse-Strings," review of *A Woman and Her Money* by Elizabeth Frazer, *New York Times*, March 14, 1926, sec. BR, 7.

98. Sereno S. Pratt, *The Work of Wall Street: An Account of the Functions, Methods, and History of the New York Money and Stock Markets*, rev. ed. (New York: D. Appleton, 1919), 89.

99. Frederic D. Bond, *Stock Movements and Speculation* (New York: D. Appleton, 1928), 173.

100. Foster, *Making Money*, 36.

101. Joel E. Thompson, "The State of Investment Analysis in 1927: On the Eve of Destruction," *Journal of Business and Behavioral Sciences* 29, no. 1 (2017): 141, 144–46; Friedman, *Fortune Tellers*, 86–87.

102. John Moody, *How to Invest Money Wisely* (New York: Office of John Moody, 1912), 74.

103. Roger W. Babson, *Business Barometers Used in the Accumulation of Money: A Text Book on Applied Economics for Merchants, Bankers, and Investors*, 5th ed. (Wellesley Hills, MA: Babson's Statistical Organization, 1912), 15.

104. Thomas Gibson, *Simple Principles of Investment* (Garden City, NY: Doubleday, Page, 1919), 6, 8.

105. Moody, *How to Invest*, 6.

106. S. A. Nelson, *The ABC of Stock Speculation* (New York: S. A. Nelson, 1902), 28.

107. Preda, *Framing Finance*, chap. 3.

108. Charles H. Dow, *Scientific Stock Speculation*, ed. G. C. Selden (New York: Magazine of Wall Street, 1920), 15.

109. G. C. Selden, introduction to Dow, *Scientific Stock Speculation*, 7–8.

110. Dow, *Scientific Stock Speculation*, 25–26.

111. William Peter Hamilton, *The Stock Market Barometer* (New York: Harper and Brothers, 1922), 8, 53, 20, 8, 42, 53, 101, 89–90.

112. Hamilton, 90.

113. See esp. "Rollo Tape" [Richard D. Wyckoff], *Studies in Tape Reading* (New York: Ticker Publishing, 1910), 127–28.

114. See, e.g., Richard D. Wyckoff, "Are Charts an Aid to Trading?" *Magazine of Wall Street* 39 (1926): 586, 598.

115. Richard D. Wyckoff, *How I Trade and Invest in Stocks and Bonds* (New York: Magazine of Wall Street, 1925), 122; see also 28–29, 36.

116. Leon Wansleben, "Inventing the Amateur Speculator: New Modes of Inclusion in the US Stock Market, 1920s to 1940s" (working paper, University of Lucerne, 2013), 13–17.

117. Richard D. Wyckoff, "William D. Gann: An Operator Whose Science and Ability Place Him in the Front Rank," *Ticker and Investment Digest* 5 (1909): 54.

118. William D. Gann, *Truth of the Stock Tape* (New York: Financial Guardian, 1923), 2, 82; emphases in original.

119. Gann, v, 1, 3, 23–24, 146, 150.

120. Jamie L. Pietruska, *Looking Forward: Prediction and Uncertainty in Modern America* (Chicago: University of Chicago Press, 2017), 199. On the interweaving of "scientific" and "superstitious" or "rational" and "irrational" worldviews in the United States around the turn of the twentieth century, see also T. J. Jackson Lears, *No Place of Grace: Antimodernism and the Transformation of American Culture, 1880–1920*, rev. ed. (Chicago: University of Chicago Press, 1994).

121. For somewhat differing views, see Alexander Elder, *The New Trading for a Living* (Hoboken, NJ: John Wiley, 2014), 15; James A. Hyerczyk, *Pattern, Price, and Time: Using Gann Theory in Technical Analysis*, 2nd ed. (Hoboken, NJ: John Wiley, 2009), chap. 2, e-book.

122. Gann, *Truth of the Stock Tape*, 32, 108.

123. Dow, *Scientific Stock Speculation*, 13, 25.

124. Gann, *Truth of the Stock Tape*, vi, 51–52, 75, 116, 149.

125. William D. Gann, *The Tunnel thru the Air, or, Looking Back from 1940* (New York: Financial Guardian, 1927), n.p.

126. For an especially elaborate recent example, see Tony Plummer, *The Law of Vibration: The Revelation of William D. Gann* (Petersfield, Hants, UK: Harriman House, 2013).

127. On occult labor, femininity, and blackness, see LaShawn Harris, *Sex Workers, Psychics, and Numbers Runners: Black Women in New York City's Underground Economy* (Urbana: University of Illinois Press, 2016), esp. chap. 3. On the predominance of women among "fortune-tellers and spirit mediums" (and their clients), see also Pietruska, *Looking Forward*, 20, 206–7.

128. See, e.g., Andrew W. Lo and Jasmina Hasanhodzic, *The Evolution of Technical Analysis: Financial Prediction from Babylonian Tablets to Bloomberg Terminals* (Hoboken, NJ: John Wiley, 2013), 93–94.

129. Gann, *Truth of the Stock Tape*, 2, 7, 51.

130. Edwin Lefèvre, *Reminiscences of a Stock Operator: With New Commentary and Insights on the Life and Times of Jesse Livermore*, ed. Jon D. Markman (Hoboken, NJ: John Wiley, 2010), 4, 73, 12, 89, 269, 3.

131. Charles Amos Dice, *New Levels in the Stock Market* (New York: McGraw-Hill, 1929), v.

132. Edgar Lawrence Smith, *Common Stocks as Long Term Investments* (New York: Macmillan, 1924), 77, 79.

133. Quoted in Robert Shiller, *Irrational Exuberance* (Princeton, NJ: Princeton University Press, 2000), 193.

134. Lawrence Chamberlain and William Wren Hay, *Investment and Speculation: Studies of Modern Movements and Basic Principles* (New York: Henry Holt, 1931), 189–90, xi.

135. Cowing, *Populists*, 157.

136. Carol J. Simon, "The Effect of the 1933 Securities Act on Investor Information and the Performance of New Issues," *American Economic Review* 79, no. 3 (1989): 296.

137. Arthur Train, *Paper Profits: A Novel of Wall Street* (New York: Horace Liveright, 1930), 3. The novel also features a transparent depiction of Jesse Livermore in the figure of William Shelton or "William the Silent." The novel's account of the rise of this "Boy Plunger" (58) (the nickname bestowed by the press on Livermore) to the status of "one of the biggest stock operators in the country" (23) who exploits what "appear[s] to be a regularity or rhythm in prices" to predict the market (57) draws heavily on Lefèvre's portrayal of Livermore's alter ego Larry Livingstone in 1923's *Reminiscences of a Stock Operator*.

138. Train, *Paper Profits*, 76, 77, 344.

139. See Traflet, *Nation of Small Shareholders*, 1–5.

140. Traflet, 4; Ott, *When Wall Street*, 2.

141. Alfred Cowles, "Can Stock Market Forecasters Forecast?" *Econometrica* 1, no. 3 (1933): 323, 314, 232.

142. Robert Rhea, "Random Comment," *Dow Theory Comment*, mailing no. 9 (January 18, 1933); reprinted in Robert W. Dimand and William Veloce, "Alfred Cowles and Robert Rhea on the Predictability of Stock Prices," *Journal of Business Inquiry* 9, no. 1 (2010): 58–60.

143. Stephen J. Brown, William N. Goetzmann, and Alok Kumar, "The Dow Theory: William Peter Hamilton's Track Record Reconsidered," *Journal of Finance* 53, no. 4 (1998): 1311–33.

144. Cowles, "Can Stock Market Forecasters Forecast?" 309.

145. Richard W. Schabacker, *Stock Market Theory and Practice* (New York: B. C. Forbes, 1930), 688–91.

146. Traflet, *Nation of Small Shareholders*, 14.

147. See, e.g., Humphrey B. Neill, *Tape Reading and Market Tactics* (New York: B. C. Forbes, 1931), viii, 145, 149–151, 220–223.

148. Neill, 9–10.

149. Neill, 23.

150. Neill, 140, 162, 225, 230.

151. Kristian Bondo Hansen discusses the importance of crowd psychology to Neill's approach in "Crowds and Speculation: A Study of Crowd Phenomena in the U.S. Financial Markets, 1890 to 1940" (PhD diss., Copenhagen Business School, 2017), 192–93. On the influence of crowd theory on approaches to financial markets in the early twentieth century, see also Christian Borch, *Social Avalanche: Crowds, Cities, and Financial Markets* (Cambridge: Cambridge University Press, 2020), esp. chap. 5.

152. Ralph Nelson Elliott, *R. N. Elliott's Masterworks: The Definitive Collection*, 3rd ed., ed. Robert R. Prechter (Gainesville, GA: New Classics Library, 2017), 87, 88, 90, 216, 218–19.

153. Elliott, 90.

154. Lo and Hasanhodzic, *Evolution*, 93–94.

155. Robert D. Edwards and John Magee Jr., *Technical Analysis of Stock Trends* (Springfield, MA: Stock Trend Service, 1948), 3, 1, 3.

156. Edwards and Magee, 5–6, 116, 139, 282, 285, 6 (emphasis in original), 5–6, 11, 86, 5, 55, 405, 10, 185, 1, 405.

157. Edwards and Magee, 6.

158. Benjamin Graham, *The Intelligent Investor: A Book of Practical Counsel*, rev. ed. (New York: HarperBusiness, 2003), ix.

159. Benjamin Graham and David L. Dodd, *Security Analysis* (New York: Whittlesey House, 1934), viii.

160. Graham and Dodd, 312, 313, 17, 18–19, 54 (emphasis in original).

161. Graham and Dodd, 352.

162. Timothy C. Jacobson, *From Practice to Profession: A History of the Financial Analysts Federation and the Investment Profession* (Charlottesville, VA: Association for Investment Management and Research, 1997), 25.

163. Investment Advisers Act, 1940, sec. 202, https://www.sec.gov/answers/about -lawsshtml.html#invadvact1940.

164. This status would later be tested—and reinforced—by a Supreme Court judgment of 1983, which held that "the Advisers Act excludes publishers of impersonal, analytical reports concerning securities from the definition of an investment adviser" (Robert W. Pontz, "SEC Release 1092 on the Investment Advisers Act of 1940: Applicability of the Investment Advisers Act to Financial Planners and Other Persons Who Provide Financial Services," *Washington and Lee Law Review* 45, no. 3 [1988]: 1149).

165. *Investment Trusts and Investment Companies: Report of the Securities and Exchange Commission Pursuant to Section 30 of the Public Utility Holding Company Act of 1935* (Washington, DC: United States Government Printing Office, 1939), 5.

166. Neill, *Tape Reading*, 141.

167. Neill, 140 (emphasis in original).

168. Roger W. Babson, *Cheer Up! Better Times Ahead!* 4th ed. (New York: Fleming H. Revell, 1932), 60.

169. John Moody, *The Long Road Home* (New York: Macmillan, 1933), 259.

170. Elliott, *Masterworks*, 216.

171. On the significance of the culture of self-help in this period, see Micki McGee, *Self-Help, Inc.: Makeover Culture in American Life* (Oxford: Oxford University Press, 2005), chaps. 1–2.

Chapter Five

1. Helen Gurley Brown, *Having It All: Love, Success, Sex, Money, Even If You're Starting with Nothing* (New York: Simon & Schuster, 1982), 415–17.

2. Macrotrends, "Dow Jones—DJIA—100 Year Historical Chart," http://www .macrotrends.net/1319/dow-jones-100-year-historical-chart.

3. James Poterba and Andrew Samwick, "Stock Ownership Patterns, Stock Market Fluctuations, and Consumption," *Brookings Papers on Economic Activity* 2 (1995): 321; and Edward N. Wolff, "Has Middle Class Wealth Recovered?" National Bureau of Economic Research, Working Paper no. 24085 (2017), http:// www.nber.org/papers/w24085.

4. Steve Fraser, *Wall Street: A Cultural History* (London: Faber and Faber, 2005), 480; and Kevin Phillips, *Wealth and Democracy: A Political History of the American Rich* (New York: Broadway Books, 2002), 78.

5. Janette Rutterford and Dimitris P. Sotiropoulos, "The Rise of the Small Investor in the United States and United Kingdom, 1895 to 1970," *Enterprise & Society* 18, no. 3 (2017): 485–535; and Janice M. Traflet and Michael P. Coyne, "Ending a NYSE Tradition: The 1975 Unraveling of Brokers' Fixed Commissions and Its Long Term Impact on Financial Advertising," *Essays in Economic & Business History* 25 (2007): 132.

6. The decision to act in these collective ways was, of course, largely a continuation of an existing pattern for middle-class Americans, for whom life insurance had been one of the keystones of personal financial investment planning in the nineteenth and early twentieth century; see *Anglo-American Life Insurance, 1800–1914*, ed. Timothy Alborn and Sharon Ann Murphy (London: Pickering & Chatto, 2012).

7. Joseph Nocera points to the "intriguing list of cities with the highest proportion of stockholders" that is buried in the stock market data about new investors in the early 1950s, and he notes that they are topped not by New York or even Washington, DC, but by those cities—Hartford, CT, Wilmington, DE, and Rochester, NY—that were home to the rapidly expanding insurance and technology companies that were leading the stock market growth in this period. Joseph Nocera, *A Piece of the Action: How the Middle Class Joined the Money Class* (New York: Simon & Schuster, 1994), 45. The coverage of the corporate workforce by these pension plans grew rapidly in the postwar period, from 22.5 percent in 1950 to 47 percent in 1970; see Jacob Hacker, *The Great Risk Shift: The New Economic Insecurity and the Decline of the American Dream* (Oxford: Oxford University Press, 2008).

8. Melinda Cooper, "Shadow Money and the Shadow Workforce: Rethinking Labor and Liquidity," *South Atlantic Quarterly* 114, no. 2 (2015): 395–423. See also Michael Szalay, *New Deal Modernism: American Literature and the Invention of the Welfare State* (Durham, NC: Duke University Press, 2000), and Martijn Konings, *The Development of American Finance* (Cambridge: Cambridge University Press, 2011).

9. Sharmila Choudhury, "Racial and Ethnic Differences in Wealth and Asset Choices," *Social Security Bulletin* 64, no. 4 (2001/2002): 1–15; Ken-Hou Lin and Megan Tobias Neely, *Divested: Inequality in the Age of Finance* (Oxford: Oxford University Press, 2020); and Ariel Education Initiative and Hewit Associates, *401(k) Plans in Living Color: A Study of 401(k) Savings Disparities across Racial and Ethnic Groups* (Lincolnshire, IL: Hewitt Associates, 2009).

10. Andrew F. Brimmer, "Blacks in the Stock Market," *Black Enterprise* (October 1983): 41.

11. Michael A. McCarthy, *Dismantling Solidarity: Capitalist Politics and American Pensions since the New Deal* (Ithaca, NY: Cornell University Press, 2017).

12. Cooper, "Shadow Money"; and Edward A. Zelinsky, *The Origins of the Ownership Society: How the Defined Contribution Paradigm Changed America* (Oxford: Oxford University Press, 2008). Participants in Kodak's 401(k) and ESOP filed a class action lawsuit in 2012 after the Kodak stock in their accounts became worthless due to Kodak's bankruptcy, and on April 27, 1990, a federal district court judge

approved a $9.7 million settlement. The suit alleged that Kodak CEO Antonio Perez held a town hall meeting three months before the bankruptcy filing, in which he told workers that the company would not file for bankruptcy and encouraged them to "hang in there"; https://www.nceo.org/employee-ownership-update/2016-05-02.

13. Kieran Heinemann, "Investment, Speculation and Popular Stock Market Engagement in 20th-Century Britain," *Archiv für Sozialgeschichte* 56 (2016): 258.

14. Phillips, *Wealth and Democracy*, 78; and Thomas Piketty, *Capital in the Twenty-First Century* (Cambridge, MA: Harvard University Press, 2014).

15. Bruce J. Schulman, *The 1970s: The Great Shift in American Culture, Society and Politics* (New York: De Capo Press, 2001), 216.

16. Rutterford and Sotiropoulos, "The Rise of the Small Investor."

17. Fraser, *Wall Street*, 480.

18. Wayne Parsons, *The Power of the Financial Press: Journalism and Economic Opinion in Britain and America* (Rutgers, NJ: Rutgers University Press, 1989), 88–89.

19. A. L. Yarrow, "The Big Postwar Story: Abundance and the Rise of Economic Journalism," *Journalism History* 33, no. 2 (2006): 58–76.

20. Heinemann, "Investment, Speculation"; Dilwyn Porter, "'City Slickers' in Perspective: *The Daily Mirror*, Its Readers and Their Money, 1960–2000," *Media History* 9, no. 2 (2003): 137–52.

21. Julia C. Ott, *When Wall Street Met Main Street: The Quest for an Investors' Democracy* (Cambridge, MA: Harvard University Press, 2011).

22. Amy Edwards, "'Manufacturing Capitalists': The Wider Share Ownership Council and the Problem of 'Popular Capitalism,' 1958–92," *Twentieth Century British History* 27, no. 1 (2016): 100–123.

23. Janice M. Traflet, *A Nation of Small Shareholders: Marketing Wall Street after World War II* (Baltimore: Johns Hopkins University Press, 2013). The Monthly Investment Plans allowed "individuals to invest from $40 quarterly to $1,000 monthly, less commissions, in a stock chosen from those listed on the exchange. An account is limited to one stock, and, where necessary, it is credited with purchases of fractional shares." "Personal Finance: Battle for Small Investor," *New York Times*, January 20, 1964.

24. Fraser, *Wall Street*, 497.

25. Chris Roush, *Profits and Losses: Business Journalism and Its Role in Society* (New York: Marion Street Press, 2006).

26. Edwin J. Perkins, *Wall Street to Main Street: Charles Merrill and Middle-Class Investors* (Cambridge, MA: Cambridge University Press, 1999), 203.

27. "From the Editor," *Kiplinger's* (January 1947): front cover.

28. "The Maddest Drug Store," *Kiplinger's* (January 1947): 12.

29. "When We Had Runaway Inflation," *Kiplinger's* (January 1947): 8. The Shays Rebellion (1786–87) was prompted by farmers' grievances about high post–Revolutionary War taxation.

30. "The Earth Worm: Nature's Soil Builder," *Changing Times* (January 1950): 31.

31. "10 Ways to Make Your Money Go Further," *Changing Times* (June 1949): 11.

32. "Fight Regimentation and War Waste: Good Accounting Can Help Us Do It," *Changing Times* (February 1951): 28.

33. "Farmer in Wall Street," *Kiplinger's* (June 1947): 16.

34. "Here Comes the Welfare State," *Changing Times* (May 1949): 8.

35. "Too Much Government?" *Changing Times* (November 1949): 21.

36. "The Truth about Health Insurance," *Changing Times* (August 1950); "A College Fund for Kids," *Changing Times* (December 1953).

37. John Hazard, ed., *Success with Your Money: How to Handle Family Money Matters* (Hoboken, NJ: Prentice Hall, 1956), 8.

38. Nocera, *A Piece of the Action*, 43.

39. Winthrop H. Smith, *Catching Lightning in a Bottle: How Merrill Lynch Revolutionized the Financial World* (New York: Wiley, 2014).

40. Traflet, *Nation of Small Shareholders*.

41. Smith, *Catching Lightning in a Bottle*, 198.

42. Gregory S. Bell, *In the Black: A History of African-Americans on Wall Street* (New York: Wiley, 2016), 47.

43. Bell, *In the Black*, 45, 49.

44. Mehrsa Baradaran, *The Color of Money: Black Banks and the Racial Wealth Gap* (Cambridge, MA: Harvard University Press, 2017), 26.

45. "Louis Engel Jr., Ex-Merrill Lynch Partner, Dies," *New York Times*, November 8, 1982, D15.

46. Louis Engel, *How to Buy Stocks* (New York: Bantam Books, 1953), ix.

47. Smith, *Catching Lightning in a Bottle*, 207.

48. Engel, *How to Buy Stocks*, 157.

49. Norton Reamer and Jesse Downing, *Investment: A History* (New York: Columbia Business School, 2016).

50. Matthew P. Fink, *The Rise of Mutual Funds* (Oxford: Oxford University Press, 2011).

51. James Poterba and Andrew Samwick, "Stock Ownership Patterns, Stock Market Fluctuations, and Consumption," *Brookings Papers on Economic Activity* 2 (1995): 321; and Steven M. Rosenthal and Lydia S. Austin, "The Dwindling Taxable Share of U.S. Corporate Stock," *Tax Notes*, May 16, 2016.

52. "Arthur Wiesenberger, Broker and Mutual Fund Adviser, Dies," *New York Times*, January 14, 197; and *Journal of Business* (January 1, 1976).

53. Arthur Wiesenberger, *Investment Companies and Their Securities* (New York: A. Wiesenberger, 1942), 5.

54. "Mutual Funds: Don't Buy Blind," *Kiplinger's Personal Finance* (June 1958): 31.

55. Joseph Lester, *How to Make More Money from Mutual Funds: A Guide for Conservative Investors* (New York: Exposition Press, 1965); Amy Booth, *How to Invest in Mutual Funds: Facts You Should Know about This Specialized Form of Investing* (Toronto: Financial Post, 1968); and David L. Markstein, *How to Make Money with Mutual Funds* (New York: McGraw-Hill, 1969).

56. Markstein, *How to Make Money*, 9, 86.

57. Matthew P. Fink, *The Rise of Mutual Funds: An Insider's View* (New York: Oxford University Press, 2011).

58. Ralph Lee Smith, *The Grim Truth about Mutual Funds* (New York: Putnam, 1963).

59. Carolo Massironi, "Philip Fisher's Sense of Numbers: An Account of the Use of Quantitative Reasoning in Philip Fisher's Qualitative Model of Equity Valuation," *Qualitative Research in Financial Markets* 6, no. 3 (2014): 302–31.

60. Philip A. Fisher, *Common Stocks and Uncommon Profits* (New York: Harper, 1958), 41, 43.

61. Joseph Granville, *Granville's New Strategy of Daily Stock Market Timing for Maximum Profit* (Englewood Cliffs, NJ: Prentice-Hall, 1960), 17, 97, 98.

62. *Kiplinger's Personal Finance* (February 1962).

63. Tracy Lucht, *Sylvia Porter: America's Original Personal Finance Columnist* (Syracuse: SUNY Press, 2013).

64. Lucht, 66.

65. J. K. Lasser and Sylvia Porter, *Managing Your Money* (New York: Henry Holt, 1953), 1, 3, 20, 180.

66. Cited in Janet Sutherland, "How to Lay a Nest Egg," *Iowa Homemaker* 30, no. 7 (1950).

67. Mabel Raef Putnam, *What Every Woman Should Know about Finance* (New York: Charles Scribner's Sons, 1955), 3.

68. Herta Hess Levy, *What Every Woman Should Know about Investing Her Money* (Chicago: Dartnell Corporation, 1968), 9.

69. Sutherland, "How to Lay a Nest Egg," 191; and Putnam, *What Every Woman Should Know*, 3.

70. Putnam, *What Every Woman Should Know*, 3.

71. Levy, *What Every Woman Should Know*, 10, 53.

72. Lucht, *Sylvia Porter*, 82.

73. Lasser and Porter, *Managing Your Money*, 276, 293.

74. Lucht, *Sylvia Porter*, 81.

75. Sylvia Porter, *Sylvia Porter's Money Book* (New York: Avon, 1975).

76. Helaine Olen, *Pound Foolish: Exposing the Dark Side of the Personal Finance Industry* (New York: Penguin, 2012).

77. Porter, *Sylvia Porter's Money Book*, 279–280.

78. True to form, Porter was an early innovator in broadcast financial journalism, launching a show on the NBC radio network in 1942. The show flopped, however,

leaving the way clear for another pioneering woman financial writer, Wilma Soss, to emerge as "the first female journalist to report regularly on business, economic, and financial news over the nation's airwaves." See Robert E. Wright, "Pioneer Financial News: National Broadcast Journalist Wilma Soss, NBC Radio, 1954–1980," *Journalism History* 44, no. 3 (2018): 143.

79. Traflet and Coyne, "Ending a NYSE Tradition," 132.

80. Harry Markowitz, "Portfolio Selection," *Portfolio Selection: Efficient Diversification of Investments* (New Haven, CT: Yale University Press, 1968).

81. Peter L. Bernstein, *Capital Ideas: The Improbable Origins of Modern Wall Street* (New York: Wiley and Sons, 1992).

82. Fraser, *Wall Street*, 536.

83. Philip Mirowski and Rob Van Horn, "The Rise of the Chicago School of Economics," in *The Road from Mont Pèlerin: The Making of the Neoliberal Thought Collective*, ed. Dieter Plehwe and Philip Mirowski (Cambridge, MA: Harvard University Press, 2009), 139–78.

84. It was an episode that has since been read as central to the "invention of neoliberal practices of gifting moral hazard to the banks and making the people pay up through the restructuring of municipal contracts and services and was to be later rolled-out through Pinochet's Chile as well as Reagan's America and Thatcher's Britain": David Harvey, *The Ways of the World* (Oxford: Oxford University Press), 276.

85. James A. Anderson, *Black Enterprise Guide to Investing* (New York: Wiley, 2016).

86. Jerry Edgerton and Richard Eisenberg, "Reagan and Your Dollars," *Money* (December 1980): 40; *Kiplinger's Personal Finance* (July 1981).

87. Pamela Reeves, "Back with the Pack," *Kiplinger's Personal Finance* (April 1982): 88.

88. Brimmer, "Blacks in the Stock Market"; Bebe Moore Campbell, "These Women Mean Business," *Black Enterprise* (June 1984): 224, and "Beating the Boys," *Black Enterprise* (December 1991).

89. Brimmer, "Blacks in the Stock Market"; and Ariel and Hewitt, *401(k) Plans in Living Color.*

90. Richard T. Griffin, "Miss Moneybags," *Essence* (March 1975): 79.

91. Howard Ruff, *How to Prosper during the Coming Bad Years: A Crash Course in Personal and Financial Survival* (Alamo, TX: Target Publishers, 1978), 24, 101.

92. Ruff, 32.

93. George Troughton, "Review of Howard Ruff's *How to Prosper during the Coming Bad Years*," *Financial Analysts Journal* (May 1, 1980).

94. In her introduction to her final book, for example, Susan Strange recommends Erdman's work not only for its satirical accounts of the danger of the financial marketplace but also for its pedagogical weight; Susan Strange, *Mad Money* (Manchester: Manchester University Press, 1998), 8. Strange's recommendation is less

idiosyncratic than it appears: other teachers of economics and business studies have recommended Erdman's work for its insightful and clear account of the workings of the financial marketplace rather than for its fictional or narrative qualities; see, e.g., Alexander E. Bracken and E. Bruce Geelhoed, "Clio and the Marketplace: Teaching American Business History," *History Teacher* 14, no. 2 (1981).

95. Arthur Donner, "Run on U.S. Dollar Assets Could Be Neutralized," *Globe* (May 4, 1981); and Paul Erdman, *Paul Erdman's Money Book* (New York: Random House, 1984), 77.

96. Adam Smith, *The Money Game* (New York: Random House, 1968).

97. Smith, 52, 53.

98. Randall Poe, *Across the Board* 38, no. 6 (November/December 2001): 60; N. R. Kleinfield, "Enduring, Not Always Endearing 'Wall Street Week,'" *New York Times*, November 11, 1990; Patricia Burstein, "Unlike His Fans, Wall Street Is a Special No-Lose Situation for PBS' Lou Rukeyser: He Plays, but Rarely the Market," *People*, February 26, 1979.

99. "The Television Audience for Selected Public Affairs Programs, Report 2; The Roper Surveys," Corporation of Public Broadcasting, 1977.

100. E. J. Ferreira and S. D. Smith, "'Wall Street Week': Information or Entertainment?" *Financial Analysts Journal* (January–February 2003); Jess Beltz and Robert Jennings, "'Wall Street Week with Louis Rukeyser' Recommendations: Trading Activity and Performance," *Journal of Financial Economics* 6, no. 1 (1997):15–27; Messod D. Beneish, "Stock Prices and the Dissemination of Analysts' Recommendations," *Journal of Business* 64, no. 3 (1991): 393–416.

101. Louis Rukeyser, *How to Make Money in Wall $treet* (New York: Doubleday, 1974), 3; Marlys Harris and Holly Wheelwright, "Louis Rukeyser's Wall Street," *Money* 15, no. 11 (1986).

102. Rukeyser, *How to Make Money*, 6.

103. Rukeyser, 37, 105, 130. The beta coefficient is a number representing the specific risk of an individual firm and is needed to carry out calculations using the CAPM model.

104. Rukeyser, 62, 65.

105. Carol Curtis, "How the Fastest Growing Funds Gather Assets," *U.S. Banker* 108, no. 7 July 1998), 57.

106. Jerry Felsen, *Cybernetic Approach to Stock Market Analysis versus Efficient Market Theory* (New York: Exposition Press, 1975), 21, 38, 23.

107. Robert Hagin, *Modern Portfolio Theory* (New York: Dow Jones Irwin, 1979), 158, 167–68.

108. John Marks Templeton (as described by John Marks Templeton to James Ellison), *The Templeton Plan: 21 Steps to Personal Success and Real Happiness* (New York: HarperCollins, 1987), 152.

109. Burton Malkiel, *A Random Walk Down Wall Street* (New York: W. W. Norton, 1972), 225.

110. Malkiel, 350.

111. Lester, *How to Make More Money*; Booth, *How to Invest in Mutual Funds*; Markstein, *How to Make Money*; Donald D. Rugg and Norman B. Hale, *The Dow Jones-Irwin Guide to Mutual Funds*, rev. ed. (Homewood, IL: Dow Jones-Irwin, 1983); and Junius Ellis, *Winning with Mutual Funds* (Birmingham, AL: Oxmoor House, 1987).

112. Amy Edwards, "'Financial Consumerism': Citizenship, Consumerism and Capital Ownership in the 1980s," *Contemporary British History* 31, no. 2 (2017): 210–29.

113. Lester, *How to Make More Money*; Booth, *How to Invest in Mutual Funds*; and Markstein, *How to Make Money*.

114. "Telling Their Secrets," *BusinessWeek* (October 16, 1965): 170–72.

115. John Train, *The Money Masters* (New York: Harper and Row, 1980), 165.

116. Peter Lynch, *One Up on Wall Street: How to Use What You Already Know to Make Money in the Market* (New York: Penguin, 1989), 14, 61.

117. Lynch, 18.

118. Malkiel, *A Random Walk Down Wall Street*, 245.

119. John C. Bogle, *Bogle on Mutual Funds* (New York: Dell Publishing, 1992), 61, 159.

120. John C. Bogle, *The Battle for the Soul of Capitalism* (New Haven, CT: Yale University Press, 2005).

121. Annie Lowrey, "Could Index Funds Be 'Worse than Marxism'?" *Atlantic* (April 5, 2021).

122. Jonathan Brogaard, Matthew C. Ringgenberg, and David Sovich, "The Economic Impact of Index Investing," *Review of Financial Studies* (July 2018), https://papers.ssrn.com/sol3/papers.cfm?abstract_id=2663398.

123. Rodney N. Sullivan and James X. Xiong, "How Index Trading Increases Market Vulnerability," *Financial Analysts Journal* 68, no. 2 (2012): 70–84.

124. Jose Azar, Martin C. Schmalz, and Isabel Tecu, "Anticompetitive Effects of Common Ownership," *Journal of Finance* 73, no. 4 (2018): 1–79.

125. Gary Becker, *Treatise on the Family* (Cambridge, MA: Harvard University Press, 2009), 32.

Chapter Six

1. Jess Walter, *The Financial Lives of the Poets: A Novel* (New York: HarperCollins, 2009), 49–51 (emphasis in original).

2. On "crunch lit," see Katy Shaw, *Crunch Lit* (London: Bloomsbury Academic, 2015).

3. David Denby, *American Sucker* (Boston: Little, Brown, 2004), 74.

4. David Gardner and Tom Gardner, *The Motley Fool Investment Guide: How*

the Fool Beats Wall Street's Wise Men, and How You Can Too (New York: Simon & Schuster, 2001), 34.

5. The decline in transaction costs predates the advent of e-trading, with the deregulatory abolishing of fixed-rate commissions in 1975 as the major spur to price competition among brokers. However, the emergence of discount broker-ages (and even no-commission operators like Robinhood) pushed costs down even further. See Charles M. Jones, "A Century of Stock Market Liquidity and Trading Costs" (2002), available at SSRN: https://ssrn.com/abstract=313681; and Hans R. Stoll, "Electronic Trading in Stock Markets," *Journal of Economic Perspectives* 20 (2006): 153–74.

6. Brad M. Barber and Terrance Odean, "Online Investors: Do the Slow Die First?" *Review of Financial Studies* 15, no. 2 (2002): 455–88.

7. See Alex Preda, *Noise: Living and Trading in Electronic Finance* (Chicago: University of Chicago Press, 2017), 6.

8. See Matt Taibbi, *Griftopia: Bubble Machines, Vampire Squids, and the Long Con That Is Breaking America* (New York: Spiegel & Grau, 2010); and Donald Mackenzie, "Dark Markets," *London Review of Books* 37 (June 4, 2015): 29–32.

9. Michael Lewis, *Flash Boys: Cracking the Money Code* (London: Allen Lane, 2014).

10. Joe Hagan, "The Dow Zero Insurgency," *New York Magazine,* September 25, 2009, https://nymag.com/guides/money/2009/59457/.

11. Hailiang Chen et al., "Wisdom of Crowds: The Value of Stock Opinions Transmitted through Social Media," *Review of Financial Studies* 27, no. 5 (2014): 1367–403.

12. On investment clubs, see Kieran Heinemann, "Popular Investment and Speculation in Britain, 1918–1987" (PhD diss., University of Cambridge, 2017), https://www.repository.cam.ac.uk/handle/1810/274603.

13. Gregory D. Saxton and Ashley E. Anker, "The Aggregate Effects of Decentralized Knowledge Production: Financial Bloggers and Information Asymmetries in the Stock Market," *Journal of Communication* 63, no. 6 (2013): 1054–69. The study used data from the 150 top financial bloggers and stock returns from the S&P 500. See also a study of the SeekingAlpha.com website: Laura K. Rickett, "Do Financial Blogs Serve an Infomediary Role in Capital Markets?" *American Journal of Business* 31, no. 1 (2016): 17–40.

14. Mark Hirschey, Vernon J. Richardson, and Susan Scholz, "How 'Foolish' Are Internet Investors?" *Financial Analysts Journal* 56, no. 1 (2000): 62–69.

15. Chen et al., "Wisdom of Crowds." However, another study (Werner Antweiler and Murray Z. Frank, "Is All That Talk Just Noise? The Information Content of Internet Stock Message Boards," *Journal of Finance* 59 [2004]: 1259–94) found that it is not necessarily possible to make money by using computational sentiment analysis of discussion boards: although bullishness on the message boards of Yahoo! Finance in the late 1990s did indeed correspond with market developments,

lively disagreement on the boards merely predicted higher trading volumes and volatility.

16. Brad M. Barber and Terrance Odean, "The Behavior of Individual Investors," in *Handbook of the Economics of Finance*, vol. 2, ed. George M. Constantinides, Milton Harris, and Rene M. Stulz (Amsterdam: Elsevier, 2013), 1565.

17. Brad M. Barber and Terrance Odean, "The Internet and the Investor," *Journal of Economic Perspectives* 15, no. 1 (2001): 41–54.

18. Helaine Olen, *Pound Foolish: Exposing the Dark Side of the Personal Finance Industry* (New York: Portfolio, 2013), 129.

19. Arvid Hoffmann and Katarina Otteby, "Personal Finance Blogs: Helpful Tool for Consumers with Low Financial Literacy or Preaching to the Choir?" *International Journal of Consumer Studies* 42 (2018): 241–54.

20. Shiller, cited in Denby, *American Sucker*, 148.

21. "Trade Wisdom for Foolishness," https://www.fool.com/how-to-invest/thirteen -steps/step-2-trade-wisdom-for-foolishness.aspx.

22. For a critique of their spurious data mining, see Grant McQueen and Steven Thorley, "Mining Fool's Gold," *Financial Analysts Journal* 55, no. 2 (1999): 61–72.

23. Don Giacomino and Michael Akers, "Examining an Online Investment Research Service: The Motley Fool," *Journal of Business and Economics Research* 9, no. 1 (2011): 37–48.

24. Gardner and Gardner, *Motley Fool Investment Guide*, 14.

25. Greg Filbeck, Alexander Lyon, and Xin Zhao, "Evaluating the Performance of the Motley Fool's Stock Advisor™," *Investment Management and Financial Innovations* 14, no. 3 (2017): 280–90.

26. Hagan, "The Dow Zero Insurgency."

27. Tyler Durden, "The Imminent Disinformation Schism," ZeroHedge.com, April 11, 2009, http://zerohedge.blogspot.com/2009/04/imminent-disinformation -schism.html.

28. Ivandjiiski briefed the *Rolling Stone* journalist Matt Taibbi, who developed the story into his book *Griftopia*.

29. The idea of "disaster capitalism" is set out in Naomi Klein, *The Shock Doctrine: The Rise of Disaster Capitalism* (London: Penguin, 2008). In the light of the cheerleading for a hard Brexit by Jacob Rees-Mogg, his father William Rees-Mogg's *Sovereign Individual* (London: Macmillan, 1997) began in retrospect to look more like a blueprint for how a hedge fund manager (as indeed Rees-Mogg Jr. is) could benefit from the economic turmoil of the United Kingdom leaving the European Union. See https://www.theguardian.com/books/2018/nov/09/mystic -mogg-jacob-rees-mogg-willam-predicts-brexit-plans.

30. "Financial Market Website Zero Hedge Knocked off Twitter over Coronavirus Story," *Reuters*, February 3, 2020, https://www.reuters.com/article/us-china -health-twitter-idUSKBN1ZW0PZ; "Twitter Restores Account of Financial Market Website Zero Hedge," *Reuters*, June 13, 2020, https://www.reuters.com/article /us-twitter-zerohedge-idUSKBN23K0H8.

31. See, e.g., Thomas Renault, "Market Manipulation and Suspicious Stock Recommendations on Social Media" (December 20, 2017), available at SSRN: https://ssrn.com/abstract=3010850; and Christian Leuz et al., "Who Falls Prey to the Wolf of Wall Street? Investor Participation in Market Manipulation," National Bureau of Economic Research (2017), Working Paper no. 24083; and David Rakowski, Sara E. Shirley, and Jeffrey R. Stark, "Twitter Activity, Investor Attention, and the Diffusion of Information," *Financial Management* (2020): 1–44.

32. "About Kris," https://www.kriskrohn.com/learn-about-kris-a.

33. For an overview of the rise of robo-advising, see Jill E. Fisch, Marion Labouré, and John A. Turner, "The Emergence of the Robo-Advisor," in *The Disruptive Impact of FinTech on Retirement Systems*, ed. Julie Agnew and Olivia S. Mitchell (New York: Oxford University Press, 2018), 13–37.

34. See https://www.statista.com/outlook/337/100/robo-advisors/worldwide; and Facundo Abraham, Sergio L. Schmukler, and Jose Tessada, "Robo-Advisors: Investing through Machines," World Bank Policy Research, Working Paper no. 134881 (2019).

35. "Invest with a Robo Advisor Today," https://www.moneyfarm.com/uk/robo-advisor/; and "Pricing at Betterment," https://www.betterment.com/pricing/.

36. See, e.g., Francesco D'Acunto, Nagpurnanand Prabhala, and Alberto G. Rossi, "The Promises and Pitfalls of Robo-Advising," *Review of Financial Studies* 32, no. 5 (2019): 1983–2020.

37. See Catherine D'Hondt et al., "Artificial Intelligence Alter Egos: Who Benefits from Robo-Investing?" (July 2019), available at SSRN: https://ssrn.com/abstract=3415981.

38. Eric Jansen, "When a Robo-Advisor Is, or Isn't, the Right Choice," CNBC, https://www.cnbc.com/2018/06/04/when-a-robo-advisor-is-or-isnt-the-right-choice.html.

39. Charlotte Cowles, "How I Get It Done: Suze Orman Gives Money Advice from Her Private Island," *The Cut*, March 20, 2019.

40. David Grainger, "The Suze Orman Show," *Fortune Magazine*, June 16, 2003, https://money.cnn.com/magazines/fortune/fortune_archive/2003/06/16/344218/.

41. Suze Orman, *Women and Money: Be Strong, Be Safe, Be Secure* (New York: Ballantine, 2019).

42. Nancy Fraser, "Contradictions of Capital and Care," *New Left Review* 100 (2016), https://newleftreview.org/issues/ii100/articles/nancy-fraser-contradictions-of-capital-and-care.

43. Suze Orman, *The 9 Steps to Financial Freedom: Practical and Spiritual Steps So You Can Stop Worrying* (New York: Three Rivers Press, 1997), 18–19.

44. Orman, 32.

45. Grainger, "Suze Orman Show."

46. Olen, *Pound Foolish*, 24.

47. The best-selling financial advice guru David Bach rode to fame on his claim that ordinary people could retire with $2 million if they merely cut out their daily

latte. See Bach, *The Latte Factor: Why You Don't Have to Be Rich to Live Rich* (New York: Atria, 2019); and Olen, *Pound Foolish*, 48–73.

48. Elizabeth Warren and Amelia Warren Tyagi, *The Two-Income Trap: Why Middle-Class Parents Are (Still) Going Broke* (Philadelphia: Basic Books, 2003), 163.

49. Warren and Tyagi, 162; and Melinda Cooper, *Family Values: Between Neoliberalism and the New Social Conservatism* (New York: Zone, 2017).

50. Elizabeth Warren and Amelia Warren Tyagi, *All Your Worth: The Ultimate Lifetime Money Plan* (New York: Simon & Schuster, 2005), 54–55.

51. Felix Salmon and Susie Poppick, "Save Like Dave, Just Don't Invest Like Him," *Money* 42, no. 9 (October 2013): 72.

52. Dave Ramsey, *The Total Money Makeover: A Proven Plan for Financial Fitness* (Nashville: Thomas Nelson, 2013), https://www.daveramsey.com/store/product /the-total-money-makeover-book-by-dave-ramsey.

53. Eleanor Laise, "Karma Chameleon," *Smart Money*, February 2003, 97–103.

54. Robert Kiyosaki and Sharon Lechter, *Rich Dad, Poor Dad: What the Rich Dads Teach Their Kids about Money That the Poor and Middle Class Do Not!* (New York: Warner Business Books, 2000).

55. Jim Cramer, *Confessions of a Street Addict* (New York: Simon & Schuster, 2003), 140.

56. Cramer, *Mad Money* (New York: Simon & Schuster, 2006), 23, 57.

57. Jim Cramer, *Real Money: Sane Investing in an Insane World* (New York: Simon & Schuster, 2005), 3.

58. Cramer, *Real Money*, 3.

59. Gonen Dori-Hacohen and Timothy T. White, "'Booyah Jim': The Construction of Hegemonic Masculinity in CNBC 'Mad Money' Phone-in Interactions," *Discourse, Context and Media* 2, no. 4 (2013): 175–83.

60. On this tradition of finance fiction, see Nicky Marsh, *Credit Culture: The Politics of Money in the American Novel of the 1970s* (Cambridge: Cambridge University Press, 2020), 50–57.

61. Cramer, *Confessions of a Street Addict*, 301.

62. Olen, *Pound Foolish*, 24.

63. Michael Markey, "Can You Imagine Averaging 18% Returns?" January 25, 2016, https://www.thinkadvisor.com/2016/01/25/can-you-imagine-averaging-18-re turns-thats-what-early-dave-ramsey-followers-were-told-to-expect-2/.

64. Cramer, *Confessions of a Street Addict*, 81.

65. Ekaterina V. Karniouchina, William L. Moore, and Kevin J. Cooney, "Impact of 'Mad Money' Stock Recommendations: Merging Financial and Marketing Perspectives," *Journal of Marketing* 73, no. 6 (2009): 244–66.

66. Gerald Sim, "Jim Cramer's 'Mad Money': Disavowals of a Late Capitalist Investor," *Rethinking Marxism: A Journal of Sociology and Culture*, March 2012, 307–16.

67. Olen, *Pound Foolish*, 12.

68. Robin Burchett, *Smart Dad, Dumb Dad* (New York: Warning Books, 2008);

and Andy Borowitz, *The Trillionaire Next Door: The Greedy Investor's Guide to Day Trading* (New York: HarperCollins, 2000).

69. Suze Orman, interview with the Television Academy Foundation, October 26, 2012, https://interviews.televisionacademy.com/interviews/suze-orman#about.

70. Suze Orman, interview on *Larry King Live*, October 2008, https://www.you tube.com/watch?v=qvgMKXq59z8.

71. Josh Compton, "Cramer versus (John Stewart's Characterization of) Cramer: Image Repair Rhetoric, Late Night Political Humor and the *Daily Show*," in *"The Daily Show" and Rhetoric: Arguments, Issues, and Strategies*, ed. Trischa Goodnow (Lanham, MD: Lexington Books, 2011).

72. Joe Neumair, "Jodie Foster Says 'Money Monster' Isn't about Jim Cramer," *Fortune*, May 13, 2016, https://fortune.com/2016/05/13/jodie-foster-money-monster-jim -cramer/.

73. Charles B. Carlson, foreword to William Peter Hamilton, *The Stock Market Barometer* (New York: John Wiley & Sons, 1998), x, xi.

74. See, e.g., the multiple endorsements of the book in Jack D. Schwager, *Market Wizards: Interviews with Top Traders* (New York: HarperBusiness, 1993).

75. Paul Tudor Jones, foreword to Edwin Lefèvre, *Reminiscences of a Stock Operator with New Commentary and Insights on the Life and Times of Jesse Livermore*, ed. Jon D. Markman (Hoboken, NJ: John Wiley & Sons, 2010), v.

76. "Paul Tudor Jones on *Reminiscences*," in Lefèvre, *Reminiscences of a Stock Operator*, 400.

77. Seth A. Klarman, "Preface to the Sixth Edition: The Timeless Wisdom of Graham and Dodd," Benjamin Graham and David L. Dodd, *Security Analysis: Principles and Technique*, 6th ed. (New York: McGraw-Hill, 2009), xxv.

78. W. H. C. Bassetti, "Preface to the Eighth Edition," Robert D. Edwards, John Magee, and W. H. C. Bassetti, *Technical Analysis of Stock Trends*, 11th ed. (New York: Routledge, 2019), xxix.

79. Klarman, "Preface to the Sixth Edition," 13, xviii.

80. Bassetti, "Preface to the Tenth Edition," Robert D. Edwards, John Magee, and W. H. C. Bassetti, *Technical Analysis of Stock Trends*, 11th ed. (New York: Routledge, 2019), xvii.

81. Bassetti, "Preface to the Eighth Edition," xxviii–xxix.

82. See, in particular, Randy Martin, *Financialization of Daily Life* (Philadelphia: Temple University Press, 2002); Paul Langley, *The Everyday Life of Global Finance: Saving and Borrowing in Anglo-America* (Oxford: Oxford University Press, 2008); Ulrich Bröckling, *The Entrepreneurial Self: Fabricating a New Type of Subject*, trans. Steven Black (London: SAGE, 2016); Lisa Adkins, *The Time of Money* (Stanford, CA: Stanford University Press, 2018).

83. Michel Foucault, *The Birth of Biopolitics: Lectures at the Collège de France, 1978–1979*, ed. Michel Senellart, trans. Graham Burchell (Basingstoke: Palgrave Macmillan, 2008), 226.

84. Herausgegeben von Trendbüro, ed., *Duden Wörterbuch der New Economy* (Duden Dictionary of the New Economy) (Mannheim: Bibliographisches Institut, 2001), 79; quoted in Bröckling, *Entrepreneurial Self*, 20.

85. Elizabeth Grace Saunders, *How to Invest Your Time Like Money* (Boston: Harvard Business Review Press, 2015), chap. 5, e-book.

86. Dorrie Clark, *Entrepreneurial You: Monetize Your Expertise, Create Multiple Income Streams, and Thrive* (Boston: Harvard Business Review Press, 2017), chaps. 1, 4, e-book.

87. Reid Hoffman and Ben Casnocha, *The Start-Up of You: Adapt to the Future, Invest in Yourself, and Transform Your Career* (New York: Crown Business, 2012), chap. 3, e-book.

88. Hoffman and Casnocha, chap. 6.

89. See Daniel Akst, "Life and Work, Codified at Last," *Wall Street Journal*, October 1, 2017, https://www.wsj.com/articles/life-and-work-codied-at-last-1506889007.

90. Ray Dalio, *Principles: Life and Work* (New York: Simon & Schuster, 2017), 53–54.

91. See Kris Frieswick, "How Tony Robbins Created an Empire by Being the Most Confident Man on Earth," *Inc.*, October 2016, https://www.inc.com/magazine/201610/most-confident-man-tony-robbins.html.

92. Anthony Robbins, *Awaken the Giant Within: How to Take Immediate Control of Your Mental, Emotional, Physical, and Financial Destiny* (New York: Free Press, 2003), 10 (emphasis in original).

93. Robbins, 326 (emphasis in original).

94. Robbins, 467, 326.

95. Robbins, 326–27 (emphasis in original).

96. Robbins, 184, 343, 36 (emphases in original).

97. Tony Robbins, *Money: Master the Game: 7 Simple Steps to Financial Freedom* (New York: Simon & Schuster, 2016), 101.

Conclusion

1. Christine Ibbotson, *Don't Panic! How to Manage Your Finances and Financial Anxieties during and after Coronavirus* (Halifax, NS: Nimbus, 2020), chaps. 2, 5, 2, e-book.

2. Robin Wigglesworth, Richard Henderson, and Eric Platt, "The Lockdown Death of a 20-Year-Old Day Trader," *Financial Times*, July 2, 2020, https://www.ft.com/content/45d0a047-360f-4abf-86ee-108f436015a1.

3. See, e.g., "Has Coronavirus Changed the Basic Income Debate?" *BBC News*, June 9, 2020, https://www.bbc.co.uk/news/uk-scotland-52967720.

4. Foundational Economy Collective, *Foundational Economy: The Infrastructure of Everyday Life* (Manchester: Manchester University Press, 2019); and Mariana

Mazzucato, *The Value of Everything: Making and Taking in the Global Economy* (London: Penguin, 2019).

5. David Bach, *The Latte Factor: Why You Don't Have to Be Rich to Live Rich* (New York: Atria Books, 2019); and Janet Nguyen, "Now That Millennials Aren't Buying Avocado Toast," *Marketplace*, August 14, 2020, https://www.marketplace.org/2020/08/14/now-that-millennials-arent-buying-avocado-toast-and-lattes-can-they-afford-a-home/.

6. Caroline Kitchener, "Women Are Missing from the GameStop News. Experts Blame This 'Fratty' Subreddit," *The Lily* [*Washington Post*], February 2, 2021, https://www.thelily.com/women-are-missing-from-the-gamestop-news-experts-blame-this-fratty-subreddit/.

7. Josh K. Elliott, "'Hold the Line': Reddit's 'Meme Stock' Traders Embrace the GameStop Chaos," *Global News*, January 28, 2021, https://globalnews.ca/news/7604872/reddit-gamestop-wallstreetbets-hold-the-line/.

8. Will Dunn, "The Big Squeeze: How Financial Populism Sent the Stock Market on a Wild Ride," *New Statesman*, January 29, 2021, https://www.newstatesman.com/business/finance/2021/01/big-squeeze-how-financial-populism-sent-stock-market-wild-ride.

9. Taylor Tepper, "What's the Endgame for GameStop?" *Forbes*, January 27, 2021, https://www.forbes.com/advisor/investing/gamestop-stock-what-is-happening/.

10. Matt Levine, "The GameStop Game Never Stops," *Bloomberg*, January 25, 2021, https://www.bloomberg.com/opinion/articles/2021-01-25/the-game-never-stops?sref=1kJVNqnU.

11. Matt Levine, "Money Stuff: GameStonk Rocket Rocket Rocket," *Bloomberg*, January 27, 2021, https://www.bloomberg.com/news/newsletters/2021-01-27/reddit-driven-surge-puts-gamestop-and-ryan-cohen-in-a-weird-spot-kkfof4sn.

12. Norma Mendoza-Denton, "'Sticking It to the Man': r/wallstreetbets, Generational Masculinity and Revenge in Narratives of Our Dystopian Capitalist Age," *Anthropology Now* 13, no. 1 (2021): 91–99.

13. Lauren Berlant, *Cruel Optimism* (Durham, NC: Duke University Press, 2011).

Index